ProDOS® Inside and Out

DENNIS DOMS AND TOM WEISHAAR

TAB TAB BOOKS Inc.
Blue Ridge Summit, PA 17214

FIRST EDITION

SECOND PRINTING

Printed in the United States of America

Library of Congress Cataloging in Publication Data

Doms, Dennis.
ProDOS inside and out.

Includes index.
1. ProDOS (Computer operating system)
2. Apple II (Computer)—Programming. I. Weishaar, Tom. II. Title.
QA76.76.O63D66 1986 005.4'465 86-6016
ISBN 0-8306-0245-3
ISBN 0-8306-2745-6 (pbk.)

Questions regarding the content of this book should be addressed to:

Reader Inquiry Branch
Editorial Department
TAB BOOKS Inc.
P.O. Box 40
Blue Ridge Summit, PA 17214

Contents

Preface

I don't know about Tom, but I didn't think this book was going to be *that* hard to write. Of course, Murphy's Law took full effect.

There were some known problems. First, the Apple documentation on ProDOS and BASIC.SYSTEM has some holes in it. Second, Apple has been demonstratably lax (reticent?) in revealing known bugs in its products. Third, as this book was started, Apple cut back its support operations. This included closing the Carrollton, Texas, facility that I used to call for tech support. Finally, Apple released a slew of new products in the latter half of 1985, just as this book was being prepared, and a new revised version of ProDOS and its utilities was forthcoming.

Still, we felt we had found some items of interest in dealing with ProDOS BASIC.SYSTEM that should be passed along. Several of these items were concerned with filling the gap between the descriptions of ProDOS and BASIC.SYSTEM left in the Apple literature. Several others were concerned with outright bugs or changes in BASIC.SYSTEM since its original description.

A significant portion of this book is drawn from articles Tom had written for *Softalk* and for his *Open-Apple* newsletter. The book has been "fleshed out" with a description of BASIC.SYSTEM commands and necessary background, along with known (or perceived) bugs and peculiarities.

We also wanted to attack, both in the course of the book and in its Appendices, the interrelationship of DOS 3.3 and ProDOS programming. Since DOS 3.3 is still very much in force (apparently in everyone's eyes but Apple's), we are assuming a significant portion of the readership will be concerned with *both* operating systems.

The style of this book developed into something like *The DOSTalk Scrapbook*, which Tom Weishaar co-authored with Bert Kersey (of Beagle Bros. Software Fame). It may seem a bit schizoid to pure neophytes, but we hope that the "free wheeling" discussion of some topics allows us to incorporate information of use to programmers that is hard to present in a more "formal" style.

There are many programming examples included, although presentation of complete programs is often delayed until all the commands contained therein are described. Hopefully, you don't have to be sitting at an Apple to read this book, although actually doing the programming is an important step in understanding the principles.

A few programs presented here do nothing but test or check BASIC.SYSTEM's reaction to certain commands, which is not always the same as what the documentation (even Apple's) states. We hope that readers see the importance of these examples in writing and testing their own programs.

ABOUT THE PROGRAM LISTINGS

Although many program listings in this book (both BASIC and assembly) are new programs, many have also have been developed over the last two years and printed in sources such as user newsletters and publications such as *Softalk* and *Open-Apple*.

All of the complete programs (other than simple descriptive examples) have been typed in and tested. They are available on a disk from the authors if you wish to avoid re-typing them. It's difficult to know everything about how even a simple program will perform at times, so please use only backups of your ProDOS disks to enter, save, and run the programs. We can't guarantee that the programs are 100% safe and usable as provided.

Entry of the BASIC examples should be easy. However, one problem which exists is the representation of spaces within the listing's PRINT statements. These are usually not visible in listings, so it is difficult to tell the difference between

```
PRINT "     " : REM 5 SPACES
PRINT "      " : REM 6 SPACES
```

unless the lines are juxtaposed. Therefore, if a screen seems improperly formatted, try adjusting the spacing of the PRINT statements.

ASSEMBLY LISTINGS

A second problem has to do with the assembly listings. The authors use different assemblers which are not totally compatible in syntax.

Tom Weishaar's TYPE command was originally assembled using the *S-C Assembler* (from S-C Software). The MLI "STARTUP" call, the Mountain Hardware Apple Clock driver, the IRQ demonstration program, and the BASIC.SYSTEM Global page disassembly were all originally done with the *Merlin Pro Assembler* (from Roger Wagner Publishing).

This left us in a quandry; using both assemblers, the listing formats would not be uniform throughout the book. We wanted to limit the editing of the output listings to reduce the chance of typographical errors. Therefore, the "TYPE" command in Chapter 20, which originally appeared in *Softalk* magazine as an *S-C Assembler* source listing, was re-assembled and appears in this book as a *Merlin Pro* source listing. It is hoped this does not greatly inconvenience anyone.

If you have neither assembler, the hex code output which appears next to the addresses at the left-hand edge of the listing can be entered manually.

TECHNICAL TALK

Time for our first editorial comment. Originally, Apple used to include several manuals with the Apple II Computer that it sold prior to the introduction of the Apple *II*e and *II*c. These manuals were dropped from inclusion in the Apple package because the Apple management felt that the manuals tended to "burden novice users with more information than they need" (a quote from a letter sent to me by Apple's Product Marketing department). This does, however, make writing ancillary books on the Apple difficult as one can no longer assume a potential reader has all the Apple documentation on hand.

Because this information is not included with the computer, we have tried to cover some of the points on a "need-to-know" basis within this book, and we have included some general information about the Apple II series computers in Appendix C. In trying to keep the size of this volume manageable, however, it is not possible to duplicate all the information in the original manuals. We hope that users will acquire and read the complete Apple documentation (available now as extra cost items). Additionally, we hope that users who feel their computer was received "under-documented" will express their feelings to Apple in writing.

Despite all of the "nay-saying," we also think it's important not to forget the power and flexibility of the Apple II series. With the exception of four figures drawn with a Macintosh, the original manuscript for this book was prepared on an Apple *II*e computer, using Apple software (primarily *AppleWriter II*).

Apple II forever!

Dennis Doms

Introduction

This book describes BASIC.SYSTEM, a program designed to facilitate Applesoft BASIC programming in conjunction with *ProDOS*, Apple's *Pro*fessional *D*isk *O*perating *S*ystem for the Apple II series of computers. To start, this book makes a few assumptions about you, the reader.

First, it is assumed that the reader is familiar with Applesoft BASIC as described in Apple's manual *The Applesoft Tutorial,* and with the elements of operating the Apple II and the disk drive as covered in that reference and in your computer's owner's manual. If you are an experienced Applesoft programmer beyond that level, all the better, but that minimum level of BASIC knowledge will be needed to use this book.

Second, you will eventually need ProDOS in the form of *The ProDOS User's Kit* (which should be available at any authorized Apple computer dealer) and/or Apple's *II*c utilities if you have an Apple *II*c. You *may* be able to evaluate your need for ProDOS from this book before buying one of the forms of ProDOS, but to *learn* and *use* ProDOS you will need one of these packages, which contains the ProDOS software (including BASIC.SYSTEM), some necessary utility programs, and an introductory manual.

Lastly, toward the end of this book there will be some machine language programming and technical descriptions of the ProDOS and BASIC.SYSTEM programs. This is connected to the intricacies of the advanced use of BASIC.SYSTEM, but is not essential to digest if you are only interested in pure BASIC programming. At times, you may be referred to other books to fill in areas that are beyond the scope of this book.

Part 1

Introduction to ProDOS and BASIC.SYSTEM

Chapter 1

What Is an Operating System?

If you have ever happened to turn on your computer's monitor and watched the screen before starting the computer, you have noticed that a lot starts happening when you turn on the power. The monitor screen flashes and things get printed and the computer generally seems to run amok until (often) the screen just sits there with some type of questioning prompt and waits for you to type something.

There are two things to learn from this—one practical and one philosophical. From a practical perspective, something has to be active to tell the computer what to do for it to get from A to B.

From the philosophical perspective, it's important to remember that you are smarter than the computer. The computer can ask you a question and get directions. Unless someone (you or another programmer) has told the computer ahead of time what to answer, you will be unable to get an intelligible reply when you ask it a question. You are (and should be) in command.

WHO'S IN CHARGE?

A computer always follows the directions given to it. The first and most basic thing a computer must have in the way of directions is a set of instructions that tells it where to look for *more* instructions and, once found, how to interpret them.

The "smartest" thing in your Apple computer is a *microprocessor unit* (abbreviated *MPU*) called a *6502*, a piece of electronically active material that has been designed to get an instruction, do *exactly* what the instruction says, get the next instruction, do *exactly* what it says, and so on, ad infinitum. This serves as the "brain" of the Apple. The problem with this "brain" that it can only do what it is told to do.

The true workhorse responsibility of a computer falls to the *software*, the sets of instructions themselves that the computer executes. It doesn't matter if you have the most elementary or most powerful computer; a bad set of instructions will perform miserably on either.

Any computer has to be told how to communicate with its "external" devices (*peripherals* such as the disk drives, printers, etc.). These devices allow sending new information to the computer, or receiving information from the computer; the information must often be processed into an acceptable form as it is either sent or received. The software that does this is called an *operating system.*

AT THE "BASIC" LEVEL

Starting with the Apple's power off, if you open your disk drive doors (so that the Apple doesn't boot a disk) and turn the power on, you will hear a "beep" and (on most current Apples) the disk drive whirs with its little "IN USE" light lit. If your Apple does this, hold down the "control" key at the left of the keyboard (labeled "CTRL" or "Control" depending on your model of Apple), press the "RESET" key at the upper right hand corner of the keyboard (unless you have a *II*c, where it is at the upper *left* hand corner), and release them both.

The disk drive "IN USE" light should go out and the drive should stop. With the monitor screen on, you should see a "]" (right bracket) at the lower left hand corner of the screen. If you have a ">" instead, you *cannot* run BASIC.SYSTEM and this book will do you no good; check with your Apple dealer about a solution.

If the disk drive doesn't start and the screen has a bunch of "trash" on the upper part of the screen (flashing characters and such), look for a "*" (asterisk) at the lower left hand corner of the screen. If it's there, hold down the "control" key, press "B" (capitol B), release both keys, and then press the "return" key at the right side of the keyboard. Again, you should see a"]"; if you see a ">", you *cannot* run BASIC.SYSTEM without some hardware changes.

YOUR BASIC OPERATING SYSTEM

The "]" indicates that we have arrived at Applesoft BASIC, a computer language built into the hardware of the Apple *II*e, *II*c, and Apple *II* Plus Computers. Applesoft BASIC accepts English-like words as commands. The ">" symbol, if that is what appeared, indicates you have an Apple *II* (no "Plus") which uses a different version of the BASIC language.

Applesoft uses a very basic type of operating system. The flashing "box" immediately to the right of the "]" symbol is the *cursor* prompting you to type something.

If you happen to type a familiar BASIC command like

```
PRINT "HELLO"
```

Applesoft will do something sensible like print the word

```
HELLO
```

on the screen. If you type something which BASIC finds unintelligible, like

```
TYPE "HELLO"
```

Applesoft will object via a "beep" and a

```
?SYNTAX ERROR
```

message. "?SYNTAX ERROR" indicates that Applesoft did not understand the command. This is reasonable since "TYPE" is not a valid Applesoft program statement.

Part of the "operating system" of the BASIC Apple is at work. When you type something on the keyboard like "PRINT", each character has to be read from the keyboard, stored in an assigned space, and sent to Applesoft when you signal you are done typing this command via the "return" key.

BASIC itself doesn't handle that task, it turns the job over to a set of programs called the *system monitor* that handle most of the menial tasks. The system monitor gets the characters you type, assimilates them into a line, and sends that line to BASIC when you hit the "return" key to show you are done (for now). Applesoft recognizes "PRINT" as something it knows how to do and does it. It doesn't understand "TYPE" and so it gives an error when it sees that entered as a command. The reason you don't get an error until you hit "return" is that BASIC hasn't seen the command until you finish it.

If you type "PRINT" at the "]" prompt and use the left-arrow key to back up to the "R", then use the right-arrow to move forward past the "T", you are interacting with the system monitor, the low man on the operating system totem pole.

BASICS WITH THE DISK

If you try typing "CAT" as an Applesoft command, again you see the dreaded "?SYNTAX ERROR" message. Applesoft has no instruction to interpret what "CAT" should mean as a command.

With the disk door still open, insert a copy of a bootable ProDOS disk with BASIC.SYSTEM (a copy of the /USERS.DISK or *II*c /UTILITIES will work) into the drive attached as drive 1 of slot 6. Use the Applesoft command "PR#6" to activate the disk drive. Notice the "IN USE" light comes on again and the drive whirs. Now, with the disk properly inserted, close the drive door.

You should see a screen display similar to Fig. 1-1; the message "PRODOS VERSION <something-or other>" (there are several versions in use) and a copyright notice from Apple Computer. You might also hear some rattling noises from the disk drive as information is read in from the disk.

If the message "UNABLE TO LOAD PRODOS" or "RELOCATION ERROR" occurs, then you either have a bad disk or a hardware problem. Try a different ProDOS disk. If the same thing happens, it is probably a hardware problem; consult an Apple dealer to help you with the problem.

Eventually, the disk drive "IN USE" light will go out and the drive will stop. Hopefully, you will see the "]" prompt. If you booted a copy of the /USERS.DISK, you'll need to press "B" to escape to Applesoft. If you booted the *II*c /UTILITIES, choose option 9 from the main menu and insist that, yes, you really want to quit to BASIC.

Leave the disk in the drive. Now type "CAT" followed by a "return". Notice that as you hit "return" the flashing cursor disappears. The disk drive "IN USE" light will glow again, the disk will spin for a few seconds, loads of stuff will be printed to the screen, and then everything will go quiet again and you will see the "]" prompt and the blinking cursor again.

Why didn't Applesoft print "?SYNTAX ERROR"? How did Applesoft know to go to the disk? The answer is that Applesoft didn't know to go to the disk. Applesoft, in fact, never *saw* the command "CAT".

RUNNING INTERFERENCE

Obviously, the use of the information on the disk loaded into the Apple's memory during the "boot" process has changed some of the capabilities of the Apple. A program has been read in from

```
              APPLE //

     PRODOS 1.1.1    18-SEP-84



COPYRIGHT APPLE COMPUTER,  INC., 1983-84
```

Fig. 1-1. ProDOS boot screen display.

the ProDOS disk that added commands to the Apple that were not originally part of Applesoft.

The first of these, ProDOS, is a program that handles the systematic use of the disk drive. It allows you store and retrieve information as *files* on the disk. In fact, the ProDOS program itself exists in a file named "PRODOS". ProDOS is the *D*isk *O*perating *S*ystem. It is an operating system that allows use of the disk.

ProDOS has a limitation, though. To directly control it, it is necessary to communicate commands to ProDOS using *machine language*, the native language of the 6502 MPU. For most people, this is too cumbersome a language to converse in on a regular basis. One of the reasons BASIC is used in many computers is so that people can avoid machine language (we'll discuss this in more detail in Chapter 17).

A second program is loaded when Applesoft is to be used with ProDOS. This second program serves as an *interpreter* that converts English-looking commands into the machine language terms that ProDOS understands, much like the Applesoft BASIC interpreter translates English-looking BASIC programs into the machine language commands that the 6502 MPU can understand. This second program is named *BASIC.SYSTEM*, and is the primary focus of this book.

You will often see commands such as "CAT" referred to as ProDOS commands. Actually, this is false; ProDOS has no idea what "CAT" means. There is not even an equivalent command in ProDOS; the same function requires several ProDOS commands to carry out. "CAT" is a *BASIC.SYSTEM* command; BASIC.SYSTEM translates the command "CAT" into the sequence of instructions needed to have ProDOS return a list of files from the disk (which is what "CAT" is supposed to do).

Since the word "ProDOS" is sometimes used to refer to the *complete* package of ProDOS, BASIC.SYSTEM, and utilities sold in combination (such as *The ProDOS User's Kit*), the program represented by the ProDOS file itself is often referred to as the *kernel*, to make it plain that *only* the ProDOS program is being discussed.

If you execute the "CAT" command again, you will probably see the names "PRODOS" and "BASIC.SYSTEM" whiz by at the left edge of the screen display.

SHARING RESPONSIBILITY

Just to show that BASIC.SYSTEM doesn't know everything, try the

```
TYPE "HELLO"
```

command again. Again, you get the same Applesoft

```
?SYNTAX ERROR
```

with a "beep". But try the command

```
CAT "HELLO"
```

(include the quotation marks). Now you get a

```
SYNTAX ERROR
```

with a "beep".

Look like the same thing? Look closely. The first message has a "?" in front of the "S" in "SYNTAX". The second message does not. That's because the first error message was sent by Applesoft; the second error message was returned by BASIC.SYSTEM.

This gives us a clue as to how commands are handled by the combination of the disk operating system (and BASIC.SYSTEM, in this case) and Applesoft. When you type a command line, the first program to "examine" the completed line is BASIC.SYSTEM. BASIC.SYSTEM decides if the command resembles one of its commands; if so, it attempts to execute the command. If, for some reason, BASIC.SYSTEM finds it cannot complete the command because of an error, it will report the error and return you to Applesoft (unless you have made other arrangements).

If BASIC.SYSTEM does not recognize the command at all, it will pass the command on to Applesoft (if we are at the "]" prompt or running a BASIC program). Applesoft then gets a chance to see if it can recognize and execute the command as an Applesoft statement. If not, Applesoft returns an error message. Applesoft error messages are always prefaced with a question mark (as in "?SYNTAX ERROR"). BASIC.SYSTEM error messages do not contain the question mark.

If you happen to be using the system monitor, which prompts you with an asterisk ("*") instead of the Applesoft prompt, BASIC.SYSTEM will still intercept any command you type and examine it. If it does not recognize it as a BASIC.SYSTEM command, it will be sent on to the monitor. An error encountered by BASIC.SYSTEM while in the monitor will cause BASIC.SYSTEM to print its error message and send you back to Applesoft.

In our example above, the first "TYPE" command was not recognized by BASIC.SYSTEM, so it was sent on to Applesoft. Applesoft will not recognize the command either, so it notifies you that it did not understand via the "?SYNTAX ERROR" message.

In the second example, "CAT" is a valid command word for BASIC.SYSTEM, but

```
CAT "HELLO"
```

is not valid because "HELLO" (in quotes) is not valid for use with the command. Therefore, BASIC.SYSTEM sent its error message and did not forward the command to Applesoft.

SO WHAT ELSE DOES IT DO?

Of course, BASIC.SYSTEM does a lot more than simply report the list of files on a disk and tell you when you've goofed. The commands will be discussed in detail over the next few chapters, but here's the nutshell description of what BASIC.SYSTEM and ProDOS do.

ProDOS is responsible for performing all disk read/write operations. Any time you wish to read something into memory from the disk or write something to the disk, ProDOS handles the chore. ProDOS also keeps track of the use of RAM memory so that it knows which part of memory are free for its use.

ProDOS also contains information on communicating with certain other devices attached to the computer, notably a clock peripheral card (if appropriate software is installed) to provide the time and date for some ProDOS operations. ProDOS also provides support for using hardware signals called *interrupts*, which will be discussed later.

ProDOS can be directly instructed to perform tasks by machine language commands sent to it's *MLI* (*M*achine *L*anguage *I*nterpreter). This method of communicating with ProDOS is available for use with or without BASIC.SYSTEM.

BASIC.SYSTEM does not actually contain programs that read the disk, but it serves as the interface between ProDOS and Applesoft programs. It also allows you to type in BASIC.SYSTEM commands directly for immediate access to the disk while you are entering a program or simply "mucking about" in BASIC or in the monitor.

ABOUT THE DISK

The 5 1/4 inch diskette, presently the standard storage medium for the Apple *II* is essentially a flat disk of very thin plastic with a coating similar to that used on recording tape (such as the familiar audio or video cassette). This disk is then encased in a square cover to protect the disk's delicate surface.

When placed within the disk drive, the disk can be rotated within the cover. The disk drive is capable of reading (and writing to) circular paths on the spinning disk called *tracks*. The information on these tracks is broken into smaller units called *sectors*.

If you remove the diskette from its protective paper sleeve as if you were going to place it in the drive, you'll notice that you can see the (usually brownish) disk through a rather large slot cut in the cover. The disk drive has a electronic sensing head that can read or record magnetic signals on the disk; it touches the disk through that slot's opening. Don't touch the brown surface; the coating will be soiled or damaged which may cause the disk to become unusable, or can in turn cause damage to the recording head inside the disk drive. Magnetic fields (including those from telephone or even toy magnets!) can also damage the disk, as can folding it, etc. Treat the disk with respect, in accordance with the manufacturer's directions.

When disks are originally manufactured, they are created without programs of any kind recorded on them. Since different computers use different ways of storing information on the disks, all disks must be *formatted* for the particular computer they are to be used on. Formatting involves writing a certain minimum amount of information on the disk to "mark off" the tracks and sectors, and organizing them in a way that allows the operating system can locate to access its files. Once the disk has been formatted, programs can be recorded on it and the disk is ready for use. The disk does not have to be reformatted unless the formatting is damaged by an electronic or mechanical problem, or by mishandling.

THE PRODOS FORMAT

Not only must disks be formatted for the particular brand of computer they are to be used on, they must be formatted for the particular operating system they are to be used with. As an example, disks that are to be used with ProDOS must be formatted as ProDOS disks; ProDOS cannot normally read files on a DOS 3.3 (an older operating system for the Apple *II*) disk, for instance, without a special program. The program "FILER" on the /USERS.DISK will prepare a disk for use with ProDOS; you can use the "format a volume" option on the "volume activities" menu. The *II*c /UTILITIES disk has a similar option.

If you decide to use the disk with DOS 3.3 later, it can be re- formatted for use with DOS, but *formatting always destroys all files and data on the disk*, so you should not format a disk unless you know it does not contain any valuable information.

The Apple Disk *II* drive and its work-alikes (like the DuoDisk, the 5 1/4"" UniDisk, and the Apple *II*c drive) divide the diskette into 35 concentric circular *tracks* during formatting. Each track is created in 16 subdivisions called *sectors*, each contains 256 bytes of storage capacity. That gives the disk a total storage capacity of 256 * 16 * 35 (a total of 143,360) bytes. Not all of this storage capacity is usable; under ProDOS, 3584 bytes are reserved for particular information about the disk used by ProDOS.

ProDOS is capable of handling larger disk drives than these, up to a maximum of 32 *megabytes* (a megabyte is 1024 * 1024 bytes; slightly over a million) for a single disk volume. ProDOS divides its disks into storage areas called *blocks*; each block is 512 bytes in size (two sectors each on the Disk *II*-type drives). ProDOS can manipulate files up to 16 megabytes in size.

THE PRODOS BOOT PROCESS

When you boot a ProDOS disk, there are several stages to the process. Most of these stages involve programs in machine language.

First, the machine language program within the disk controller card's ROM memory is executed, which positions the disk drive's read/write head to read track 0 (the first track). The first block (block 0) of information from the ProDOS disk is read into RAM memory at $800 (2048) and executed.

Block 0 on a ProDOS disk contains the *ProDOS loader*; this program examines the computer to see if it is being booted on an Apple *II* or an Apple *III* computer. On an Apple *III*, the loader attempts to load an operating system named *SOS*. On an Apple *II*, the loader looks for the file named "PRODOS" on the diskette; if that program is found, it is loaded into RAM at $2000 (8192) and executed. If the file is not found, or an error occurs trying to load it, you will see an "*** UNABLE TO LOAD PRODOS ***" error message on the screen.

The PRODOS program prints the "boot screen" identifying itself. It then attempts to move (relocate) the ProDOS kernel into the RAM card area of the Apple *II* (this is why ProDOS requires a 64K Apple); if ProDOS detects an error while doing this, an error message will be printed and the system will be unresponsive to keyboard commands other than "reset" (the system will "hang").

During this boot process, PRODOS also attempts to identify various devices attached to the computer, specifically disk drives and a clock card, and record their presence for later access. PRODOS also attempts to identify the type of Apple it is being booted on (Apple *II*, 64K *II*e, 128K *II*e, or *II*c) and the presence of an Apple *II*e-compatible

80-column text card. On a 128K Apple *II*e or *II*c system, PRODOS will turn most of the "extra" 64K RAM memory into an area named "/RAM" that it can access as if it were a small disk drive.

If PRODOS relocates itself successfully, it will then attempt to load a special type of file called a *system program* and execute it. The way ProDOS chooses this file will be described in Chapter 3, after we discuss the ProDOS *file system* and *file types*. In this book, we usually assume that the program we want loaded is BASIC.SYSTEM.

ProDOS files can contain programs, ASCII text, binary (machine language) data or programs, etc. ProDOS can maintain a very large number of files on a disk (up to the capacity of the disk). The manner in which ProDOS organizes these files will be discussed in the next chapter.

If you are familiar with DOS 3.3 (as we assume some of you are), there are some advantages to ProDOS and BASIC.SYSTEM over DOS. All is not gravy, however. We have reserved further comments about ProDOS for discussion in an Appendix, where we compare ProDOS to the older (but still widely used) DOS 3.3 operating system.

Chapter 2

The ProDOS File System

ProDOS uses a relatively complicated method of identifying a single file out of the thousands (or more!) it can maintain on a disk. Here, by way of a fable, is how the system is supposed to work.

GETTING ORGANIZED

Let's assume we have the classic kind of "files", the basic manilla folder-type that people carry around large business offices and dump on some horrified person's desk (who then opens it with all the enthusiasm of someone hunting water-moccasins). If we are a BIG company, we might have a few thousand folders to store away for later reference. How do you find one folder among thousands?

The first thing you do is *label the folders*, hopefully in a recognizable and systematic manner. A file containing monthly information on purchases would be labelled "PURCHASES", one containing receipts would be labeled "RECEIPTS", etc. If you switch the names and the folders are filed away, woe be to you when you to find it again.

You then can throw the files into a large stack (let's call it "Big Stack") and it will not take too long to find a particular folder in the stack, as long as there aren't too many total file folders. Let's say the corporate management has made it an absolute edict that no more than 51 file folders are ever allowed to be used, just to make sure the number stays manageable. And, of course, the day arrives when the 52nd category has arisen and you need 52 file folders.

Now you have to change the system. You can't have more than 51 folders, but you need 52. The only way you can do this is with a new product: *magic file folders* that hold other file folders. As long as the magic folder is closed, the files within it aren't visible so they can't be counted as part of Big Stack. Once you get into the file, though, you can read all the names of the file folders it contains, but none of the names of files outside of that specific folder.

Strange rules—but that's the way it is with magic. One advantage of the "magic" file folder is that it can hold any number of other files, including other magic file folders. The disadvantage is that you can't see what's in the magic folder until it's open, and then you can *only* see what's in it until you close it to look at another folder.

This doesn't seem like too much of a limitation at first, so you start consolidating the original 52 files into groups so that you can use the magic folders. For example, you take the files "US Orders" and "Overseas Orders" and save them into a magic file folder labeled just "Orders", which becomes a part of Big Stack. When you look at Big Stack, "Orders" is visible but not the two files it contains. You can at any time, however, pull out "Orders", open it, and see the other two files. This works fine for a time.

MORE AND MORE FILES

Then, due to the advent of Intergalactic Travel, one day you have to put a *bunch* of files into "Orders". Let's say, for the sake of argument, that you decide to try and keep the number of files you have in any file folder at once, magic or otherwise, reasonably low. Too many files and you are back to the basic problem of finding one file among hundreds.

By now, you know the solution: nothing bans the use of magic files within magic files, so you split the *bunch* of files into smaller groups and put these into new magic files. Say that you split the files within "Orders" into two new groups named "Orders from Earth" and "Other Orders". Then "US Orders" and "Overseas Orders" could be placed within the magic file labeled "Earth", and that file in turn could be concealed within "Orders". See Fig. 2-1 for an illustration of this principle.

How to find a file? Just refer to it in the sequence of file folders that you have to open to get to it. You could fetch "US Orders" by going to Big Stack, looking inside for "Orders", looking inside "Orders" for "Orders from Earth", and looking inside "Orders from Earth" for "US Orders". Hopefully, the information you need is in there.

PRODOS AS GO-FER

A set of disk files under ProDOS works just like the set of file folders above. The "Big Stack" becomes the ProDOS disk "volume name". ProDOS uses names for its disks so that each can be identified. If we had two stacks of files in an office, we might have to name them "Big Stack" and "Paper Mill" to differentiate them. Similarly, ProDOS needs a separate name for each disk volume it works with.

ProDOS has the same restriction on the number of files as "Big Stack" above. ProDOS calls a collection of file names a "directory" (or sometimes "catalog").The first list of up to 51 files for the ProDOS volume, corresponding to the files we can read in Big Stack before looking inside any of the magic folders, is called the *volume directory.*

ProDOS can have no more than 51 file names in a volume directory, although it may have fewer. When more than 51 files are needed within a volume directory you must open a *subdirectory* (for "subordinate" directory) which is very close to our magic file above; it is *not* limited to 51 files as for the volume directory. A subdirectory may in turn hold more subdirectories as part of its list of files.

At this level, hunting a file on a ProDOS volume is just like hunting a file in Big Stack; you look for the file in the volume directory (Big Stack), if the file is not there you search the subdirectories (magic files) to see if the file you want is there. If not, you search the subdirectory within the subdirectory (magic files within magic files) until you find the file you are looking for.

A FILE BY ANY OTHER NAME

ProDOS does have some peculiarities of its own. For one thing, it's very particular about how you name your disk volume and its files.
Basically, the rules are these:

1. The name must begin with a letter; 'A' through 'Z'. Lowercase 'a' through 'z' can be typed with commands, but will be changed to uppercase when the file name is placed in the directory.

2. The name can contain only letters, numbers, and the period ('.'). No other characters are allowed—not even a blank space.

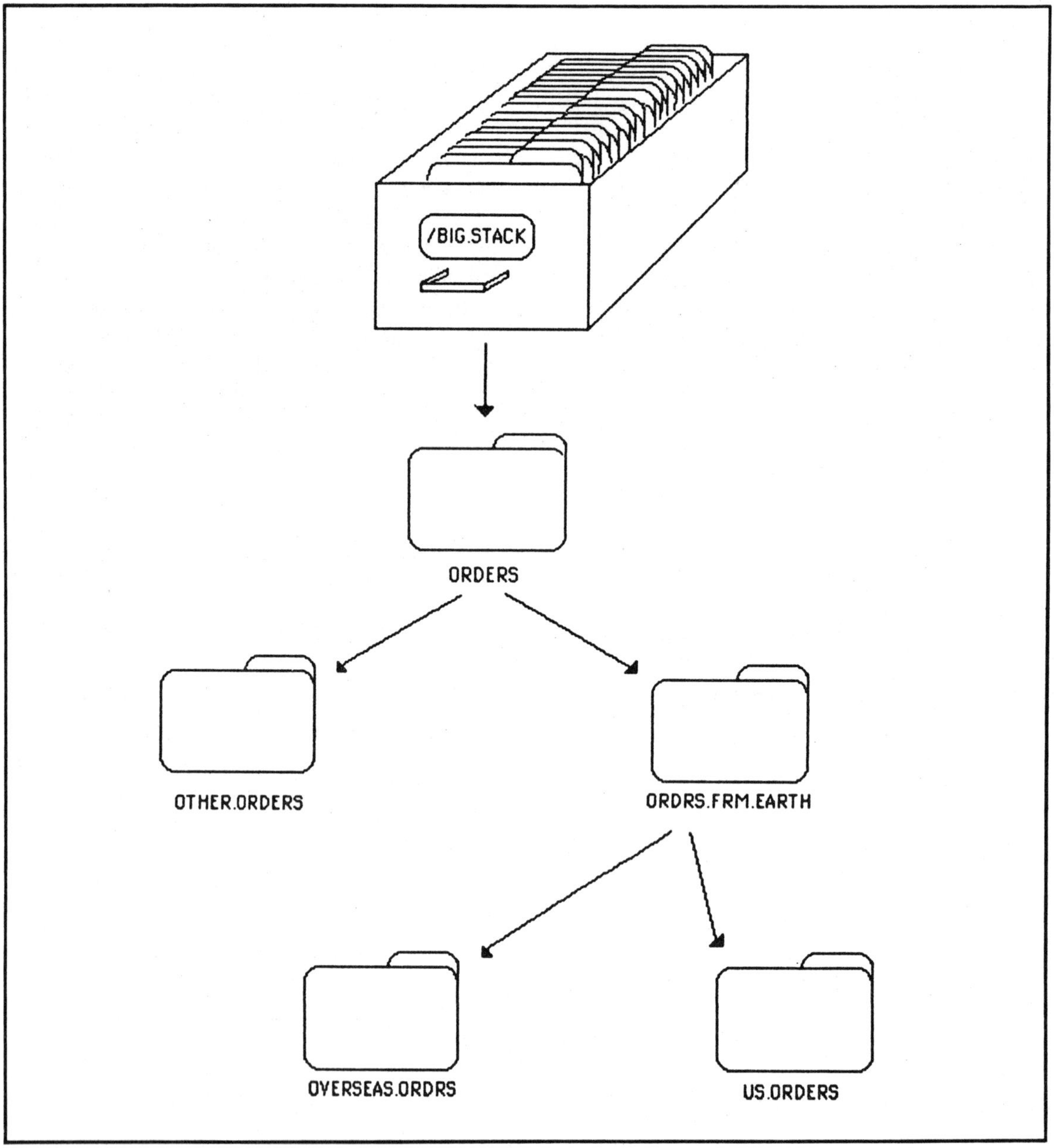

Fig. 2-1. The hierarchy of /BIG.STACK.

3. The name can be a maximum of fifteen characters in length.

Examples of *legal* names (the quotes used here to denote the name are not typed as part of the name) are "BIG.FAT.DISK","MY.WORLD.1", and "FILES . . . " (no rule against successive periods). Examples of *illegal* names are "1.FOR.ALL" (does notstart with a letter), "SPACED OUT" (contains a space, which is not a legal character), and "TOO.BLOODY.LONG.TO.USE" (22 characters long, which is over the 15 character limit).

PATHNAMES

If we look at what it takes to look through the magic files in our fable, we realize that a single filename may not take us where we need to go. For example, in our search for "US Orders" we have to look through three of the magic folders first. The search order was "Big Stack", "Orders", "Orders from Earth", and finally "US Orders".

Let's look at the equivalent exercise under ProDOS. First, we change the filenames to valid ProDOS filenames; they become "BIG.STACK", "ORDERS","ORDRS.FRM.EARTH" (we had to abbreviate to get that one down to 15 characters),and "US.ORDERS".

"BIG.STACK" becomes the volume name, representing the ultimate 'File That Leads to All Files'. This stack would correspond to the volume name of a disk. To show that this is the *first* name used for any *complete* description of a search, ProDOS expects a volume name to be the first name in the list and to be preceded by a "/" ("slash" character). Therefore, the truly proper ProDOS designation for the name of our volume directory is "/BIG.STACK".

Each of the magic files holds the names of other files. These magic files are also directories, but are also called *subdirectories*. The magic files are all subordinate to the volume directory that contains them; plus, any directory that is contained in another directory is subordinate to it. ProDOS uses the same "/" character to separate subdirectories, so that our search designator becomes

/BIG.STACK/ORDERS/
ORDRS.FRM.EARTH/US.ORDERS

We search the volume directory /BIG.STACK, find its subdirectory ORDERS, search it, find the subdirectory ORDRS.FRM.EARTH, and search its files until we find the file US.ORDERS. If we try to do the search in any other order, we won't find the right file.

This arrangement of the names into an ordered list is called a *pathname* because it describes a path to the designated file though the directories.

THE PREFIX

Suppose we are already at the subdirectory file "ORDRS.FRM.EARTH" and just need to go from "US.ORDERS" to "OVERSEAS.ORDRS" (another file in the directory "ORDRS.FRM. EARTH"). There is no need to know the *entire* pathname since we already know we are in the directory reached by the path

/BIG.STACK/ORDERS/ORDRS.FRM.EARTH/

Therefore, there should be no need to specify the entire pathname just to reach a file in the same directory.

And there isn't. If so instructed, ProDOS will maintain the first portion of the pathname in a *prefix*. The prefix defines the *start* of the pathname. It's a *partial pathname*. The remainder of the pathname forms a second partial pathname. The two parts can be joined to make a whole pathname.

Our path to US.ORDERS can be broken in several ways to form sets of a prefix and a second partial pathname:

/BIG.STACK/ and ORDERS/ORDRS.FRM.
EARTH/US.ORDERS
/BIG.STACK/ORDERS and
ORDRS.FRM.EARTH/US.ORDERS
/BIG.STACK/ORDERS/ORDRS.FRM.EARTH/ and
US.ORDERS

Notice that the trailing "/" for the prefix can either be present or absent when you define it; as ProDOS assembles the prefix and partial pathname to form the complete pathname, it will add the separating "/" after the prefix if it isn't specified. There is never a "/" before the partial pathname, however. That would cause the first name listed in the partial pathname to be interpreted as a volume name and the partial pathname would become a name for a *complete path*.

ALL HAIL THE KING

When all the subdirectories and files on a volume are mapped by their pathnames, a overall file structure begins to take form as previously seen in Fig.2.1. This file structure is known as a *hierarchical file structure*, since it resembles the hierarchy of a chain of command. The volume (/BIG.STACK, in this case) turns out to be the 'Big Cheese' which lords over all the subordinate files and directories. In turn, each subdirectory of the volume may have subdirectories of its own, and so on.

THOUGHTS ON THE DIRECTORY STRUCTURE

From time to time, it will be necessary to talk about advantages and limitations of ProDOS and BASIC.SYSTEM. A few things are obvious now about pathnames and the ProDOS directory structure.

First, this system can handle a *large* number of files. Even though limited to 51 files in the volume directory, you can simply keep expanding the number of subdirectories until you have enough to store all your files. The only limit is disk space and the maximum permissible length of a pathname (128 characters). The latter limit is not severe for present Apple *II* storage devices.

Second, once you get that *large* number of files, finding a file in the hierarchy is like hunting a needle in a haystack. Indeed, if you decide to beclever and use as many subdirectories as possible (whether you need them or not), you can make looking for one file among fifty an adventure.

Third, if you do bury a file deep in a series of subdirectories, it's going to take a very long pathname to get to it. That means more typing, and more chances for typographical errors (or to forget where the file is).

Ultimately, you are better off to minimize the number of subdirectories you use to keep such confusion to a minimum. There are two legitimate purposes for using subdirectories: to make sufficient room for filenames on a large disk volume, and to group/organize files of a similar purpose. If you don't have an overwhelming need for either of these uses, stay away from subdirectories. It just makes it harder for you (and others) to find things on a disk. Additionally, when creating new directories, use logical groupings for files so that if you do need to find one, you can make an educated guess where to look.

Chapter 3

Learning To Be In Command

The initial step in giving commands is to know how to do so in a manner that the recipient of the command can understand what you want. BASIC.SYSTEM only understands its BASIC.SYSTEM language. Since we are smarter than the computer, we will have to learn BASIC.SYSTEM's language in order to speak to it. BASIC.SYSTEM can't learn ours.

A NON-COMMAND

Schematically, the normal generalized form of a command to BASIC.SYSTEM is

COMMAND <name>, <opt1>, <opt2>, . . . , <optn>

where "COMMAND" represents the name of the command (naturally), "<name>" represents a volume name or pathname that may or may not be required, and the "<opt#>" terms represent various command options (separated by commas) that may be present.

The addition of extra spaces (or *no* spaces) between the "COMMAND" and "<name>" is usually insignificant; BASIC.SYSTEM will ignore the number of spaces and attempt to decipher the command line as typed, if possible. Usually, commands are shown as being separated by a single space from their arguments.

TABLE OF BASIC.SYSTEM COMMANDS

The "COMMAND" portion is a word known to BASIC.SYSTEM that tells it to perform a certain action. Table 3-1 provides a nickel tour of all of the BASIC.SYSTEM commands and a brief description of what each command does.

If you use DOS 3.3 already, most of these commands will be familiar. The biggest changes are the use of pathnames for ProDOS commands, and some additional changes in parameter use with the ProDOS commands.

COME TO THE CONVENTIONS

It sometimes facilitates description of a BA-

Table 3-1. BASIC.SYSTEM Command "Words."

CAT	(or the long form, CATALOG) lists the files in a directory.
PREFIX	is used to display the prefix (as described in Chapter 2) or "set" it to a default value.
CREATE	is used to make new subdirectories and other types of files.
RENAME	changes file and directory names (including volume names).
DELETE	removes files and frees the disk space they occupied for re-use.
LOCK	protects files from being altered as a result of other BASIC.SYSTEM commands.
UNLOCK	reverses the effects of LOCK.
SAVE	saves a copy of the BASIC program in memory onto the disk.
LOAD	loads a copy of a BASIC program into memory from its disk file.
RUN	executes BASIC files specifically.
STORE	copies the currently defined BASIC variables into a disk file of type VAR.
RESTORE	copies a VAR file's data into BASIC variables.
CHAIN	is used within a BASIC program to execute a second BASIC program without destroying variable data from the first program.
BSAVE	copies binary data from memory to a disk file.
BLOAD	copies binary data from a disk file to memory.
BRUN	loads and executes a binary (machine language) file.
-	(that's the command, sometimes pronounced "dash" and also known as the "smart RUN" command) will execute several types of program files.
OPEN	prepares a file for use in transferring text (ASCII characters).
READ	causes a BASIC program to take its input (including INPUT and GET input) from a disk file.
WRITE	causes a BASIC program to send its output (via PRINT statements) to a file.
APPEND	causes a BASIC program to WRITE new information to the end of a file.
POSITION	allows you to change your position in an OPEN file.
FLUSH	updates any incomplete WRITE operations.
CLOSE	updates any incomplete WRITE operations and seals the file from further use (until it is OPENed again).
PR#	sets a slot number that output is to be "printed" to.
IN#	sets a slot number that input is to be "read" from.
FRE	"cleans up" memory wasted by unused string variables.

SIC.SYSTEM activity to use a command word in a verb or adjective form. Although BASIC.SYSTEM will accept commands in upper or lower case (so that "cat" is equivalent to "CAT" as a command), capital letters will be used to emphasize a command in a body of text, so that when you see the phrase "get the CAT off the disk," you know that the phrase is talking about using the BASIC.SYSTEM command to read a directory, and not implying that your feline mopes about on your computer supplies. Similarly, Applesoft statements will be capitalized when used in the same manner.

NAMES AND PLACES

The "<name>" can be a volume name or a full or partial pathname to a directory or file (which of these depends on the type of command) that may be required by the command. This name will conform to the rules of legal filenames (and pathnames) covered earlier. Not all commands need a name specified, and some commands that do not work on files or directories (including volumes) will insist that you not give them a name.

The use of a pathname and the uniqueness of the name are an essential part of the bookkeeping that ProDOS and BASIC.SYSTEM use to find a disk volume and/or a file on the disk.

PARAMETERS

Common *options* (which also might be called "*parameters*", "*arguments*" or "*modifiers*") include "S6", which specifies that slot number 6 is to be accessed, or "A8192", which indicates that a memory address of 8192 is to be used as a parameter. Unfortunately, it is necessary to memorize what the abbreviations mean in the context of the command that's being issued. As with pathnames, not all commands require (or accept) options.

Incidentally, if you know hexadecimal notation, any numeric parameter can be entered as its hexadecimal equivalent by placing a "$" directly in front of the number. For example, the above "S6" could have been specified as "S$6" and the "A8192" could have been given as "A$2000". We will be using hexadecimal numbers rather than decimal on occasion because ProDOS and BASIC.SYSTEM intermix the two number systems at times; at the point you feel it necessary, you can divert yourself to Appendix A1 (which briefly explains number systems) at the back of this book.

Just as with volume names or pathnames, lower case letters can be used when specifying options so that "a8192" is interpreted to mean the same thing as "A8192".

A SECOND CONVENTION

As a second convention for this book, a filename or other argument or parameter of the command which is not optional (that is, *must* be specified) will be *italicized* when we define a command's syntax to distinguish it from optional parameters that can be entered or omitted.

FINALLY, A PREVIEW

Here is a look at a valid BASIC.SYSTEM command:

```
CAT /BLOODY.BIG.DISK/MORE.FILES,S6,D2
```

"CAT" is the command, "/BLOODY.BIG.DISK/MORE.FILES" is the (optional) pathname, "S6" is the (optional) slot we want specified, and "D2" is the (optional) drive we want specified. This tells BASIC.SYSTEM to do a CAT of the specific subdirectory /BLOODY.BIG.DISK/MORE.FILES, a disk volume that is supposed to be in the drive attached to slot 6 as drive number 2. The commands will be covered in detail starting in Chapter 4.

BASIC.SYSTEM AND ERRORS

If you specify a command incorrectly, BASIC.SYSTEM will normally "beep" the Apple speaker and print "SYNTAX ERROR" to the screen. "*Syntax*" is a fancy word referring to the form of the command; whether the command line includes a recognizable command word, whether a required pathname was provided, etc.

If you specify a command correctly, but for some reason BASIC.SYSTEM cannot fulfill your wish, it may say other nasty things to you; for example, if you ask it to do something involving the volume "/BIG.DISK.2" while that volume is on the shelf behind you and not in the disk drive, you will hear a beep and see "PATH NOT FOUND" (which means the pathname wasn't found on a disk in a drive) printed to the screen.

The full complement (or insult, if you prefer) of BASIC.SYSTEM errors are listed in Table 3-2.

COMMONLY OCCURRING ERRORS

You need to keep in mind that several of these errors are common to certain BASIC.SYSTEM operations. Any time you specify a command, you can receive a "SYNTAX ERROR", "RANGE ERROR", "INVALID OPTION", or "NO DEVICE CONNECTED" message for the respective error. BASIC.SYSTEM will report these types of errors *before* it even tries to access the disk, with an occasional exception granted to "SYNTAX ERROR".

Any time you use a pathname in a command, or have a prefix set (so that it becomes at least part of a pathname), you can receive a "PATH NOT FOUND" error after BASIC.SYSTEM searches the disk(s) and the specified path was not found.

"I/O ERROR" indicates there is a problem with the disk (usually) or the disk drive (rare). Often, removing and carefully re-inserting the diskette *after the drive has stopped completely* will solve the problem. If it fails the second time and you *know* the proper disk is in the drive, you may need to reboot ProDOS to eliminate the problem.

If you attempt to read information from the disk, you may receive an "I/O ERROR" or, very occasionally, a "NO BUFFERS AVAILABLE".

There is a more detailed discussion of what causes the "NO BUFFERS AVAILABLE" error later in this book. If you are loading a program file into RAM, the self- explanatory "PROGRAM TOO LARGE" error is also possible. If you are attempting to write information to the disk or change information that is already on the disk, "WRITE PROTECTED", "DIRECTORY FULL", "DISK FULL", "FILE TYPE MISMATCH", "FILE LOCKED", and "DUPLICATE FILENAME" errors are all possible, as well as the errors mentioned with reading information from the disk.

None of these errors are particularly catastrophic; except for "FILE(S) STILL OPEN", where the files must be closed or you might lose data, and "I/O ERROR", which may indicate a disk has been physically damaged and that you have "lost" at least a portion of a file.

As mentioned in the first chapter, Applesoft error messages always begin with a "?", so you can distinguish them from BASIC.SYSTEM error messages.

SPECIAL FILENAMES

One mystical type of error that can occur can be caused by misuse of filenames. Generally, you can use any name for a file that you wish, but there are exceptions. There are three special filenames that may have special significance, especially during the "boot" process. These names should not be used so as to retain their function in the boot process.

As mentioned in Chapter 1, when a ProDOS disk is booted, the first file to be searched for is a file named "PRODOS" in the *volume* directory. If it is found, it will be loaded and executed. This name should be reserved for the file containing the ProDOS kernel.

If the ProDOS kernel is loaded and executed, it will look for the *first* file (in the directory currently defined for use by ProDOS) which is a *system* file, and which has a name ending in ".SYSTEM". ProDOS detects a system file via inspection of information it has stored regarding the file at the time of the file's creation, this information can also be viewed using BASIC.SYSTEM commands we'll discuss in the next chapter.

After booting a new disk, the directory defined for use is the volume directory. In most of our discussions, the assumption will be that the first system file with a name ending in ".SYSTEM" will be the file "BASIC.SYSTEM", so that ProDOS will load and execute the BASIC.SYSTEM interpreter for use automatically. In turn, the BASIC.SYSTEM interpreter will search for a file in the currently defined directory named "STARTUP"; if a file with that name is found it will auto-

Table 3-2. BASIC.SYSTEM Error Messages.

RANGE ERROR	you specified a number for a parameter that was too large or small to be used, such as "D888" for a drive number parameter.
NO DEVICE CONNECTED	usually seen when you try to access a disk drive that doesn't exist at the slot or drive you specified.
WRITE PROTECTED	Usually this means ProDOS is unable to write anything on the disk because the write-protect notch has been covered up.
END OF DATA	(within a program) you have instructed ProDOS/BASIC.SYSTEM to read more data from a file than the file contained.
PATH NOT FOUND	the requested pathname or prefix could not be found on a disk volume.
I/O ERROR	ProDOS was unable to read the disk with the specified pathname or in the specified drive. This may mean the drive is empty (no disk), or that the disk is not properly seated in the drive (the drive door is not open or the disk has not been centered properly), or that the disk in the drive is damaged, or that it is not a formatted ProDOS disk.
DISK FULL	in the process of attempting to store something on the disk, ProDOS discovered that there was no room for it.
FILE LOCKED	the command could not be completed because the individual file has been "protected" from modification.
INVALID OPTION	you used a parameter that does not exist for the command.
NO BUFFERS AVAILABLE	ProDOS/BASIC.SYSTEM was unable to create a required workspace to use with the file.
FILE TYPE MISMATCH	you attempted to use a command on a file of a type not designed for that command.
PROGRAM TOO LARGE	(for BASIC programs) the program is too large to fit in the available Apple memory.
NOT DIRECT COMMAND	you used a deferred-only mode command in direct mode.
SYNTAX ERROR	the command is not in the correct form to be executed, possibly from a spelling error, etc.
DIRECTORY FULL	you tried to put more than 51 files into a volume directory.
FILE NOT OPEN	(within a program) you tried to access a file that was not prepared for access.
DUPLICATE FILENAME	you tried to create a second file with the same pathname as another existing file in the directory.
FILE BUSY	you tried to open a file for use (or alter a file) that was already open.
FILE(S) STILL OPEN	(at termination of a program) you did not close all open files at the end of your program, or the program was stopped by an error before all files were closed.

matically be executed by BASIC.SYSTEM. Usually, the file is a BASIC program (similar in function to the "HELLO" program on a DOS 3.3 disk), but it is not restricted to this.

You can name other files "PRODOS" or "BASIC.SYSTEM", but it can cause problems and it is wise to reserve these names for files containing the ProDOS kernel and BASIC.SYSTEM interpreter specifically.

Chapter 4

Finding Files

The manipulation of data with the disk drive implies that you have ways of getting the files to and from the disk. Although ProDOS handles the intricacies of the actual storage and retrieval, BASIC.SYSTEM is the linguist that takes a command made up of (almost) English words and turns it into commands that ProDOS can understand. The first set of these BASIC.SYSTEM commands to discuss are the ones that allow us to locate information on a disk.

In the following discussion, the errors that are described will usually *not* include the general errors mentioned at the latter part of Chapter 3. Be aware that, although not specifically mentioned, errors like "I/O ERROR" may occur for the reasons covered in the last chapter.

THE "CAT" AND "CATALOG" COMMANDS

Since the whole point of the game is to work with the files on the disk, it is of paramount importance to be able to find the names of files on the disk(s). The *CATALOG* command or its shorter version *CAT* are used to this end. The command is given in either the long form:

```
CATALOG pathname,Dn,Sn
```

or the short form

```
CAT pathname,Sn,Dn
```

where "pathname" is a full or partial pathname defining a *directory* (type DIR) file. If a partial pathname is used, the current value of the prefix is "prepended" to the front of the name and the entire name is used as the name of the directory to search for.

The "D" and "S" stand for a specific *drive* and *slot* number and the "n" signifies a number for the slot or drive. You can specify (at this writing) an integer slot number of 1 to 7, and an integer drive number of 1 or 2. Any integer value outside of these ranges will cause a "RANGE ERROR" message. If a disk drive is not found at the specified location, BASIC.SYSTEM will return a "DEVICE NOT

CONNECTED" error.

If *only* the directory name is specified as a parameter in the command (this includes a directory name determined by a set prefix, discussed later), ProDOS will search all attached disk drives for that directory name. The search starts with the boot drive's slot and, if the correct directory is not found, ProDOS will go back and search the remaining drives starting at slot 7 and proceeding downward to slot 1. If the directory is not found, BASIC.SYSTEM will return a "PATH NOT FOUND" error message. For example, the command "CATALOG /MY.DISK" would search all disk drives for the volume "/MY.DISK" and, if found, display its volume directory.

If the drive and/or slot parameters are specified along with a *full* pathname specifying a directory name, BASIC.SYSTEM will search only the specified drive for that directory. If the directory file isn't there, BASIC.SYSTEM will again give a "PATH NOT FOUND" error. For example, "CAT /MY.DISK,D1" would only check drive one of the last slot accessed for the volume "/MY.DISK".

If the drive and/or slot parameters are specified along with a *partial* pathname specifying a directory name, BASIC.SYSTEM will "pre-pend" the volume name of the specified drive to the pathname and search for that directory. For example, even if the prefix is currently set to "/MY.DISK", if the command "CATALOG SUBDIRECTORY.1,S5,D2" is issued and the volume in drive 2 attached to slot 5 is named "/MY.OTHER.DISK", BASIC.SYSTEM will attempt to CATALOG the directory "/MY.OTHER.DISK/SUBDIRECTORY.1" in that slot and drive. If the directory is not found, the "PATH NOT FOUND" message will again be printed.

If the slot and/or drive is specified but no pathname is specified, then BASIC.SYSTEM will attempt to print the list of files in the *volume* directory of the specified drive attached to the specified slot, regardless of any defined prefix. If no prefix has been set and no options are used, ProDOS will return the volume directory listing of the volume in the last disk drive accessed.

In any of the above circumstances, if BASIC.SYSTEM returns an "I/O ERROR" message that is an indication that ProDOS was unexpectedly unable to read the volume in a drive. Possible reasons: the drive door is open, the disk is damaged or blank, or the disk is not a ProDOS-format disk (you cannot CATALOG a DOS disk using BASIC.SYSTEM's CATALOG command, for example).

It is *very* wise to get in the habit of labeling any ProDOS disks you use with their volume name. Although BASIC.SYSTEM will allow you to read the volume name, some other programs that run under ProDOS aren't so accommodating.

LOOKING AT THE RESULT

Now that we've beat the alternatives silly, let's look at the short form of the command. The command

```
CAT
```

will display the "short" form of the disk directory (or "catalog") as is shown in Fig. 4-1 (this example is from the /USERS.DISK found in Apple's *ProDOS User's Kit*). This display is conveniently about the same width as the Apple's normal video display format when the Apple is in 40-column mode. If the 80-column card is active and displaying 80 columns, the longer command

```
CATALOG
```

will display even more information as shown in Fig. 4-2.

If CATALOG is used with the 80-column card "off", the extended display format will still be used but it will "wrap" at the right edge of the screen to look like the display in Fig. 4-3. With a little practice you can read even this "folded" listing; it becomes important because the extra information of CATALOG versus CAT may be needed. Generally, the listings in this book will be given in the 80-column format so you can see all of the data.

CONTROLLING THE SCROLL

If you have a CATALOG listing with a lot of

```
/USERS.DISK
 NAME            TYPE  BLOCKS  MODIFIED

*PRODOS           SYS       30  18-SEP-84
*BASIC.SYSTEM     SYS       21  18-JUN-84
*FILER            SYS       51  18-JUN-84
*CONVERT          SYS       42  24-SEP-85
*STARTUP          BAS       24  15-OCT-83
*MOIRE            BAS        3  15-OCT-83
*HYPNOSIS         BAS        3  15-OCT-83
*ANIMALS          BAS       10  15-OCT-83

BLOCKS FREE:    89      BLOCKS USED:   191
```

Fig. 4-1. 40-Column CAT display.

filenames you may find that the top of the listing "scrolls off" the top of the screen before you can read the first few files. To temporarily stop the scrolling during a CATALOG, type a control-S, which will pause the listing on the screen until you press another key.

If you happen to spot the file you are looking for in the first few entries, you can type control-C to abort the rest of the listing. BASIC.SYSTEM will not print any more filename entries, but will instead just print the "disk free space" information line and then exit back to the Applesoft prompt.

THE FILE ENTRIES

Well, what does all this gibberish represent? Starting with the "BASIC.SYSTEM" entry from the CAT listing, let's examine the five items of data presented. From left to right, the items represent the following:

1. The presence of an asterisk at the far left end of the line means that this file is "protected" against certain BASIC.SYSTEM commands that might erase or alter it.
2. Next, we have the file*NAME* of up to 15 characters.
3. Then we have a file *TYPE*, in this case "SYS" to show that it is a "system" file.
4. Then comes the number of disk *BLOCKS* used by the file. This is a measure of the amount of

```
/USERS.DISK
 NAME            TYPE  BLOCKS  MODIFIED              CREATED              ENDFILE SUBTYPE

*PRODOS           SYS       30  18-SEP-84  0:00  20-DEC-84  8:28     14848
*BASIC.SYSTEM     SYS       21  18-JUN-84  0:00  20-DEC-84  8:29     10240
*FILER            SYS       51  18-JUN-84  0:00   8-APR-85 11:35     25600
*CONVERT          SYS       42  24-SEP-85 22:32   8-APR-85 11:36     20481
*STARTUP          BAS       24  15-OCT-83  0:00  15-OCT-83  0:00     11465
*MOIRE            BAS        3  15-OCT-83  0:00  15-OCT-83  0:00       941
*HYPNOSIS         BAS        3  15-OCT-83  0:00  15-OCT-83  0:00       637
*ANIMALS          BAS       10  15-OCT-83  0:00  15-OCT-83  0:00      4578

BLOCKS FREE:    89      BLOCKS USED:   191       TOTAL BLOCKS:   280
```

Fig. 4-2. 80-Column CATALOG display.

```
/USERS.DISK
 NAME             TYPE  BLOCKS  MODIFIED
       CREATED            ENDFILE SUBTYPE

*PRODOS           SYS      30  18-SEP-84
 0:00  20-DEC-84  8:28     14848
*BASIC.SYSTEM     SYS      21  18-JUN-84
 0:00  20-DEC-84  8:29     10240
*FILER            SYS      51  18-JUN-84
 0:00   8-APR-85 11:35     25600
*CONVERT          SYS      42  24-SEP-85
22:32   8-APR-85 11:36     20481
*STARTUP          BAS      24  15-OCT-83
 0:00  15-OCT-83  0:00     11465
*MOIRE            BAS       3  15-OCT-83
 0:00  15-OCT-83  0:00       941
*HYPNOSIS         BAS       3  15-OCT-83
 0:00  15-OCT-83  0:00       637
*ANIMALS          BAS      10  15-OCT-83
 0:00  15-OCT-83  0:00      4578

BLOCKS FREE:   89      BLOCKS USED:   191
    TOTAL BLOCKS:  280
```

Fig. 4-3. 40-Column CATALOG display.

space that the file occupies on disk (1 block = 512 bytes).

5. Then there is a date for the last time the file was *MODIFIED* (changed).

If we look at the same file entry from the "CATALOG" list, we see the first five entrys across are the same as for "CAT", but there are some new ones, too. The additional items are:

6. A time for when the file was last *MODIFIED*.
7. A date for when the file was *CREATED*.
8. A time for when the file was *CREATED*.
9. A value for *ENDFILE*, which essentially tells us how big ProDOS believes the file to be (the bigger the number, the bigger the file) in bytes.
10. An area called *SUBTYPE*, which holds additional data for certain types of files.

Additionally, look at the left of the very first line of the "CAT" listing and you will see the volume name "/USERS.DISK". CATALOG also displays this at the top of its listing; this tells us what volume or subdirectory we are listing the files for.

The line directly below this gives the titles for the various information we found in the file entry (described above); then there is a blank (empty) line and then the file entries.

At the end of the file entries another blank line is printed and finally we are told about the number of blocks free and the number of blocks used in the CAT entry, and also the number of total blocks in the last line of the CATALOG listing. This gives us a running account on how much room we have on the disk.

TYPES OF FILES

In the directory listing examples produced by

Table 4-1. BASIC.SYSTEM File Type Specifiers.

BAS	A stored Applesoft BASIC program file. single space; blank line between entries
TXT	A file of text data.
BIN	A file of binary data; possibly a program, data, or possibly just an "image" of an area of memory saved to disk.
SYS	A file containing a special type of program called a "system" program. These programs are usually designed to utilize ProDOS directly as does BASIC.SYSTEM, which is itself a system file.
DIR	A directory file which contains a list of grouped filenames which are not listed in the current directory (the one you are reading). These correlate to the "magic folders" we discussed in Chapter 2.
VAR	A file used by BASIC.SYSTEM to save information on Applesoft BASIC variables.

CAT and CATALOG earlier, the file "type" appears just to the right of the filename. The five most common types of files and what they generally represent are presented in Table 4-1.

There is additionally a file type called *REL* (for RELocatable) used for relocatable machine language program files.

As you may have noticed, the file type attempts to categorize the files in such a way as to tell you (and ProDOS) something about their probable function. The types listed are not all of the types of files available; some programs (notably *AppleWorks*) have special file types to use specifically with their data. ProDOS even allows a user to define up to eight of these "special" file types for his own use.

SUBDIRECTORIES AND PREFIX

As mentioned, every ProDOS disk volume has a name associated with it which becomes a part of the complete pathname to the file you are interested in. Naturally, before you begin rummaging around on a disk to find your copy of a "MY.BEST.PROGRAM" file you will need to have the proper volume name at hand to start the search from. The *PREFIX* command of BASIC.SYSTEM facilitates displaying the volume name for you.

If you are brave enough to be working heavily with subdirectories, PREFIX will also allow you to set a partial pathname that is always "prefixed" to the filename or partial pathname that you enter. As with the volume name, this "PREFIX" pathname can be displayed later if you happen to forget what directory you are working within. The generalized form of the command is

PREFIX pathname,Dn,Sn

where the optional "pathname" can be a full or partial pathname or, for this command, the null path ("/"). The different forms of the PREFIX command allow you to set the prefix in various ways.

Using the command with no arguments if no prefix name is set (which is usually the case immediately after we boot up ProDOS and BASIC.SYSTEM) will cause BASIC.SYSTEM to read the volume name of the last drive accessed and report it to you; but the prefix will *not* be set to that value. To set (or change) the value of the prefix, the PREFIX command must be issued with either a pathname or slot and drive values explicitly used.

Using "PREFIX" with no argument if a prefix value has been set will cause BASIC.SYSTEM to report the currently set value. For example, if we have just booted "/USERS.DISK/" and it remains in slot 6, drive 1, the command

```
PREFIX
```

will cause BASIC.SYSTEM to read the volume name of the last drive accessed (which was drive 1 attached to slot 6) and report it as "/USERS.DISK/".

Typing "PREFIX /USERS.DISK" will cause BASIC.SYSTEM to check all drives for the presence of the volume "/USERS.DISK" and, if the volume is found, BASIC.SYSTEM will set the value of the prefix to "/USERS.DISK". Subsequently, typing "PREFIX" by itself will cause "/USERS.DISK/" to be displayed without BASIC.SYSTEM having to read the disk again. Until you change the prefix, BASIC.SYSTEM remembers the current value of the prefix.

You can, of course, change the value of the prefix at any time; it may be mandatory to do so if you change disks so that BASIC.SYSTEM can recognize the new disk.

Let's imagine we want to try and disturb BASIC.SYSTEM's equilibrium a bit; let's switch "/USERS.DISK/" to drive 2 and placing an imaginary volume named "/MY.OTHER.DISK/" in drive 1. Assuming the prefix was set to "/USERS.DISK/" as we did above (so that drive 1 was the last drive accessed), if we issue a "CAT" command (with no arguments) BASIC.SYSTEM first spins the disk in drive 1 (which now contains "/MY.OTHER.DISK/"), but it doesn't print the CAT; it remains silent and spins the disk in drive two (which now contains "/USERS.DISK/") and prints its CAT! After the prefix has been set, BASIC.SYSTEM remembers it and silently issues it as the first part of the argument following the command. This means that the above "CAT" command was actually interpreted as if you had typed "CAT /USERS.DISK/" and BASIC.SYSTEM felt compelled to hunt for "/USERS.DISK/" before it displayed the directory.

If you had removed "/USERS.DISK/" before issuing the above "CAT" command, BASIC.SYSTEM would have searched every disk drive attached to the system and attempted to read in every disk volume name on the system before it decided that "/USERS.DISK/" was no longer available, at which time ProDOS would have told BASIC.SYSTEM to print the dreaded "PATH NOT FOUND" error message (with a "beep" of the speaker to impress you).

This points out a complication of having the prefix set to a specific volume or pathname; in using ProDOS commands that access files after the prefix is set, you must explicitly provide the complete pathname to reach any file that does not exist within the path set by the current prefix. In other words, to get the catalog of "/MY.OTHER.DISK/" with the prefix set to "/USERS.DISK/", you must use "CAT /MY.OTHER.DISK/" so that ProDOS knows you wish to look at "/MY.OTHER.DISK/" rather than at the volume currently defined in the prefix.

Note that "CAT /MY.OTHER.DISK" (no trailing "/" after the volume name) will also work since we don't need the latter "/" to separate the volume from a further path definition, but "CAT MY.OTHER.DISK" will not work since ProDOS will interpret this as meaning "CAT /USERS.DISK/MY.OTHER.DISK" after it adds the current prefix to the command. The first "/" before the "M" in the command "CAT /MY.DISK" tells ProDOS that "MY.DISK" is the volume name and that the prefix is not to be used in conjunction with it.

SETTING THE PREFIX WITHOUT A PATHNAME

It becomes apparent from this exercise that there must be ways of changing the prefix so that BASIC.SYSTEM can be notified that a new disk is now being put to use. One way to do this for a new volume in a specific drive is to order BASIC.SYSTEM to return the prefix of that drive using a command such as

```
PREFIX,D2
```

which will set the prefix to the *volume* name of the disk in drive 2 of the last slot accessed. In this case BASIC.SYSTEM does *not* print the value of the prefix automatically after reading the disk, it simply sets the prefix. To display the result, use the command "PREFIX" (no parameters) to force BASIC.SYSTEM to display the current prefix. Notice that the "S" parameter can also be used to force selection of a particular slot.

CLEARING THE PREFIX SETTING

All this setting of the prefix helps if you are planning to work with a specific disk directory. However, if the prefix is set to a specific volume or path, you may decide it is becoming awkward to always have to type a volume name or complete pathname as an argument to the various ProDOS commands. An easy solution is to type

```
PREFIX /
```

which cleverly sets the prefix to "/", which is the same as no prefix at all!

SETTING LONGER PATHNAMES AS PREFIX VALUES

Going deeper into the file system, if you have a subdirectory of interest, you can set the prefix to the value of the path to that directory. For example, if "/USERS.DISK/" is in drive 2 and has in its volume directory the subdirectories "DIRECTORY.1" and "DIRECTORY.2", and you want to always refer to files in "DIRECTORY.2", you can type

```
PREFIX /USERS.DISK/DIRECTORY.2
```

to attempt to set the prefix to that pathname. ProDOS will read the disk to see if the pathname is valid (that is, that the named volume and subdirectory exist so that the path exists) and, if so, will set the prefix to that value. A subsequent issuing of the command "CAT" will produce the directory listing of the contents of "/USERS.DISK/DIRECTORY.1". The command "CAT,D2" with "/USERS.DISK" in drive 2 will produce the directory listing of "/USERS.DISK/", as will "CAT /USERS.DISK/", but neither of these commands will alter the current prefix setting. To set the prefix back to "/USERS.DISK/" requires a "PREFIX /USERS.DISK/" or "PREFIX,D2" (with "/USERS.DISK" in drive 2) command.

ADDING TO THE PREFIX

If you wish to set the prefix to a directory that is a subdirectory within the current value of the prefix path, you can use the prefix command to simply add this additional portion of the path to the current prefix. For example, if the current value of the prefix was already set to "/USERS.DISK/" for the case above, then

```
PREFIX DIRECTORY.1
```

will attach (append) "DIRECTORY.1" to the "end" of the current prefix to generate "/USERS.DISK/DIRECTORY.1" as the entire value of the current prefix.

Note that "DIRECTORY.1" does not begin with a "/" since we are defining a subordinate directory name to be added to the current prefix. BASIC.SYSTEM (and ProDOS) assume that any pathname that does not begin with a "/" is intended to be used with the current value of the prefix.

DOWN THE LONG PATH

Although we have used short paths, a prefix may be set to any pathname up to 64 characters so that

```
PREFIX /USERS.DISK/DIRECTORY.1/
ANOTHER.NAME/STILL.MORE
```

followed by a "CAT" command will cause the catalog of directory "STILL.MORE" within the directory "ANOTHER.NAME" within the directory "DIRECTORY.1" within the volume directory "/MY.DISK" to be displayed. And, just to add to the depths to which ProDOS can probe, if we issued the command

```
CAT YET.MORE/AND.MORE/FINALLY
```

with the above prefix set, we would be looking for

the list of files in the directory "FINALLY" which is a subdirectory of "AND.MORE" which is within the directory "YET.MORE" which is a subdirectory of "STILL.MORE" (the last directory defined in the current prefix setting) . . . ad nauseum. This partial pathname can also be 64 characters in length, which allows a full pathname (prefix plus the partial pathname) of 128 characters!

Although this seems like overkill to the point of confusion, the reason for allowing such a long combination of prefix and partial pathname into a 128 character pathname is to facilitate the storage of files on a very large disk drive, such as a hard disk drive which may have a storage capacity exceeding 10 megabytes (that's over 10 million bytes of data!).

PROBLEMS WITH LONG PATHS

In addition to the caveats of using subdirectories in the first place, there are some additional problems with using *long* pathnames. On any disk, and especially if you are using a hard disk, think about arranging your directory structure to avoid using a pathname of over 64 characters to reach any file. The reason: a pathname of over 64 characters will *require* the use of the prefix and a partial pathname. To construct a pathname of over 64 characters, you must use both a set prefix and a partial pathname. Second problem; if you go one subdirectory beyond the length of that "maximum length" prefix, you will have to set the prefix to reach that directory. Then you will have to type the complete remaining portion of the pathname *every time you want to access a file in that subdirectory*. If you have a 128 character pathname, that means you *must* set the prefix and then you will still have *64 characters* to type to finish getting to the file represented by that path.

It might be argued that someone this deep in the directory structure might not plan to "jump over" to another directory deep in the hierarchy with a different prefix path. If you do decide to do so, you will have to set a new prefix every time you change directories. This adds an extra step to every file access. So, plan ahead on two counts: try to divide up your first few directories into enough subdirectories that no pathname to a file has to use a pathname over 64 characters, or, failing that, make sure that associated files kept in different subdirectories deep in the directory structure have at least the prefix in common. It will simplify programs that have to reach files in remote directories.

THE LONG AND SHORT OF IT (OR, HOW MANY IS 128?)

The division of a hard disk also brings up the question of how many directories and/or files the 64 character prefix plus 64 character partial pathname can allow you to reach. This has something to do with how long you make your names. If you use the full 15 characters for *all* filenames, the maximum number of filenames you can use in the prefix is *3*; 64/15 = 4 4/15; and more than 4/15 of a filename is needed to hold the "/" separators. As an example:

/VOL.DIRECTORY.1/SUB.DIRECTORY.1/
SUB.DIRECTORY.2/SUB.DIRECTORY.4/

is 65 characters long (ProDOS will add the last "/" if you don't!). So the longest legal prefix we can set for this path is

/VOL.DIRECTORY.1/SUB.DIRECTORY.1/
SUB.DIRECTORY.2/

We can set a final partial pathname of length 63:

SUB.DIRECTORY.4/SUB.DIRECTORY.5/
SUB.DIRECTORY.6/FINAL.FILENAME1

since the initial and final "/" are not used in its definition.

The length of the partial pathname that can be appended to this is also 64 characters. This means you can go six directory levels deep and still get to a file. The levels would include the prefix of the volume name plus 2 subdirectories (3 15 character filenames plus 4 "/" characters in total), and the appended partial pathname of three more subdirectories plus the final filename to access.

```
10  REM *** FIND PREFIX SIZES ***
20 A$ = "/XXXXXXXXXXXXXXX": REM "/" PLUS 15
      CHARACTERS.
30  FOR I = 2 TO 16
40 B$ =  LEFT$ (A$,I)
50 C$ = ""
60 A = 0
80  IF  LEN (B$ + C$) < 64 THEN C$ = C$ + B$:A =
      A + 1: GOTO 80
90 C$ = C$ + "/": REM ADD FINAL SEPARATOR.
100  IF I = 2 THEN  PRINT "NAME LEN.  PREFIX
      LEN.  PREFIX NAMES"
110  IF I = 2 THEN  PRINT "========
      ===========  ============": PRINT
120  PRINT  SPC( 6 - ( LEN (B$) - 1 > 9)); LEN
      (B$) - 1; SPC( 12); LEN (C$); SPC( 12);A
130  NEXT I
```

Listing 4-1. Calculate prefix sizes.

How much do you gain by going to shorter names? Well, if you go to 1 character filenames you start getting bound up by the number of "/" characters needed, so a name of the type

/A/B/C/D/E/F/G/H/I/J/K/L/M/N/O/P/Q/R/S/T/U/V/W/X/Y/Z/A/B/C/D/E/

(at 63 characters) is the longest prefix we can ènter.

To examine the possibilities, we can use a program to test the length of a prefix created by using names of various fixed lengths, such a program is presented in Listing 4-1. The program creates a screen listing similar to Table 4-2 for the average subdirectory name length used, maximum prefix length allowed for names of that length, and maximum number of names within the prefix.

MAKING NEW FILES

The files that are being discussed obviously have to be created on the disk in some manner. The next chapter will cover how BASIC.SYSTEM will make files when asked to save information, but since we are playing mostly with directories now let's look at the *CREATE* command, which can be used to make a new (empty) directory. The syntax is

CREATE *pathname*,Sn,Dn,Ttyp

Notice the pathname is *not* optional. The "*T*"ype option stands for the three-letter designation of one of the ProDOS file types, such as "TXT", "DIR", "BAS", etc. Actually, CREATE normally assumes you want to make a DIRectory file unless you tell it different, so the commands "CREATE DIR.FILE,TDIR" and "CREATE DIR.FILE" are

Table 4-2. Maximum Prefix Length as a Function of Average Directory Name Length.

NAME LEN.	PREFIX LEN.	PREFIX NAMES
1	63	31
2	64	21
3	61	15
4	61	12
5	61	10
6	64	9
7	57	7
8	64	7
9	61	6
10	56	5
11	61	5
12	53	4
13	57	4
14	61	4
15	49	3

equivalent. Either command creates a directory of name "DIR.FILE" in the directory specified by the currently set prefix. If no prefix is set, the new directory will be placed in the volume directory of the last disk accessed.

If we happen to have the prefix "/MY.DISK/VOLUME.1/CHAPTER.2" set at the time "CREATE DIR.FILE" is issued, then the resulting directory file made will be "/MY.DISK/VOLUME.1/CHAPTER.2/DIR.FILE. DIR.FILE" will contain no files until they are placed there later.

ProDOS insists that we have unique filenames within a directory, so you must not try to create a file with the same pathname as one that already exists in that directory or BASIC.SYSTEM will send you a "DUPLICATE PATHNAME" error and refuse to make the file.

CREATE can also be used to make a directory entry for a file of another type; for example "CREATE BIN.FILE,TBIN" would make a binary file. Again, no data exists in the file until another command puts it there. CREATE only creates a space for the file in the specified directory.

Chapter 5

BASIC Program Files

BASIC.SYSTEM has several commands available for use on BASIC files. The commands SAVE, LOAD, and RUN are used to store and retrieve Applesoft BASIC programs as files on the disk. Also discussed will be the DELETE, RENAME, LOCK, and UNLOCK commands that allow us to delete unused files, change file names, and to protect files from such changes. These commands can be used with files other than BASIC ("BAS") program files.

BASIC PROGRAMS ON DISKS

Let's start by imagining we have a short BASIC program in memory that we've just typed in. To make the shortest one there is, type "NEW" at the Applesoft prompt and then don't type anything else. This clears the old BASIC program from memory.

Now that we have a very small program, we can afford to store it on a disk. After all, we ought to have plenty of room (since there is essentially no program in memory), but you could use CAT to check the free space (blocks free) on your current ProDOS disk. If you were to use the command

SAVE NOTHING

Applesoft's flashing cursor will disappear, the disk drive "IN USE" light should glow, the disk make a few noises, and then the light should go out and the cursor start blinking happily again. You can then CAT the disk again to show that NOTHING has indeed been saved; the name will appear in the directory.

SAVE, then, is a BASIC.SYSTEM command used to save a BASIC program on disk as a file of type "BAS". The general form of the command is:

SAVE *pathname*,Sn,Dn

The pathname (either a full or partial pathname) is required for reasons we'll look at in a moment; remember that any value of the prefix will be added to a partial pathname.

The possible errors that can occur are "SYNTAX ERROR" (make sure you typed the correct command; also, remember the rules for legal pathnames), "WRITE PROTECTED" (the disk's write-protect notch is covered, which keeps BASIC.SYSTEM/ProDOS from writing to the disk), "PATH NOT FOUND" (the prefix or specified path was not found), "FILE LOCKED" (a file by that name exists and is protected against being overwritten by the new information), "FILETYPE MISMATCH" (there is a file of that pathname on the disk and it is not a BASIC file) and the dreaded "I/O ERROR" (ProDOS can't read the disk).

If you SAVE this "null" program and CATALOG the disk, assuming all went well, you will see an anomaly of computer life; the non-program "NOTHING" takes up 1 block of disk space! This is the minimum space allotted by ProDOS for *any* disk file; even an empty one.

When the BASIC.SYSTEM *SAVE* command stores a BASIC program on the disk, it works by copying the area of memory specified as the Applesoft program area out to the disk and making that disk image of the memory as a file of type *BAS* (for "BASIC program" file). Even though the area of memory used by our program is nil, the minimum area ProDOS can allot to a file is always one disk block. BASIC.SYSTEM is not concerned with the fact that no program is there.

A LOADED DECK

If you'd like a 'longer program', you could use

```
10 PRINT "THIS IS A TEST."
20 PRINT "THIS IS THE SECOND PART OF
THE TEST."
```

and save this program as "TEST" via a "SAVE TEST" command.

After the file is SAVEd, LISTing the program will show it is still there in memory, all well and good. The SAVE command *copies* the program to disk, but it does not affect the program in memory. This is fortunate and important to remember; as long as the computer is up and operating with your program and you don't alter memory, you can SAVE it without fear of destroying the program in memory. If an error does occur (like a "WRITE-PROTECTED" error), just correct the error (remove the write-protect tab and re-insert the disk) and try SAVEing the program again.

You can check the directory of the disk with CAT to make sure the program is on the disk. Notice that if you LIST the program it is still there. Like SAVE, CAT does not affect the program in memory.

Let's say we want to recover our first file, "NOTHING". We can copy our disk file for "NOTHING" back into memory by using the *LOAD* command. The syntax is

LOAD *pathname*,Sn,Dn

We can issue a "LOAD NOTHING" command to get back our original file. The drive will spin, lights flash, and then all will quiet down. LISTing the program reveals a crisis.

Nothing will be there, our program is gone. Actually, "NOTHING" is there; we have just discovered that LOADing a program overwrites the BASIC program (or lack of one) in memory. The program SAVEd as "NOTHING" replaced "TEST" in memory. However, being the clever people that we are, we had SAVEd our program "TEST" disk so that the command "LOAD TEST" will restore our program, which can be LISTed to verify that it's there. Try it.

Other than our "normal" errors, you might run into a BASIC.SYSTEM "PROGRAM TOO LARGE" or "NO BUFFERS AVAILABLE" error. Either error means BASIC.SYSTEM had trouble allocating RAM memory space to allow LOADing the program.

If you don't see a BASIC.SYSTEM error message with LOAD or SAVE, but the disk drive doesn't activate and you hear two "beeps" separated by a long pause, you may be having another problem.

WHEN A SAVE IS NOT A SAVE

If you have an Apple *II*c, just realize that typing "SAVE" or "LOAD" as a command without specifying the pathname will result in a BASIC.SYSTEM "SYNTAX ERROR". You can then skip a few paragraphs to the next topic.

If you have an Apple *II* Plus or *II*e, and issue

the SAVE command without a pathname you will hear a beep, a few seconds will pass, and another beep will sound. No error message will be printed, but the disk drive won't come on, either. What were the beeps, then?

BASIC.SYSTEM doesn't recognize a non-program, but is smart enough to recognize its own commands. "SAVE TEST" is a BASIC.SYSTEM command which implies use of the disk drive to save the program as a file named "TEST". "SAVE" (no filename) is an *Applesoft* command that specifies you are trying to save the program to a tape recorder connected to the back of the Apple. The two beeps signify the start and end of the Applesoft SAVE process. LOAD without a filename will also not be recognized as a BASIC.SYSTEM command. Remember, the pathname is *required* to save the file to disk with SAVE.

RUNNING A PROGRAM FROM DISK

While a program is still in memory, whether by LOAD or if it was freshly typed in, you can execute it with the Applesoft RUN command without any intervention by BASIC.SYSTEM. There is an equivalent BASIC.SYSTEM command called *RUN* that combines the (BASIC .SYSTEM) LOAD and Applesoft RUN commands. If you type "NEW" to clear the program, then try the command

RUN TEST

(notice the filename; "RUN" without a filename is the Applesoft command) BASIC.SYSTEM will get into the act and attempt to automatically LOAD the program from disk, then start it executing as if the Applesoft RUN command had been issued immediately after the LOAD. The general form of the BASIC.SYSTEM RUN command is

RUN *pathname*,Sn,Dn,@ln

The "@" option lets you start execution of the program at a specified line number (specified by "ln"). You don't like to start at the beginning of the program? Using the command "RUN TEST,@20" for our program "TEST" has the effect of LOADing the program and issuing the Applesoft command "RUN 20", which means the first line (line 10) will be "passed by" and only the sentence "THIS IS THE SECOND PART OF THE TEST." will be printed.

The BASIC.SYSTEM RUN command can have the same errors as LOAD. In addition, if there is something wrong with the program itself, any of the normal Applesoft errors will also be possible. Notice that specifying a non-existent line number with the "@" parameter will cause an Applesoft "UNDEF'D STATEMENT" (undefined statement) error, which tells you Applesoft can't find the requested line number.

THE "-" ("SMART RUN") COMMAND

There is another command that is similar to RUN, of the form

- *pathname*,Sn,Dn

The command "- TEST" has the same effect as "RUN TEST" for the Applesoft program "TEST".

The command "-" is sometimes called the "dash" command, or the "smart RUN" command. The term "smart" is used because the "-" command can load and execute types of programs other than Applesoft programs.

Notice that the "@" parameter is not available with the "-" command.

GENERAL FILE COMMANDS

The commands SAVE, RUN, and LOAD are all restricted to use with Applesoft BASIC programs. There are, obviously, other file commands desired to keep things in order; the following BASIC.SYSTEM commands work on most files regardless of file type.

Suppose we are getting tired of the name TEST for a SAVEd Applesoft program. It would be easy to LOAD the file and SAVE it under a new name, but there is an easier way. BASIC.SYSTEM has the *RENAME* command to directly change the name of a file:

RENAME *pathname1, pathname2*,Sn,Dn

will change the name of the file specified by "pathname1" to "pathname2". For example, "RENAME TEST,NEWTEST" changes the name of the file "TEST" to "NEWTEST".

RENAME requires *two* pathnames separated by a comma; the first pathname must be an existing pathname to a file or a directory (*any* directory, including the volume), and the second name must be a unique new name *within the same directory level*. By "unique", we mean that you can't give the file the same name as a file that already exists within the directory.

Notice that you can't pull a stunt like

RENAME/THIS.DISK/FILENAME.1,/THIS.DISK/A.NEW.DIRECTORY/FILENAME.2

because this involves *moving* the file to a new directory, not just RENAMEing it. Only the last name in the pathname can be changed, as in

RENAME/THIS.DISK/FILENAME.1,/THIS.DISK/FILENAME.2

which is perfectly legal unless /THIS.DISK/FILENAME.2 already exists (if it already exists, you'll get a "DUPLICATE PATHNAME" error).

BYE BYE FILE

As mentioned, you could issue a sequence of commands like "LOAD TEST" and "SAVE SON.OF.TEST" to make a copy of the program with a new name. The LOADed file ("TEST") would be left in memory as a result of this operation.

If you happen to LOAD TEST, use NEW to clear it, and then SAVE SON.OF.TEST, "SON.OF.TEST" will no longer contain a program. If "SON.OF.TEST" is LOADed and LISTed, you find that it no longer is a copy of "TEST"; it's gone! What occurred is that the "cleared" (NEWed) copy of memory was SAVEd "on top" of the original program SAVEd in "SON.OF.TEST", and the original program was replaced with the new (empty) program.

This gives us a way to "empty" a file, but not get rid of it completely; the filename still appears in the directory and it still eats a block of disk space. Again, BASIC.SYSTEM has a command, *DELETE*, to help us out:

DELETE *pathname*,Sn,Dn

The command "DELETE SON.OF.TEST" will *completely* remove the file from the directory display, and free up that one block of space.

There are utility programs and methods that can be used to *try* to recover a DELETEd file, but they are usually only successful if used *before* any changes involving creating new files have been performed on the disk. Be very careful with DELETE.

LOCKING THE DOOR

Suppose we had wanted to *keep* the original "SON.OF.TEST". To protect a file from being overwritten by SAVE, DELETEd, or RENAMEd, we can use the *LOCK* command

LOCK *pathname*,Sn,Dn

which will access the disk and change some information in the file's directory entry to prevent those things from being done. LOCK can be undone by the *UNLOCK* command

UNLOCK *pathname*,Sn,Dn

which removes the protection offered by LOCK.

You could protect the file "SON.OF.TEST" via a "LOCK SON.OF.TEST" command. This is very fragile protection, as the command "UNLOCK SON.OF.TEST" will undo the protection. These commands are sort of like "software write-protect tabs" for individual files; LOCK puts the protection on a file, UNLOCK removes it.

These commands do *not* have any effect on a disk if the disk is re-formatted. Re-formatting a disk will erase *all* files on the disk, whether or not they are LOCKed.

Both commands require that the disk with the

specified file not be write-protected as they do make minor modifications to the file entry on the disk. You can check the status of the file with the CAT or CATALOG command; LOCKed files appear in the directory listing with an asterisk ("*") to the left of their filename. UNLOCKed files have a space character (no asterisk) to the left of their name.

PHILOSOPHY OF THESE COMMANDS

The BASIC commands can be used to load BASIC programs from a disk for modification or execution and to save BASIC programs for future reference or use. It is very important when working on BASIC programs to SAVE your work to disk periodically, since a power failure or careless NEW or (BASIC.SYSTEM) LOAD command will destroy the program you have in RAM memory. A good practice is to SAVE a file frequently to a disk (or even different disks) under separate names (such as PROGRAM.1 the first time, PROGRAM.2 a few minutes later, etc.). Never add more to a program between SAVEs than you think you can afford to lose should a catastrophe occur.

Apple's *BASIC Programming with ProDOS* manual mentions SAVEing interim versions of a program to /RAM; *this is unsafe* unless the program is *expendable* since /RAM will also be lost in event of a power outage (realistically, power failures are rare but it only takes *one* to lose a lot of work).

RENAME, LOCK, UNLOCK, and DELETE can be used on nearly *all* files to keep things organized on the disk. The exception to these is for the disk volume; which cannot be DELETEd or LOCKed (or UNLOCKed). The volume can be RENAMEd, however, just like a file . Just remember to use valid volume names (preceded with a "/"), such as

```
RENAME /USERS.DISK,/BACKUP
```

(If you have a *II*c, notice that the *II*c /UTILITIES will not let you change a volume's name, but you can rename a volume by exiting to BASIC and using RENAME in this manner).

Other directory files (other than the volume directory, that is) can be LOCKed or UNLOCKed to allow or disallow RENAMEing or DELETEing them. LOCKing a directory does not prevent its listings from being updated through the addition of new files or the removal of old files, however.

Additionally, you cannot DELETE a directory that contains any other files (we say it's "*non-empty*"); all files and subdirectories must be DELETEd from a directory before it can be DELETEd itself. Curiously, you will get a "FILE LOCKED" error if you try to DELETE a non-empty directory, even if the CAT shows the directory is not locked.

Chapter 6

The Binary File Commands

In addition to the file commands SAVE, LOAD and RUN we used in the last chapter, ProDOS has special forms of the commands to use with *binary files* files (usually) made up of images of the Apple's memory copied to disk.

If you have been using DOS 3.3, one of the big changes you will notice with BASIC.SYSTEM is the number of parameters which can be used with the binary file commands. We'll start off with the examples of the commands.

BSAVE

Imagine that Applesoft has been used to draw pictures on each of the Apple's two displayable high-resolution graphics pages. To show the simplest form of the "BSAVE" command, let's move the picture in high-res page 1 to the disk. One way to do this is to use the command line

```
BSAVE PIC.1,A$2000,L$2000
```

Notice that this looks similar to the "SAVE" command for Applesoft programs except for the extra parameters "A" and "L". These parameters are important because they specify where the address in memory at which we want to start saving, and the length of memory we want to save. "A$2000" specifies a starting address of $2000 hexadecimal (8192), which is the starting location of the first high-res page. "L$2000" specifies that the length of the program we want to save is $2000 hexadecimal (8192) bytes.

Hexadecimal is used here because it gives "nice, round numbers", but decimal numbers could also be used so that the command reads "BSAVE PIC.1,A8192,L8192".

Notice that we are saving the area from $2000 to $3FFF of our memory *inclusive*; the length reflects that the number of bytes we are saving is equal to *one more* than the last byte's address ($3FFF) minus the starting byte's address ($2000).

Why the need for the "A" and "L" parameters? Unlike BASIC programs, for which Applesoft keeps tab of the start and length of the program, machine language (or binary) programs and data are not intrinsically "visible" to any other software in the Apple, including ProDOS, BASIC.SYSTEM, and Applesoft. Such a program can exist in memory and never be accessed until another program specifically utilizes it. Since such information is "invisible" until specifically called upon, it is also "invisible" to BASIC.SYSTEM. Therefore, BASIC.SYSTEM needs to know where the program is in memory and its length in order to save it to disk. If you don't tell BASIC.SYSTEM those things (via "A" and "L", for example), BASIC.SYSTEM will report a "SYNTAX ERROR".

There is an exception; if binary data is saved to a filename that already exists then the previous address and file length will be assumed. A second "BSAVE PIC.1" with no "A" and "L" parameters will save out the same memory area indicated by the current file "PIC.1".

If you verify that you have indeed saved the file by CATALOGing the disk, you should see a file listing. Notice in the listing that in addition to the "ENDFILE" specification of 8192 for the decimal length of the file we have BSAVEd, we have an entry under "SUBTYPE" of "A=$2000"; this is our original "A" value in hexadecimal (why is "ENDFILE" given in decimal and "SUBTYPE" in hexadecimal? . . . a good question?).

The above "BSAVE" example was used because the "A" and "L" parameters correspond to the "BSAVE" command used in DOS 3.3. Here is an example where BASIC.SYSTEM under ProDOS shows a little more "smarts" than DOS 3.3: suppose we didn't feel like counting the length of the above memory block in bytes just to save it. With BASIC.SYSTEM, we can specify the end of the program rather than the length using the "E" (for "End") parameter thusly:

```
BSAVE PIC.1,A$2000,E$3FFF
```

and forgo counting or calculating the length of the block to save; BASIC.SYSTEM will save the same version of the program as it did using the "A" and "L" parameters mentioned previously. Note that we still need two parameters for the save; one to specify the start and one to determine the length. But given the last byte's location via the "E" parameter, BASIC.SYSTEM can save the proper number of bytes. Sometimes it may be easier to specify a starting and ending address for a binary file.

Let's look quickly at the complete set of parameters for the BSAVE command:

BSAVE *pathname*, *Aaddr*, *Lnbyt*,Bnbyt,Sn,Dn,Ttyp

or

BSAVE *pathname*, *Aaddr1*, *Eaddr2*,Bnbyt,Sn,Dn,Ttyp

Notice that there are two possible sets of required parameters. The first uses "A" and "L" to specify the starting address and length of the segment to be saved. The number "addr" ("address") associated with "A" must correspond to a valid Apple memory address, and the value of "nbyt" ("number of bytes") associated with "L" must be non-negative. The total of the two numbers cannot exceed the Apple's normal memory size of 64K bytes without generating an error. It *is* legal to BSAVE a file of length 0 ("L0").

In the second case, the "L" parameter has been replaced with "E". The use of "A" and "E" causes the memory area included in the address range from "addr1" to "addr2" to be saved. Both arguments must contain valid integer addresses, and the value of "addr2" must be greater than or equal to "addr1". If the two addresses are equal, a file of length 0 will be BSAVEd under the specified name.

The "S" and "D" parameters have their usual meaning. The "T" parameter has the same use as it did under CREATE; it allows the use of the BSAVE command to save a block of memory into a file of a type other than "BIN". If no type is specified, the default file type is assumed to be "BIN". In order to use the "T" parameter to save to a file of type other than "BIN", that file must have been CREATEd first. Remember the use of the command

CREATE/MY.DISK/DIRECTORY.1/DUMMY.PROG,TBAS

to make a file of name "DUMMY.PROG"? The ability to use binary file commands on BASIC (and other) files is the reason for that capability of the CREATE command. A file of any type may be created and then data later moved into it with the BSAVE command.

The "B" parameter specifies the number of bytes to offset into a file before saving the specified data. For example, if the binary file DATA already exists on the disk, the command

BSAVE DATA,A$300,L$20,B100

will save $20 (32) bytes of data into the file DATA starting at location number 100 within the file, which leaves the first 100 bytes of the file DATA undisturbed.

This provides a means of overlaying a portion of an existing file with new data from memory (if DATA is over 100 bytes in length), or appending ("tacking-on") the new segment if DATA is exactly 100 bytes long, or (important) reserving 100 bytes at the beginning of the file DATA for future use. Additionally, the permitted range for the "B" parameter is 0 to 16,777,215 (16 megabytes minus one byte)! This gives us a very powerful feature; we can access any portion of any type file (as binary data) at will with a single command.

BLOAD

To load a binary segment of a file, or a portion of a file that has been previously saved to a disk, we use the BLOAD command in the form

BLOAD *pathname*,Aaddr,Lnbyt,Bnbyt,Sn,Dn,Ttyp

or

BLOAD *pathname*,Aaddr1,Eaddr2,Bnbyt,Sn,Dn,Ttyp

where "pathname" specifies an existing file. All the other options have a similar meaning as for BSAVE: the "A" parameter refers to where the file (or segment) will be loaded into memory, the "E" or "L" parameter specifies the ending address or length (in bytes) respectively of the file to be loaded, and the "B" parameter specifies how many bytes of the file to read and discard before reading the specified number of bytes into memory. If none of these latter parameters are provided, the file will be loaded into the same location of memory that was recorded in the directory as its original starting location, and the entire length of the file will be loaded.

Let's reload our picture we saved above with the command

BLOAD PIC.1,A$2000

If we issue the HGR command first, we can see the program load into high-resolution graphics page 1.

By using the "A" parameter, we can modify the address at which the file is loaded; for example "BLOAD B.PROGRAM,A$4000" for our demo file will cause the entire file to be loaded to a starting location of $4000 (into the high-res page 2 area of memory, initialized with the Applesoft HGR2 command), so that the data occupies memory locations $4000 through $5FFF rather than $2000-$3FFF as for the original picture (before it was saved). Since the disk directory for the entry still has the original starting add ress recorded as its default reference, the address ("A") parameter must be specified if a load address other than the default is desired.

BRUN

Finally, as for BASIC programs, there is a command to cause a binary *program* file to be loaded and then executed. If we use the form

BRUN *pathname*,Aaddr,Lnbyt,Bnbyt,Sn,Dn

or:

BRUN *pathname*,Aaddr1,Eaddr2,Bnbyt,Sn,Dn

the program specified by "pathname" will be loaded at its default starting address and execution will begin at the starting address specified with the "A" parameter. If the "A" parameter is not used the entire file will be loaded at the address it was originally saved from and executed there. The command

```
BRUN B.PROGRAM
```

will cause B.PROGRAM to be loaded at its default address and then be executed starting at the first byte of the program.

The problem with BRUN is that there is no way to tell a binary program file containing executable 6502 machine code from a binary *data* file (such as a high-resolution graphics image) simply from the files appearance in the directory listing. Both kinds of files are listed as type "BIN" with no distinguishing features. If you happen to BRUN a data file the exact results are unpredictable, but usually the computer will either "lock up" (the disk will stop spinning, the cursor will disappear, and the key board will be ignored except for "Reset") or you will hear a "beep" and be looking at a pair of lines which indicate the "program" aborted with an "error" (actually, a 6502 BRK) and left you in the monitor program. To get back to BASIC, the best solution is to re-boot; the program may have caused other damage to any programs in RAM memory, including possibly catastrophic changes to ProDOS and BASIC.SYSTEM.

A value for the "A" parameter other than the original starting address can be specified with "BRUN", but this assumes that the program will execute properly at the starting address specified by the "A" parameter. Binary (machine language) programs can be so designed to do this, but not all programs are, so that

```
BRUN B.PROGRAM,A$1000
```

may not execute properly if B.PROGRAM was not originally designed to be executed when it resides at address $1000 in memory.

ONLY TAKE WHAT YOU NEED

With either programs or data files, a portion only of the program can be loaded. If *both* high resolution pages 1 and 2 were saved as one file with the command "BSAVE PIC.1.AND.2,A$2000, L$4000", it is still possible to reload *only* the first or second picture to high-res page 1.

The command "BLOAD PIC.1.AND.2, A$2000,A$2000" will load only the first $2000 bytes of the file as specified by the "L" parameter's value. To load the second picture to page 1, use "BLOAD PIC.1.AND.2,A$2000,B$2000" which offsets $2000 bytes into the file as directed by the "B" parameter, then loads the remainder of the file to the address $2000. "L" could have also been specified, but is not necessary since we want the entire remainder of the file to be loaded.

The same parameters can be specified with the BRUN command, but the program segment loaded will be executed after it is loaded. This gives the opportunity to save several short machine language programs in a single file to use less disk space. Since ProDOS always reserves a minimum of 512 bytes for a file, you could put 10 50-byte routines in a single file occupying only 1 block of disk space. If you put these same routines into 10 files, they would use up 10 disk blocks and waste over 90% of that space. With BASIC.SYSTEM, you directly can load segments of this conglomerate file to anywhere in memory you would like; with normal DOS 3.3 commands you would have had to load the entire file as a unit and move the individual segments to their final destinations after they were in memory.

DASHING OFF

Another way to execute a binary file is with the "-" command discussed before; the syntax is the same as for the example given in the section on LOAD, SAVE and RUN. The command

```
- B.PROGRAM
```

will cause the file B.PROGRAM to be loaded and executed at its original location. As for BASIC programs, the only optional parameters permitted with the "dash" command are "S" and "D"; so the complete program will be loaded and executed at its original address.

In addition, the "-" command can be used to load and execute *system* (SYS) programs, such as BASIC.SYSTEM itself. You can simulate re-booting (including the re-initialization of the Apple's memory) by using the command "- PRODOS" with the appropriate disk in the default drive.

That wraps up the section on the BASIC.SYSTEM commands most often used in immediate mode. Part II starts a new topic; the discussion of using these commands within Applesoft programs, and further commands that are available.

Part 2

BASIC Programming with BASIC.SYSTEM

Chapter 7

BASIC.SYSTEM Commands In BASIC Programs

So far we've talked about entering BASIC.SYSTEM commands immediately at the Applesoft prompt. This is referred to as *immediate mode* since BASIC.SYSTEM attempts to execute the command line immediately, as soon as you hit the "return". All of the previously discussed BASIC.SYSTEM commands can also be entered into BASIC programs for *deferred* (as opposed to immediate) execution. When placed within a BASIC program, the BASIC.SYSTEM command will not be executed until the program is RUN and the BASIC statement containing the command is encountered.

The syntax used to enter these commands into BASIC programs is different than the syntax used when Applesoft statements are entered. You cannot simply enter "CAT" into a BASIC program as if it were an Applesoft statement. First, let's look at how the commands discussed thus far can be included in BASIC programs, and how to handle the additional errors that they can generate when the program is running. Then we'll increase our vocabulary of BASIC.SYSTEM with other commands that become more useful when used within programs.

A DEFERRED BASIC.SYSTEM COMMAND

Incorporating BASIC.SYSTEM commands within a BASIC program is done very simply. Let's look at a one-line program.

```
10 PRINT CHR$(4);"CAT,D1"
```

If you type in and RUN this program, the CAT listing of the disk in drive one will be displayed on the screen unless you get an error message. You could get "beeped" with a "?SYNTAX ERROR IN 10" from Applesoft if there was a typographical error. Or you could get "I/O ERROR IN 10" from BASIC.SYSTEM if there was a problem reading the disk. The "IN 10" part of the message tells us which line the error occurred in. The possible BASIC.SYSTEM and APPLESOFT error messages are summarized in Appendix A1; the possible causes of BASIC.SYSTEM errors have already been listed in Chapter 3.

Notice the difference between the deferred-mode form and the immediate-mode command

```
CAT,D1
```

which executes as soon as you hit the "return" key to end the line.

Within a program, BASIC.SYSTEM commands are included as *string variables* within a specially-constructed PRINT statement; in our program the "CAT,D1" string (in quotes) contains the actual BASIC.SYSTEM command we wish to use. The "special" item in the PRINT statement is the "CHR$ (4)" between the "PRINT" and the BASIC.SYSTEM command string. "CHR$(4)" evaluates to "control-D" which the designers of BASIC.SYSTEM have used as a "wake-up" character to tell BASIC.SYSTEM that one of its commands is about to be used.

When an Applesoft program is RUNning under BASIC.SYSTEM, BASIC.SYSTEM looks for the occurrence of the Applesoft PRINT command word followed *immediately* by a control-D character. If that sequence occurs, BASIC.SYSTEM will assume the rest of the PRINTed line is meant as a BASIC.SYSTEM command. The literal use of "CHR$ (4)" itself is not mandatory, we can also use a variable defined as equal to "CHR$ (4)", so that the program

```
10  D$ = CHR$ (4) :REM Control-D.
20  PRINT D$;"SAVE THIS"
```

will save itself to the disk under the filename "THIS" (unless a BASIC.SYSTEM error interferes). "D$" is almost universally used by Apple programmers as the variable to hold control-D, which provides a nice consistency among programs. The BASIC.SYSTEM command can also be represented, in whole or part, by normal Applesoft strings and properly defined string variables, so that

```
10  D$ = CHR$ (4) :REM Control-D.
20  C$ = "SAVE"
30  PRINT D$;C$;" TEST,D";1
```

is also perfectly legal.

[DOS 3.3 programmer's note: the control-D must be the *first* item to occur after the "PRINT". Often under DOS, D$ was defined as "CHR$ (13) + CHR$ (4)" to prevent all kinds of problems. This will *not* work under ProDOS. BASIC.SYSTEM sees a "CHR$ (13)" (control-M or "return") character instead of a control-D immediately after the "PRINT" and assumes that what follows isn't a disk command.]

USING OTHER COMMANDS

All of the BASIC.SYSTEM commands we covered in the last three chapters, with one exception (PREFIX, which we'll attack in a few paragraphs), perform in the same manner when issued within a program as they do when typed as immediate mode commands. Therefore, all you need to do to use one of these commands within a program is place it within a PRINT statement as we have described.

Some points to be aware of: issuing a command such as RUN or LOAD within a program will *replace* the BASIC program that issues the command with the program that is LOAD or RUN. This terminates execution of the program that issued the command. Thus, RUN can be used to "link" one BASIC program to another. We can even choose between programs, as in this short program

```
10  REM *** IIe (IIc) OR NOT IIe (IIc)? ***
20  D$ = CHR$ (4) : REM Control-D.
30  IF PEEK(-1101) = 6 THEN PRINT D$;"RUN
    NEW.VERSION"
40  PRINT D$;"RUN OLD.VERSION"
```

Line 30 of this program PEEKs at an identification location in the Apple's monitor ROM (the hexadecimal equivalent is $FBB3) that is always equal to "6" on an Apple *II*e or *II*c computer. If the computer is a *II*e or *II*c, then the new version of the program is RUN (we've named it "NEW.VERSION"), otherwise "OLD.VERSION" is selected. In either case the current program is terminated. This allows you to tailor two versions of the same program for use on the different types of Apple computers.

THE SPECIAL "STARTUP" FILE

Whenever BASIC.SYSTEM is executed,

whether by a "- BASIC.SYSTEM" command or as a result of booting a ProDOS disk, BASIC.SYSTEM examines the directory specified by the current prefix and looks for a file named "STARTUP". If the file is found, BASIC.SYSTEM *automatically* loads it into memory and executes it. STARTUP may be any type of executable file; a "BAS" or "SYS" file as well as "BIN" and "TXT" program files ("TXT" program files are discussed in Chapter 14).

If the "-" is used to execute BASIC.SYSTEM with the prefix set to a specific directory, then BASIC.SYSTEM will search for STARTUP in the directory specified by the prefix.

When a disk is booted and BASIC.SYSTEM is the first "SYS" program executed by the freshly-loaded ProDOS kernel, any STARTUP file in the volume directory will be executed.This allows us to have a program or series of programs automatically executed when a disk is booted up.

For example, let's imagine taking our "*II*e or not *II*e" program and SAVEing it as "STARTUP" on a ProDOS disk containing the files "PRODOS", "BASIC.SYSTEM", "NEW.VERSION" and "OLD.VERSION". When we boot this disk, BASIC.SYSTEM will execute the "STARTUP" program, which will in turn execute either "NEW.VERSION" or "OLD.VERSION". Thus we have *completely* automated the process of RUNning the proper version for the computer the disk is booted on.

"PREFIX" IN PROGRAMS

Programming with the PREFIX command is slightly different from using the other BASIC.SYSTEM commands. Setting the prefix with a pathname is done in the same manner as in immediate mode; simply take the PREFIX command you would use in immediate mode and put it in the form of a BASIC.SYSTEM program statement. The immediate mode command "PREFIX /MY.DISK" becomes

```
10 PRINT CHR$(4); "PREFIX /MY.DISK"
```

The Applesoft program line that contains the PREFIX command, when executed, will search for "/MY.DISK" just as the immediate mode command does, and report an error if "/MY.DISK" is not found in a drive. All other tricks work, such as

```
10  D$ = CHR$ (4) : REM CONTROL-D
20  PRINT D$; "PREFIX DIRECTORY.1"
```

to set the prefix above ("/MY.DISK") to "/MY.DISK/DIRECTORY.1". All parameters can be included as normal.

APPLESOFT "INPUT" REMINDER

An advantage within a program is the ability to use Applesoft string commands and variable assignments to manipulate the pathname and parameter values (actually, this can be done in immediate mode, too, but seldom is truly useful).

The prefix string you attempt to set can also be entered using an INPUT statement, within the normal restrictions of the Applesoft INPUT

```
10  D$ = CHR$ (4) : REM Control-D
20  INPUT "Pathname?: ";PN$
30  PRINT D$;"PREFIX ";PN$
```

Notice that we could enter only the prefix pathname directly, not the entire command including drive number parameter, as the Applesoft INPUT statement does not allow the use of the comma within an input line except to separate distinct variables. We could, however, have substituted

```
20 INPUT "PREFIX?: "PF$,D1
```

to input BOTH variables. The problem is, this forces the input of the drive number or Applesoft will not have enough input variables to satisfy line 20 (and will insist you give it two).

There are Applesoft "input anything" routines, including several in the public domain, that allow overriding the restriction of INPUT's use with commas and colons. If you feel the need, seek out one of these utilities; we have included one in Appendix G. Most of these are written at least partially in machine language. In addition, Bruce Tognazzini's program "MAGIC MENU" that is documented in *The Applesoft Tutorial* manual from Apple Computer contains a "blinking underline cursor" input subroutine that could be adapted for this purpose. It is slow in response but is written in BASIC if you prefer to avoid machine language.

An easy way to avoid the problem is to preface your reply with a single quote (" " ") mark, which allows INPUT to read the entire line following the quote (up until the next quote mark or ASCII NUL) as a single string variable.

This will be a sometimes-headache with BASIC programming for BASIC.SYSTEM; how to flexibly handle all possible pathname and parameter combinations via INPUT. A program presented at the end of Chapter 16 attempts to show some ways to allow the person using the program to enter pathnames and drive and slot numbers within its subroutines.

READING THE CURRENT PREFIX

Attempting to read the set prefix within a program is where PREFIX acts a bit differently. Following our general form for ProDOS commands; the PREFIX command can be used in a simple program to read and report the current setting of the prefix

```
10  D$ = CHR$ (4)
20  PRINT D$;"PREFIX"
30  INPUT PF$
40  PRINT "THE CURRENT PREFIX IS: ";PF$
```

If you type this short program in and RUN it (in a case where a valid PREFIX exists or can be read from a disk), you notice that the Applesoft string variable "PF$" contains the name for the prefix. Also, you may have noticed that the prefix was printed by the program, not by BASIC.SYSTEM as it was in immediate mode. You can verify this by deleting line 40 and RUNning the program again; PF$ will again be set to the current prefix, but the prefix will not be displayed on the screen. To display the final value of PF$ (after the program has stopped RUNning and the Applesoft prompt returns), type "PRINT PF$" in immediate mode, and the value set by RUNning the program will be displayed on the screen.

"PREFIX" AND "INPUT"

Why wasn't the prefix value printed to the screen when line 40 was DELETEd? How did "PF$" become set to the value of the prefix? Again, this has to do with the fact that watchdog BASIC.SYSTEM is always checking the progress of Applesoft commands to see whether there is some task that needs the attention of ProDOS.

When you typed the PREFIX command in immediate mode, BASIC.SYSTEM directed the printout of the current prefix to the monitor's (and Applesoft's) current output device (in this case, the screen) since that is the logical place for it if you wish to read the resulting value.

When the program was executing, however, BASIC.SYSTEM routed the data to the next INPUT statement in the program, since it is assumed that you wish to have the value for the current available to be used later within the program. There's no need (or desire) for BASIC.SYSTEM to print it to the screen since you can easily do this within the same program.

In our original example above, line 20 issues the BASIC.SYSTEM command to have the prefix displayed. Line 30 contains the INPUT statement used to read the value returned for the prefix into the variable "PF$" (which, obviously, MUST be a string variable or you will get Applesoft's dreaded "TYPE MISMATCH ERROR"), and line 40 was used to print the value to the screen.

READING THE VOLUME NAME

Think of a situation where you might need to identify a volume in a drive and set its volume pathname as the current prefix. Take a theoretical case: you have loaded a program from the volume in drive 1 and wish to substitute a differently-named volume into the same drive as a data disk. To read the prefix within a program when you KNOW the disks are going to be changed, you simply clear the former prefix and read in (and save) the new value, as outlined in Listing 7-1.

```
10 D$ = CHR$ (4)
100 REM Body of program starts here.
 ...
200 REM Prompt for new (data) volume.
210 PRINT "Insert new volume and press a key: ";
220 GET A$
230 PRINT
300 REM Read prefix of new volume.
310 PRINT D$; "PREFIX,D1": REM Read volume name
      as prefix.
320 PRINT D$; "PREFIX" : REM Ask for new volume
      name.
330 INPUT NP$ : REM Read new prefix.
400 REM On with'work...
 ...
```

Listing 7-1. Reading the volume name with PREFIX.

The ability to read the volume's name into a string variable gives us the power to "hold" it for later use, and to use distinct volume names as a means for a ProDOS/BASIC.SYSTEM program to identify different disks. You could have the program come back later and ask you to re-insert the original disk and use the PREFIX command to read the prefix and verify that it is the same volume name as the original.

To request a SPECIFIC volume without first reading the prefix, you can manually clear the current prefix and attempt to set a new value as shown in Listing 7-2. The problem with the latter method is that line 220 cannot execute successfully until volume "/NEW.VOLUME" is available to BASIC.SYSTEM in drive 1. The "PREFIX/NEW.VOLUME,D1" command will check for the presence of the volume and will cause a "PATH NOT FOUND ERROR" and stop your BASIC program if the volume is not on-line at the time the command is issued.

One thing these programs haven't addressed thus far is how to keep an error (such as an open drive door, causing an "I/O ERROR") from giving us an error and stopping the BASIC.program. For our next trick, we're going to pursue this problem: how to make a program tell you (nicely, if you prefer) when you have given it the wrong disk.

BASIC ERROR HANDLING

Programming is not always as easy as it might be. Errors can occur at several places when BASIC.SYSTEM, Applesoft BASIC, and ProDOS are

Listing 7-2. Setting a specific volume name as the prefix.

```
10 D$ = CHR$ (4)
100 REM Body of program starts here.
 ...
200 REM Prompt for new (data) volume.
210 PRINT "Insert new volume and press a key: ";
220 GET A$
230 PRINT
300 REM Set prefix to new volume.
310 PRINT D$; "PREFIX /": REM Clear old volume
      as prefix.
320 PRINT D$; "PREFIX /NEW.VOLUME,D1" : REM Set
      new volume name.
400 REM On with work...
```

all interacting. The two main foes we have to worry about are BASIC.SYSTEM and Applesoft, since they are controllable using, essentially, an extension of the Applesoft error-handling routines mentioned in the Applesoft manuals. Any error serious enough for *ProDOS* to send us an error directly will probably require re-booting to "clear".

The attack plan on errors is this: Applesoft maintains memory locations that store the status of its error-handling routines and data from errors that occur during program execution. When BASIC.SYSTEM attempts to execute a command and encounters an error, it uses these same locations to notify Applesoft of the error and pass its (BASIC.SYSTEM's) error code to the BASIC program.

RUDE INTERRUPTIONS

As an example, the program in Listing 7-3 will set the prefix value to the volume name of the disk in drive 1. The program will report the prefix/volume name each time you insert a disk and press the "RETURN" key. But what happens to the program if the disk isn't there? If the program is running, removing the ProDOS disk in drive one and pressing "RETURN" will cause the disk drive to chatter (no harm is done), and the program will stop with a "I/O ERROR" message. Notice that the type of error is reported as well as the BASIC line number which the program was executing when the error occurred.

It's a lot nicer if the program can simply "trap" the error and continue to run; hopefully allowing you to re-try the operation. In this case, you could re-insert the disk properly and the program could let you attempt to read the volume name again. A short program that allows this is presented in Listing 7-4. If a disk input/output error occurs while this program is running, it will ignore it and continue, trying to read another volume name.

"ONERR GOTO" AND BASIC.SYSTEM

The key statement that sets up the BASIC

Listing 7-3. Reading a volume name without error handling.

```
1000  REM *** ERROR DEMO ***
1010  TEXT : PRINT  CHR$ (21): HOME
1020  D$ =  CHR$ (4): REM CTRL-D.
1030  VTAB 3: PRINT "Insert ProDOS disk in drive
        1 and"
1040  VTAB 5: PRINT "press <RETURN> to read
        volume name: ";
1050  GET A$: PRINT : IF A$ <  >  CHR$ (13) AND
        A$ <  >  CHR$ (27) THEN  GOTO 1040
1055  IF A$ =  CHR$ (27) THEN  GOTO 1190: REM
        Exit on "ESC".
1100  REM Read volume name as new prefix.
1110  HOME
1120  PRINT D$;"PREFIX,D1"
1130  PRINT D$;"PREFIX"
1140  INPUT PF$
1150  VTAB 3: PRINT "The current disk (and
        prefix) name is:": PRINT : PRINT  CHR$
        (34);PF$; CHR$ (34)
1160  VTAB 22: PRINT "Press <RETURN> to read
        another disk,": PRINT : PRINT "or <ESC>
        to quit: ";
1170  GET A$: PRINT : IF A$ <  >  CHR$ (13) AND
        A$ <  >  CHR$ (27) THEN  GOTO 1160
1180  IF A$ =  CHR$ (13) THEN  HOME : GOTO 1030
9999  HOME : END
```

```
1000  REM *** ONERR DEMO ***
1005  ONERR  GOTO 10000
1010  TEXT : PRINT  CHR$ (21): HOME
1020 D$ =  CHR$ (4): REM CTRL-D.
1030  VTAB 3: PRINT "Insert ProDOS disk in drive
       1 and"
1040  VTAB 5: PRINT "Press <RETURN> to read
       volume name: ";
1050  GET A$: PRINT : IF A$ <  > CHR$ (13) AND
       A$ <  > CHR$ (27) THEN  GOTO 1040
1055  IF A$ =  CHR$ (27) THEN  GOTO 1190: REM
       Exit on "ESC".
1100  REM Read volume name as new prefix.
1110  HOME
1120  PRINT D$;"PREFIX,D1"
1130  PRINT D$;"PREFIX"
1140  INPUT PF$
1150  VTAB 3: PRINT "The current disk (and
       prefix) name is:": PRINT : PRINT  CHR$
       (34);PF$; CHR$ (34)
1160  VTAB 22: PRINT "Press <RETURN> to read
       another disk,": PRINT : PRINT "or <ESC>
       to quit: ";
1170  GET A$: PRINT : IF A$ <  > CHR$ (13) AND
       A$ <  > CHR$ (27) THEN  GOTO 1160
1180  IF A$ =  CHR$ (13) THEN  HOME : GOTO 1030
1190  POKE 216,0: REM Clear "ONERR" flag.
9999  HOME : END
10000  REM Error handler.
10010  IF  PEEK (222) = 8 THEN  CALL  - 3288:
       HOME : GOTO 1030: REM Disk I/O error.
```

Listing 7-4. Reading a volume name with error handling.

error-handler is the "ONERR GOTO 10000" statement in line 1005, where "10000" is the starting (entry) line number of your error-handling routine. Once this ONERR statement has been issued, any Applesoft error will cause the program to "jump" to the line specified. BASIC.SYSTEM, with its watchful eye, also monitors that a BASIC program is in progress and will let BASIC attempt to handle any errors that occur for its commands.

At line 10010, the "PEEK (222)" is used to recover the error number of the last error that occurred, which BASIC.SYSTEM placed in Applesoft's normal zero page location for the error code. It so happens that BASIC.SYSTEM represents an I/O ERROR by the number 8 as an error code. "PEEK (222)" allows you to determine *what* error occurred, which you may need to know to help the program recover.

In line 1190, we use another POKE ("POKE 216,0") to tell ONERR we no longer want to use the ONERR GOTO line number we defined. This returns control to normal Applesoft error-handling. During a program, we can tell if ONERR is in effect by using "PEEK (216)", if the value is greater than 127 then ONERR GOTO is in use.

You can also calculate the line number in which the error occurred by using the expression "PEEK (218) + PEEK (219) * 256", which reads the line number in which the error occurred from information Applesoft maintains. This may be useful to use within the error handler to determine what action your program needs to take to fix things.

Just for your information, the ONERR GOTO statement should be the LAST statement on the BASIC program line. Due to the way the Applesoft interpreter works, any other statements after the

ONERR GOTO statement on the same line will LIST but will not be executed when the program is RUN.

CALL -3288

There are several ways to exit the error-handling routine. One is to simply allow the error routine to "clean up" the mistake, notify the user, etc., and then END the program.

Another is to use a GOTO statement to return to a specific section of the program, you can decide which section based on the line number where the error occurred. This gives you more freedom to attempt to correct the problem before proceeding, and to re-try the last operation.

Another method is to use a special statement provided to exit the error routine and go back to the statement in the program in which the error occurred. The "RESUME" statement causes this action, it works similarly to the "RETURN" statement used to exit a subroutine called with "GOSUB" with the exception that RESUME is used specifically with error-handling subroutines, and that it returns to the same *statement* (not line) that caused the error.

There is one historical problem with GOTO versus RESUME. The Applesoft interpreter does not have any control over where the error "interferes" with things, and some data used by Applesoft to keep track of the BASIC program's status may become slightly scrambled (for you techies, it has to do with the Applesoft control stack's operation). Apple Computer used to supply a short machine-language subroutine to use to correct the problems, but later they released a CALL to an Applesoft interpreter subroutine that served the equivalent function, which is "CALL -3288". This CALL should be included in all error subroutines if a GOTO, rather than RESUME, is used to exit.

A BIGGER "ONERR" ROUTINE

Sometimes, when debugging programs, it is nice to have a do-all error handler. Listing 7-5 contains a subroutine which can be used to return the error code, the line number in which the error occurred, and an error message corresponding to the

```
3230  REM *** ERROR HANDLER ***
3240  REM RESERVED VARIABLES:
3250  REM      ECODE  (FOR ERROR NUMBER)
3260  REM      EMESSAGE$ (FOR ERROR MESSAGE
       STRING)
3270  REM      EFLAG  (FOR ERROR FLAG, = 1 IF
       ERROR)
3280  REM      ELINE (FOR ERROR LINE NUMBER)
3290  GOSUB 3330: REM get error info.
3300  IF EFLAG = 1 AND ECODE = 255 THEN  VTAB
       20: HTAB 1: CALL  - 958: PRINT EMESSAGE$:
       PRINT "at # ";ELINE".": VTAB 22: CALL  -
       3288: POKE 216,0: END : REM EXIT ON
       CONTROL-C.
3310  RESUME
3320  STOP : REM shouldn't happen.
3330  REM *** MAKE UP ERROR STRING ***
3340 ECODE =  PEEK (222)
3350 ELINE =  PEEK (218) +  PEEK (219) * 256
3360 EMESSAGE$ = ""
3370  REM APPLESOFT ERRORS
3380  IF ECODE = 0 THEN EMESSAGE$ = "NEXT
       WITHOUT FOR"
```

Listing 7-5. A "generalized" error handling subroutine.

```
3390  IF ECODE = 16 THEN EMESSAGE$ = "INCORRECT
       SYNTAX"
3400  IF ECODE = 22 THEN EMESSAGE$ = "RETURN
       WITHOUT GOSUB"
3410  IF ECODE = 42 THEN EMESSAGE$ = "OUT OF
       DATA"
3420  IF ECODE = 53 THEN EMESSAGE$ = "ILLEGAL
       QUANTITY"
3430  IF ECODE = 69 THEN EMESSAGE$ = "OVERFLOW"
3440  IF ECODE = 77 THEN EMESSAGE$ = "OUT OF
       MEMORY"
3450  IF ECODE = 90 THEN EMESSAGE$ = "UNDEFINED
       STATEMENT"
3460  IF ECODE = 107 THEN EMESSAGE$ = "BAD
       SUBSCRIPT"
3470  IF ECODE = 120 THEN EMESSAGE$ =
       "REDIMENSIONED ARRAY"
3480  IF ECODE = 133 THEN EMESSAGE$ = "DIVISION
       BY ZERO"
3490  IF ECODE = 163 THEN EMESSAGE$ = "TYPE
       MISMATCH"
3500  IF ECODE = 176 THEN EMESSAGE$ = "STRING
       TOO LONG"
3510  IF ECODE = 191 THEN EMESSAGE$ = "FORMULA
       TOO COMPLEX"
3520  IF ECODE = 224 THEN EMESSAGE$ = "UNDEFINED
       FN"
3530  IF ECODE = 255 THEN EMESSAGE$ = "CONTROL-C
       ABORT"
3540  REM BASIC.SYSTEM ERRORS
3550  IF ECODE = 2 THEN EMESSAGE$ = "RANGE
       ERROR"
3560  IF ECODE = 3 THEN EMESSAGE$ = "NO DEVICE
       CONNECTED"
3570  IF ECODE = 4 THEN EMESSAGE$ = "WRITE
       PROTECTED"
3580  IF ECODE = 5 THEN EMESSAGE$ = "END OF
       DATA"
3590  IF ECODE = 8 THEN EMESSAGE$ = "I/O ERROR"
3600  IF ECODE = 9 THEN EMESSAGE$ = "DISK FULL"
3610  IF ECODE = 10 THEN EMESSAGE$ = "FILE
       LOCKED"
3620  IF ECODE = 11 THEN EMESSAGE$ = "INVALID
       OPTION"
3630  IF ECODE = 12 THEN EMESSAGE$ = "NO BUFFERS
       AVAILABLE"
3640  IF ECODE = 13 THEN EMESSAGE$ = "FILE TYPE
       MISMATCH"
3650  IF ECODE = 14 THEN EMESSAGE$ = "PROGRAM
       TOO LARGE"
3660  IF ECODE = 15 THEN EMESSAGE$ = "NOT DIRECT
       COMMAND": REM SUPERFLUOUS.
3670  IF ECODE = 16 THEN EMESSAGE$ = "INCORRECT
       SYNTAX": REM REDUNDANT.
3680  IF ECODE = 17 THEN EMESSAGE$ = "DIRECTORY
       FULL"
3690  IF ECODE = 18 THEN EMESSAGE$ = "FILE NOT
       OPEN"
```

```
3700  IF ECODE = 19 THEN EMESSAGE$ = "DUPLICATE
       FILENAME"
3710  IF ECODE = 20 THEN EMESSAGE$ = "FILE BUSY"
3720  IF ECODE = 21 THEN EMESSAGE$ = "FILE(S)
       STILL OPEN"
3730 EFLAG = 1
3740  IF (ECODE = 0 OR ECODE > 21) THEN
       EMESSAGE$ = "A/S error: " + EMESSAGE$
3750  IF (ECODE > 0 AND ECODE < 21 AND ECODE <
       > 16) THEN EMESSAGE$ = "BASIC.SYSTEM
       error: " + EMESSAGE$
3760  IF (ECODE = 16) THEN EMESSAGE$ = "A/S or
       BASIC.SYSTEM error: " + EMESSAGE$
3770  RETURN
```

Applesoft or BASIC.SYSTEM error message. This subroutine (with appropriate renumbering of line numbers) can be used during debugging of a program. Then, when the program is debugged, the inappropriate error messages can be "stripped out" to reduce the size of the subroutine, or the program can be replaced with a more compact error handler.

[Note: The "CALL -958" in line 3300 invokes a routine in the system monitor that causes the lower portion of the Apple text screen to be cleared from the location of the cursor to the end of the screen. A reference to the routine can be found in Apple's technical reference manuals for the Apple *II* or *II*e.]

USING "VERIFY" TO CONTROL ERRORS

There is a useful command named *VERIFY* that allows us to check for a file on a disk before trying to do a lot of fancy work with the file. The command has the syntax

VERIFY pathname,Dn,Sn

and is used with the optional pathname to detect the presence of a file, usually (within programs) in conjunction with the ONERR command. VERIFY will return a "PATH NOT FOUND" message if the specified file does not exist; otherwise it apparently does nothing and lets its silence bespeak the fact that the file indeed exists. The "PATH NOT FOUND ERROR" can be used within a program to detect whether the file exists before proceeding with various operations.

The uses of VERIFY with a pathname are obvious, the use of VERIFY without a pathname (in the absence of a set prefix) is perplexing. If no pathname is specified and the prefix is clear, VERIFY returns a message identifying BASIC.SYSTEM as copyrighted by Apple Computer!

VERIFYING A VOLUME

To demonstrate the use of VERIFY, let's use it to provide a friendly way to use a very unfriendly BASIC.SYSTEM command named *BYE*.

The manner in which the BYE command works is hard to justify. What it DOES is easy; the command "BYE" (no options) issued in immediate or deferred mode calls up an "exit" routine called the *quit code* that ProDOS (note:*not* BASIC.SYSTEM!) keeps internally. The quit code is designed to prompt a person for both a prefix and pathname when they desire to exit a program; it is usually used when transferring a user from one program on a disk to the next program, possibly on a new disk.

The problem with BYE is within ProDOS's quit code itself; the quit code as supplied with ProDOS will not let you exit except by specifying the prefix and pathname of a new (executable) program or booting a new disk from scratch. The quit code will read and incorporate the prefix value which exists at the time of its "invocation", but from there on you're on your own.

On an Apple *II* with an Autostart ROM, you cannot exit the quit code by booting without turn-

```
10  REM *** "BYE" DEMO ***
20 EF = 0: ONERR  GOTO 1000
100  TEXT : PRINT  CHR$ (13) +  CHR$ (21): HOME
110 D$ =  CHR$ (4)
200  REM GET CURRENT VOLUME NAME
210  IF  NOT EF THEN  PRINT D$;"PREFIX,D1"
215  IF EF THEN  VTAB 22: PRINT "Can't read
       disk! (Press a key) ";: GET A$: PRINT :EF
       = 0: GOTO 210: REM Try again.
220  PRINT D$;"PREFIX"
230  INPUT PF$: REM Read prefix and hold.
240  PRINT "Current volume name is: ";PF$
250  PRINT : PRINT
260  PRINT "Do you wish to boot a disk?: ";
270  GET A$
280  IF A$ <  > "Y" AND A$ <  > "y" AND A$ <  >
       "N" AND A$ <  > "n" THEN 270
290  PRINT : PRINT : IF A$ = "N" OR A$ = "n"
       THEN 400
300  REM *** FORCE REBOOT ON <RESET> ***
310  PRINT "Insert disk and press 'RESET' while"
320  PRINT "holding the 'CONTROL' key down."
330  POKE 1012,0: REM Trash power-up byte.
340  GOTO 340
400  REM *** GET NEXT APPLICATION ***
410  HOME : PRINT "Insert next disk and press
       <RETURN>:";
420  GET A$: IF A$ <  >  CHR$ (13) AND A$ <  >
       CHR$ (27) THEN 420
425  IF A$ =  CHR$ (27) THEN  PRINT : HOME :
       PRINT "Aborted.": VTAB 22: END
430  PRINT : IF  NOT EF THEN  PRINT
       D$;"PREFIX,D1"
435  IF EF THEN  VTAB 22: PRINT "Can't read
       disk! (Press a key) ";: GET A$: PRINT :EF
       = 0: GOTO 410: REM Try again.
440  PRINT D$;"PREFIX"
450  INPUT PF$
460  HOME : PRINT "Current volume name is: ";PF$
470  PRINT : PRINT "Pathname of program to run
       (type a"
480  PRINT "<RETURN> by itself for a CAT of the"
490  INPUT "disk)?: ";NM$
500  IF NM$ = "" AND  NOT EF THEN  PRINT D$;"CAT
       ";PF$;",D1": PRINT : INPUT "PATHNAME?:
       ";NM$: IF NM$ = "" THEN 410
505  IF EF THEN  VTAB 22: PRINT "Can't read
       disk! (Press a key) ";: GET A$: PRINT :EF
       = 0: GOTO 410: REM Try again.
510  HOME : IF  NOT EF THEN  PRINT
       D$;"VERIFY";NM$;",D1"
520  IF EF THEN  VTAB 22: PRINT "Can't find
       file! (Press a key) ";: GET A$: PRINT :EF
```

Listing 7-6. Simulating "BYE" (with the option to CATALOG a directory).

```
      = 0: GOTO 410: REM Try again.
530  POKE 216,0: REM Clear ONERR flag.
540  IF  NOT EF THEN  PRINT D$;"- ";NM$;",D1":
      REM Run it (or at least try).
999  END
1000  REM Cheap error handler.
1010 EF = 1
1020 EC =  PEEK (222)
1030  RESUME
```

ing off the computer's power, which results in additional wear-and-tear on the power supply's switch and electronics. Luckily, on a *IIe* or *IIc* you can use the "control-open-Apple reset" sequence to reboot (maybe Apple forgot the multitude of Apple *II*'s still in use).

The quit code will otherwise force you to enter the prefix (or accept the current prefix as the "default") and pathname of a program to exit; it will not even do the courtesy of allowing you to view the files on the disk once the quit code is running (this is one reason we recommend labeling all ProDOS disks with their volume names, and possibly the name of the first ".SYSTEM" file on the disk).

You might enjoy trying the "BYE" command, but make sure you have saved any work in RAM memory to disk before issuing the command, or it will be lost.

Very likely, the command was placed in BASIC.SYSTEM to give program developers (those programmers who write programs to sell on the commercial market) easy access to the quit code, which they often custom modify to improve. But the "raw" quit code supplied with ProDOS is a very user-hostile way to end a program.

We cannot recommend using BYE without modifying the quit code to make it serviceable; anybody smart enough to do that is smart enough to call the quit code from machine language which obviates the presence of BYE. The command appears largely useless.

There is no reason to subject the average user to the indignity of this command from within a BASIC program. If the user cannot be trusted to be allowed to exit to the wilds of BASIC by a simple "END" command, at least give him or her a chance to identify the next disk and choose between an exit via ProDOS pathname or booting a new disk.

Listing 7-6 contains a short example of routines which can substitute for BYE. They use VERIFY to check for any requested program to be executed on exit. Line 510 demonstrates the most common use of VERIFY within a program, to identify if a file is present. Since ONERR is in effect, the occurrence of an error in line 510 will send us to line 1000, which simply sets the error flag variable "EF" to 1 and RESUMEs at the errant statement. If line 520 finds "EF = 1" is true, then the file could not be VERIFYed and the program asks you to try again.

Chapter 8

Programs In Pieces

Normally, BASIC programs are stored on disk using the SAVE command and brought back into memory using LOAD or RUN (or "-"). The program reserves a certain "chunk" of the available RAM memory. Most of the remaining RAM memory is still available for other uses by Applesoft and BASIC.SYSTEM.

There is a continual battle fought between the programmer and his computer; the battle for space. The programmer always wants more space to expand the performance of his creation; the computer may or may not have room to grant his wish. Eventually, if enough "buzzers and bells" are added to a program, size constraints start to become noticeable. When the "PROGRAM TOO LARGE" error occurs, the battle enters a new level.

BASIC.SYSTEM has three commands to facilitate managing programs in less memory than they would require if handled as a single large entity. These commands are *CHAIN*, *STORE* and, *RESTORE*.

DIVIDE AND CONQUER

Sometimes you get really involved in adding improvements to a program to the point where the program starts to outgrow the computer. With Applesoft BASIC under ProDOS and BASIC.SYSTEM, you have a maximum of about 34K bytes of space to program; this can be much less due to space you need to store your variables, any machine language support routines, etc. At the point where you run out of room, you have to make a decision: reduce the memory requirements of your single program by improving its size efficiency or by removing features, or split the program into smaller subsections.

Examples of the first approach are removing unneeded REM statements, combining program lines, defining variables to use the minimum space (including use of arrays), and so forth. This will provide some help in many cases.

But a truly BIG program, such as a database, will require that you split up the program's functions. A database program will have routines for setting up the database format, entering data, storing the data on disk (usually in text files, something we haven't covered but will in Part III), and retrieving the data; and usually an extensive set of routines to allow printing reports, which opens a whole extra set of data to store for report and printer formats. Such a program can easily fill the Apple memory by itself, without leaving any room for the data. And without room for the data, there may as well not be a program.

If you think about it, though, most of the sections of the database program do not really overlap in responsibility. You can only work with one section of the program at a time. For example, if you are entering names and addresses you aren't going to be setting up a printer format at the same time since that is a separate operation. Why not, then, put the sections of the program that you are not using on disk, out of the way, and call them in only when needed?

THINKING "TRADE-OFF"

The disadvantage of having sections of the program on disk is the delay in reading a new section you need into memory. There's also the irritation of having to have the disk with all the program sections "handy". The delay factor is not a big concern if the program is broken up into intelligent sections, especially since ProDOS only takes a few seconds to load a file at BASIC.SYSTEM's request. And, using ProDOS's ability to identify disks and files by name, the program can always check to see if the right disk and program are present. What you get for all this irritation is the ability to easily "run" a bigger program in sections than you could possibly fit into memory at one time. Also, you can keep more of the memory free as space for your variables and support routines.

One other problem: the Applesoft RUN command clears all variables from memory when starting execution of the program. BASIC.SYSTEM's RUN command does the same thing. It is really going to slow things down if we have to save all of our variables before we can RUN the next section, which will then have to re- read all of the data. It would be better if we could keep our diligently entered variable data in memory and just "switch" BASIC programs.

LINKING THE SEGMENTS

There is, happily, a BASIC.SYSTEM command to allow this, called *CHAIN*. It has the syntax

CHAIN *pathname*,@In,Sn,Dn

This command is similar to the BASIC.SYSTEM RUN command except that it does not clear the current variables. A variable defined in a program that executes a second program via CHAIN can be referenced by the same name in the second program and will have the same value.

As an example, let's think of a "first" program (shown in Listing 8-1) saved to disk as "CHAIN.DEMO.1", and a second program (shown in Listing 8-2) saved to the same disk as "CHAIN.DEMO.2". If we RUN CHAIN.DEMO.1, it will set the value of NAME$ to "JOHN DOE" and then execute CHAIN.DEMO.2 via the CHAIN command. CHAIN.DEMO.2 enters memory with the value of variable NAME$ held in memory intact, and uses that value when it prints the statement in line 30. If "RUN" is substituted for "CHAIN" in line 50 of CHAIN.PART.2 to use the normal BASIC.SYSTEM RUN command, you'll see that NAME$ is cleared to an empty string before being printed in line 30 of CHAIN.DEMO.2.

This same approach can be used for a much larger program to break it into manageable pieces that will fit in memory. All of the segments may use common names for specific variables and CHAIN to the required segment at will.

[Note: although this demo works, Peter Meyer reported a bug in CHAIN in the June 1985 issue of *Call-A.P.P.L.E.* magazine, in the article "A Bug in the ProDOS CHAIN Command" on page 30. Briefly, his observation is that the first variable defined in a program may be "lost" during a CHAIN operation. His recommendation is to define an unused "dummy" variable at the beginning of any program which issues the CHAIN command.]

```
10  REM *** CHAIN DEMO (PART 1 OF TWO) ***
20 D$ =  CHR$ (4): REM CTRL-D
30  TEXT : HOME
50 NAME$ = "JOHN DOE"
60  PRINT D$;"CHAIN CHAIN.DEMO.2"
```

Listing 8-1. A CHAIN demonstration, part one.

"STORE" AND "RESTORE"

One major use of the remaining memory by Applesoft during the execution of most BASIC programs is for storage of variables. If you are used to working with BASIC programs, you know that a lot of programming statements can be dedicated to defining initial values for variables, and that all variables defined in the program are stored as a part of the program itself. When the BASIC program is executed these values are moved into the variable space area of RAM; the value of each variable is associated with an area of RAM memory used to contain its representation. In addition, a certain amount of "bookkeeping" information is used to keep track of the location and length of string variables, etc.

SINGLE-ENTRY BOOKKEEPING

One way to decrease the size of a program, were it possible, would be to eliminate the double-bookkeeping of having variables defined in the program and also in the RAM area assigned for the variables would be to create most (or all) of the variables to be used, save those variables out to disk in a compact form, and then erase the definitions from the BASIC program. Then, in our ideal world, the program could later re-load the set of initialized variables when needed. BASIC.SYSTEM provides for such a system using two commands, *STORE* and *RESTORE*.

The STORE command compresses ("tokenizes") the current defined set of BASIC variables within the variable space area of RAM (*not* within the program itself) into a block and saves that block to disk under a specified filename. The command syntax is

STORE *pathname*,Sn,Dn

The command can be used in the immediate mode, but would normally be used in conjunction with a BASIC program to place the current set of defined values within the variable space into a disk file of type "VAR" (for "variable"). This is one way of storing data from a BASIC program. Another, more conventional, manner is with text files (to be discussed later). Binary ("BIN") files are also used, normally to store data that exists as a raw image of a section of memory.

A variable file created with the STORE command can be re-called into memory using the RESTORE command so the data can be re-used

RESTORE *pathname*,Sn,Dn

Variables stored with the original command can now be accessed with the same variable names; that is, the value of an arbitrary variable named "MI$(11)" saved with the STORE command can again be referenced as "MI$(11)" after RESTORE

```
10  REM *** CHAIN DEMO (PART 2 OF TWO) ***
20  TEXT : HOME : PRINT "THE VALUE OF 'NAME$'
      IS:"
30  PRINT : PRINT  SPC( 10); CHR$ (34);NAME$;
      CHR$ (34)
40  VTAB 22: END
```

Listing 8-2. A CHAIN demonstration, part two.

is used to re-load the same variable file. In fact, you *must* use the same variable name for a defined value that was in effect when "STORE" was used to create the file.

Additionally, the VAR file loaded by RESTORE will replace *all* currently defined variables in memory. This includes "D$ = CHR$ (4)"; if you want "D$" to have the same value in your program after RESTORE you must save it as part of the file when using STORE, or define it again after the RESTORE command has been issued.

One valid application of STORE and RESTORE is to save space as mentioned above; the variable file uses disk space efficiently (*very* efficiently versus text files) since the data is compressed prior to being saved on disk. One disadvantage to the compression is that there may be a brief "pause" between the time the "STORE" command is issued and the variable file can be created due to the time spent in preparing the variable data for storage. All the Applesoft statements defining variables in the program can then be removed (saving space within the program) and replaced with an initial BASIC.SYSTEM "RESTORE" command to load in the pre-determined values.

A second application is the ability to define two or more different sets of variables for a single program, save each under a different filename, and load the desired set dependent upon conditions tested by the program.

"STORE" AND DEBUGGING

A third, less obvious use is in debugging a BASIC program. When a program is stopped with an END statement (or by encountering the last statement in the program's flow), with a control-C ("break") typed from the keyboard, or via an error, the current values of the variables remain in RAM in the variables space. Any changes to the program to change an errant line will cause Applesoft to "clear" the current values of the variables. STOREing the variables will allow RESTOREing them for later examination.

Since a change in a program line forces Applesoft to update its accounting for the location of the start and end of the program, Applesoft may have to re-assign the start and end of the variable space and therefore Applesoft clears the current variable space and starts anew when a program line is changed or re-entered.

"Resetting" the Apple also causes the variable space to be cleared due to BASIC.SYSTEM's initialization routines. To allow yourself to edit a line AND still retain the variable definitions, you can issue a STORE command such as "STORE DEBUG.1" to save the current variable values, edit the line, then use a RESTORE DEBUG.1 to read in the variable set. Actually, you could save the state of the variables at several different stages of the program by using different names, and RESTORE each set by name if you like.

ESCHEW OBFUSCATION

A last, more insidious, use of STORE and RESTORE is to make a program very hard to read and modify. Since the variable definitions can be removed completely from a program by using variable files, the (usually non-trivial) documentation value of the definitions is no longer extant in such a program. Undocumented programs are a bad practice; we will say no more.

A "STORE" DEMO

For an example of the STORE command, try the program in Listing 8-3. RUN it, and the program will create a file named "STRING.DATA" of type "VAR" (verify this by using the CAT or CATALOG command, if you like).

The file can be read in by the program in Listing 8-4. When this program is run, notice that the values printed for the strings before the "RESTORE" command is issued are all the null string. After RESTORE, the values are the same as those values STOREd into the file "STRING.DATA" by the previous program.

Notice also the difference between this command and the CHAIN method of "holding" variables over for use by another program. CHAIN keeps the values of the variables in RAM memory only; if power is lost to the computer or memory

```
10  REM *** VARIABLE FILE DEMO PART 1 ***
20  TEXT : HOME :D$ =  CHR$ (4)
30  FOR I = 1 TO 5
40 A$(I) = "THIS IS STRING #" +  STR$ (I) + "."
50  NEXT I
60  PRINT D$;"STORE STRING.DATA"
99  END
```

Listing 8-3. The use of STORE to create a VAR file.

```
10   REM *** VARIABLE FILE DEMO PART 2 ***
20   TEXT : HOME :D$ =  CHR$ (4)
30   PRINT "BEFORE 'RESTORE':"
40   PRINT : GOSUB 1000
50   VTAB 22: PRINT "PRESS A KEY: ";
60   GET A$: PRINT
100  HOME
110  PRINT "AFTER 'RESTORE':"
120  PRINT D$;"RESTORE STRING.DATA"
130  PRINT : GOSUB 1000
140  VTAB 22: END
199  END
1000  REM PRINT STRING VALUES.
1010  FOR I = 1 TO 5
1020  PRINT  SPC( 5);"A$(";I;") = "; CHR$
        (34);A$(I); CHR$ (34)
1030  NEXT I
1040  RETURN
```

Listing 8-4. The use of RESTORE to read a VAR file.

is otherwise "cleared" the value of these variables is lost just as a BASIC program is lost from memory under similar circumstances. STORE and RESTORE use the disk to store their variable table and values, so that the record of the variables' values is as permanent as the disk file.

Chapter 9

"FRE"; Taking A Poke At The Garbageman

There is a very useful command in BASIC.SYSTEM called *FRE* (no options) which is used to clear up string storage. Why this command is so useful, and why the string storage needs "cleaning" in the first place requires some background.

THE GARBAGEMAN (SLOWLY) COMETH

Everybody has a nemesis. Hamlet has his stepfather, Batman and Robin have the Riddler, Peter Rabbit has Mr. McGregor. Applesoft programmers working under DOS 3.3 have the Garbageman.

When the Garbageman strikes, your Applesoft program comes to a sudden and complete halt. Your keyboard will go dead. Your face will look confused and angry. You will probably hit control- reset, unless you've met the Garbageman before. In that case you will sit and wait. After a pause of something between a few seconds and a few minutes, the Garbageman, his can full of electronic detritus, suddenly flees. Your Apple will mysteriously start working perfectly again.

WHAT STRINGS?

Consider the following famous program, which originally appeared in a *Softalk* "DOStalk" column:

```
10 INPUT "WHAT? ";A$
20  GOTO 10
```

When you run this program, the word "WHAT?" appears on your screen with a cursor beside it. You type "WITCHES" and press return. Applesoft puts the word "WITCHES" in an empty place inside your computer. It also stores the length and location of "WITCHES" in a table used to keep track of such stuff. It's called a *variable table*.

The empty place where strings are stored extends from where the variable tables end to where BASIC.SYSTEM starts. The first string is placed right up against BASIC.SYSTEM. The next one is tucked in next to the first. Figure 9-1 will help you figure out where this string storage place is inside your computer.

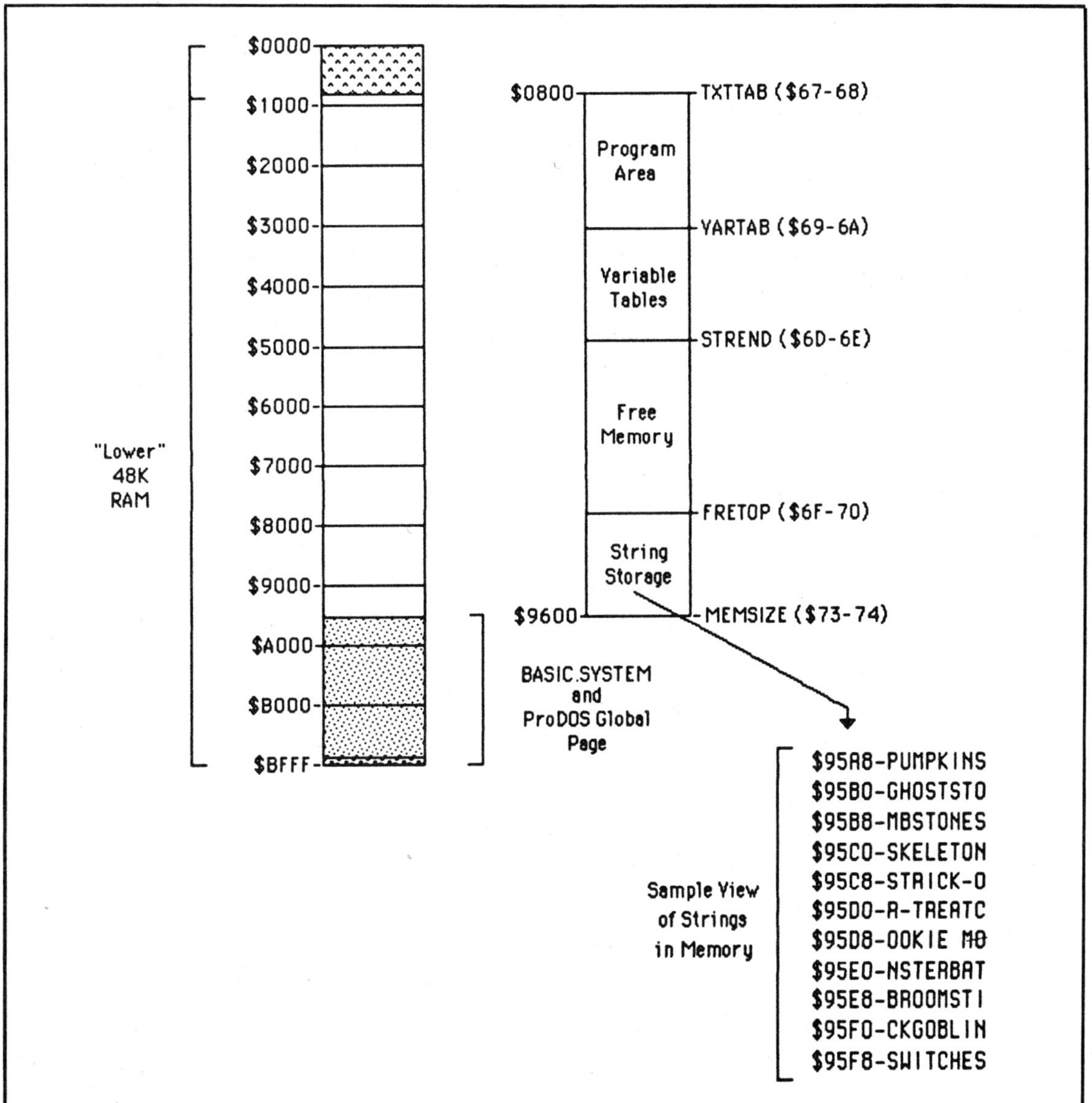

Fig. 9-1. BASIC string variable storage in memory.

The left-most bar of Fig. 9-1 represents the entire range of Apple II memory and shows its standard uses. The middle bar shows how Applesoft splits up the "free" memory area from byte $800 (in decimal that's 2048) to byte $9600 (38400). Applesoft uses this area for storing your actual program and your program's variable tables and strings. The right-most bar of Fig. 9-1 (the "sample view" of the strings) gives you a peek inside the string storage area itself.

Usually memory maps are presented with the high addresses at the top. Some of you may think this map is upside down. We do it that way because it matches what you see when you examine memory using the monitor program. It takes only a few minutes of trying to match what you see in the monitor's memory display with what you see in a standard memory map to realize that it's the standard maps that are upside down.

Since the first string is stored right next to DOS and the second next to the first, the order in which they appear in memory is backward from the order in which they are used. Note in the right-most bar of Fig. 9-1 that our first string, "WITCHES", appears as the last word in the bar. If line 20 of our famous little program said "PRINT A$", Applesoft would look in the variable table until it found the entry for A$, then would use the length and address stored there to retrieve "WITCHES".

WHY THE GARBAGEMAN TAKES SO LONG

Ah, but the next command isn't "PRINT", it's "GOTO 10". Our input statement is repeated. In response to the second "WHAT?", you type in "GOBLINS". Applesoft now stores "GOBLINS" in unused memory, right next to "WITCHES", and changes the length and address for A$ in the variable table.

Applesoft keeps track of where the edge between empty memory and the string storage area is by means of a pointer kept at bytes $6F-70 (111-112). This pointer is called *FRETOP* in the Applesoft literature. It, too, is shown in Fig. 9-1, along with several other interesting pointers. Whenever you enter a new string, Applesoft refers to FRETOP to figure out where to store the string.

Since your program has changed the value of A$ from "WITCHES" to "GOBLINS", Applesoft correctly assumes you are no longer interested in "WITCHES". The word "WITCHES" is still in memory, but because its length and address have been overwritten by the length and address of "GOBLINS", Applesoft can no longer find it. "WITCHES" is now an *inactive* string.

"WHAT?" You type in "BROOMSTICK" and a couple thousand similar words. Eventually Applesoft will go to store a word you have typed in and find the strings have bumped into the variable tables—there is no more empty memory left. At that point, Applesoft calls on the Garbageman to examine the variable table, find all the "active" strings, and consolidate them down at the BASIC.SYSTEM end of memory. After the consolidation, FRETOP will be changed to point to the new boundary between the active strings and the rest of memory. All the memory held by "inactive" strings will be freed and made available for reuse.

The Applesoft Garbageman has a lot of work to do. He can't just go in, find the first active string in the variable table, and move it next to BASIC.SYSTEM. If he did, he might overwrite *another* active string. So what he does is search through the *entire* variable table and find the active string that is already closest to BASIC.SYSTEM. Then he moves it into the first position in the string storage area. This happens in a flash with the little program we've been using. Since there is only one string variable being used (A$), the Garbageman quickly finds its active value, moves it, and disappears. You probably wouldn't even notice he had stopped by.

But, programs that have a lot of string variables, particularly programs with large string arrays, really slow the Garbageman down. For *each* variable in the table, he must look through the *entire* variable table once. The more variables in the table, the more times he must look *and* the longer it will take to look through it each time.

A DEMONSTRATION

If you'd like to measure the effects of the Garbageman yourself, try the little program (designed for both DOS and ProDOS, if you want to compare) in Listing 9-1.

Line 10 determines how many strings our program will have. Line 20 dimensions a string array of length I. Lines 30 through 60 fill the array with strings. Lines 70 through 90 allow us to measure how long the Garbageman takes to clean up this many strings.

You may be somewhat puzzled by lines 80 and 85. To understand these two lines, you first have to know that BASIC.SYSTEM includes its own Garbageman. He is quite a bit faster than the one built into Applesoft, as we'll soon see. A program

```
10  I=250
20  DIM G$(I)
30  FOR X=0 TO I
40  : G$(X)=STR$(X)
50  : PRINT G$(X)
60  NEXT
70  PRINT "COLLECTING GARBAGE"; CHR$(7)
80  IF PEEK(978)<>190 THEN X=FRE(0) : REM
       Applesoft/DOS 3.3
85  IF PEEK(978)=190 THEN PRINT CHR$(4);"FRE" :
       REM BASIC.SYSTEM
90  PRINT "GARBAGE COLLECTED"; CHR$(7)
```

Listing 9-1. Garbage collector (for DOS or BASIC.SYSTEM).

can tell if it is running under ProDOS or DOS 3.3 by taking a peek at byte 978 ($3D2). If this byte is equal to 190, then BASIC.SYSTEM is active. If it is anything else, then you are running under DOS 3.3.

If you are running with DOS 3.3, you can call the Applesoft Garbageman and ask him to clean up with the command "X = FRE(0)". To call the BASIC.SYSTEM Garbageman, however, you have to use a BASIC.SYSTEM command. Thus, in line 85, we say

PRINT CHR$(4);"FRE"

If you are running the program with BASIC.SYSTEM and do not have DOS 3.3 for a comparison, you can force the program to use the Applesoft Garbageman (which is actually the one used under DOS 3.3) by deleting line 85 and replacing line 80 with "80 X = FRE (0): REM Applesoft.". This avoids calling the much faster BASIC.SYSTEM routines.

After typing in the program and running it, increase the value of "I" in line 10. This will increase the number of strings in the program. Garbage collection will take longer and longer. Table 9-1 contains some sample timings.

SPEEDING UP THE GARBAGEMAN

Back in January 1981, *Call -A.P.P.L.E.* published a program by Randy Wiggington (one of the very first Apple employees, currently famous as the author of *MacWrite*) that could make the DOS 3.3 Garbageman fly. The program worked by finding the *16* active strings closest to DOS on each scan of the variable table, rather than just the closest *one*. Rather than searching through the entire variable table once for each variable, the new technique scanned once for each 16 variables.

Apple's programmers used a similar technique

Table 9-1. Comparison of Garbage-Collection Times (DOS versus BASIC.SYSTEM).

	Garbage collection time in seconds	
number of strings	DOS 3.3	BASIC.SYSTEM
250	5	0.1
500	19	0.2
1000	114	0.5

```
10 REM*** CALC FREE MEMORY ***
20 D$ = CHR$ (4) : REM CTRL-D
30 PRINT D$;"FRE": REM CLEAR GARBAGE FAST.
40 LM = PEEK (109) + PEEK (110) * 256 : REM
       START OF "FREE" RAM.
50 HM = PEEK (111) + PEEK (112) * 256 : REM END
       OF "FREE" RAM.
60 FM = HM - LM : REM NET "AVAILABLE" RAM.
99 END
```

Listing 9-2. A program to force garbage collection and calculate free RAM.

in the ProDOS BASIC.SYSTEM software. That's why the BASIC.SYSTEM Garbageman is so much faster than the one built into Applesoft. Thus, the obvious way to escape the lulls caused by Applesoft garbage collection is to use ProDOS and BASIC.SYSTEM rather than DOS 3.3.

BASIC.SYSTEM will watch the progress of the string storage and automatically call its (fast) garbage collection routines before Applesoft has a chance to call its (lethargic) routines. Therefore, there is no real need to use "FRE" explicitly just to do the garbage collection.

One common use of the Applesoft Garbageman was to return the amount of "free" RAM memory available for variables, in a program line such as

```
10  X = FRE (0) :REM X = FREE MEMORY.
```

which sets "X" equal to a number representing the amount of memory available for variables. Unfortunately, this invokes the lethargic Applesoft Garbageman.

To utilize the speed of BASIC.SYSTEM's Garbageman, the use of Applesoft's "FRE (0)" should be avoided altogether. You can calculate free memory directly from the Applesoft pointers for the start and end of available memory, as shown in the program in Listing 9-2.

The variable "FM" will hold the available free memory calculated from "LM" (the end of the variable array space that starts in memory after the end of the program storage) and "HM" (the highest memory position available, from FRETOP). Remember that these locations only know about BASIC program and variable usage of memory,

```
10  REM *** TEST FOR FREE MEMORY ***
20 I = 0
30 MEM = ( PEEK (112) * 256 +  PEEK (111)) - (
       PEEK (110) * 256 +  PEEK (109)): REM CALC
       FREE MEMORY.
40  IF LMEM - MEM < 0 AND I <  > 0 THEN  PRINT
       CHR$ (7);"GARBAGE COLLECTED!!!"
50  PRINT "Free memory = ";MEM: PRINT "Strings
       defined = ";I: PRINT
60 A$ = "ONE BLOODY BIG SENTENCE JUST TO TEST
       THIS THING OUT ONCE AND FOR ALL SO THAT
       WE KNOW HOW MUCH SPACE IS BEING USED IN
       MEMORY AT THE DEFINITION OF SENTENCE
       NUMBER " +  STR$ (I)
70 LMEM = MEM: REM SAVE LAST MEM VALUE.
80 I = I + 1: REM NEW DEFINITION FOR STRING.
90  GOTO 30
```

Listing 9-3. A program to show the "loss" of memory to "garbage."

however; items like the memory used by Applesoft's high-res graphics pages are not included in the figure.

MORE GARBAGE COLLECTED

Listing 9-3 contains a program that lets us determine how much memory is used before BASIC.SYSTEM does its garbage collection. It stores successive values of "A$" into memory until BASIC.SYSTEM is forced to "clean up" the garbage produced.

Type in and RUN the program. It will print a number representing the number of "A$"'s that have been stored into memory and a value for the "free" memory remaining. When you hear a "beep" from the Apple speaker, you'll see a message "GARBAGE COLLECTED!!!". The last "free memory" value before this message is the minimum amount of free memory allowed by BASIC.SYSTEM before garbage collection. If you watch the "free memory" figures that appear before and after this message, you'll see a dramatic increase after garbage collection. You can RUN the program and watch it continuously "fill" and then "clean" the Apple's string space in memory.

You'll now notice the reason why the first "CALC FREE MEMORY" program used the "FRE" command before reading the Applesoft pointers and calculating free memory. If "FRE" had not been explicitly used, garbage collection would not necessarily be up-to-date when the calculation was done, and you would likely have arrived at too small a number for the amount of "cleaned" memory actually available.

Chapter 10

The New "IN#" And "PR#"

The use of peripherals and the "slots" of the Apple *II* series computers have been mentioned before. Now let's take a further look at Applesoft's and BASIC.SYSTEM's interaction with these "extra" devices.

THE APPLESOFT SLOT I/O COMMANDS

Applesoft uses the familiar "IN#" and "PR#" to re-direct input and output (respectively) to specific "slots". On the Apple *II* Plus and Apple *II*e computers, these slots actually exist in the computer (just lift the lid and see). The Apple *II* Plus contains actual (physical) slots numbered 0-7. The Apple *II*e contains physical slots numbered 1-7 and a new interface slot known as the "auxiliary" slot.

On the Apple *II*c there are *no* physical slots, but the Applesoft "IN#" and "PR#" commands are still valid because the *II*c design makes its input/output devices appear to use essentially the same system as the *II*e. This was done so that the *II*c could run most of the existing software available for the *II* Plus and *II*e.

The respective syntax for the Applesoft commands is

```
IN#n
```

and

```
PR#n
```

where "n" is an integer value for the slot number from 0 to 7 inclusive. An improper value for "n" results in a "?ILLEGAL QUANTITY" error message if Applesoft is active without BASIC.SYSTEM; BASIC.SYSTEM issues a "RANGE ERROR" message instead.

The command "PR#3", whether used in immediate or deferred mode, causes Applesoft to activate the peripheral device in slot 3 and to send all output there until told otherwise (or until the computer is reset). The command "IN#2" causes Applesoft to attempt to take input from the device in slot 2, until otherwise instructed.

With BASIC.SYSTEM, if no device is present

in the slot you specify with one of these commands, the computer will cause a "DEVICE NOT CONNECTED" error.

The commands "IN# 0" and "PR# 0" have a special meaning, since they do not actually refer to a "physical" slot 0. The command "IN# 0" means that Applesoft should take its input from the standard input device, the Apple keyboard, via the system monitor's KEYIN routine at $FD1B. The "PR# 0" command means that the Apple should send its output to the standard output device, normally this is the Apple 40-column text screen. Thus the command "PR#1", used to send output to a device attached to slot 1, can be cancelled with a "PR#0" command.

THE *II*E AND *II*C 80-COLUMN DISPLAY

There is an important exception to this last point: the Apple *II*e and Apple *II*c treat the 80-column by 24-line screen as a peripheral card device in slot 3, even though the Standard or Extended Apple *II*e 80-column Text Cards (from Apple Computer) and their clones are installed in the *II*e's auxiliary slot, and the *II*c has no physical slot 3 at all. This was done as a noble gesture by Apple to keep the newer Apple *II* series computers compatible with older models, where slot 3 had become the de-facto standard slot to install an 80-column display device or remote console (terminal).

Therefore, "PR# 3" activates the 80-column display mode on the *II*e (with 80-column text card) and *II*c computers. The firmware also has a 40-column display mode which leaves the 80-column firmware active; to see this mode, type a "PR#3" to activate the firmware, then an "ESC" followed by a "4" to switch to the 40 column display. Notice that the cursor in this display is a solid white "box", as opposed to the "flashing checkerboard" of the "standard" 40-column display. Typing "ESC" and then "8" will return you to the 80-column mode.

"PR# 0" cannot be used to switch from the 80-column firmware (in either 80-column or 40-column modes) to the standard 40-column display on a *II*e or *II*c due to the manner in which the 80- column firmware controls the computer. Always use the sequence "ESC Control-Q" from the keyboard, or "PRINT CHR$ (21)" from within a program, to de-activate the 80-column firmware and return to the 40-column display.

NEW GAME IN TOWN: BASIC.SYSTEM

The BASIC.SYSTEM *forms* of the standard immediate mode commands of "IN#" and "PR#" are the same as for Applesoft. However, within a program, it becomes important not to confuse BASIC.SYSTEM's forms with the standard Applesoft syntax.

Try the following. With BASIC.SYSTEM active, type "NEW" to clear memory, then enter and run this program line:

```
10  IN# 0 : PR# 0 : REM Set "standard" I/O.
```

Done? Try to view the disk directory using an immediate mode "CAT" command. You should hear a beep and see "?SYNTAX ERROR" on the screen. Note the leading "?"; that means it's an Applesoft (and not BASIC.SYSTEM) error.

Surprised? Don't adjust your set, the problem is in your program. When ProDOS and BASIC.SYSTEM take up residence in your computer, they "take over" control of the input and output routines. Actually, what happens is that BASIC.SYSTEM inserts itself in the input/output stream so that it can see your commands. For a complicated reason, the simple program above has "disconnected" BASIC.SYSTEM, so that it no longer sees what you type!

When you first "power up" your Apple (before ProDOS or other disk operating system loads in), the monitor has control of all input and output; it sets the keyboard and screen up as input and output device. In the course of doing this, the monitor stores an execution address corresponding to *COUT1*, its internal machine language subroutine to output "printed" data, in the low end of the Apple memory. These low memory locations $36 and $37, or 54 and 55 if you prefer decimal, are referred to as the "output hook" or *CSW*.

The address assigned to CSW is available as a "pointer" or "vector" used by other programs to print characters to the screen. Normally, Applesoft eventually sends the character to the subroutine at the address specified by this vector, but Applesoft can change the value of the output vector in CSW to point to a new output routine. That routine then is responsible for outputting characters.

A similar vector, called the "input hook" or *KSW*, is assigned to $38 and $39 (56 and 57 in decimal) which points to the subroutine used to read a character from the input device; the monitor normally keeps this vector pointed at a routine named KEYIN that reads a character from the Apple keyboard when summoned. Applesoft also may redefine this vector for its use.

When BASIC.SYSTEM loads into the Apple, it needs to be able to "see" what is being typed at the keyboard so that it can intercept its commands before Applesoft has a chance to say "?SYNTAX ERROR". The use of the input/output vectors mentioned allows this. All BASIC.SYSTEM (or any other program) has to do to be able to "preview" any input and to insert data into the output stream to be printed is to take possession of these vectors and point them to its own routines.

This is exactly what happens. When BASIC.SYSTEM "installs" itself in your Apple's memory, it takes the original contents of these vectors and installs them internally in itself. The vector in KSW is moved to $BE32-BE33 and used for character input; the CSW vector is moved to $BE30-$BE31 and referenced for output. Then it changes the value of the vectors in CSW and KSW to point to its own command interpreter subroutines.

When you type a command (in answer to the Applesoft prompt) at the keyboard with BASIC.SYSTEM active, BASIC.SYSTEM will "echo" each printable character you type on the screen just as the monitor would, using the monitor's original input/output vectors that BASIC.SYSTEM now keeps internally. But when you press the RETURN key to finish the command, before Applesoft sees the command line, BASIC.SYSTEM looks to see if it recognizes the command. If so, it checks the syntax; if the syntax is correct, executes the command, if the syntax is incorrect it prints a "SYNTAX ERROR" message. If BASIC.SYSTEM doesn't recognize the command, it passes it on to Applesoft just as if BASIC.SYSTEM wasn't there. The same order of events is true if BASIC.SYSTEM is active and you are in the monitor ("*" prompt), but any commands BASIC.SYSTEM doesn't recognize are passed to the monitor instead of BASIC.

Long detour ended; so what happened above? The "IN#" and "PR#" commands in the program line above were issued as *Applesoft* commands, not as BASIC.SYSTEM commands. Applesoft, knowing nothing about BASIC.SYSTEM, set the low memory input/output vectors back to their original values; that is, they were set back to point directly at the monitor's input/output routines, bypassing BASIC.SYSTEM. So BASIC.SYSTEM never saw the "CAT" you typed; and when Applesoft saw the word "CAT" issued as a command, it knew it was not a valid statement and issued the error message.

So, how do you get BASIC.SYSTEM back? Execute a "reset". As part of the reset cycle issued when BASIC.SYSTEM is active, BASIC.SYSTEM will check the I/O vectors and put them right, as well as setting the default I/O devices (the keyboard and the screen) as the devices in use. After "reset", "CAT" should again work as expected.

This is a very long but important lesson: any time BASIC.SYSTEM is active, its "IN#" and "PR#" commands must be issued rather than Applesoft's or BASIC.SYSTEM will become "unhooked" from the input or output stream, respectively. The proper BASIC.SYSTEM form of the normal (slot-directed) commands is illustrated by

```
10  D$ = CHR$ (4) : REM CTRL-D.
20  PRINT D$; "IN# 0" : PRINT D$; "PR# 0"
```

You can type in and RUN this program to demonstrate that it will not disconnect BASIC.SYSTEM as the earlier single-line program did, because this program issues the commands using the proper BASIC.SYSTEM "control-D" form.

BASIC.SYSTEM I/O REDIRECTION

The purpose of the "A" parameter is to allow purposeful re- direction of input or output using a machine language subroutine at the specified address. For example, some older printers require what are called "software drivers", which are machine language s subroutines installed in the Apple's RAM memory. These drivers typically processed the output character and then directed the resulting output stream to the printer's actual slot.

Suppose we have a printer interfaced to slot 1 that requires a driver (named "DRIVER"). Such a routine could be installed with BASIC.SYSTEM with the sequence

```
10  D$ = CHR$ (4) : REM CTRL-D
20  PRINT D$; "BLOAD DRIVER, A$300"
```

and then activated with the program statement

```
PRINT D$; "PR# A$300"
```

which re-directs output to that address.

In a more generic sense, it would be nice if we could use the standard slot number syntax. This can also be done, by this sequence:

```
10  D$ = CHR$ (4) : REM CTRL-D
20  PRINT D$; "BLOAD DRIVER,A$300"
30  PRINT D$; "PR# 1,A$300"
```

Line 30, where both a slot number and an output address are specified, does *not* cause the printer routine to be activated for output as either the lone address parameter or slot number would. Line 30 tells BASIC.SYSTEM to assign the routine at $300 to be responsible for all output directed to slot 1. Later, when BASIC.SYSTEM sees a

```
PRINT D$;"PR# 1"
```

statement within the BASIC program, it will automatically re- direct the output to the routine at $300. This is a very useful feature of BASIC.SYSTEM.

Another use of the command would be to redirect output from one slot to another. For example, if a BASIC program is loaded with references to "PR# 1", and you wish to use a printer in slot 4, you can issue a

```
PR# 1,A$C400
```

statement in immediate mode, then RUN the program (the slot assignment is a feature of BASIC.SYSTEM and not Applesoft BASIC; therefore "RUN" does not clear this definition!) and all output meant for slot 1 will be redirected to slot 4 (unless the program changes the assignments again). This works because the address "$Cn00" corresponds to the entry point of a device in slot n (for n=1 to 7), so that the specified address "$C400" implies we want to use the slot 4 device for output.

VIRTUALLY CHANGING SLOTS

Listing 10-1 contains a program using such redirection. On an Apple *II*e or *II*c, identified by the "PEEK (-1101) = 6" test, the lowercase letters in A$ will be converted to uppercase when the string is printed the second time. On other Apples, the lowercase letters will be converted to inverse uppercase text. The subroutine at line 100 installs a short machine-language driver routine that does the "case conversion". Line 40 assigns the subroutine (installed at address $300) to be used when output is directed at slot 2. In line 70, A$ is PRINTed using the standard Applesoft BASIC method; in line 80 the "slot 2" device (actually, our driver) is activated and A$ is printed again. Line 95 changes the routine address associated with "PR# 0" back to the address of COUT1, the system monitor's normal screen output routine. Line 99 de-activates the output re-direction (sets the normal screen output) and ends the program.

THE 80-COLUMN (RE-)CONNECTION

If you have an Apple *II*e or *II*c and wish to use your printer from a program using the 80-column text display, you may run into a dilemma. Apple recommends that you turn the 80-column display

```
10  REM *** PR# DEMO ***
20 D$ =  CHR$ (4): REM CTRL-D
30  GOSUB 100
40  PRINT D$;"PR#0,A$300"
50  TEXT : PRINT  CHR$ (13) +  CHR$ (21): HOME
60 A$ = "This is a test."
70  PRINT A$
80  PRINT D$;"PR#0"
90  PRINT : PRINT A$
95  PRINT D$;"PR#0,A$FDF0": REM SET TO COUT1
      WHEN DONE.
99  PRINT D$;"PR#0": END
100  REM INSTALL ML SUBOUTINE.
110  FOR I = 768 TO 777: READ J: POKE I,J: NEXT
      I
120  IF  PEEK ( - 1101) <  > 6 THEN  POKE 774,31
200  DATA 216,201,224,144,2,41,223,76,240,253
299  RETURN
```

Listing 10-1. Redirecting output to a user routine via PR#.

firmware functions *off* before sending output to another slot.

The first problem is that they don't tell you in the *Apple IIe 80-column Text Card* manuals how to disable the firmware functions from within a program. That is easy to solve; the correct procedure *from within a BASIC program* is to use an Applesoft "PRINT CHR$ (21)" statement which will disable the firmware and put you back in 40-column mode. The correct procedure *from immediate mode* is to type an "escape" character (via the "Esc" key), then a control-Q. "PRINT CHR$ (21)" in immediate mode will also work, as will (usually) resetting the Apple.

The next problem is that as you move to 40-column mode, your carefully-formatted 80-column screen display is cut in half. The other half is lost. When we reactivate the 80-column display with a "PR# 3" command, the entire screen is "blanked". We must then re-construct our original display. Some of us get tired of re-writing the 80-column screen every time we wish to send a few lines to the printer, so Listing 10-2 is a demonstration of how to dump the contents of the (*II*e or *II*c) 80-column display to a printer without exiting 80-column mode and without destroying our screen. This program uses commands designed for an Apple Parallel Interface Card (or equivalent) installed as a printer interface in slot 1. As luck (or good forethought) would have it, Apple's Super Serial Card also understands the commands we are using.

Lines 100-120 set up an array with the starting memory address of each of the 24 screen lines; the POKEs in lines 330 and 350 choose whether we PEEK the value of the columns in main memory or auxiliary memory assigned to the text page. Gradually, each line is built up in the variable L$ and then printed.

The "PRINT CHR$ (9)" in line 260 tells this interface card *not* to "echo" characters to our screen. The "90N" immediately following in the same line tells the interface card that we do not want it to issue an extra carriage return at the end of a PRINTed line unless the line length exceeds 90 characters between carriage returns. By these commands, we have eliminated the problems (for this interface card) that Apple was trying to avoid by advising the de-activation of the 80-column firmware while printing printing to a slot.

If you do not have a printer interface card that follows the conventions of the Apple parallel interface, it may still have commands that perform the same function; check the owner's manual for your interface card.

The re-connection of the 80-column firmware (so we can again send output to the screen) is per-

```
10  REM *** DUMP 80 ***
20  REM (DUMPS 80 COLUMN //E OR //C SCREEN
30  REM TO PRINTER IN SLOT 1.)
100  DIM LADR(23)
110  FOR I = 0 TO 23 : READ X : LADR(I) = X :
      NEXT
120  DATA
      1024,1152,1280,1408,1536,1664,1792,1920,10
      64,1192,1320,1448,1576,1704,1832,1960,1104
      , 1232,1360,1488,1616,1744,1872,2000
200  IF  PEEK (78) = 190 THEN 250: REM DOS OR
      PRODOS?
210  POKE 43602,0: REM BRUTE FORCE <CR> FOR DOS
      3.3.
250  PRINT  CHR$ (4);"PR#1": REM PRINTER ON.
260  PRINT  CHR$ (9);"90N": REM DON'T MESS UP
      SCREEN.
300  FOR LINE = 0 TO 23
305 :L$ = ""
310 : FOR CHR = 0 TO 39
320 ::ADR = LADR(LINE) + CHR
330 :: POKE 49237,0: REM PEEK EVEN COLUMNS.
340 ::L$ = L$ +  CHR$ ( PEEK (ADR)):
350 :: POKE 49236,0: REM READ ODD COLUMNS.
360 ::L$ = L$ +  CHR$ ( PEEK (ADR)):
370 : NEXT
380 : PRINT L$
390  NEXT
400  REM RE-HOOK 80 COLUMN SCREEN WITHOUT
      ERASING IT.
410  REM SEE TIP ON PAGE 6 OF JANUARY
      OPEN-APPLE.
420  IF  PEEK (978) = 190 THEN 450: REM 3.3 OR
      PRODOS?
430  POKE 54,7: POKE 55,195: CALL 1002: REM DOS
      3.3.
440  GOTO 500
450  PRINT  CHR$ (4);"PR#A$C307": REM
      BASIC.SYSTEM.
500  END
```

Listing 10-2. Non-destructively printing and re-enabling the //e (or //c) 80-column text display.

formed in line 450, which sets $C307 as the output vector to be used by BASIC.SYSTEM. This happens to point to the normal location used to "print" characters to the 80-column screen, and bypasses the initialization that "PR# 3" performs (which includes clearing the screen).

Chapter 11

Using Binary Files

The advantages of a disk drive over the formerly popular cassette storage are primarily restricted to speed and ease of storing and loading programs unless you employ data files. Data files can be of type VAR (the variable files created with STORE and recovered with RESTORE), TXT (text files, which is a large category dealt with in Part III), and BIN (binary) files.

Why use BIN files for data storage? First, since BIN files can copy any data that is in the computer memory, they give us a lot of flexibility. VAR files can contain only data from variables, TXT files can store only text data. BIN files are not so restricted. For another reason, look to the speed of ProDOS, and the flexibility of the BASIC.SYSTEM binary file parameters.

PRODOS AND BASIC.SYSTEM VERSION NUMBERS

Before we start, let's talk about the various versions of ProDOS, since there are some version differences in how the binary commands work. Before we can even talk about versions, however, let's review something even more elementary: the difference between different versions of the ProDOS kernel and BASIC.SYSTEM.

The ProDOS kernel is part of the file called *PRODOS*. When this book was written there were four official versions; 1.0.1 (1-JAN-84), 1.0.2 (15-FEB-84), 1.1 (17-AUG-84), and 1.1.1 (18-SEP-84). You can tell which version is on a disk by CATALOGing the d disk and looking at the date the file was last *modified* (not *created*, that's when the FILER put it on your disk). You can also tell by booting the disk and watching the screen carefully. The version number of the ProDOS kernel and a copyright notice appear for about 4 seconds while the disk is booting.

BASIC.SYSTEM lives in a file called BASIC.SYSTEM . It's been officially released in only two versions; 1.0 (15-NOV-83) and (15-MAR-84) and 1.1 (18-JUN-84). You can tell which version is on a disk by CATALOGing the disk and checking the date. You can also start up BASIC.SYSTEM in such a way that it can't find a "STARTUP" file (temporarily RENAME the STARTUP file to something else); BASIC.SYSTEM prints its version number at the top of the screen after booting if there's nothing to start up.

A difference between BASIC.SYSTEM 1.0 and 1.1 is what happens when a file already exists and you save something new into it that begins at a *new* address range. With 1.0, as with DOS 3.3, the old address range is thrown out and the new one is used. If the new range is shorter than the previous one, any unneeded disk blocks are released. With 1.1, on the other hand, the old address range is retained. (If the new material makes the file longer, however, the file length will be increased as required.)

Sandy Mossberg (letter in *Nibble*, June 1985, page 7) and Glen Bredon (letter in *Open-Apple*, May 1985, page 40), both competent authorities on such stuff, say this is a bug in BASIC.SYSTEM 1.1 But Ken Kashmarek and Cecil Fretwell, also competent authorities, argue in letters to *Open-Apple* that it's not a bug at all. More about this in a moment.

IT'S PAINFUL TO "B" MISUNDERSTOOD

First, though, let's examine the use of the "B" (byte) parameter in conjunction with the binary file commands BLOAD and BSAVE.

The "B" parameter allows you to quickly and easily move the position-in-file pointer to any byte in a file. BASIC.SYSTEM allows you to use "B" with BLOAD and BSAVE, an option unavailable with DOS 3.3 commands. "B" can also be used (under both DOS 3.3 and BASIC.SYSTEM) with the text file commands READ and WRITE, but this is more complicated; for a complete discussion see Chapter 15.

When you use "B" and "L" (or "E") together, you suddenly have some amazing new binary-file-handling abilities. You can put several graphics in the same file and access them one at a time. You can put several programs in one file, too.

The best part, though, is using "B" and "L" (or "E") and "T" together at the same time. This allows you to read and write records to and from any part of a text file at binary-file speeds. For example, imagine a hard-disk based data file with 1,000 records ("record" is used as a name for a block of associated data), each 1,200 bytes long. Reading in a 1,200 byte record with BASIC.SYSTEM from a text file *accessing it as a binary file* is very rapid using

```
PRINT D$;"BLOAD DATA.FILE, TTXT, A$4000,
L1200, B";R*1200
```

That command would load the 1,200 byte record specified by "R" into the memory range beginning at $4000 in a fraction of the time normal text-file commands (which will be described in Part III) would take.

But consider for a moment the equivalent command for saving to the data file, and you'll understand why our correspondents Kashmarek and Fretwell don't see a bug where Mossberg and Bredon do:

```
PRINT D$;"BSAVE DATA.FILE, TTXT, A$4000,
L1200, B";R*1200
```

If BASIC.SYSTEM's BSAVE works like DOS 3.3's in this situation, all the data in the file beyond the current record gets cut off and thrown away. That's not an acceptable alternative. But, on the other hand, if BSAVE doesn't adjust the length of binary files, you'll often end up with files that have junk tacked on the end (as frequently happens with text files).

If the ProDOS modification team thinks like we do, someday they'll fix BSAVE so it cuts off the end of the file, but *only if no file type parameter is given*. Treat the "T" like Mr. T, we say, and don't cut anything from files when a BSAVE uses it.

THE APPLE TEXT SCREEN

One common use of BIN files is to store hi-resolution graphics images from the Apple memory. The normal Apple *II* 40-column text display page (which is also used as the low-resolution graphics display when the Applesoft "GR" command is issued) can also be BSAVED and re-loaded, but the re-loading process is a bit tricky. Hidden within the text page are several ranges of memory that are used by peripheral cards to store data. At least a few of the bytes in these areas will always be in use by the disk drive controller card and possibly by other peripheral cards.

The number of these "hidden" bytes (sometimes called *screenhole* bytes) works out to be 64 (or $40) bytes, equal to the size of the area used to hold one page of the text display minus the actual number of bytes displayed as characters. The size of the area reserved for the primary text screen is $400 (1024) bytes, located in memory from location $400-$7FF (or 1024-2047 in decimal). Since the normal display uses a total of 24 lines of 40 characters each, the total number of characters displayed is 24 times 40 or 960 characters. The total number of "hidden" bytes is 1024 minus 960 or 64 bytes.

We can BSAVE a text screen, but cannot BLOAD it directly back into the text page without a risk of altering the screenhole bytes in effect at the time of the BLOAD command. In fact, ProDOS will not *allow* us to BLOAD a page in such a manner for our protection; attempting to do so causes a "NO BUFFERS AVAILABLE" error.

The demonstration program in Listing 11-1 creates a single file containing four text screens which are then loaded by request. The screens are each BSAVEd as normal by simply saving out the block of memory containing the text screen data.

When re-loading a screen, we want to insure that we don't disturb the peripheral card locations which are currently in use. So instead we create a buffer area in line 250 by telling Applesoft (and BASIC.SYSTEM) that we want the text screens to be LOADed into memory at location $2000, into the low end of the high-resolution screen memory area, when they are recovered later. Since our program does not use this area, it's safe to use for demonstration purposes.

Our re-loaded text screens will be put here when loaded so that we don't destroy the peripheral card data within the current text screen; the subroutine beginning at line 3000 installs a short machine language routine which moves ONLY the text data (not the peripheral card data) "down" into the text display page 1 area of memory.

The routine from line 100 through line 160 makes four numbered text screens and saves them to disk. The important factor is the "B" parameter used in line 150. The "B" offset value is set to the screen number minus 1 times 1024 bytes for each screen; this means screen 1 is stored starting at byte offset 0 (at the first of the file), screen 2 is stored after moving the position-in-file pointer 1024 bytes into the file, etc. This has the effect of sequentially attaching (or *appending*) each new screen of the four screens saved into the file onto the end of the last screen saved.

Lines 200 through 290 re-load a screen for display. First, in line 250, the position-in-file pointer is moved to the starting byte of our text screen (screen number minus one * 1024 bytes/screen), then the 1024 byte section of "PAGEFILE" containing the screen number we request is BLOADed into our buffer area at $2000.

Line 270 CALLs the machine language subroutine which copies the text data from the buffered screen into the actual text display area of memory, leaving the peripheral card data bytes untouched. Pressing the "ESC" key will end the program.

What would a program of this type be useful for? It could be used to create a large file of "help" screens to be BLOADed from within a complicated program. Putting the same information within the program might use up too much memory; CHAINing or RUNning a "help" program might not be as convenient. This technique only uses the 1024 bytes for the buffer (plus the BASIC statements to BLOAD the screens) and doesn't require shuffling programs (or variables) to and from disk.

A second consideration is that you will save approximately one block of disk space for each text screen you save to the same file as opposed to a new file. If you BSAVE a text screen, it requires 3 blocks of memory. Notice that the length of "PAGEFILE" created by this program is not 12 (three blocks times four screens) blocks, but only 10 blocks, representing a saving of one kilobyte of disk space. This saving could be significant if disk space is becoming cramped.

The presence of the screen buffer at location $2000 could present some problems if our program

```
10  REM *** TEXT PAGE SAVER DEMO ***
20  TEXT : PRINT : PRINT  CHR$ (21): HOME
30 D$ =  CHR$ (4)
40  GOSUB 3000: REM INSTALL ML ROUTINE.
100  REM *** MAKE AND SAVE 4 PAGES ***
110  FOR I = 1 TO 4
120  GOSUB 1000
130 A$ = "THIS IS PAGE NUMBER " +  STR$ (I) +
     "."
140  GOSUB 2000
150  PRINT D$;"BSAVE
     PAGEFILE,A$400,L$400,B";1024 * I
160  NEXT I
200  REM *** PROMPT FOR PAGE ***
210  HOME : VTAB 3
220  PRINT "PAGE NUMBER TO LOAD (1-4 OR 'ESC')?:
     ";
230  GET A$: IF A$ <  >  CHR$ (27) AND ( VAL
     (A$) < 1 OR  VAL (A$) > 4) THEN 230
235  IF A$ =  CHR$ (27) THEN 900
240  PRINT :I =  VAL (A$)
250  PRINT D$;"BLOAD
     PAGEFILE,A$2000,L$400,B";1024 * I
260  CALL 768: REM MOVE PAGE TO DISPLAY AREA.
270  POKE  - 16368,0: REM CLEAR KEYBOARD DATA
     STROBE.
280  IF  PEEK ( - 16384) < 128 THEN 280: REM
     WATCH FOR KEYPRESS.
290  POKE  - 16368,0
299  GOTO 200
900  REM *** EXIT ***
910  HOME
920  VTAB 22
999  END
1000  REM *** MAKE BORDER ***
1010  VTAB 1: FOR K = 0 TO 39: PRINT I;: NEXT K
1020  FOR K = 2 TO 22: VTAB K: HTAB 1: PRINT I;:
      HTAB 40: PRINT I;: NEXT K
1030  VTAB 23: HTAB 1: FOR K = 0 TO 39: PRINT
      I;: NEXT K
1040  RETURN
2000  REM *** CENTER STRING ***
2010  VTAB 11: HTAB  INT ((40 - ( LEN (A$)) /
      2)
2020  PRINT A$
2030  RETURN
3000  REM *** ML DATA TO RESTORE TEXT PAGE FROM
      BUFFER ***
3010  FOR I = 768 TO 823: READ X: POKE I,X: NEXT
      I
3020  DATA 162,119,189,0,32,157,0,4,189
3030  DATA 128,32,157,128,4,189,0,33,157
3040  DATA 0,5,189,128,33,157,128,5,189
3050  DATA 0,34,157,0,6,189,128,34,157
```

Listing 11-1. A program to store text screens into a BIN file.

```
3060  DATA 128,6,189,0,35,157,0,7,189
3070  DATA 128,35,157,128,7,202,224,255,208
3080  DATA 203,96
3099  RETURN
```

BASIC is expanded, however. We'll provide a solution to this along with a second version of the program in Chapter 19.

"BLOAD", "BSAVE" AND A SPECIAL VOLUME: "/RAM"

The /RAM disk that ProDOS automatically installs on 128K Apples is a feature that can be hard to take advantage of. If you have a very big program, you can theoretically split the program into sections, put the sections on /RAM, and use the CHAIN command to quickly move from one section to another. Or, if you have a small program but a large data file, you can theoretically put the data file on /RAM and access it at the speed of light (well, the speed of RAM) instead of your disk drive's 300 RPM.

To change these ideas from theory to practice, however, requires a program that will copy files from disk to /RAM when you start up your computer, and from /RAM back to disk just before you turn it off. You *can* use the ProDOS *FILER* for this, but it doesn't give the kind of automatic operation most computer users are looking for.

Something that would be useful, then, is a BASIC program that can copy files from disk to /RAM and back. Such a program turns out to be extremely simple to write because of the powerful parameters BASIC.SYSTEM provides for binary file commands.

Based on the use of BLOAD and BSAVE with the "A", "L", "B", and "T" parameters under BASIC.SYSTEM, let's write a quick routine for copying files from disk to /RAM and back. We'll BLOAD the files with one prefix, then quickly BSAVE them with another prefix. Just one problem; *where* in memory do we load them? Our program and its variables will be in memory somewhere; it's important that we don't load a file on top of anything.

Refer back to the memory map in our chapter on "FRE". The map shows that there's an area of free memory between a BASIC program's variable tables and its string storage area. The map shows what bytes to peek at to find the boundaries of this free area. And, as explained earlier, the FRE command makes this area as large as possible.

So, to get some memory we'll execute a FRE command; PEEK into the locations known as STREND at 109-110 ($6D-6E) to get an "A" (address) parameter; and PEEK into the locations known as FRETOP at 111-112 ($6F-70) and subtract 1 to get an "E" (end) parameter . The program presented in Listing 11-2 is the finished product. Don't mess with line 400. It makes sure all the variables used in the routine have been allocated space in memory *before* we find out how much free space we have. If a variable is used for the first time *after* we do our peeks to determine A, the variable table will get moved up into our free space with not inconsequential consequences.

Since BSAVE, when used with the "T" parameter, can't create files, we have to CREATE a file for our /RAM copy in line 440. If the file already exists, (as it most certainly will when we copy from /RAM back to disk), a "DUPLICATE PATHNAME" error will occur and line 430's ONERR will take us to line 500. The error code for duplicate pathname is 19; line 500 deletes the file and RESUMEs back to the CREATE command.

Line 450 BLOADS the file. If the file is *shorter* than what we have specified with the "E" parameter, no error will occur. If it is *longer,* "E" sees to it that we load only as much of the file as will fit. Loading begins with the first byte of the file (byte 0).

Line 460 peeks at a BASIC.SYSTEM location known as RWTRANS at 48859-60 ($BEDB-DC) to find out how many bytes actually were loaded by the BLOAD command. The actual loading Address

```
10 REM ***  BASIC.COPY  ***
100 D$=CHR$(4)
110 P1$="/JLY/"  : REM prefix of volume that
      files are to be copied FROM
120 P2$="/RAM/"  : REM prefix of volume that
      files are to be copied TO
130 F$="FILE1" : T$="TXT" : GOSUB 400 : REM
      names and types of
140 F$="FILE2" : T$="BAS" : GOSUB 400 : REM
      files to be copied
150 F$="FILE3" : T$="BIN" : GOSUB 400
200 END
400 B=0 : A=0 : E=0 : L=0 : REM
      Important--messing with this line can be
      fatal
405 X1=0 : X2 = 0 CMD = 0
410 PRINT D$;"FRE"
420 A=PEEK(109) + PEEK(110)*256
425 E=PEEK(111) + PEEK(112)*256
430 ONERR GOTO 500
440 PRINT D$;"CREATE"; P2$;F$; ",T";T$
450 PRINT D$;"BLOAD"; P1$;F$; ",T";T$; ",A";A;
      ",E";E-1; ",B";B
455 CMD=196 : GOSUB 600 : X1=PEEK(48825) :
      X2=PEEK(48826)
460 L=PEEK(48859) + PEEK(48860)*256
470 PRINT D$;"BSAVE"; P2$;F$; ",T";T$; ",A";A;
      ",L";L; ",B";B
475 CMD=195 : POKE 48820,7 : POKE 48825,X1 :
      POKE 48826,X2 : GOSUB 600
480 IF L=(E-A) THEN B=B+L : GOTO 450
490 POKE 216,0 : RETURN
500 IF PEEK(222)=19 THEN PRINT D$;"DELETE";
      P2$;F$ : RESUME
510 IF PEEK(222)=5  THEN CALL -3288 : GOTO 490
520 PRINT "ERROR #";PEEK(222);" IN LINE
      ";PEEK(218) + PEEK(219)*256
530 END
600 REM *** MLI caller for use with
      BASIC.SYSTEM ***
610 POKE 48728,169 : POKE 48729,CMD : POKE
      48730,32
620 POKE 48731,112 : POKE 48732,190 : POKE
      48733,176
630 POKE 48734,170 : POKE 48735,96 : CALL 48728
      : RETURN
```

Listing 11-2. A file copy program in BASIC.

can be found at 48855-56 ($BED7-D9).

Line 470 BSAVES the file using its actual length via assignment of the "L" parameter. This length will transfer to the new copy of the file correctly. However, if the file really is a binary file, the copy's loading address, as shown in the CATALOG, will be wrong. So will the record length ("R=") of text files. BASIC.SYSTEM 1.0 shows the address we used in parameter "A", not the one on the original file, for both address and record length. Version 1.1, on the other hand, sets both to zero. (Incidentally, if you try to BLOAD a file with a loading address of zero, you get a "NO BUFFERS AVAILABLE" error. This message is quite confusing, because the problem has nothing to do with buffers; the ProDOS Kernel simply refuses to load files into that address because the area is "protected" in the "system bit map". See Chapter 23 for a further discussion.

These problems have been fixed by lines 405, 455, 475, and 600- 603, which request information from ProDOS itself. An explanation of these lines appears in Chapter 23, where the ProDOS machine language interface (*MLI*) is discussed. For now, always specify "A" and "L" when using files copied copied by this technique.

Line 480 looks to see if we got the whole file or if there is more of it still on the disk. If the actual "L" (length) we got was less than the "E" (end) minus the "A" (address), we got it all. If these values are equal, the file was either exactly the same size as our free memory area, or there is more. In either case, adjust the "B" parameter so it points to the first byte we didn't get, and go back to line 450.

The second time we execute BLOAD, the "B" parameter points well inside the file. We'll get a bunch more of it; this will continue until we have the whole file. If we should run across a file that accidentally has the same number of bytes as our free space, line 450 will get an "END OF DATA" error. Line 430's ONERR will then take us to line 510, where we clear the stack (see Chapter 7), and return to the caller.

There you have it, a basic BASIC copy routine.

Part 3

BASIC.SYSTEM and Text Files

Chapter 12

Text Files

Probably the most common type of data file used by the average person is the *text* file, which contains the ASCII codes for text characters. Such files are used by word processing programs such as *Applewriter*; even *Appleworks*, which uses its own special file types for storing its workfiles, has been designed to read and write standard text files.

There are two major distinct types of text files used with BASIC.SYSTEM. The first and most common is called *sequential access*, the second is named *random access*. To understand the difference, we have to look at a schematic of how ASCII data is stored in the files.

STRINGS, RECORDS, AND FIELDS

As an (at least part-time) Applesoft programmer, you are no doubt familiar with string variables. Part of the connotation of the word "string" may come from the comparison of a phrase such as

THE APPLE COMPUTER

stored in a variable to a "string" of ASCII characters tied together, one after the other. The attachment is (hopefully) secure in Applesoft's eyes so that if the "T" in the word "THE" is moved to a new location 100 bytes away in memory, each of the rest of the characters is also moved the same 100 byte (relative) distance and the entire string is intact, now 100 bytes away from its original location (if it didn't work this way, we'd be in trouble).

Text files are also made up of strings of ASCII characters. BASIC.SYSTEM commands allow the re-direction of the output from BASIC PRINT statements to text files. The question is, then, what does the file look like when all the characters are strung together, one after the other?

If you wanted such a model that you could hold in your hands, you could make a "bead-string" model of our phrase by attaching together 18 properly lettered beads in order; the first bead with a "T", the second with a "H", etc. until you recreated the above phrase's letters in order.

If we join several such phrases we should get a model of a file containing several strings, so let's make a few more bead-strings out of the phrases

IS A VERY
NICE COMPANION
FOR DOING SOME
OF OUR WORK.

Let's put these together and see what the result looks like.

SEQUENTIAL STORAGE

Imagine PRINTing the data from each of these phrases to the screen in sequential order as per the program:

```
10  REM PRINT STRINGS.
20  PRINT "THE APPLE COMPUTER"
30  PRINT "IS A VERY"
40  PRINT "NICE COMPANION"
50  PRINT "FOR DOING SOME"
60  PRINT "OF OUR WORK."
```

If we re-directed the output to a file, how would you construct a bead-string to imitate the above effect?

If we put these strings together end-to-end, keeping them in "proper" order (that is, without reversing the ends), get a set of beads, mark a letter on each bead, and string them together in order, we could make "real" bead-strings out of them and lay them end-to-end. The resulting string of letters would look like

THE APPLE COMPUTERIS A VERYNICE COM
PANIONFOR DOING SOMEOF OUR WORK.

making (almost) a sentence. Well, there's a problem; the words run together.

Actually, though, each of the original phrases PRINTs on a separate line. If we ran our BASIC program to print the phrases, we wouldn't see the above result, we'd see something more like

THE APPLE COMPUTER
IS A VERY
NICE COMPANION
FOR DOING SOME
OF OUR WORK.

rather than having all five phrases printed in one long line.

The difference between the "separated" phrases and the "strung together" sentence is that each PRINTed string is terminated by a carriage return. Unfortunately, we don't have a way to put the abstract carriage return at the end of each bead-string, but we could use a symbol such as "]" to represent the "return" character. We can write this character on some beads, then tack one of these "return" beads on the end of each bead-string and put them together again:

THE APPLE COMPUTER]IS A VERY]NICE COM
PANION]FOR DOING SOME]OF OUR WORK.]

The individual phrases now are separated by a discernible character ("]"), which represents the carriage return that would be placed at the end of each string if it were PRINTed to the screen.

If you've gotten this far, you now understand sequential files! A sequential text file is formed by PRINTing ASCII data (characters or strings) to a file on disk. If the PRINT statement is terminated with a "return" character, which occurs unless you end the PRINT statement with a semicolon character (";") or space statement such as "SPC (8)", then that carriage return is also sent into the disk file to end the string and separate it from the next string. Notice that the carriage return is not *part* of the string; it is used in the file to separate individual strings from each other.

The use of a semicolon at the end of the PRINT statement causes the carriage return to be *suppressed*; that is, it isn't "tacked on" automatically at the end of the string being PRINTed. If the carriage return *is* suppressed, then the string written to the screen (or file) will be written *without* the carriage return. The statements

```
10  PRINT "THIS IS O";
20  PRINT "NE PHRASE."
```

which would print

THIS IS ONE PHRASE

if RUN, would be stored as the single joined string

THIS IS ONE PHRASE]

(using our visible carriage return symbol) if redirected to a text file. There is no carriage return between the "O" and "N" because the semicolon at the end of line 10 suppresses the use of a carriage return after the first string. The second string *is* followed by a carriage return. This placement of carriage returns becomes important when we attempt to re-read the data from the file.

If line 10 were ended with a SPC(n) statement, there would also be no carriage return placed at the end of the first string because the SPC(n) statement suppresses the final carriage return on a line, whether or not a ";" is used to end the line.

Apple's older version of *BASIC Programming with ProDOS* says (on page 94) that when PRINTing string variables to a file, a comma separating two strings will have the same effect that a semicolon would; that the normal "comma-tabbing" will not occur. Cross that statement out; it's incorrect (at least with BASIC.SYSTEM 1.1). Commas between strings will add spaces between the strings when they are PRINTed to a file (there *is* a problem with this, discussed in Chapter 16).

The word "sequential" is used to describe these files because each segment is stored sequentially at the precise end of the segment before, unless we force it to be stored elsewhere. We'll hold off on the discussion of how to do the latter trick until we actually describe the text file commands.

RANDOM ACCESS FILES

With sequential access files, the length of each segment of data is variable. This means that you don't know *exactly* where (at what byte number) in the file the data belonging to the 577th string begins until you actually "look through" the file.

Suppose we don't want each new portion of data to start exactly after the point where the previous carriage return occurs. A good example of this situation is if you had 1000 sets of data to look through and knew you wanted to look at the 577th set.

If the space used to store each set of data was always the same, then the problem becomes easier. Say we define the storage area for each set of data at a standard 100 bytes (characters) per set. To find the start of the 577th set you simply multiply the number of the set of data, minus 1, times the length of the standard set length (storage space). The "minus 1" is needed because the first set of data will start at byte 0, the second set at byte 100, and the "nth" set at byte (100 * n-1). Therefore, the 577th set starts at byte 57600.

We can define this same-sized unit of data as a *record*. Each record will take up the same amount of space within the large file, and contain a certain systematic amount of information.

With sequential files, the "record" (a liberal use of the term) length is not standard so in order to find the 577th record we have to look at each of the first 566 records, find each separating carriage return, throw the record away, and proceed. With a standard record length, we simply move 57600 bytes into the file (we don't have to look at the intervening records). This is called a *random access* file, because we now can find a specific record without having to sequentially read all previous records to determine its location.

There is a second division that can be done. If the record length is large enough, it can be divided into a small sequence of strings separated by carriage returns. For example, we can define a record length of 20 and set up a file called "RHYMES":

```
Record 1 = BRIGHT]WHITE]xxxxxx
Record 2 = NIGHT]LIGHT]xxxxxxx
Record 2 = TRY]BELIE]xxxxxxxxx
```

(the "x"'s denote unused space within each record) where we have two "subrecords" within each record. These "subrecords" are called *fields* to distinguish them from the fixed-length record; notice that the fields are stored almost like a miniature sequential file within the record.

The grouping of fields within fixed length records gives a way to access several associated fields rapidly; each field being accessible. You access the record using the random access method of "jumping" to the correct position in the file, then read the individual fields (similar to the way you read a sequential file) until you have recovered the data you need.

RANDOM VERSUS SEQUENTIAL

The major *advantage* of sequential files is that, for data that is likely to be read in "all at once" (that is, where all or most of the file is to be read in at one time), sequential storage is much more efficient in terms of disk use; there is no "dead space" in the "records" to use up precious disk space. It is also a little easier to access sequential files since the records can be read in one after another (no "fields" to worry about).

The major *disadvantage* of sequential files is that it is hard to access a record far into the file quickly. Accessing and modifying specific records within a large file can be extremely slow; it usually involves copying the entire sequential file into a new file.

The major *advantage* of random access text files is that a specific record can be accessed very quickly if the record number desired is known. The ability to create a group of fields within the record is very handy for constructing certain data files.

The *disadvantages* of random access files: once the record length is defined, changing it requires re-copying a file's data into a newly structured file. Writing a too-long record into a file will damage information in the next (following) record in the disk file. Random access files waste disk space for unused bytes within the record space. And random access files require extra programming care. The techniques of accessing a record are different than accessing a field within a record.

Chapter 13

Text File Programming

In the "olden days", the Apple used cassette tapes to SAVE and LOAD programs. Data could also be saved but it was usually an awkward process, especially for string variables which could not be saved directly.

The big advantage of a disk drive is the ability to generate files from string data. These files are called *text files* because they store the information as readable text, PRINTed to the file just as you would PRINT text to the screen. Any ASCII character can be printed to the file; even not-printing characters such as control-G will be stored in the file.

Well, almost. Control-D plays a part with the text file commands just as it does with other BASIC.SYSTEM commands within programs. Let's look at that first.

"D$" AND TEXT FILE COMMANDS

A high proportion of all problems that Applesoft programmers are likely to have with using disk commands are associated with *D$*. As discussed in previous chapters, BASIC.SYSTEM fails to execute a command we send from inside a program if the statement containing the command does not conform to the sequence: PRINT, then a control-D, then the BASIC.SYSTEM command string. If the control-D is not the *first* character printed by the PRINT statement, then the command will *not* be recognized and executed. If the command string is not a recognizable BASIC.SYSTEM command, you will get a "SYNTAX ERROR" message.

When a BASIC.SYSTEM command within a running program appears on your display screen rather than being intercepted by BASIC.SYSTEM, there is a problem with this sequence. The problem will usually be that you forgot to define D$ as equal to a control-D or that you accidentally changed it.

With DOS 3.3, it was often recommended that you insert a carriage return character (ASCII code equal to 13) before each control-D like this:

```
D$ = CHR$ (13) + CHR$ (4)
```

Discard this technique with BASIC under ProDOS; it absolutely *does not work* with BASIC.SYSTEM because BASIC.SYSTEM *doesn't require a return* before the control-D as the older commands syntax of Apple DOS did. In fact, putting one there with this method actually causesBASIC.SYSTEM to assume that what follows couldn't possibly be a DOS command (after all, it doesn't *begin* with a control-D).

When using this technique with DOS 3.3, the value of D$ was usually defined in the first few lines of the program. If you later convert such a program to use with BASIC.SYSTEM/ProDOS, simply remove the "CHR$(13)" from the D$ definition.

THE TEXT FILE COMMANDS

Beginning programmers quickly get the hang of using LOAD and SAVE with program files and BLOAD and BSAVE with binary files. The OPEN, APPEND, READ, WRITE, and CLOSE commands associated with text files, however, are a different story. These commands have far more options, and far more quirks, than the others. In addition, these commands can't be typed directly on the keyboard; they can only be used within programs. There are only two text file commands, CLOSE and FLUSH, that can be entered as immediate mode commands.

Whenever you want to deal with a text file, the first thing you have to do is open it, with a command of the form

OPEN *pathname*,Lnbyt,Sn,Dn,Ttyp

The "L" parameter is *not* the "length" parameter that was used with binary files; here it has a different meaning, and is used only with a special file format called *random access* files. It specifies the record length of the file. If omitted (or if the record length is specified as 0), the file is assumed to be a sequential access text file.

The BASIC.SYSTEM OPEN command performs several functions. First it sets aside some memory space, called a *file buffer*, that is used to store information about the file itself while the file is open. Then it looks for the file you specified; if the file doesn't exist, BASIC.SYSTEM creates a new one.

The file buffer is actually created by ProDOS, which is ordered to do so by BASIC.SYSTEM as BASIC.SYSTEM attempts to execute your command. You may OPEN up to eight files at one time if you have enough memory available. Remember that the CAT and CATALOG commands also require a file buffer area, so if you have eight files open and issue a CAT command (which needs another buffer), you will get a "NO BUFFERS AVAILABLE" error.

When the file you specified does exist, on the other hand, OPEN checks to make sure it is a text file and sends you a "FILE TYPE MISMATCH" error if it's not. You can override this feature with BASIC.SYSTEM, *if* the file already exists, by using the "T" parameter and the file's type (BIN, BAS, DIR, and so on), like this:

```
400 PRINT D$;"OPEN WEATHER, TDIR"
```

Once you get a non-text file open with this technique, you can read it normally *if* the file contains ASCII characters (otherwise, you can use the Applesoft "GET" statement within a loop to read *any* data a byte at a time). You can also write ASCII characters to any type of file except a directory. If you use the "T" parameter with OPEN and the file doesn't exist, you receive a "PATH NOT FOUND" message.

If you try to OPEN a file that is already open, BASIC.SYSTEM refuses to proceed and sends you the error message "FILE BUSY". Similarly, BASIC.SYSTEM does not allow you to RENAME, EXEC (another text file command to be covered in the next chapter), or DELETE files that are open. It *does* allow this kind of shenanigan with LOCK, UNLOCK, and VERIFY, leaving the file open.

There are a number of other error messages you might see when you try to open a file. With most of them, it's clear what's wrong, but one deserves special mention: "NO BUFFERS AVAILABLE" means there is no memory space left for file buffers. With ProDOS, this message usually means your program has outgrown your Apple's memory, either in pure size (filling memory) or in using too many file buffers (more than eight at once).

IT'S NOT POLITE TO POINT, BUT . . .

The final feature of the OPEN command is that the *position-in-file pointer* is set to the first byte of the file.

The position-in-file pointer is like a pointing finger that holds your place in the file. Every open file has one. The pointer actually points to the *next* character to be read. When writing, it points to the position where the next written character will go. There are several ways you can move the pointer to other parts of a file.

One place people commonly want the pointer to be is at the *end* of the file. This makes it easy to add new material to a file without overwriting what's already there. BASIC.SYSTEM includes an *APPEND* command that works just like OPEN, except that the position-in-file pointer ends up pointing one byte beyond the last byte in the file. It uses the same form:

APPEND *pathname*,Lnbyt,Sn,Dn,Ttyp

Because ProDOS writes down the exact length of each file in the file's directory entry, the BASIC.SYSTEM APPEND command is fast and accurate. In addition to opening the file you specify (or creating it, if it doesn't exist) and setting the pointer, the BAS BASIC.SYSTEM APPEND command also executes an automatic WRITE to prepare the file to be used for output from the next PRINT. If the file being opened is a random-access file, the pointer will automatically be set to the beginning of the record immediately following the last record in the file.

CONTROLLING FILE BIRTHS

As mentioned already, both OPEN and APPEND will create a new file for you if the file you specify doesn't exist. In some situations this isn't much help. For example, consider what happens when a user of your program misspells the name of a pre-existing data file he or she wants to use. If you accept the spelling and open a file by that name, you will create a new, empty file. Moreover, as soon as your program tries to read the new file, it will expire with an "END OF DATA" error.

To avoid this problem, you must take some action to assure that the file actually exists before opening it. One way to do this with BASIC.SYSTEM is to use the "T" parameter. As mentioned earlier, whenever you use the BASIC.SYSTEM "T" parameter with OPEN, only pre-existing files can be accessed. This is true even if you specify "TTXT". Another way to guarantee a file exists is to VERIFY the file before opening it. If you don't get a "PATH NOT FOUND" error (which can be trapped by an error-handling routine), then the file is present and accounted for.

READ, WRITE, AND NULL

The command to read a text file is, naturally enough, READ. The syntax is

READ *pathname*,Rn,Fn,Bnbyt

The "R", "F", and "B" parameters refer to the number of *R*ecords, *B*ytes, and/or *F*ields to "skip" before starting to read data from the file.

The corresponding command to write to a file is

WRITE *pathname*,Rn,Fn,Bnbyt

The READ and WRITE commands have been well documented by Apple and others, but unless you've been reading your manuals quite carefully, you've probably never heard of the "null" command. Nonetheless, a good understanding of the command is critical to getting to your reads and writes to work correctly.

WHEN DOING "NOTHING" IS DOING SOMETHING

The READ and WRITE commands don't actually do any reading or writing. Instead, the READ command tells BASIC.SYSTEM to use the specified file as the source of characters for any subsequent Applesoft INPUT or GET commands. Likewise, WRITE tells BASIC.SYSTEM to send any characters subsequently PRINTed to the specified *file* rather than to your screen or printer.

Both READ and WRITE supposedly stay in effect until another BASIC.SYSTEM command is issued. However, PRINTing to the screen while WRITEing to a file, or trying to INPUT or GET characters from the keyboard while READing from a file will obviously be impossible, since READ and WRITE assign input and output (respectively) to a file.

The "*null*" command consists of a simple control-D followed by a return. It is used to turn off READs and WRITEs on purpose, without mystery. Unnecessarily active and mysteriously inactive READs and WRITEs are probably the biggest contributors to intractable Applesoft bugs. You can avoid all this by taking just one simple step: always use the *null* command to turn off READs and WRITEs *immediately* after using them.

For example, say you decide to print something to the screen in the middle of WRITEing to a file. To do this reliably, you have to turn off the WRITE before trying to PRINT to the screen. For example, examine Listing 13-1.

Look carefully at line 60. It turns off line 40's WRITE. If you leave out line 60, what you PRINT in line 70 never makes it to the screen, but goes to the file instead. As written, the printed sentence in line 50 goes into the text file "PRINT.DEMO. TXT", but the printed sentence in line 70 goes to the Apple's screen.

The use of control-D in line 60 has disabled the WRITE instruction but has left the file open for further use; to enable the file for output again we simply issue another WRITE command for the file. For example, if we add the line

```
65 PRINT D$;"WRITE PRINT.DEMO.TXT"
```

to the program, both sentences will be written to the file.

Just as you can't PRINT and WRITE at the same time, you can't simultaneously READ from a file and get INPUT from the keyboard without control-D (unless you CLOSE the file first). Solve the problem by organizing the program lines like those in Listing 13-2.

Line 50 reads a line from the file; then line 60 turns off the READ operation momentarily so that you can enter a line from the keyboard in line 70. If line 60 is omitted, the program will try to read *two* lines from the file.

READ and WRITE may experience other problems with INPUT (and GET) and PRINT. If you make a habit of using this technique to turn off READs and WRITEs immediately after using them, you will save yourself hours of "bug hunting" over the course of your life.

WHAT BUFFERS ARE GOOD FOR

When you begin to read a file with an INPUT command, a small piece of the file is loaded into the file buffer that your OPEN command created. BASIC.SYSTEM sends characters to your INPUT statement from this buffer rather than directly from the disk. When all the characters in the buffer have

```
10  REM *** PRINT DEMO WITH FILE OUTPUT ***
20 D$ =  CHR$ (4): REM CONTROL-D.
30  PRINT D$;"OPEN PRINT.DEMO.TXT"
40  PRINT D$;"WRITE PRINT.DEMO.TXT"
50  PRINT "This line to file.": REM THIS LINE
       PRINTED TO FILE.
60  PRINT D$: REM TURNS OFF "WRITE".
70  PRINT "This line to screen." : REM THIS LINE
       PRINTED TO SCREEN.
80  PRINT D$;"CLOSE"
99  END
```

Listing 13-1. Sample of PRINTing to a text file.

```
10  REM *** INPUT DEMO WITH FILE INPUT ***
20 D$ =  CHR$ (4): REM  CONTROL-D.
30  PRINT D$;"OPEN PRINT.DEMO.TXT"
40  PRINT D$;"READ PRINT.DEMO.TXT"
50  INPUT FILE$: REM INPUT LINE FROM FILE.
60  PRINT D$: REM TURN OFF "READ".
70  INPUT KEYBD$: REM READ LINE FROM KEYBOARD.
80  PRINT D$;"CLOSE"
99  END
```

Listing 13-2. Sample of READing INPUT from a text file.

been passed to you, BASIC.SYSTEM and ProDOS load the next section of the file into the buffer and the process continues.

You may have noticed when reading text files that your disk drive constantly turns on and off. This is because it takes Applesoft a while to collect the contents of the buffer with INPUT statements. By the time it's done, the drive has stopped. ProDOS then restarts it to retrieve the next section of the file.

With ProDOS, the buffer holds a *block* of 512 bytes. The buffer itself takes up 1024 bytes of memory, however; the extra 512 bytes is used to hold information ProDOS needs, such as where within the file the current buffered block is stored, etc.

When you are WRITEing to a file, BASIC.SYSTEM collects the stuff you PRINT and puts it in the buffer. Only when the buffer is full are its contents actually written on the disk.

CLOSING COMMENTS

The *CLOSE* command is used to tell BASIC.SYSTEM you are done working with a file. When BASIC.SYSTEM receives the CLOSE command, it tells ProDOS to finish processing the file, write the file's buffer contents to disk, and release the file's buffer. If you have been WRITEing to the file, it's possible the buffer will contain the last few lines you have written; the CLOSE command gets these written on the disk.

Unlike other text-file commands, CLOSE can be entered directly on the keyboard. If CLOSE is used with a filename, only the specified file is closed. You can also use CLOSE without a filename, in which case *all* open files are closed.

BASIC.SYSTEM includes a command called *FLUSH*, which is similar to CLOSE. FLUSH is used when writing to files, it can also be issued in immediate mode like CLOSE. It forces ProDOS to send the contents of the file buffer to the disk. FLUSH doesn't release the file buffer, however, so writing can continue later without reopening the file.

As previously mentioned, every OPEN file *must* be CLOSEd before it can be OPENed again under BASIC.SYSTEM, or you will get a "FILE BUSY" error. This is a change from the older versions of Apple DOS, which did not require such action. It is, however, good programming practice to *always* CLOSE files not actually in use, in case of an error. An open file may lose data if the computer "crashes" before the file is CLOSEd.

With BASIC.SYSTEM/ProDOS, most errors that halt a program will leave an open file open. If such an error halts your Applesoft program, or if your program ends without CLOSEing everything, BASIC.SYSTEM will send you a handy "FILE(S) STILL OPEN" message. You can then type "CLOSE" in immediate mode to close all open files.

If you don't CLOSE an open file, several bad things can happen. The file's buffer won't be released and will take up precious memory. If you've been writing to the file, the last buffer full of information won't be written on the disk and may be lost (unless you have used FLUSH to write it to the file). Unclosed files are particularly a problem for people who turn their computers off or who do open-Apple-control-RESET boots while the files are still open.

Chapter 14

EXEC Files

We have said that there are two basic types of text files. One type is called "random-access" and the other is called "sequential". Sequential files are ideal for applications that start a session by reading a file from beginning to end (sequentially) into the computer's memory. Later in the session, a modified version of the entire file may be resaved. This is, of course, exactly how a word processor works.

In the next chapter we'll talk about random-access files in more detail. In the meantime we'll take a close look at a special kind of sequential file; the kind that holds keystrokes.

You've probably never heard of a *keystroke file* before. That's because we just made them up (We make stuff up all the time around here.). Most discussions of text files, such as those in the ProDOS manuals, explain text files as if they were only used to store inventories and mailing lists. In fact, one of the most important uses for sequential text files is to store keystrokes.

A keystroke file is a text file that contains the keystrokes needed to do some task on your computer. A good image for explaining this concept is that of the player piano. If sitting at a computer and typing in commands is like playing a piano, then running a keystroke file through a computer is like listening to a player piano.

EXEC "EXEC"

You can thank our old friend BASIC.SYSTEM for giving your Apple the power to press its own keys. We've discussed previously how BASIC.SYSTEM intercepts all messages between your programs and your keyboard and screen. Whenever a program tries to read the keyboard through the standard I/O link, BASIC.SYSTEM will know about it. You can get him to send the program something from a file rather than something from the keyboard by using the *EXEC* command.

The EXEC command follows the syntax

EXEC *pathname*,Sn,Dn,Fn,Rn

The optional "F" and "R" parameters specify the

number of records or fields to "throw away" before the file input is issued to BASIC.SYSTEM as if it came from the keyboard. The required pathname must refer to a ProDOS "TXT" file, or you will receive a "FILE TYPE MISMATCH" error from BASIC.SYSTEM.

The BASIC.SYSTEM "dash" command can be used, too. "-TEXTFILE", where "TEXTFILE" is a sequential text file, will cause the file to be EXECed. "S" and "D" options (only) are permitted.

Text files for use by EXEC can be created in your word processor, if it can read and write standard ProDOS "TXT" ASCII files. If you don't yet have a word processor, or if your favorite uses binary files, try the simple program in Listing 14-1 to enter the text strings. This EXEC.MAKER program, though not as convenient as a word processor, can be used to enter most of the examples in

```
10  REM *** MAKE EXEC FILE ***
20 D$ =  CHR$ (4)
30  DIM IN$(1000)
40  TEXT : PRINT  CHR$ (21): HOME
100  REM  *** INSTRUCTIONS ***
110  PRINT "Enter your commands at the '?'
       prompt."
120  PRINT
130  PRINT "Command strings are limited to
       about"
140  PRINT "238 characters each. Strings that
       will"
150  PRINT "contain ',' or ':' characters must"
160  PRINT "begin with a '"; CHR$ (34);"'
       (quote), as in:"
170  PRINT
180  PRINT  SPC( 5); CHR$ (34);"See, an
       example!"
190  PRINT
200  PRINT "Enter a carriage return on a line
       by"
210  PRINT "itself to end entering strings."
220  VTAB 22: HTAB 1
230  PRINT "Press a key to continue: ";: GET A$:
       PRINT
240  HOME
300  REM *** GET STRINGS ***
310 SCOUNT = 0
320  PRINT SCOUT + 1;
330  INPUT IN$(SCOUNT)
340  IF IN$(SCOUNT) <  > "" THEN SCOUNT = SCOUNT
       + 1: GOTO 320
350  IF SCOUNT = 0 THEN  HOME : END
400  REM *** WRITE FILE ***
410  PRINT
420  INPUT "Name for EXEC file?: ";NAME$
430  PRINT D$;"OPEN ";NAME$
440  PRINT D$;"WRITE ";NAME$
450  FOR I = 0 TO SCOUNT
460  PRINT IN$(I)
470  NEXT I
480  PRINT D$;"CLOSE ";NAME$
490  HOME
499  END
```

Listing 14-1. A program to make simple text (EXEC) files.

this chapter except one (we'll notify you of the exception).

The EXEC command is useful for easily entering frequently used command sequences. For example, we all know that the safest way to write programs is to keep two or more backup copies of your work. Having earlier versions of a program available is a good feeling when you realize the last set of modifications you made did more harm than good. Backups also decrease the chances of pure disaster when the power company's transformer blows. Few people consistently rotate earlier versions when saving their work, however, because the commands are so tedious.

But by using a simple keystroke file and the EXEC command, you can simplify things immensely. If you are working on a program called "EGGNOG", for instance, sit down at your word processor and create the following text file and save it under the name BACKUP:

```
DELETE EGGNOG.BKUP2
RENAME EGGNOG.BKUP1,EGGNOG.BKUP2
RENAME EGGNOG,EGGNOG.BKUP1
SAVE EGGNOG
```

Now, instead of entering "SAVE EGGNOG" when you want to save your program, enter "EXEC BACKUP". The oldest copy of EGGNOG will be deleted, newer copies will be rotated, and a copy of the current version of the program will be saved—all with a single command command.

Notice that the commands in the BACKUP file look exactly as they would if you typed them on your keyboard. There is no need for a control-D or a PRINT statement, as there would be inside a BASIC program. Also notice the commands should be in uppercase letters, unless you are sure the program is only going to be used on Apple computers that can utilize lowercase. BASIC.SYSTEM will recognize lowercase commands, but older Apple *II* computers (pre-*II*e and *II*c) may not be able to display small letters (and it's nice to be able to see what you're doing). Applesoft in Apple *II* Plus and un-enhanced Apple *II*e computers also does not recognize lowercase BASIC commands.

If your word processor has an option to display the carriage returns in a file, use it when creating EXEC files. In particular, make sure you have a "return" after the last line in the file. If there is no carriage return there, the last line won't be executed until you press "return" on your keyboard. By then things are usually a mess.

THE EXECUTIVE PRINTER RIBBON

EXEC files are also handy for little commands you may not use frequently but, for that very reason, are hard to remember. Here is a file we use for the Apple Dot Matrix printer called "BOLDFACE".

```
PR#1
PRINT CHR$(27) + "!"
PR#0
```

The program should also work as-is on an Apple Imagewriter. To convert the program for your printer, just change the PRINT statement to cause your printer to use boldface (check your printer manual).

This little file turns on the boldface feature of an Apple Dot Matrix Printer. It's very handy when you need a new printer ribbon but just can't break away from the keyboard long enough to buy one. Of course, you could write a BASIC program that would do the same thing, but using an EXEC file instead has a simple advantage. EXEC files don't disturb the program you already have in memory. If "BOLDFACE" was a BASIC program, it would destroy the program in memory whenever it was used.

WHERE WILL IT ALL END?

Since EXEC files don't disturb what's in memory, you can use them as a sort of external subroutine from within programs, but this requires a special trick. This trick is not recommended for polished work, but it is handy for QDS (quick and dirty software), particularly if you have a library of useful EXEC files already written.

Normally when you try to EXEC a file from

within a BASIC program nothing happens. This is because BASIC is running your program rather than looking for commands entered on the keyboard. BASIC.SYSTEM can't pass keystrokes to an Applesoft program unless the program asks for them.

Normally, an EXECed file will only send data to INPUT and GET statements while a BASIC program is running. If we want our "external subroutine" function to be useful, we have to find a way to make BASIC pay attention to the BASIC statements in the EXEC file.

BASIC will ignore the commands in the EXEC file, just as it does commands you type on your keyboard, while a program is running. To get it to pay attention, put an "END" right after the EXEC command. That may seem drastic at first, but follow along. BASIC sees your END command, goes to the keyboard for input, finds your EXEC file, and executes it. To restart your program where it left off, put the virtually unknown Applesoft command *CONT* at the end of your EXEC file.

CONT will cause execution to continue at the next instruction after the END statement. It works exactly like a "RETURN" from a subroutine, with one exception: BASIC can't continue if the EXEC file did something that caused an error message. The technique is also useless for modifying the program in memory itself; adding, deleting, or editing a program line renders the CONT command powerless.

EXEC files can be linked together, but they can't be nested. This means one EXEC file can start a second one, but there is no command that can return to the first one and have it continue where it left off. (You can use the EXEC command with the "R" parameter to start execution of a file somewhere other than the beginning. It is quite difficult to envision situations in which people would want to do that, however.)

A limitation you have when working with EXEC files is that several Applesoft BASIC commands don't work from immediate mode. The most important of these are "INPUT" and "GET". (If they did work it would be useless anyhow, since they would just pick up the next string of characters in your EXEC file.) Like all computer problems, there is a long way around this one.

HOW TO STAY EXECUTION

Let's begin with a simple case. Say you want an EXEC file to stop in the middle of execution and wait until you give it permission to continue. Maybe you want to put a new envelope in your printer or something. Try this:

```
PRINT "PRESS <ANY KEY> TO CONTINUE."
POKE -16368,0
WAIT -16384, 128
POKE -16368,0
```

"POKE -16368" sets the value of the keyboard data register to less than 128 to indicate that keyboard data is not waiting to be "picked up" by BASIC. WAIT is an often-overlooked Applesoft command that allows testing a byte location in the Apple; in this case we use it to test the value in the keyboard data register. "WAIT -16384, 128" causes Applesoft to pause until the value at memory location -16384 (which receives keyboard data any time you type a character) is greater than or equal to 128, which indicates a key has been hit.

Expand this technique a little and you have conditional execution:

```
PRINT "PRINT A GREETING MESSAGE?
<Y/N>"
POKE -16368,0
WAIT -16384, 128
I=PEEK(-16384)
POKE -16368,0
IF CHR$(I-128)="Y" OR CHR$(I-128)="y"
THEN PRINT "Hello! This is an EXEC program!"
```

In the sixth line, where the keyboard data value was compared to the ASCII characters "Y" and "y", we subtracted 128 from the value read because Applesoft doesn't recognize ASCII letter codes above 127. If the character corresponds to a "Y" or "y", the message is printed.

One subtle effect EXEC files like these could have if you used them from inside a program is jumbling your variables. If your program had set "I" to a special value, for example, it would be scrambled when the EXEC file was done with it.

PROGRAM PROCESSING

So far all our EXEC file samples have used "immediate mode" BASIC statements. You can also fill a file up with statements that have line numbers. When you EXEC a file like this, the BASIC statements are added to your program in memory (overwriting any statements with duplicate line numbers).

The implications of this are astounding. You can write programs on your word processor! Use all of your word processor's neat features for finding and replacing variable names, for scrolling up and down, and for moving things around. Save your program into a text file and then EXEC it into memory. A long program will take a while to load using this method, but it is a very powerful feature. If you have a program that's already half-written and you want to start using this technique tonight, here's a little EXEC file that will turn BASIC programs into text files. It's a modified version of a program that appears in Apple's venerable old *DOS Programmer's Manual* (the old DOS 3.3 version) on page 97:

```
0 D$ = CHR$ (4) : TEXT : INPUT "PATH
   NAME? ";F$ : PRINT D$;"OPEN";F$ :
   PRINT D$;"CLOSE";F$ : PRINT D$;"DE
   LETE";F$ : PRINT D$;"OPEN";F$ : PRINT
   D$;"WRITE";F$ : POKE 33,33 : LIST 1, :
   PRINT D$;"CLOSE";F$ : TEXT : END

RUN
```

The BASIC program line is typed in as a single line, the only carriage return is after the END statement. "RUN" is then typed on a new line. After creating this file on your word processor (this is the program that EXEC.MAKER can't handle, because it contains quote marks *and* colons and commas), save it. Then load your BASIC program. EXEC the file shown above.

It will insert our complete one-line BASIC program (line 0) to your program in memory. Then it will run the little one-liner. One caution: it will overwrite any line 0 that you have in your original program!

In response to the "FILENAME?" question give a name for the new text file that will hold your program lines. (If you have an extra carriage return after the RUN command that's in the EXEC file, that will be used as the filename and we'll die of "syntax erroritis" . . . just one "return" please.)

Most readers will easily figure out how the program works. The "POKE 33,33" moves the right edge of the display screen window to the 33rd column; this prevents extra spaces from appearing within long program lines.

Now you know how to convert a BASIC program file into a text file so you can edit it in a word processor. And you know how to convert a text file back into a BASIC program. It is also possible to have a BASIC program that writes another BASIC program and puts it in a text file.

Listing 14-2 contains one which can be used to capture machine language programs for use by a BASIC program. The program asks for the (decimal) starting and ending addresses of a block of memory and a starting line number. It then creates a BASIC subroutine starting at the specified line number containing the data found within the specified address range in DATA statements. The subroutine will automatically POKE the data back into memory at its original location, which provides a method of restoring memory data from a BASIC program.

EXECUTIVE SOPHISTICATION

The most sophisticated use of EXEC files is to provide input for programs. You can enter the following lines into a text file named "EXEC.-INPUT":

```
RUN RECEIVE.EXEC
/BOOK.PROGRAMS
```

Then type in and save the program in Listing 14-3 under the name "RECEIVE.EXEC".

If you type the command "EXEC EXEC.IN-

```
10  REM MAKE DATA STATEMENTS.
20  TEXT : PRINT : PRINT  CHR$ (21): HOME
30 D$ =  CHR$ (4): REM CTRL-D
100  INPUT "STARTING LOCATION?: ";A$
110  PRINT
120  INPUT "  ENDING LOCATION?: ";B$
130 A =  VAL (A$):B =  VAL (B$)
140  IF A >  = B THEN  END
150  PRINT : PRINT : INPUT "STARTING LINE
       NUMBER?: ";C$
160 C =  VAL (C$)
200  REM
210  PRINT D$;"OPEN DATA.FILE"
220  PRINT D$;"WRITE DATA.FILE"
230  PRINT C;"REMML DATA"
240 C = C + 10
250  PRINT C;"FORI=";A;"TO";B;":READ
       X:POKEI,X:NEXTI"
260 C = C + 10
300  REM WRITE DATA STATEMENTS.
310 COUNT = 1
320  FOR I = A TO B
330  IF COUNT > 10 THEN COUNT = 1:C = C + 10:
       PRINT
350  IF COUNT = 1 THEN  PRINT C;"DATA";
360  PRINT  PEEK (I);
370 COUNT = COUNT + 1
380  IF COUNT <  = 10 AND I <  > B THEN  PRINT
       ",";
390  NEXT I
400  REM CLOSE UP SHOP.
410  PRINT : REM END FILE WITH CARRIAGE RETURN.
420  PRINT D$;"CLOSE DATA.FILE"
499  END
```

Listing 14-2. A program to save a machine language subroutine in DATA.FILE which can later be EXECed into a BASIC program.

PUT", the first line of the EXEC file will run the BASIC program "RECEIVE.EXEC". The EXEC file is not through, however; it has one more line to deliver. It waits until the BASIC program asks for INPUT in line 110; then it sends the second line "/BOOK.PROGRAMS" to the program and terminates the EXEC function. The program, still running, prints the INPUT string in line 210, then ends.

This technique can be used with any program that uses the standard I/O Links for receiving commands. Programs that directly read the keyboard

```
10  REM *** RECEIVE MESSAGE ***
100  REM *** READ STRING FROM EXEC FILE ***
110  INPUT "Tell me the disk's name. ";NAME$
120  PRINT
200  REM *** PRINT THE NAME ***
210  PRINT "The name is "; CHR$ (34);NAME$; CHR$
       (34);"."
220  END
```

Listing 14-3. A program to accept input from an EXEC file.

```
10  REM *** SON OF RECEIVE MESSAGE ***
20  PRINT  CHR$ (4);"EXEC EXEC.INPUT,F1"
100  REM *** READ STRING FROM EXEC FILE ***
110  INPUT "Tell me the disk's name. ";NAME$
120  PRINT
200  REM *** PRINT THE NAME ***
210  PRINT "The name is "; CHR$ (34);NAME$; CHR$
       (34);"."
220  END
```

Listing 14-4. A program which EXECs a file and uses its data as input.

(as per our "WAIT" example earlier) can't use this technique.

If you like, you can start the execution of the EXEC file from within a program instead. With "EXEC.INPUT" still on the disk, try typing in and RUNning the program in Listing 14-4. Line 20 EXECs the file and discards the first line ("field") via the "F1" parameter, which skips the "RUN RECEIVE EXEC" command in the EXEC file. These-cond line is still fed the the INPUT statement in our new program.

One problem with EXEC files is that once set into motion, they tend to execute until all the commands contained within have been sent. Neither errors, control-C, nor reset will stay the EXECutioner from his appointed rounds.

"MONITORING" EXEC FILES

Try entering the following lines into a sequential text file:

```
CALL-151
300L
300.37F
3DOG
```

EXEC (or "-") the file with these commands and watch the screen. *Whatwasthat?*

The file demonstrates the use of the Apple system monitor from within an EXEC file. If you are not familiar with monitor commands, the middle of the file will look like gibberish. But don't worry, it works.

"CALL -151" invokes the Monitor from BASIC. The "300L" statement causes the Monitor to print a disassembled listing of 20 6502 instruction mnemonics starting at location $300; the "300.37F" statement cause the program to display the hexadecimal contents from $300 through $37F. Finally, "3D0G" re-activates Applesoft via BASIC.SYSTEM.

Those of you who are more familiar with the monitor may be pleasantly surprised that you can send commands to it from an EXEC file just as if the commands were typed at the keyboard.

Chapter 15

Parameters And File Pointers

Now let's continue our investigation, with emphasis on the *parameters* that can be used with text file commands. Most of these parameters have come to be associated with *random access* text files, so we'll examine those rascals at the same time.

DRAWING A BEAD ON TEXT FILES

Let's go back to our "bead string" analogy, but on a bead-by-bead basis this time. Imagine, for the moment, a bag of marbles. There are important differences between a file full of characters and a bag full of marbles, although they may not be immediately obvious. If you shake up a bag of marbles ten times, and after each shake open the bag and examine the top marble, you'll probably find a different marble on top each time. But if you do the same thing to a file, the first character out of the file will always be the same one.

In addition, the second character out of the file will always be the same, as will the third, and so on; but the second marble out of the bag one time might be the seventeenth one out the next time. So let's take all our marbles, drill holes in them, string them together like beads, and put them back in the bag. Now we have something more like a file. A string of beads could be pulled out the bag the same way everytime, just like a file of characters.

Simple text files don't amount to much more than a string of beads in a bag. The beads come in 128 colors, one for each ASCII character. When you write a simple text file, you are simply stringing the beads together. When you read a simple text file, you take the beads out of the bag and translate them back into characters.

As discussed earlier, this kind of file is called a *sequential* file. Sequential files are good for computerized information you store and retrieve all in one hunk. As this chapter was developed, for example, it is was stored in a sequential text file. The entire file had to be loaded into a word processor before so much as one character could be changed. After a change, the entire file had to be resaved. This is a simple, effective technique for dealing with the development of text documents, since us usually many changes are made to the file, in random places, each time it is loaded.

RANDOM ACCESSIBILITY

For other kinds of files, however, a simple sequential structure is often inadequate. Imagine Brother Bob's furniture inventory (substitute your favorite fast-talking advertiser if you like). Brother Bob has a list somewhere that goes something like that in Table 15-1.

The numbers represent how many of each item ole Brother Bob has on hand. If he gets in a new shipment of five cheap red sofas, for example, that first 4 will have to be changed to a 9. In this situation, it would be nice if Brother Bob could go directly to the part of the file about cheap red sofas, change just that number, and leave the rest of the file untouched. To do this easily, we need to invent a way to jump from one part of our bead string to another part. Pull that long string of beads out of that big bag over there, and let's look into this a little.

Extend the string out on a table. Now imagine the beads at the beginning of the string have the numbers on Brother Bob's overstuffed mattresses and the beads at the end of the string hold a count of love seats. Somewhere in the middle are our sofas. Now just imagine that we happened to know that cheap red sofas were item number 77 in the string, and that each item had been allotted exactly 30 beads.

A little quick math (77 times 30) would tell us that cheap red sofas start at bead 2,310. Furthermore, if we knew that names took up the first 25 beads of each item's allotted 30, and that the quantity-on-hand was stored in the last five beads, we could do a little more math (2,310 + 25) and know exactly where to find the number of cheap red sofas in Brother Bob's inventory.

Table 15-1. Brother Bob's Inventory.

```
cheap red sofas              4
cheap yellow sofas          12
really cheap red sofas       6
really cheap blue sofas      1

  and so on....
```

This same kind of math works with files as well as beads. ProDOS uses a position-in-file pointer that designates the current bead position. When you read from or write to a file, this pointer automatically moves down the string. When working with simple sequential files this is the only method used for moving the pointer.

As Brother Bob knows, however, there are other ways to move the pointer around. OPENing a file always moves the pointer to the file's beginning. The APPEND command moves it to the file's end. The READ and WRITE commands' "R" and "B" parameters, in conjunction with OPEN's "L" parameter, allow you to move the pointer anywhere you like.

WHAT THE "L" (IS ALL ABOUT)

It is helpful in this context to remember that the READ and WRITE commands don't actually read or write anything. The READ command tells BASIC.SYSTEM to supply data from the specified file to any subsequent INPUT or GET commands. If you use the "R" or "B" parameters with READ, you are also telling ProDOS to move the file pointer before supplying data. Similarly, the WRITE command tells BASIC.SYSTEM to place anything subsequently PRINTed in the specified file, at the position specified by the "R" and "B" parameters.

When you open a file, you can specify a length parameter for DOS to use with that file. The length parameter represents the number of beads, or bytes, allotted to each item, or record, in the file. Brother Bob specifies his record length like this

```
520 PRINT "OPEN BEDBUGS, L30"
```

With BASIC.SYSTEM you can use any length value you like when you open a file. Just because a file was originally opened with one value doesn't mean you can't reopen it later with another value. Doing so may cause you all kinds of confusion, but ProDOS insists it's your confusion; it knows what *it's* doing. (There really are reasons you might do this that we'll get to in a moment.)

ProDOS keeps track of the record length you

use when OPENing a random-access file. You can determine the record length a file was created with by using the BASIC.SYSTEM CATALOG (note: not CAT) command. The final entry on each line of the catalog, the entry in the column labeled *SUBTYPE*, is where you'll find this information. For some reason known only to the ProDOS development team, the "L" parameter used when the file was created appears there with the prefix *R*= (presumably to signify "*R*ecord length").

If you neglect to specify an "L" value when you open a file, ProDOS will set it to whatever was specified when the file was created. If you OPEN a new file with BASIC.SYSTEM without specifying an "L" value, the file will be assigned a length of zero. Under ProDOS, files with a length of zero (SUBTYPE listed as "R=0") are considered sequential files; all others are considered random-access files.

In and of itself, the length value you assign to a file is absolutely meaningless. It has meaning only when you also specify a *R*ecord parameter with a READ or WRITE command. The "L" and "R" parameters always occur together; either one alone is useless.

"R" YOU READY FOR THIS?

When you use the "R" parameter with READ or WRITE, the pointer for the specified file is moved according to the following formula

POINTER = (L * R)

If you OPEN a file with "L" specified as *1*, you can use "R" to move the file's pointer to any byte in the file. The first byte in the file is always called byte zero. Specify "R" as zero and the pointer gets set to the (1 × 0) byte. Specify one and the pointer moves to (1 × 1). Specify 2310 and the pointer moves to (1 × 2310). Using this technique, you can move the pointer to any byte of the file within the range of the "R" parameter (65535 for ProDOS). To reach beyond that, OPEN the file with a slightly bigger "L" and do the appropriate math.

Brother Bob doesn't use this technique because he hates math. He would much rather open the file with a length of 30 and then tell BASIC.SYSTEM he wants to access record 77. There are a few crazy people around, however, who think it's fun to have Applesoft multiply the record length by the record number and give the total to BASIC.SYSTEM. Gives them a feeling of control, they say. Either way, the results are the same. Multiplication, after all, is multiplication.

TWO "B"S OR NOT TWO "B"S?

Folks who like to have lots of control over the file pointer can also move it around with the *B*yte parameter. They rarely do, however, because of the problems in descriptions of the "B" parameter. Nonetheless, the "B" parameter is a reliable little critter that can be quite useful if you know how to use it.

"B" got off on the wrong foot in the original DOS 3.3 documentation, *The DOS Manual.* That book had a two-page section on the "B" parameter that began, "Note: the following section is *not* for beginners . . .", and which consisted mostly of warnings about all the problems you could create by using the "B" parameter inappropriately.

In the later *DOS Programmer's Manual,* this two-page section is missing. To add insult to injury, what little information on "B" that *is* presented is only partially correct.

In *BASIC Programming with ProDOS,* the "B" parameter loses even its entry in the index! No examples of how to use the parameter are given. And the tradition continues in Gary Little's ProDOS series running in *A+* magazine and in Lee Swoboda's series running in *inCider;* neither of them say much about "B" and both of them have its maximum value wrong.

The "B" parameter allows you to quickly and easily move the position-in-file pointer to any byte in a file. Unlike DOS 3.3, BASIC.SYSTEM allows you to use "B" with BLOAD and BSAVE, as demonstrated in Chapter 11. "B" can also be used (under both DOS 3.3 and ProDOS) with READ and WRITE, but this is more complicated.

As originally designed, the "B" parameter is supposed to allow you to bump the file pointer a specific number of bytes beyond the beginning of the file (sequential files) or the beginning of a record (random files). Brother Bob, for example, actually reads the cheap red sofa data with commands like these

```
520  PRINT "OPEN BEDBUG, L30"
525  PRINT "READ BEDBUG, R77, B25"
```

As long as you take the proper precautions (to be explained momentarily), the "B" parameter always enters the pointer-positioning formula in a very precise way. The formula becomes

POINTER = (L * R) + B

Something most people don't realize is that the "B" parameter can be used to move the pointer vast distances as well as to tap it slightly. For example, it is entirely possible to have a file that consists of four 2,500 byte sequential sections and 400 30-byte records. To access the various parts of the file you would use commands like those in Listing 15-1. The final command may puzzle you. It appears we are trying to read 10,000 bytes beyond the beginning of record 100. In fact we are skipping over the 10,000 sequential bytes at the beginning of the file, and then going to record 100. This works because (30 × 100) + 10000 (what we specify in the command), is mathematically the same as 10000 + (30 × 100) (the file position we actually want).

Note carefully that each of the commands shown above includes *both* the "R" and "B" parameters. This is the precaution you should take when using "B"; never use it alone, *always* specify "R" when you use B. If you are dealing with a sequential file, where "R" is usually not used, specify "R" as zero. If you are using BASIC.SYSTEM and you neglect to specify "R", the file pointer moves "B" bytes beyond the *current pointer position*. As an exercise for the reader, see if you can find a practical application for this feature; we can't think of any.

With BASIC.SYSTEM, the minimum permissible "B" value is zero but the maximum value varies. At any moment it is the difference between the current file position and the last byte in the file. (Thus, if the pointer is at the end of your file, the maximum allowable "B" value is zero.). With BASIC.SYSTEM you can't use "B" to move the pointer beyond the end of the file when accessing it as a sequential file. If you try you'll get a "RANGE ERROR", even when writing. You can get around this while using BASIC.SYSTEM by simply opening a file and using big "L" and "R" values with a WRITE and a PRINT to move the end of the file into hyperspace.

Table 15-2 summarizes the possible values you can use with the "L", "R", and "B" parameters for ProDOS. Note that under ProDOS, the largest record number you can have is the smaller of 65,535 or 16 megabytes (16,777,216 bytes—the largest possible ProDOS file, which is also the ultimate maximum for "B") divided by the record length. If, for example, your records were 1,000 bytes long, the maximum record number you could have would be 16,777.

BAD FIELD POSITION

Another way to move the position-in-file pointer is with the *POSITION* command. You can use POSITION to move the pointer forward only (never backward) a specified number of *fields*. A field is a bunch of characters that end with a carriage re-

```
540  PRINT "OPEN CURIOSITY, L30"
550  PRINT "READ CURIOSITY, R0, B0"          1st sequential section
550  PRINT "READ CURIOSITY, R0, B2500"       2nd sequential section
550  PRINT "READ CURIOSITY, R0, B5000"       3rd sequential section
550  PRINT "READ CURIOSITY, R0, B7500"       4th sequential section
550  PRINT "READ CURIOSITY, R0, B10000"      record zero
550  PRINT "READ CURIOSITY, R100, B10000"    record 100
```

Listing 15-1. Sample program lines using the "R" and "B" parameters.

Table 15-2. Allowable "L," "R," and "B" Values.

	default value	minimum value	maximum value
Length of records	0	0	65535
Record Number	---	0	smaller of 65535 or 16M / L
Byte offset	0	0	length of file - current position

turn. BASIC.SYSTEM/ProDOS place no limit on the maximum number of characters in a field, although if you intend to read your file with BASIC INPUT statements you'd better not exceed INPUT's 239-character limitation. A field can contain as few characters as none; this happens when you have two carriage returns in a row.

With BASIC.SYSTEM, you use the "F" parameter to specify how many fields POSITION should skip over (starting from the current position). If you specify *zero*, the pointer won't move at all. If you specify *one*, ProDOS will zip through the file's characters from the current position to the next occurrence of a carriage return within the file; the pointer will end up at the first character following the "return". If you specify *two*, ProDOS will stop after two "returns", and so on.

In DOS 3.3, POSITION used an "R" parameter for relative field position rather than "F". There is absolutely *no* relationship between POSITION's *relative fields* and READ and WRITE's *record numbers* (even though they share the use of "R" as the parameter character). BASIC.SYSTEM uses the "F" to minimize confusion. With BASIC.SYSTEM, the "F" parameter can also be used with READ and WRITE commands. This makes the POSITION command itself unnecessary; it was included in ProDOS only for DOS 3.3. compatibility.

Imagine you want to move the file pointer to record 93 of a file and then read the 2nd field. Here's how you do it

```
525 PRINT "READ SUNTAN, R93, F1"
```

You set "F" to 1 because you want to skip one field. This puts you at the beginning of the second field.

In actual practice, the POSITION command and the "F" parameter usually create more confusion than they dissipate. Their existence makes it appear that a file organized as a series of variable-length fields can be usefully accessed one field at a time. But this is extremely difficult because of the problem of WRITEing to such a field.

Say a file has a field with a 10-character name in it. If you replace that10-character name with a 5-character name, you'll create *two* fields—one with the new 5-character name, one with the final characters of the old 10-character name (including the carriage return that ended the original field).

Similarly, if you overwrite an existing field with a longer name, you'll destroy part of the following field. Consider these problems awhile and you'll probably come to the conclusion that files with fields that need to be accessed one at a time *need* fixed-length, *not* variable-length, fields. Fixed-length fields can be accessed more easily and quickly with the "B" parameter than with position or the "F" parameter.

If you decide to ignore our warnings about the uselessness of POSITION, remember that it always starts counting from the current file position. If the pointer is in a record's tenth field and you specify "R" as two, you end up at the beginning of the twelfth field. You can't go backward. To get to a record's second field from the tenth you must first reset the pointer to the beginning of the record and then use position or the "F" parameter.

This gets very tricky if you actually use the POSITION command, since a POSITION command will turn off the READ or WRITE command you use to specify the record you want. The solution is to use a second READ or WRITE, after the POSITION command. When you execute the second READ or WRITE you'll want to leave the file pointer right where it is, so don't use *any* parameters with it.

That's it for this topic. Brother Bob says to tell you he'll pay you the difference *in cash* if you can find a cheaper parameter anywhere in the city . . .

Chapter 16

Putting It All Together

Since we've been through all the text file commands and most of the idiosyncrasies, let's try putting some text in a file and shoving it around a little. Let's start by creating a sequential file and random access file from the same data, illustrating their differences.

MAKING A SEQUENTIAL TEXT FILE

The first project will be to create a sequential text file with some realistic but unusable data. The file we are going to create will function like a "genuine" name/address list; but the names and places we use will be fictitious and even somewhat strange. In the sequential format, we will save the data into the file in the form

First name
Last name
Street address
City
State
Zip Code
ID Number

Everything in that list should be self-explanatory except for "ID Number", which was thrown in as an index to the position in which this person was entered at the original creation of the file. We'll call this set of seven data items a "record" for the sequential file, although this has a less distinct meaning than a record in a random access text file.

Lines 100 through 370 in the program in Listing 16-1 create six items of information (all except the ID, which is determined by a counter) by selecting items randomly from the information in the DATA statements. Then seven items are written into the file for each name; so that when we read the file back later we know that, starting from the beginning of the file, each time we have read seven items from the file we have completed one address. The program continues to write addresses until it has done 100 of them.

Since we've attacked the commands already, there is little more to say. Listing 16-1 contains a program to write the file "NAMEFILE.S" from our phony data. Simply type in the program, SAVE it

```
10  REM *** MAKE SEQUENTIAL FILE ***
20 D$ =  CHR$ (4)
30  ONERR  GOTO 10000
100  REM *** SET UP ARRAYS FOR NAMES ***
110  DIM N1$(10),N2$(10),SN$(10),CN$(10),ST$(10)
120  FOR I = 1 TO 10: READ N1$(I): NEXT I
130  FOR I = 1 TO 10: READ N2$(I): NEXT I
140  FOR I = 1 TO 10: READ SN$(I): NEXT I
150  FOR I = 1 TO 10: READ CN$(I): NEXT I
160  FOR I = 1 TO 10: READ ST$(I): NEXT I
200  REM *** OPEN THE FILE ***
210  PRINT D$;"OPEN NAMEFILE.S"
220  PRINT D$;"WRITE NAMEFILE.S"
230 ID = 1: REM  INDEX NUMBER.
300  REM *** MAKE UP A NAME AND ADDRESS ***
310 N1$(0) = N1$( INT (9 *  RND (1) + 1))
320 N2$(0) = N2$( INT (9 *  RND (1) + 1))
330 SA$ =  STR$ ( INT (9998 *  RND (1) + 1))
340 SN$(0) = SN$( INT (9 *  RND (1) + 1))
350 CN$(0) = CN$( INT (9 *  RND (1) + 1))
360 ST$(0) = ST$( INT (9 *  RND (1) + 1))
370 ZC$ =  STR$ ( INT (99998 *  RND (1) + 1)):
      IF  LEN (ZC$) < 5 THEN ZC$ =  LEFT$
      ("00000",5 -  LEN (ZC$)) + ZC$
400  REM *** WRITE OUT THE NAME, ADDRESS, AND
      INDEX NUMBER ***
410  PRINT N1$(0)
420  PRINT N2$(0)
430  PRINT SA$ + " " + SN$(0)
440  PRINT CN$(0)
450  PRINT ST$(0)
460  PRINT ZC$
470  PRINT ID
500  REM *** CHECK FOR 100 ADDRESSES ***
510  IF ID < 100 THEN ID = ID + 1: GOTO 300
600  REM *** CLOSE FILE ***
610  PRINT D$;"CLOSE NAMEFILE.S"
999  END
1000  REM *** DATA ***
1010  DATA
      "FRED","MARY","SUE","BARNEY","BETTY","ALBE
      RT","QUINTON","MARSHA","BOB","CAROL": REM
      FIRST NAMES.
1020  DATA
      "JONES","SMITH","JOHNSON","AMES","BOOKER",
      "NELSON","FINSTER","SIMON","QUEST","WILSON
      ": REM LAST NAMES.
1030  DATA "OAK","PARK
      LANE","MAIN","ELM","WILLOW","GRAND","WESTC
      HESTER","LARCH","NORTON","FIFTH AVENUE":
      REM STREET NAMES.
1040  DATA "KOKOMO","NEW YORK","KANSAS
      CITY","ST. LOUIS","PHOENIX","LOS
      ANGELES","WICHITA
      FALLS","PITTSBURG","MIAMI","HONOLULU":
```

Listing 16-1. A program to create NAMEFILE.S, a sequential text file.

```
        REM CITIES.
1050  DATA
        "MO","KS","PA","HA","NY","AZ","CA","TX","F
        L","WI": REM STATES.
10000   REM *** IMPOLITE ERROR ROUTINE ***
10010   IF  PEEK (222) < 22 THEN  HOME : PRINT
        "DISK ERROR!": VTAB 22: CALL  - 3288:
        GOTO 600
10020   POKE 216,0: RESUME : REM GO BACK AND LET
        APPLESOFT ERROR SHOW ITSELF.
```

to disk, and RUN it. It will create the sequential "NAMEFILE.S" with 100 (phony) addresses.

READING THE DATA BACK

Now that we have our data file made up, it would be real handy to be able to read the data back. With sequential files, the problem with reading *selected* data from the file is that you usually have to read all of the information in the file and discard it, up to the point where you find the information you need. This points to sequential files being more useful with programming situations where the entire file is going to be read into memory at once.

```
10  REM *** READ NAME/ADDRESS FILE (SEQ) ***
20 D$ =  CHR$ (4):OD = 0
30  TEXT : PRINT  CHR$ (21): HOME
40  ONERR  GOTO 10000
100  REM *** GET "RECORD" NUMBER ***
110 QF = 0: VTAB 8: HTAB 1: CALL  - 958
120  INPUT "RECORD # TO RETRIEVE (0 = ALL)?:
       ";RN$
125  IF RN$ = "" THEN  GOTO 900: REM  EXIT ON NO
       INPUT.
130 RN =  VAL (RN$)
140  IF  STR$ (RN) <  > RN$ THEN  GOTO 110: REM
       MAY NOT BE A NUMBER.
150  IF RN < 0 THEN 110: REM OUT OF RANGE.
170  IF RN = 0 THEN  GOSUB 300: GOTO 110
200  REM *** SEARCH FOR A SPECIFIC "RECORD" ***
210  GOSUB 1000
220  GOSUB 2000
230  GOSUB 3000
240  GOTO 110
300  REM *** RETRIEVE AND DISPLAY (ALL) ***
310 RN = 1
320  GOSUB 1000
330  GOSUB 2000
340  GOSUB 3000
350  IF QF THEN  GOTO 110
360 RN = RN + 1: GOTO 320
900  REM *** EXIT ***
910  PRINT D$;"CLOSE": REM JUST IN CASE.
920  VTAB 22: END
1000  REM *** GO GET A RECORD ***
1010  PRINT D$;"OPEN NAMEFILE.S"
1020  PRINT D$;"READ NAMEFILE.S"
```

Listing 16-2. A program to read NAMEFILE.S.

```
1030 I = 1
1040  IF ( NOT OD) AND I <  = RN THEN  INPUT
       "";N1$,N2$,AD$,CT$,ST$,ZC$,ID
1050  IF OD THEN  PRINT : PRINT D$;"CLOSE":OD =
       0: PRINT "RECORD #";RN;" DOES NOT
       EXIST.": GOSUB 3000: GOTO 110
1060  IF I < RN THEN I = I + 1: GOTO 1040
1070  PRINT  CHR$ (4);"CLOSE"
1080  RETURN
2000  REM *** DISPLAY A RECORD ***
2010  VTAB 8: HTAB 1: CALL  - 958
2020  INVERSE : PRINT "RECORD #";ID;: NORMAL :
       PRINT
2030  PRINT
2040  PRINT N1$;" ";N2$
2050  PRINT AD$
2060  PRINT CT$;",";ST$;"     ";ZC$
2070  RETURN
3000  REM *** PAUSE BETWEEN "RECORDS" ***
3010  VTAB 22: PRINT "PRESS A KEY ('ESC'
       ABORTS): ";
3020  GET A$: IF A$ =  CHR$ (27) THEN QF = 1
3030  RETURN
10000  REM *** CHEAP ERROR ROUTINE ***
10010  IF  PEEK (222) < 22 THEN  PRINT
       D$;"CLOSE": HOME : PRINT "BASIC.SYSTEM
       ERROR: "; PEEK (222): CALL  - 3288: GOTO
       900
10020  IF  PEEK (222) > 21 THEN  PRINT
       D$;"CLOSE": HOME : PRINT "APPLESOFT
       ERROR: "; PEEK (222): CALL  - 3288: GOTO
       900
```

The program in Listing 16-2 works by handling the file in the "read and discard" manner. This is extremely wasteful compared to the equivalent method for a random access text file, which can "skip past" the inconsequential records. The program works by asking for you to give it a "record number" which corresponds to the ID number of the address you want to find. The program then reads data from the file and counts until it has read and discarded all the data up to the data you requested. It then reads in the seven items of data for the address you requested and displays it on the screen. Just type in the program, SAVE it, and RUN it; it will ask for a "record" number. Type in a number and it will try to locate it. Too large or too small a number will result in an error, a "0" will retrieve all the addresses one at a time. Incidentally, you'll notice some of the cities don't go with the states, etc.; some of the results may be amusing (that's the way with random data . . .).

The search time is not as agonizing for this program using BASIC.SYSTEM, as opposed to DOS 3.3, since ProDOS handles text files much faster than DOS. But since the program cannot detect the end of the file until it runs out of data to read, we need a mechanism to detect the end of the file's data. In the program, this is trapped by the ONERR GOTO routine; if the variable OD becomes non-zero in line 1040 and 1050 then an "OUT OF DATA" error has occurred and the fact that you specified too large a number is reported. The trouble is, you have to read the whole file to determine this!

MAKING A RANDOM ACCESS FILE

After playing with the sequential file, you might be interested in the creation of a similar *random access* text file. This can be done easily by reading each "record" from our sequential file NAMEFILE.S and writing it to a newly created random access text file named NAMEFILE.R100. We'll do this with the program in Listing 16-3. The program reads each sequential "record" in and immediately writes it out to the new random access file. In addition, the count of the total number of addresses is stored into record number 0 of the random access file (lines 4010-4030). The number of addresses is one less than the total number of records in the file; we have stored addresses in record numbers 1-100 and the count in record 0, for a total of 101 records.

READING THE RANDOM ACCESS TEXT FILE

The advantages of the random access file are tied to having a standard length; in the case of NAMEFILE.R100, the length is $100 (or 256)

```
10  REM *** SEQ. TO R/A COPY ***
20 D$ =  CHR$ (4)
30  ONERR  GOTO 10000
1000  REM *** OPEN FILES/START LOOP ***
1010  PRINT D$;"OPEN NAMEFILE.S"
1020  PRINT D$;"OPEN NAMEFILE.R100,L$100"
1030 RN = 1
2000  REM *** READ DATA FROM SEQ. ***
2010  PRINT D$;"READ NAMEFILE.S"
2015  INPUT "";N1$,N2$,AD$,CT$,ST$,ZC$,ID
3000  REM *** WRITE TO R/A FILE ***
3010  PRINT D$;"WRITE NAMEFILE.R100,R";RN
3020  PRINT N1$
3030  PRINT N2$
3040  PRINT AD$
3050  PRINT CT$
3060  PRINT ST$
3070  PRINT ZC$
3080  PRINT ID
3090 RN = RN + 1: GOTO 2000
4000  REM *** CLOSE UP SHOP ***
4005  ONERR  GOTO 20000
4010  PRINT D$;"WRITE NAMEFILE.R100,R0"
4020  PRINT RN - 1
4025  PRINT D$;"CLOSE NAMEFILE.R100"
4030  HOME
4040  PRINT "DONE!..."
4050  VTAB 22
4060  POKE 216,0
4099  END
10000  REM *** ERROR/EXIT ROUTINE ***
10010  IF  PEEK (222) = 5 THEN : PRINT D$;"CLOSE
       NAMEFILE.S": CALL  - 3288: POKE 216,0:
       GOTO 4000
20000  REM *** OTHER ERRORS ***
20010  POKE 216,0
20020  IF  PEEK (222) < 22 THEN  HOME : PRINT
       "BASIC.SYSTEM ERROR: "; PEEK (222): PRINT
       D$;"CLOSE": VTAB 22: END
20030  IF  PEEK (222) > 21 THEN  HOME : PRINT
       "APPLESOFT ERROR: "; PEEK (222): VTAB 22:
       END
```

Listing 16-3. A program to make NAMEFILE.R100 (a random access text file) from the data in NAMEFILE.S.

bytes. One advantage was demonstrated by being able to easily save the count of the number of addresses written to the beginning of the random access file without disturbing the addresses. This can't be done with a sequential access file without copying (appending) the file contents to a new file which begins with the count number.

The other advantage to the fixed length is the ability of ProDOS to skip to the start of any record without having to read all the intervening records. This speeds up access tremendously on *large* files. The program in Listing 16-4 can be used to read addresses from NAMEFILE.R100.

You can see that the routine to move us to a

```
10  REM *** READ NAME/ADDRESS FILE (R/A) ***
20 D$ =  CHR$ (4)
30  TEXT : PRINT  CHR$ (21): HOME
40  ONERR  GOTO 10000
50  REM ***READ NR FROM FILE ***
60  PRINT D$"OPEN NAMEFILE.R100,L$100"
70  PRINT D$"READ NAMEFILE.R100,R0"
80  INPUT "";NR
90  PRINT D$;"CLOSE"
100  REM *** GET "RECORD" NUMBER ***
110 QF = 0: VTAB 8: HTAB 1: CALL  - 958
120  INPUT "RECORD # TO RETRIEVE (0=<ALL>)?:
       ";RN$
125  IF RN$ = "" THEN  GOTO 900: REM  EXIT ON NO
       INPUT.
130 RN =  VAL (RN$)
140  IF  STR$ (RN) <  > RN$ THEN  GOTO 110: REM
       MAY NOT BE A NUMBER.
150  IF RN < 0 THEN 110: REM OUT OF RANGE.
170  IF RN = 0 THEN  GOSUB 300: GOTO 110
180  IF RN > NR THEN  PRINT : PRINT "RECORD
       #";RN;" DOES NOT EXIST!": GOSUB 3000: ON
       QF GOTO 900: GOTO 110
200  REM *** SEARCH FOR A SPECIFIC "RECORD" ***
210  GOSUB 1000
220  GOSUB 2000
230  GOSUB 3000
240  GOTO 110
300  REM *** RETRIEVE AND DISPLAY <ALL> ***
310 RN = 1
320  GOSUB 1000
330  GOSUB 2000
340  GOSUB 3000
350  IF QF THEN  GOTO 110
360 RN = RN + 1: GOTO 320
900  REM *** EXIT ***
910  PRINT D$;"CLOSE": REM JUST IN CASE.
920  VTAB 22: END
1000  REM *** GO GET A RECORD ***
1010  PRINT D$;"OPEN NAMEFILE.R100,L$100"
1020  PRINT D$;"READ NAMEFILE.R100,R";RN
1040  INPUT "";N1$,N2$,AD$,CT$,ST$,ZC$,ID
1070  PRINT  CHR$ (4);"CLOSE"
1080  RETURN
2000  REM *** DISPLAY A RECORD ***
```

Listing 16-4. A program to read NAMEFILE.R100.

```
2010  VTAB 8: HTAB 1: CALL  - 958
2020  INVERSE : PRINT "RECORD #";ID;: NORMAL :
       PRINT
2030  PRINT
2040  PRINT N1$;" ";N2$
2050  PRINT AD$
2060  PRINT CT$;",";ST$;"     ";ZC$
2070  RETURN
3000  REM *** PAUSE BETWEEN "RECORDS" ***
3010  VTAB 22: PRINT "PRESS A KEY ('ESC'
       ABORTS): ";
3020  GET A$: IF A$ =  CHR$ (27) THEN QF = 1
3030  RETURN
10000  REM *** CHEAP ERROR ROUTINE ***
10010  IF  PEEK (222) < 22 THEN  PRINT
       D$;"CLOSE": HOME : PRINT "BASIC.SYSTEM
       ERROR: "; PEEK (222): CALL  - 3288: GOTO
       900
10020  IF  PEEK (222) > 21 THEN  PRINT
       D$;"CLOSE": HOME : PRINT "APPLESOFT
       ERROR: "; PEEK (222): CALL  - 3288: GOTO
       900
```

record does not have to do the "read and discard" loop that was used with the sequential file. We simply tell BASIC.SYSTEM the record length ("R$100") in our OPEN statement and what record number we want; BASIC.SYSTEM and ProDOS do the work of moving the pointer to the start of that record. Then we just read the fields. Notice that the INPUT statement in line 1040 that reads all seven fields of the record looks like the same INPUT used to read seven items from a sequential file. The fields within a record in a random access file are accessed just like a miniature sequential file. You can type "100" to see how long it takes for this program to find the last record, versus the same exercise for the sequential file. The times may seem to be relatively close; but, as we see next, there are extenuating circumstances.

MAKE ROOM, MAKE ROOM

There are two main drawbacks to random access files. The first is that if you attempt to write (for our file) $120 bytes to record number 1, you are going to overwrite the first $20 bytes at the beginning of record number 2. ProDOS and BASIC.SYSTEM will do nothing to stop you, and you will discover the error when you try to read in record number 2 later.

The second is size; a random access text file always reserves the defined number bytes for a record whether or not the entire space is used. That means that if you have 10 records of 256 bytes each, they will consume 2560 bytes of filespace even if you only store 1 byte of data in each record. A sequential file does not leave such "holes" unless you manually space your data out.

To demonstrate, Fig. 16-1 is a CATALOG listing containing the two files created with our programs. Notice the size of NAMEFILE.R100 (52 blocks and 25648 bytes) versus NAMEFILE.S (11 blocks and 4618 bytes)! Obviously there was a *lot* of space wasted in NAMEFILE.R100 just for the privilege of faster access, even allowing for the one extra 256 byte record for the record number count.

SPARSE FILES

In order to keep unused space in random access text files from getting ridiculous, Apple added a special type of file storage to ProDOS called *sparse files*.

Sparse files work by having ProDOS only allot disk blocks for file records that actually contain information. We won't discuss the internal struc-

```
/TEXT.DEMOS
 NAME            TYPE  BLOCKS  MODIFIED          CREATED           ENDFILE SUBTYPE

*BASIC.SYSTEM     SYS      21  18-JUN-84  0:00   30-NOV-85 17:46     10240
*PRODOS           SYS      30  18-SEP-84  0:00   30-NOV-85 17:46     14848
*DATA.MAKER       BAS       3  19-NOV-85 18:46   30-NOV-85 17:47       622
*BAS.TO.TXT       TXT       1  14-OCT-85 10:35   30-NOV-85 17:47       107 R=      0
*MAKE.NAMEFILE.S  BAS       5  20-NOV-85 15:00   30-NOV-85 17:47      1569
*READ.NAMEFILE.S  BAS       4  20-NOV-85 15:10   30-NOV-85 17:47      1256
*NAMES.S.TO.R     BAS       3  20-NOV-85 15:07   30-NOV-85 17:47       826
*READ.NAMEFILE.R  BAS       4  20-NOV-85 15:05   30-NOV-85 17:48      1342
*MAKE.SPARSE      BAS       1  28-NOV-85 23:25   30-NOV-85 17:48       234
*TEST.COMMA.SEQ   BAS       1  30-NOV-85 11:32   30-NOV-85 17:48       416
*PRINT.DIR        BAS      22  30-NOV-85 11:19   30-NOV-85 17:48     10507
 BIGFILE          TXT      20  28-NOV-85 23:25   30-NOV-85 17:48    922651 R=   1024
 NAMEFILE.S       TXT      11  30-NOV-85 17:51   30-NOV-85 17:51      4618 R=      0
 NAMEFILE.R100    TXT      52  30-NOV-85 17:53   30-NOV-85 17:53     25648 R=    256

BLOCKS FREE:    95      BLOCKS USED:   185      TOTAL BLOCKS:   280
```

Fig. 16-1. Sample directory containing "BIGFILE."

ture of these files, but you should notice the anomaly with the file entry for "BIGFILE" in the CATALOG above. Notice that there are 20 blocks of disk space assigned to the file. Then look at the ENDFILE value of 922,651 bytes. That's almost *6.5 times* the storage capacity of the standard 280-block Apple 5 1/4″ diskette that this file was created on!

This file was created with a program that only ended up writing data to nine records in the file, but the file was created with 1000 records of 1024 ($400) bytes each. Since only nine records contain data, only the blocks used by those nine records plus a couple of blocks for overhead were actually allotted on the disk. When one of those nine records is read, ProDOS goes to its place in the file and recovers the data from the disk.

When you request data from one of the empty records, ProDOS checks the file and recognizes that no data was written to that record. Therefore, ProDOS can return a null entry. When creating the file, ProDOS did not bother reserving disk space for these null records, but their presence is reflected in the "ENDFILE" value. Indeed, if you use POSITION to move the pointer around in the file, it functions just as if the entire file was there on the disk.

The use of the sparse file format is handled automatically by ProDOS and is transparent to the program accessing the file, *unless* you copy data from the file on a byte-by-byte basis (using POSITION, for example) into another file. If you do, the file will expand and attempt to take up the disk space that its ENDFILE value indicates it should. The ProDOS FILER program can copy sparse files without making them larger. For curiosity's sake, the program that generated BIGFILE is contained in Listing 16-5.

TEXT FILE INPUT AND "?EXTRA IGNORED"

The section titled "INPUT" on page 207 Apple's *BASIC Programming With ProDOS* claims that the INPUT command will allow the use of commas and/or colons within the string being INPUT. It doesn't! You get the good old Applesoft "?EXTRA IGNORED" error. The reason lies in the way INPUT reads a line into its variables. The use of a comma in the string input is intended to signify a list of variables, such as replying

```
10  REM *** MAKE SPARSE FILE ***
20 D$ =  CHR$ (4)
30  PRINT D$;"OPEN BIGFILE,L$400"
100  REM *** SAVE EVERY 100TH RECORD ***
110  FOR I = 1 TO 1000 STEP 100: REM TAKE GIANT
       STEPS.
120  PRINT D$;"WRITE BIGFILE,R";I
130  PRINT "This is record number ";I;".
140  NEXT I
210  PRINT D$;"CLOSE"
```

Listing 16-5. The program used to create BIGFILE (a sparse file).

"One,Two,Three" to the line

10 INPUT "TELL ME THE FIRST THREE NUMBERS: ";FI$,SE$,TH$

which places "One" in "FI$", "Two" in "SE$", and "Three" in "TH$". An answer like "One,Two,Three,Four" will result in an ?EXTRA IGNORED error since no variable exists for the "Four" (after the third comma) to be read into.

The program in Listing 16-6 demonstrates that the problem is still there in BASIC.SYSTEM. When you RUN this program, it writes the data "YES, WE HAVE A COMMA HERE." to the file "COMMA.TEST.FILE." When it is read back in in line 230, you'll see an "?EXTRA IGNORED" message on the screen, and the final string printed back to you will only consist of "YES". Everything after the comma was lost by INPUT.

There are two ways around this problem. The first is to use GET to read a character at a time and build the string from the individual characters. The string is assumed to be ended by a carriage return character. You can do this by deleting line 230 from the program and adding the lines

```
230   IN$ = " ": REM NULL STRING TO START.
235   GET A$ : IF A$ < > CHR$ (13) THEN IN$
= IN$ + A$ : GOTO 235
```

A separate solution is to use Applesoft's ability to read a string in as-is if it is prefaced with a quotation mark. We add a quote mark to the "front" of the string before it is written to the file

```
10  REM *** TEST "INPUT" WITH "," ***
20  TEXT : HOME
100  REM *** WRITE "," STRING ***
110  PRINT  CHR$ (4);"OPEN COMMA.TEST.FILE"
120  PRINT  CHR$ (4);"WRITE COMMA.TEST.FILE"
130  PRINT "YES, WE HAVE A COMMA HERE."
140  PRINT  CHR$ (4);"CLOSE"
200  REM *** READ BACK STRING ***
210  PRINT  CHR$ (4);"OPEN COMMA.TEST.FILE"
220  PRINT  CHR$ (4);"READ COMMA.TEST.FILE"
230  INPUT "";A$
240  PRINT  CHR$ (4);"CLOSE"
300  REM *** SHOW IT ***
310  PRINT "THE STRING READ BACK WAS:"
320  PRINT : PRINT
330  PRINT  CHR$ (34);A$; CHR$ (34)
340  VTAB 22
350  END
```

Listing 16-6. Testing the use of INPUT with commas.

by changing line 130 in the *original* program to read

```
130 PRINT CHR$ (34);"YES, WE HAVE A COMMA HERE."
```

which stores the string in the file as

```
"YES, WE HAVE A COMMA HERE.
```

It can then be read properly by the original INPUT statement, which will discard the leading quote and read all characters up to the next quote in the string, or the first carriage return or control-@ (ASCII *NUL*) character.

The penalty for using the GET statement is that it's slow, and that it may force garbage collection to occur more often (also slowing the program). The advantage is that the file does not have to have any extraneous quote characters saved in it, making the file more space-efficient. GET can also be used to read *any* character from the file, and (in a loop) any number of characters. This gets around INPUT's 239 character limit, if you store the characters you GET directly into memory or into several Applesoft strings. Another reason to use GET instead of the "leading quote" trick is that you don't want to have the quotes in a file that may have to be loaded into a word processor; you'll probably have to remove them. An additional advantage to GET is that it will work on existing files; the use of the "quote" trick assumes the quote marks have been placed in the file at the time of its creation.

Finally, GET can be used to read in a sequence of characters (between RETURN characters) that is too long to be read into an Applesoft INPUT statement. INPUT cannot read more than a maximum of 239 characters (a total of 255 characters will be "accepted", but the final input string will be truncated to the first 239 characters). A single Applesoft string variable cannot hold more than 255 characters, so the information from the GET loop will have to be "split" between string variables or POKEd directly into a memory buffer reserved for the purpose.

There is another "solution" pointed out by Ken Kashmarek in an article titled "ProDOS Input Anything Routine", published on page 30 of the December 1985 issue of *Call-A.P.P.L.E* magazine. It turns out that a "secret" provision of BASIC.SYSTEM 1.1 allows the use of an "L" parameter with READ commands, so that the command "READ TEXTFILE,L50" will read 50 characters from a file ignoring whether they are commas, colons, or even carriage returns (but not quotes; the BASIC.SYSTEM routine uses something akin to the "leading quote" trick). The utility of this with text files is questionable for our purposes, since you would have to know how long the string is before you could read it in. That, and some other problems, may be why the feature is not officially documented.

TEXT FILE OUTPUT AND COMMAS

As mentioned in Chapter 12, Apple's *BASIC Programming with ProDOS* says that comma tabbing to a file is not supported. "Comma tabbing" refers to the insertion of extra spaces between PRINTed quantities separated by commas, such as in "PRINT 1,4". For whatever reason, BASIC.SYSTEM 1.1 *does appear* to support comma tabbing. Unfortunately, it and Applesoft do not seem to agree upon the spacing.

Again, let's use an example to demonstrate, presented in Listing 16-7. This program, when RUN, creates a file named "TAB.FILE.TEST" and PRINTs the strings "ONE", "TWO", "THREE", and "FOUR" using commas as separators. The program then PRINTS the same line directly to the screen, and re-reads and PRINTs the line resulting from the "PRINT-to-disk-file" operation. The results in 40-column mode on an enhanced Apple *II*e look something like Fig. 16-2. In In this instance, BASIC.SYSTEM appears to tab to *approximately* every 19th column, while Applesoft tabs to every 16th column! There is nothing like predictability.

It doesn't get any better in 80 columns on an *enhanced IIe* (old *II*e's will act differently), as shown in Fig. 16-3. Here, Applesoft tabs to columns 0, 16, 32, and 48: predictably every 16th column. BASIC.SYSTEM has tabbed to columns 0, 19, 38, and 59 (?). In other words, every 19th column except for "FOUR"!

```
10  REM *** TEST "COMMA TABBING" ***
20 D$ =  CHR$ (4): REM CONTROL-D.
30  PRINT D$;"OPEN TAB.FILE.TEST"
40  PRINT D$;"WRITE TAB.FILE.TEST"
50  PRINT "ONE","TWO","THREE","FOUR"
60  PRINT  CHR$ (4);"CLOSE"
100  REM *** COMPARE FILE/SCREEN TAB ***
110  PRINT "Screen PRINT:"
120  PRINT "ONE","TWO","THREE","FOUR"
130  PRINT
140  PRINT "File PRINT:"
150  PRINT D$;"OPEN TAB.FILE.TEST"
160  PRINT D$;"READ TAB.FILE.TEST"
170  INPUT F$
180  PRINT D$;"CLOSE"
190  PRINT F$
199  END
```

Listing 16-7. Testing comma-tabbing to a file.

If you format your documents to text files via comma tabbing, you are going to find BASIC.SYSTEM's method worse than useless. The best recommendation for now is that BASIC programmers using BASIC.SYSTEM should discard comma tabbing in favor of manual formatting (insert spaces manually or by calculation) when PRINTing reports to disk files.

READING "DIR" FILES

The "T" parameter used with the OPEN command can be used to read other types of files as ASCII data; the particular file of interest is likely going to be a directory file. Listing 16-8 is a program that is meant to read *all* the directories on a disk recursively and "print" their respective CATALOGs to a sequential text file with the same filename as the volume being read.

The program assumes that we wish the filename that the data to be written to does not exist. If it already exists and is a file of type TXT, the new data will be APPENDed onto the old file (which may result in *strange* listings if it is a random access file!). If it exists and is not a text file, the program will abort after notifying you that it cannot write on the output file.

Second, the program uses the current setting of the prefix to identify which directory the output file is to be placed in. It is limited to the 64 characters allowed a ProDOS prefix; if you try to run it from a directory deeper in the hierarchy than that, only the prefix for that directory's complete pathname will be retained. For reasons explained in the introductory chapters, we do not feel this is an unfair limitation.

Lastly, a trick is used to determine the current slot number when the program is first RUN. It in-

```
Screen PRINT:
ONE             TWO             THREE
FOUR

File PRINT:
ONE                TWO                TH
REE                FOUR
```

Fig. 16-2. Results of comma-tabbing to a file (40-columns).

```
Screen PRINT:
ONE            TWO            THREE          FOUR

File PRINT:
ONE                 TWO                 THREE               FOUR
```

Fig. 16-3. Results of comma-tabbing to a file (80-columns).

```
1000  REM *** INITIALIZATION ***
1010  TEXT
1020  IF  PEEK ( - 1101) = 6 THEN  PRINT  CHR$
        (21): REM TURN OFF //E OR //C 80-COL.
1030  HOME
1040 D$ =  CHR$ (4)
1050  DIM NAME$(1000),SDIR$(1000): REM ARRAYS
        FOR PATHNAMES, SUBDIRECTORIES.
1060 VDIR = 1: REM FLAG FOR VOLUME DIRECTORY.
1070 SDIR = 0: REM FLAG/COUNT FOR SUBDIRECTORIES
        FOUND.
1080 PAD$ = "...............": REM PAD FOR
        PATHNAMES.
1090  ONERR  GOTO 3230
1100  REM *** TITLES ***
1110  PRINT
        "---------------------------------------"
1120  PRINT : PRINT  SPC( 2);"ProDOS Directory
        to Textfile Program": PRINT
1130  PRINT
        "---------------------------------------"
1140  PRINT
1150  PRINT "This program will read a ProDOS
        disk"
1160  PRINT "and write the contents of all
        direct-"
1170  PRINT "ories into a text file."
1180  PRINT
1190  PRINT "Limitations: The output pathname
        will"
1200  PRINT "be limited to a prefix of a
        maximum"
1210  PRINT "64 characters. Also, duplicate
        file-
1220  PRINT "names for the output file are not"
1230  PRINT "expected."
1240  VTAB 22: HTAB 1
1250  PRINT "Hit a key to continue (ESC exits):
        ";
1260  GET A$: PRINT
1270  IF A$ =  CHR$ (27) THEN  HOME : PRINT
        "Bye...": VTAB 22: HTAB 1: END
1280  HOME : VTAB 10: HTAB 1
```

Listing 16-8 Program to print a list of all files on a volume to a text file.

```
1290  PRINT "Determining default
       congiguration..."
1300  REM *** GET CURRENT DISK'S PREFIX ***
1310  IF EFLAG = 0 THEN  PRINT D$;"PREFIX"
1320  IF EFLAG = 1 THEN  HOME : PRINT EMESSAGE$:
       STOP : REM SHOULDN'T HAPPEN.
1330  INPUT PREFIX$: REM CURRENT PREFIX.
1340  GOSUB 1820: REM GET VOLUME NAMES (CURRENT
       SLOT).
1350  GOSUB 1720: REM CHECK FOR DRIVES.
1360  REM *** PRINT CURRENT SETUP ***
1370  HOME
1380 OSLOT$ = ",S" +  STR$ (OSLOT)
1390  IF OSLOT = 0 THEN OSLOT$ = ""
1400  VTAB 1: HTAB 1: PRINT "Output Prefix =
       ";OPREFIX$
1410 ISLOT$ = ",S" +  STR$ (ISLOT)
1420  IF ISLOT = 0 THEN ISLOT$ = ""
1430  IF IPREFIX$ = "" THEN IPREFIX$ = "<NO
       VOLUME>"
1440  VTAB 5: HTAB 1: PRINT "Last Volume Read =
       ";IPREFIX$;ISLOT$;",D";IDISK
1450  VTAB 7: HTAB 1: INVERSE : PRINT  SPC( 39):
       NORMAL : PRINT : REM DIVIDING "BAR".
1460  REM *** DO MAIN MENU ***
1470  VTAB 10: HTAB 1: PRINT "Select one of the
       following:"
1480  VTAB 13: HTAB 10: PRINT "S) To set
       slot/drive to read."
1490  VTAB 15: HTAB 10: PRINT "P) To set output
       prefix."
1500  VTAB 17: HTAB 8: PRINT "ESC) To quit the
       program."
1510  VTAB 20: PRINT "or <SPACE> to read
       <VOLUME>";ISLOT$;",D";IDISK;":";
1520  GET A$: IF A$ <  > "P" AND A$ <  > "p" AND
       A$ <  > "S" AND A$ <  > "s" AND A$ <  >
       CHR$ (27) AND A$ <  > " " THEN  GOTO 1520
1530  PRINT
1540  IF A$ = "P" OR A$ = "p" THEN  GOSUB 1930:
       GOTO 1360: REM SET OUTPUT PREFIX.
1550  IF A$ = "S" OR A$ = "s" THEN  GOSUB 2040:
       GOTO 1360: REM SET SLOT/DRIVE FOR I/O.
1560  IF A$ = " " THEN  GOSUB 2270: GOTO 1360:
       REM READ DIRECTORY.
1570  IF A$ <  > CHR$ (27) THEN  GOTO 1360: REM
       LOOP THROUGH AGAIN.
1580  REM *** EXIT TO BASIC ***
1590  HOME
1600  IF EFLAG = 0 THEN  PRINT D$;"PREFIX
       ";OPREFIX$: PRINT "Bye...": VTAB 22: POKE
       216,0: END : REM SET PREFIX TO OUTPUT
       DIRECTORY ON EXIT.
1610  IF EFLAG = 1 THEN EFLAG = 0: VTAB 10: HTAB
       1: CALL  - 958: PRINT "Please insert disk
       with path: ": PRINT : PRINT OPREFIX$:
       PRINT : PRINT "and press <RETURN>: ";
1620  GET A$: IF A$ <  >  CHR$ (13) AND A$ <  >
```

```
      CHR$ (27) THEN  GOTO 1620
1630  PRINT
1640  IF A$ =  CHR$ (13) THEN  GOTO 1590
1650  HOME
1660  PRINT "Bye ..."
1670  VTAB 22
1680  END
1690  REM
1700  REM *** SUBROUTINES, ETC. ***
1710  REM
1720  REM *** DETERMINE INPUT AND OUTPUT PREFIX
       ***
1730  IF V1$ = "" THEN  GOTO 1780
1740  IF V1$ =  LEFT$ (PREFIX$ + PAD$, LEN
       (V1$)) THEN ODRIVE = 1:OPREFIX$ = PREFIX$
1750  IF V1$ <  >  LEFT$ (PREFIX$ + PAD$, LEN
       (V1$)) THEN IDISK = 1:IPREFIX$ = V1$
1760  IF V2$ =  LEFT$ (PREFIX$ + PAD$, LEN
       (V1$)) THEN ODRIVE = 2:OPREFIX$ = PREFIX$
1770  IF V2$ <  >  LEFT$ (PREFIX$ + PAD$, LEN
       (V1$)) AND D2 THEN IDISK = 2:IPREFIX$ =
       V2$
1780  IF V2$ = "" AND V1$ <  > "" AND D2 THEN
       IDISK = 2:IPREFIX$ = V2$
1790  IF D1 AND  NOT D2 THEN IDISK = 1:IPREFIX$
       = V1$
1800  IF V1$ = "" AND V2$ = "" OR PREFIX$ <  >
       OPREFIX$ THEN  STOP : REM SHOULDN'T
       HAPPEN.
1810  RETURN
1820  REM *** READ PREFIX VOLUME(S) ***
1830 V1$ = "":V2$ = "": REM CLEAR VOLUME NAMES.
1840 D1 = 1:D2 = 1: REM ASSUME TWO DRIVES EXIST
       FOR CURRENT SLOT.
1850  IF EFLAG = 0 THEN  PRINT D$;"PREFIX,D1"
1860  IF EFLAG = 1 AND ECODE = 3 THEN D1 =
       0:EFLAG = 0: GOTO 1880: REM DEVICE NOT
       CONNECTED (DRIVE 1).
1870  IF EFLAG = 0 THEN  PRINT D$;"PREFIX":
       INPUT V1$
1880  IF EFLAG = 0 THEN  PRINT D$;"PREFIX,D2"
1890  IF EFLAG = 1 AND ECODE = 3 THEN D2 =
       0:EFLAG = 0: GOTO 1910: REM DEVICE NOT
       CONNECTED (DRIVE 2).
1900  IF EFLAG = 0 THEN  PRINT D$;"PREFIX":
       INPUT V2$
1910 EFLAG = 0: IF EFLAG = 0 THEN  PRINT
       D$;"PREFIX";PREFIX$
1920  RETURN
1930  REM *** SET PATHNAME TO WRITE ***
1940  VTAB 10: HTAB 1: CALL  - 958
1950  PRINT "Pathname?: ("; SPC( 64);")"
1960  VTAB 10: HTAB 13
1970  INPUT "";PN$
1980  IF PN$ = "" THEN  RETURN
1990  IF EFLAG = 0 THEN  PRINT D$;"PREFIX ";PN$
2000  IF EFLAG = 0 THEN  PRINT D$;"PREFIX":
       INPUT "";PN$
```

```
2010  IF EFLAG = 1 THEN EFLAG = 0: PRINT : PRINT
       "Unable to find path:": PRINT : PRINT :
       PRINT PN$: VTAB 22: PRINT "Press any key
       to exit to menu: ";: GET A$: PRINT :
       RETURN
2020 OPREFIX$ = PN$: REM SET AS NEW OUTPUT
       PREFIX.
2030  RETURN
2040  REM *** (RE)SET SLOT/DRIVE TO READ ***
2050 CDRIVE$ =  STR$ (IDISK): REM  CURRENT INPUT
       DRIVE NUMBER.
2060 CSLOT$ =  STR$ (SLOT): REM  CURRENT INPUT
       SLOT NUMBER.
2070  IF SLOT = 0 THEN CSLOT$ =  STR$ ( PEEK
       (48700)): REM DON'T KNOW SLOT (YET),
       CHEAT TO READ IT.
2080  VTAB 10: HTAB 1: CALL  - 958
2090  PRINT "Set new slot/drive to read:"
2100  VTAB 12: HTAB 8: PRINT "Slot?: ";CSLOT$
2110  VTAB 14: HTAB 7: PRINT "Drive?: ";CDRIVE$
2120  VTAB 12: HTAB 15: GET A$: IF A$ < "1" AND
       A$ > "7" AND A$ <  >  CHR$ (13) THEN 2120
2130  IF A$ =  CHR$ (13) THEN A$ = CSLOT$
2140 CSLOT$ = A$: PRINT CSLOT$
2150  VTAB 14: HTAB 15: GET A$: IF A$ < "1" AND
       A$ > "2" AND A$ <  >  CHR$ (13) THEN 2150
2160  IF A$ =  CHR$ (13) THEN A$ = CDRIVE$
2170 CDRIVE$ = A$: PRINT CDRIVE$
2180  VTAB 17: HTAB 1: PRINT  SPC(
       20);"Correct?: ";
2190  GET A$: IF A$ <  > "Y" AND A$ <  > "y" AND
       A$ <  > "N" AND A$ <  > "n" THEN 2190
2200  PRINT : IF A$ = "N" OR A$ = "n" THEN 2080
2210 EFLAG = 0: IF EFLAG = 0 THEN  PRINT
       D$;"PREFIX,S";CSLOT$;",D";CDRIVE$
2220  IF EFLAG = 0 THEN  PRINT D$;"PREFIX":
       INPUT IPREFIX$:IDISK =  VAL
       (CDRIVE$):ISLOT =  VAL (CSLOT$)
2230  IF EFLAG = 1 AND ECODE = 8 THEN EFLAG =
       0:IPREFIX$ = "<NO VOLUME>":IDISK =  VAL
       (CDRIVE$):ISLOT =  VAL (CSLOT$): REM
       DRIVE THERE BUT EMPTY (I/O ERROR).
2240  IF EFLAG = 1 AND ECODE = 3 THEN EFLAG = 0:
       VTAB 19: PRINT  CHR$ (7);EMESSAGE$: PRINT
       : PRINT "Press any key to continue: ";:
       GET A$: PRINT : GOSUB 2050: REM NO DEVICE
       AT SPECIFIED LOCATION.
2250  RETURN
2260  REM *** READ/WRITE A DIRECTORY LIST ***
2270  REM *** READ NEW VOLUME ***
2280  VTAB 10: HTAB 1: CALL  - 958: PRINT
       "Insert volume to read and press a key:
       ";: GET A$: PRINT
2290  IF A$ =  CHR$ (27) THEN  PRINT D$;"CLOSE":
       RETURN
2300 EFLAG = 0: IF EFLAG = 0 THEN  PRINT
       D$;"PREFIX";ISLOT$;",D";IDISK
```

```
2310  IF EFLAG = 1 THEN EFLAG = 0: GOTO 2280:
       REM <<I/O ERROR, ETC.>>
2320 EFLAG = 0: IF EFLAG = 0 THEN  PRINT
       D$;"PREFIX";ISLOT$;",D";IDISK
2330  PRINT D$;"PREFIX"
2340  INPUT "";IPREFIX$
2350  REM VERIFY CORRECT VOLUME.
2360  PRINT : PRINT
2370  PRINT "This is volume:"
2380  PRINT : PRINT IPREFIX$
2390  PRINT : PRINT "Is this the correct volume?
       (Y/N)";
2400  GET A$: IF A$ <  > "Y" AND A$ <  > "y" AND
       A$ <  > "N" AND A$ <  > "n" AND A$ <  >
       CHR$ (27) THEN  GOTO 2400
2410  PRINT : IF A$ =  CHR$ (27) THEN  RETURN
2420  IF A$ = "N" OR A$ = "n" THEN  GOTO 2270:
       REM TRY AGAIN.
2430  REM READY TO READ.
2440 IPREFIX$ =  LEFT$ (IPREFIX$, LEN (IPREFIX$)
       - 1)
2450 OFILE$ =  RIGHT$ (IPREFIX$, LEN (IPREFIX$)
       - 1)
2460  GOSUB 2550: REM READ DIRECTORY.
2470 VDIR = 0: REM NO LONGER READING VOLUME
       DIRECTORY.
2480 NSUB = 1: REM  NUMBER OF SUBDIRECTORY WE
       ARE READING.
2490  IF ((SDIR) AND (NSUB <  = SDIR)) THEN
       IPREFIX$ = SDIR$(NSUB): GOSUB 2550:NSUB =
       NSUB + 1: GOTO 2490
2500 SDIR = 0:VDIR = 1: REM BACK TO VOLUME
       DIRECTORY.
2510 IPREFIX$ = "/" + OFILE$ + "/": REM
       REGENERATE INPUT VOLUME NAME.
2520  HOME
2530 A$ = "": REM INSURE NO GARBAGE HERE.
2540  RETURN
2550  REM *** READ A DIRECTORY ***
2560  IF EFLAG = 0 THEN  GOSUB 3130: REM CHECK
       FOR LONG PATHNAME.
2570  IF EFLAG = 0 THEN  PRINT D$;"VERIFY
       ";IPREFIX$
2580  IF EFLAG = 1 THEN EFLAG = 0: VTAB 10: HTAB
       1: CALL  - 958: PRINT "Please insert:":
       PRINT : PRINT IPREFIX$: PRINT : PRINT
       "and press <RETURN>: ";: GET A$: IF A$ <
       >  CHR$ (13) AND A$ <  >  CHR$ (27) THEN
       2580: PRINT
2590  VTAB 10: HTAB 1: CALL  - 958: PRINT
       "Reading directory pathname:": PRINT :
       PRINT LPREFIX$;IPREFIX$
2600  GOSUB 3130: REM CHECK FOR LONG PATHNAME.
2610 NL = 4: REM FIRST LINE OF FILENAME.
2620  ONERR  GOTO 2760: REM ONERR FOR READ
       OPERATION.
2630  PRINT D$;"OPEN ";IPREFIX$;",TDIR"
```

```
2640  PRINT D$;"READ ";IPREFIX$
2650  INPUT NAME$(1),NAME$(2),NAME$(3): REM READ
       HEADER DATA.
2660  INPUT NAME$(NL): REM READ FILENAME.
2670  IF NAME$(NL) <  > "" THEN NL = NL + 1:
       GOTO 2660: REM IF NON-NULL, READ NEXT
       FILENAME.
2680 NL = NL + 1: REM POINT TO LAST LINE.
2690  INPUT NAME$(NL): REM READ SPACE STATS.
2700  PRINT D$;"CLOSE ";IPREFIX$: REM CLOSE DIR
       FILE.
2710  ONERR  GOTO 3230: REM GO BACK TO GENERAL
       ERROR HANDLER.
2720  GOSUB 2770: REM FIND AND SAVE SUBDIRECTORY
       PATHNAMES.
2730  GOSUB 2920: REM WRITE OUT DIRECTORY INFO.
2740  RETURN
2750  REM ONERR FOR READ ERROR OR MEMORY FULL
2760  GOSUB 3330: VTAB 10: HTAB 1: POKE 216,0:
       PRINT D$;"CLOSE": CALL  - 958: PRINT
       CHR$ (7);EMESSAGE$: PRINT : PRINT "Can't
       continue reading - aborted.": VTAB 22:
       CALL  - 3288: END : REM MEMORY FULL,
       I/OERROR, ETC.
2770  REM *** SCAN FOR SUBDIRECTORIES ***
2780  REM CHECK LINES WITH FILENAMES ONLY.
2790  FOR CL = 4 TO NL - 2
2800  REM SEE IF IT HAS "DIR" IN THE FILETYPE
       FIELD.
2810  IF ( MID$ (NAME$(CL),18,3) <  > "DIR")
       THEN 2900
2820  REM SCAN FILE INFO FOR FILENAME.
2830 A$ = ""
2840  FOR K = 2 TO 16
2850  IF ( MID$ (NAME$(CL),K,1) = " ") THEN 2870
2860 A$ = A$ +  MID$ (NAME$(CL),K,1)
2870  NEXT K
2880 SDIR = SDIR + 1:SDIR$(SDIR) = IPREFIX$ +
       "/" + A$
2890  IF  LEFT$ (SDIR$(SDIR),1) <  > "/" THEN
       SDIR$(SDIR) = LPREFIX$ + SDIR$(SDIR)
2900  NEXT CL
2910  RETURN
2920  REM *** PRINT DIRECTORY TO FILE ***
2930  REM CHECK FOR OUTPUT FILE.
2940  IF EFLAG = 0 THEN  PRINT D$;"PREFIX
       ";OPREFIX$: GOTO 2990
2950  IF EFLAG = 1 THEN EFLAG = 0: VTAB 10: HTAB
       1: CALL  - 958: PRINT "Please insert disk
       with path: ": PRINT : PRINT OPREFIX$:
       PRINT : PRINT "and press <RETURN>: ";
2960  GET A$: IF A$ <  >  CHR$ (13) AND A$ <  >
       CHR$ (27) THEN  GOTO 2960
2970  PRINT : IF A$ =  CHR$ (27) THEN  PRINT
       D$;"CLOSE": END
2980  IF A$ =  CHR$ (13) THEN 2940
2990  REM ADD FILENAMES TO END OF OUTPUT FILE.
```

```
3000  ONERR  GOTO 3120: REM ONERR SPECIFIC FOR
       "WRITE" PROBLEMS.
3010  PRINT D$;"APPEND ";OFILE$
3020  IF VDIR THEN  PRINT "Files for volume
       directory:"
3030  IF  NOT VDIR THEN  PRINT "Files for
       subdirectory pathname:": PRINT
       SDIR$(NSUB)
3040  PRINT : REM ONE LINE TO SEPARATE TITLE
       FROM DIRECTORY.
3050  FOR N = 1 TO NL
3060  PRINT NAME$(N)
3070  NEXT N
3080  PRINT : PRINT : REM TWO LINES TO SEPERATE
       DIRECTORIES.
3090  PRINT D$;"CLOSE ";OFILE$
3100  ONERR  GOTO 3230: REM GO BACK TO GENERAL
       ERROR HANDLER.
3110  RETURN
3120  GOSUB 3330: VTAB 10: HTAB 1: POKE 216,0:
       PRINT D$;"CLOSE": CALL  - 958: PRINT
       CHR$ (7);EMESSAGE$: PRINT : PRINT "Can't
       write on output file - aborted.": VTAB
       22: CALL  - 3288: END : REM DISK FULL,
       I/OERROR, ETC.
3130  REM *** PARSE LONG PATHNAME ***
3140  IF  LEN (IPREFIX$) < 64 THEN  RETURN : REM
       LENGTH OK.
3150 LPREFIX$ = "": REM PATHNAME PREFIX.
3160 A$ = "": REM WORKING VARIABLE.
3170 I = 64: REM START AT UPPER LIMIT.
3180  IF  MID$ (IPREFIX$,I,1) <  > "/" THEN I =
       I - 1: GOTO 3180
3190 LPREFIX$ =  LEFT$ (IPREFIX$,I): REM FIRST
       SECTION.
3200  IF EF = 0 THEN  PRINT D$;"PREFIX
       ";LPREFIX$: REM SET PREFIX TO READ.
3210 IPREFIX$ =  RIGHT$ (IPREFIX$, LEN
       (IPREFIX$) - I): REM SET PATHNAME "tail".
3220  RETURN
3230  REM *** ERROR HANDLER ***
3240  REM RESERVED VARIABLES:
3250  REM      ECODE  (FOR ERROR NUMBER)
3260  REM      EMESSAGE$ (FOR ERROR MESSAGE
       STRING)
3270  REM      EFLAG  (FOR ERROR FLAG, = 1 IF
       ERROR)
3280  REM      ELINE (FOR ERROR LINE NUMBER)
3290  GOSUB 3330: REM get error info.
3300  IF EFLAG = 1 AND ECODE = 255 THEN  VTAB
       18: HTAB 1: CALL  - 958: PRINT EMESSAGE$:
       PRINT : PRINT "at # ";ELINE".": VTAB 22:
       CALL  - 3288: POKE 216,0: END : REM EXIT
       ON CONTROL-C.
3310  RESUME
3320  STOP : REM shouldn't happen.
3330  REM *** MAKE UP ERROR STRING ***
3340 ECODE =  PEEK (222)
```

```
3350 ELINE =  PEEK (218) +  PEEK (219) * 256
3360 EMESSAGE$ = ""
3370  REM APPLESOFT ERRORS
3380  IF ECODE = 0 THEN EMESSAGE$ = "NEXT
       WITHOUT FOR"
3390  IF ECODE = 16 THEN EMESSAGE$ = "INCORRECT
       SYNTAX"
3400  IF ECODE = 22 THEN EMESSAGE$ = "RETURN
       WITHOUT GOSUB"
3410  IF ECODE = 42 THEN EMESSAGE$ = "OUT OF
       DATA"
3420  IF ECODE = 53 THEN EMESSAGE$ = "ILLEGAL
       QUANTITY"
3430  IF ECODE = 69 THEN EMESSAGE$ = "OVERFLOW"
3440  IF ECODE = 77 THEN EMESSAGE$ = "OUT OF
       MEMORY"
3450  IF ECODE = 90 THEN EMESSAGE$ = "UNDEFINED
       STATEMENT"
3460  IF ECODE = 107 THEN EMESSAGE$ = "BAD
       SUBSCRIPT"
3470  IF ECODE = 120 THEN EMESSAGE$ =
       "REDIMENSIONED ARRAY"
3480  IF ECODE = 133 THEN EMESSAGE$ = "DIVISION
       BY ZERO"
3490  IF ECODE = 163 THEN EMESSAGE$ = "TYPE
       MISMATCH"
3500  IF ECODE = 176 THEN EMESSAGE$ = "STRING
       TOO LONG"
3510  IF ECODE = 191 THEN EMESSAGE$ = "FORMULA
       TOO COMPLEX"
3520  IF ECODE = 224 THEN EMESSAGE$ = "UNDEFINED
       FN"
3530  IF ECODE = 255 THEN EMESSAGE$ = "CONTROL-C
       ABORT"
3540  REM BASIC.SYSTEM ERRORS
3550  IF ECODE = 2 THEN EMESSAGE$ = "RANGE
       ERROR"
3560  IF ECODE = 3 THEN EMESSAGE$ = "NO DEVICE
       CONNECTED"
3570  IF ECODE = 4 THEN EMESSAGE$ = "WRITE
       PROTECTED"
3580  IF ECODE = 5 THEN EMESSAGE$ = "END OF
       DATA"
3590  IF ECODE = 8 THEN EMESSAGE$ = "I/O ERROR"
3600  IF ECODE = 9 THEN EMESSAGE$ = "DISK FULL"
3610  IF ECODE = 10 THEN EMESSAGE$ = "FILE
       LOCKED"
3620  IF ECODE = 11 THEN EMESSAGE$ = "INVALID
       OPTION"
3630  IF ECODE = 12 THEN EMESSAGE$ = "NO BUFFERS
       AVAILABLE"
3640  IF ECODE = 13 THEN EMESSAGE$ = "FILE TYPE
       MISMATCH"
3650  IF ECODE = 14 THEN EMESSAGE$ = "PROGRAM
       TOO LARGE"
3660  IF ECODE = 15 THEN EMESSAGE$ = "NOT DIRECT
       COMMAND": REM SUPERFLUOUS.
3670  IF ECODE = 16 THEN EMESSAGE$ = "INCORRECT
```

```
        SYNTAX": REM REDUNDANT.
3680  IF ECODE = 17 THEN EMESSAGE$ = "DIRECTORY
        FULL"
3690  IF ECODE = 18 THEN EMESSAGE$ = "FILE NOT
        OPEN"
3700  IF ECODE = 19 THEN EMESSAGE$ = "DUPLICATE
        FILENAME"
3710  IF ECODE = 20 THEN EMESSAGE$ = "FILE BUSY"
3720  IF ECODE = 21 THEN EMESSAGE$ = "FILE(S)
        STILL OPEN"
3730 EFLAG = 1
3740  IF (ECODE = 0 OR ECODE > 21) THEN
        EMESSAGE$ = "A/S error: " + EMESSAGE$
3750  IF (ECODE > 0 AND ECODE < 21 AND ECODE <
        > 16) THEN EMESSAGE$ = "BASIC.SYSTEM
        error: " + EMESSAGE$
3760  IF (ECODE = 16) THEN EMESSAGE$ = "A/S or
        BASIC.SYSTEM error: " + EMESSAGE$
3770  RETURN
```

volves PEEKing at the BASIC.SYSTEM Global Page, a subject we'll cover in detail in Part IV.

The actual routine that reads the directory begins at 2560; it sets the appropriate prefix for the pathname (including a pathname of up to 128 characters!), checks for the path, and starts reading the directory. Line 2630 OPENs the file of type DIR and reads the first three lines (thedirectory name, column headings and "blank line" separator). Lines 2660-2670 read each line as filename data until a blank line (which separates the last filename from the "disk space" data) is read. Then the disk space statistics are read in as the last line in lines 2680-2690. Line 2700 then CLOSEs the directory file.

Many REM statements have been added throughout the program (some for the author's benefit) which may help trace the rest of the program's activities. A good portion of the program is concerned with detecting and parsing input and output pathnames, along with error checking.

If the program is used with a hard disk drive with a *lot* of files, it may terminate with an Applesoft "?MEMORY FULL" error; the exact limitation in terms of the number of files the program can handle within a directory is untested. Each directory is read and "printed" to the disk file in sequence, but the number of subdirectory names could theoretically also accrue to fill memory.

Part 4

BASIC.SYSTEM and Machine Language

Chapter 17

Speaking Native to the 6502

This book is essentially about BASIC.SYSTEM, but here we start to wrestle quite a bit with machine language. One common question among BASIC programmers is why *anyone* would want to go through the headaches of programming in machine (or assembly) language. It's certainly a lot easier to enter the Applesoft statement PRINT "HELLO" than the equivalent machine language code. Why would anyone want to work harder than they have to?

The secret is *not* to work any harder than you have to. If you are an ace hacker, you might prefer to do all your coding in assembly language. But, for the large majority of us, the trick is to do as much as possible in the high level language (BASIC, in this case) and only use machine language routines when absolutely necessary. In particular, we need to know where to split the duties with BASIC.SYSTEM. So let's see what criteria help us make the choice.

BASIC POWER

BASIC is often spoken of as a *powerful* language. *Powerful* is an oft-misused and misinterpreted adjective found in advertisements for computer software (usually, the equally misleading term *user-friendly* can be found nearby). What "power" are they referring to?

First, realize that "power" is a relative term. My Apple is a lot more powerful than my programmable pocket calculator in terms of text processing, but the calculator will beat the Apple into the ground on several types of calculations in terms of both accuracy and speed. The "power" of BASIC, or any computer language, has to always be considered relative to another computer language. It boils down to the comparative ability of the two languages to perform a certain task or set of tasks.

BASIC is one of a set of *high level* computer languages. Other high-level languages are FORTRAN, Pascal, FORTH, LISP, and COBOL; this is only a small list of a burgeoning group of languages developed over the last 30 to 40 years. Each of these these languages has strengths and weaknesses; FORTRAN is best at calculations (number crunching), COBOL was designed for business uses, FORTH was designed for programming mechanical control functions, etc.

An adept programmer in any of these languages can do almost anything with it, including things it possibly was not designed for, and may indeed insist that his one favorite language is the best at all things. Still, the fact that so many different languages have survived indicates that none of them is "the best", or the others would simply crawl off and die.

BASIC started out as a "training" language to help people learn about programming. It borrowed a lot of its mathematical functions from FORTRAN; and additional features were added to help with handling string data, which was awkward to do in the original FORTRAN.

BASIC had the advantage of usually being used as an *interpretive* language, where each time you entered a command or program statement it was immediately prepared in an executable form so that commands could be issued directly from the keyboard, and a program, once entered, could be executed without any additional processing.

Most of the older high-level languages, like COBOL and FORTRAN, were usually implemented as *compiled* languages. The program was entered as text just as if you were writing a letter, then the non-executable text file had to be specially processed by a program called a *compiler* to make a separate, executable form of the program when you were ready to test the program. The executable form could be saved, but anytime the program had to be changed, the original text file had to be edited, saved, and then subjected to the compiler again to produce a new executable file which contained the changes to the program. The procedure is just as complicated and time consuming as it sounds.

WHY YOU HAVE A BASIC PERSONAL COMPUTER

The attractive features of BASIC for personal computers were these:

1. The language was easy to learn. Personal computers were, by definition, intended to be used by individuals. Most individuals, contrary to some of the present distressing opinions of computer manufacturers, are capable of learning and using BASIC to help them solve problems themselves, in their own glorious way.
2. The language's interpreter was able to "fit" into the relatively small memory space of the first personal computers. It could even be made a semi-permanent part of the computer by putting it into ROM memory, as has been done on the Apple.
3. The language was powerful enough (there's that phrase again!) to be able to do most things that people needed to do. That is, the commands available in the language could be put together in programs that would do most of the useful things that people wanted to do with the computer.

There are now larger personal computers that can run other languages, but BASIC has been retained because of the ease with which the language can be learned and used, and the fact that it still can "get the job done" for a lot of programming.

BASIC PROBLEMS

Now, to balance things out, we have to cover the *bad* points of BASIC.

First, it's usually *slow*. This is true because of the way BASIC interpreters are written; in other words, it's usually difficult to write an interpreted language that's as fast as a compiled language. The interpreter has to translate every BASIC action each time the program is RUN and a statement is executed; a compiler does this translation only *once* when the program is compiled. You can find compilers that will operate using BASIC as their language, but that eliminates much of the simplicity of the language.

Second, you just can't *do* certain things easily with BASIC. You can't write an operating system (like ProDOS) in Applesoft BASIC. Part of this has to do with BASIC's slowness; part has to do with the inability of BASIC to access certain features of the Apple hardware directly.

Third, BASIC programs take up a lot of space; they just aren't very efficient at memory usage. You may not think that PRINT "HELLO" takes up more room than the equivalent machine code, but you have to remember that (in the case of Applesoft) you have to have the 10 kilobyte interpreter present in order to translate the program. Without that 10K interpreter, the program won't run.

Still, BASIC will work nicely for a lot of microcomputer work. The *computer* is so fast that even "slow" BASIC seems fast enough. Memory space usage is not a big hassle for a lot of programs. So why use assembly language?

ASSEMBLING FOR FUN AND PROFIT

We now come to a *low level language* which solves the three limitations of BASIC. This langauge is known, sometimes interchangeably, as *machine language* or *assembly language*. Actually, machine language and assembly language *aren't* the same thing. *Machine language* is the more abstract form, it consists of the actual codes that have to be fed to the microcomputer chip in order to make the chip perform certain functions. These "codes" we represent on paper (or on the monitor) usually in some kind of numeric format; in the case of the Apple we use *hexadecimal* codes. In real life, however, all our little 6502 MPU sees is the electrical signals that these codes actually produce when they are used.

Assembly language is what programmers use to avoid entering machine code directly. Assembly language uses English-like statements that are easier to read than the hex codes that machine code requires. Assembly language programs are entered as text commands and later processed by a program called an *assembler* that converts the text into a set of codes that the MPU understands. This code set can then be loaded into the computer memory and executed.

As an example, the hex codes "A9 00" when executed as instructions tell our friendly 6502 mentor to load a value of "00" (hex) into a memory cell in the 6502 for later use. The equivalent assembly language instruction is "LDA #$00", which would be converted to the code form by the assembler. Since the distinction is sometimes not as clear as all of this implies, you will probably find us using the phrases "machine code", "machine language", and "assembly language" nearly interchangeably. The previous information will allow you to discern that we are not always being literally correct in our usage.

MACHINE LANGUAGE ADVANTAGES

The advantages of machine language are, in three words: *speed, flexibility*, and *efficiency*. Machine language is the ultimate language of the MPU chip, so it requires no further translation. We are already speaking the MPU's language. Since no translator is needed, there is no slowdown while we wait for an instruction to be converted to use the MPU's vocabulary. That means more speed.

Also, machine language can use *only* those features of the computer that it needs and *only* the precise instructions needed to perform a task. That usually means fewer instructions, which means smaller, faster programs. We also do not need the memory required by an interpreter for a high-level language.

We should also mention that compilers are usually not 100% efficient. Since a compiler has to be able to handle a wide variety of commands with a limited number of permitted "phrasings" for its text statements, it usually ends up compromising on efficiency by making its translations as general as possible. This means the compiler's output code file may include a lot of "safety" code to handle conditions that will never arise from our program. Since machine code is always being told *directly what we specifically mean, it does not put in this "extra" code, and should use the minimum amount of memory.*

Lastly, machine code has full access to the MPU. Whereas BASIC cannot give the MPU direct instructions outside of what the interpreter allows, machine language can command the MPU to do any task the MPU can be programmed for. Therefore, in terms of the *true* power to be able to command the MPU, machine code is "king".

IF IT'S SO GREAT, WHY NOT USE IT?

Machine code is used a great deal: the Applesoft BASIC interpreter is made up of it, as is BASIC.SYSTEM, ProDOS, and the monitor program. But use of machine code has one *big* disadvantage. There are about 150 individual instruction codes available for the 6502 (more for the 65C02 processor used in the *II*c and enhanced *II*e computers), comparable to the many commands for BASIC. But each 6502 command doesn't do very much. And there's the rub.

Looking back at PRINT, if we tell BASIC to PRINT "HELLO", the BASIC interpreter does all the work of PRINTing the word HELLO. If we try to do the same function in machine language, here's a rough approximation of the procedure:

1. Determine the starting address of "HELLO" in memory.
2. Point to and get the first character of "HELLO" (the "H").
3. Put the character on the output device (the screen, for example).
4. Get the next character of "HELLO" (the "E").
5. Put the character on the output device.
6. Get the next character of "HELLO" (the first "L") . . .

You get the idea. *Almost*, because the actual program has to be broken down into many more and simpler steps than those above to actually work! Obviously, this becomes tedious.

Secondly, the BASIC interpreter handles a great many things for you painlessly. It decides where to put things in memory so that they don't collide, it finds them for you later, it knows where to get input and where to send output (usually), etc. If you use machine language, even with the help of an assembler, *you must keep track of all memory usage yourself*, on a byte- by-byte basis.

Lastly, assembly language programs are often troublesome to debug. BASIC catches most common errors and notifies you; most of this help is absent from assembly language work. Additionally, a machine language program presented to you *only* as the finished binary file (that is, without the source text listing) can be *very* cryptic if you have to figure out how it functions and modify it.

MACHINE LANGUAGE WITH BASIC.SYSTEM

In particular, there are a few tasks that cannot be satisfactorily handled entirely from BASIC programs using BASIC.SYSTEM because they have been designed as responsibilities for the ProDOS MLI.

Some operations are best performed by using ProDOS MLI calls. For example, retrieving some file information (such as the "R" and "ENDFILE" information listed in the directory) can be tedious from BASIC, which would require reading in the directory, selecting out the filename string with the information we need, and parsing the string for the specific items desired. There is an equivalent MLI function (GET_FILE_INFO) that can perform the same task more efficiently in terms of both program space and speed.

Some tasks can *only* be performed by MLI calls. The MLI GET_TIME call that updates the ProDOS time and date values in memory has no equivalent in BASIC. Proper support of *interrupts* (special signals to the 6502, described in Chapter 25) also requires the use of MLI calls.

THE BEST COMPROMISE

With the above in mind, it seems that the best thing to do is to stick with a high-level language until you need machine language's abilities. You can then "turn over" control to a machine language subroutine via Applesoft's "CALL" statement, and let the machine language program do its thing. When it finishes, it sends control back to BASIC. It's this compromise approach that we generally will try to use when programming the Apple under either DOS or ProDOS/BASIC.SYSTEM.

Despite occasional diatribes by some Apple programmers that BASIC is "unsuitable" for commercial software, much commercial software for DOS and ProDOS continues to be based on at least partial use of BASIC, usually with assembly language support routines.

Chapter 18

The BASIC.SYSTEM Global Page

Direct access to BASIC.SYSTEM internals is possible but not recommended. Unlike DOS 3.3, BASIC.SYSTEM and ProDOS were both designed so that the internal location of routines could be moved at will to facilitate changes in the respective programs. It has already happened at least once with the BASIC.SYSTEM program; the locations of internal routines were changed in moving from BASIC.SYSTEM version 1.0 to version 1.1.

Fortunately, as part of the new ProDOS design, several of the common functions of BASIC.SYSTEM (and ProDOS) were made accessible through the creation of *global pages* which contain ongoing status information for each of the respective system programs, and allow for interfacing machine language routines directly to each. Also, a series of page 3 locations from $3D0 to $3FF have been set aside for accessing various system functions.

The BASIC.SYSTEM global page is established as locations $BE00 to $BEFF of the BASIC.SYSTEM interpreter. For most of the addresses we describe, we will also provide the decimal equivalent of the address (or address range) to facilitate accessing the locations via Applesoft PEEKs. The initial description is primarily a narration; a disassembly of a sample BASIC.SYSTEM global page is provided at the end of this chapter.

ENTERING BASIC.SYSTEM

Several vectors exist in the BASIC.SYSTEM global page which allow calling BASIC.SYSTEM functions. Some of these are accessible from BASIC and some require machine language to use. The addresses of these routines will be given in decimal (for BASIC CALL statements) and in hexadecimal (for machine language JSR usage).

There is a "warmstart" reentry to BASIC.SYSTEM at $BE00 (48640), which has the same effect as an entry vector at $3D0 (976). This vector will activate BASIC.SYSTEM. It can also be called from the monitor with a "BE00G" or "3D0G" command— in this case, the Applesoft prompt will replace the monitor's prompt and BASIC.SYSTEM will be hooked into the I/O stream. If an Applesoft program was in memory before you entered the monitor and you have left the program and its pointers undisturbed, it will *not* be cleared from memory by this vector. Any active *variables*, however, will be cleared (from recognition by Applesoft) from the BASIC variable workspace.

Two JMP vectors in page 3 point directly to this warmstart vector. Under DOS 3.3, performing a "3D0G" command while in the monitor would cause you to re-enter DOS with your Applesoft program intact. "3D3G" would cause you to re-enter Applesoft but your program would be gone and the Applesoft workspace would be initialized. With BASIC.SYSTEM, *both* of these commands return you to BASIC.SYSTEM with the program intact, as will a direct "BE00G". In addition to these vectors, the Apple's "reset" vector at $3F2-$3F4 is pointed to $BE00 (the last of the three bytes is used to verify the validity of the vector). There is no equivalent to the "3D3G" entry.

There is also no equivalent to the "3EAG" command (or "CALL 1002") used to re-install DOS 3.3 into the input/output "hooks" when it stopped recognizing commands. BASIC.SYSTEM is a little harder to "unhook", so this is less of a problem.

CALLING CAPTAIN BASIC

Remember all the talk of the "I/O stream" that BASIC.SYSTEM monitors? Here is the main routine that keeps throwing "SYNTAX ERROR" messages at all your typos. At 48643 ($BE03) there is a vector named *DOSCMD* used to call the BASIC.SYSTEM command line interpreter routine (named *SYNTAX*). SYNTAX is the routine that takes the current input line and attempts to execute it as input to BASIC.SYSTEM.

There is another use for this vector; it can be exploited to "trick" BASIC.SYSTEM into thinking a command issued as a line of text from machine language has been "typed" at the keyboard. The trick goes like this; store the text of your command as negative (high-bit set) ASCII into the input buffer at $200, including the terminating carriage return. For example;

```
RUN STARTUP]
```

(the "]" signifies the carriage return). This is where a normal command goes when you type it into the computer in immediate mode. When the command is ready, do a JSR $BE03 and BASIC.SYSTEM will execute the command just as if it had been typed in.

THE ERROR RETURNS

If your command has a problem executing, BASIC.SYSTEM will *still* return you to your machine language program after the JSR $BE03 call, just as with any subroutine ending with an RTS. It is then *your* responsibility to find out what happened.

The 6502 accumulator will hold the error code on BASIC.SYSTEM's return from attempting to execute the command. If the code is non-zero, then something went wrong. The numeric value of the error code conveniently matches that of the normal BASIC.SYSTEM error codes that you see appear in zero page location 222 after an error. Location $BE0C is also used directly by BASIC.SYSTEM to hold the error code, and should contain the same number.

Unless you want to write your own error-handler to provide notification of the type of error, you can have BASIC.SYSTEM print out its standard error message for you from machine language while you still have the error code in the accumulator. Just do a JSR $BE0C with the error code still fresh in the accumulator; this calls a subroutine in BASIC.SYSTEM that prints its error message corresponding to the code in A.

If you wish BASIC.SYSTEM's normal error handling to be called just as if the command had been issued from a BASIC program PRINT statement, you can JSR $BE09, which turns control over to the BASIC.SYSTEM error handler.

If you don't "take care of business" and the machine language subroutine that executed the errant command was CALLed from a BASIC program, the error will still be waiting for you when you return to BASIC with an RTS. As soon as the next statement after the CALL is ready to be executed, BASIC.SYSTEM will let you know that something went awry.

Listing 18-1 contains a short sample program

```
                ********************************
                *                              *
                * Sample call to BASIC.SYSTEM  *
                * Assembler: Merlin Pro        *
                *                              *
                ********************************
                                        ;
                DOSCMD   =     $BE03    ; BASIC.SYSTEM
        "input" call.
                PRINTERR =     $BE0C    ; Print BASIC.SYSTEM
        error.
                INPUT    =     $200     ; Input buffer.
                                        ;
                                        ;
                         ORG   $803
0803: 20 1D 08           JSR   SENDCMD  ; Send next string to
        buffer.
0806: D2 D5 CE           ASC   "RUN STARTUP"
0809: A0 D3 D4 C1 D2 D4 D5 D0
0811: 8D                 HEX   8D
0812: 20 03 BE           JSR   DOSCMD   ; Call BASIC.SYSTEM
        command line scanner.
0815: D0 01              BNE   BASERR   ; If A non-zero on
        return, print error.
0817: 60                 RTS
                                        ;
0818: 20 0C BE  BASERR   JSR   PRINTERR ; Have BASIC.SYSTEM
        print error message.
081B: 18                 CLC            ; Clear carry for
        Applesoft.
081C: 60                 RTS
                                        ;
081D: 68        SENDCMD  PLA            ; Pull call address
        off stack and save.
081E: 85 06              STA   $06
0820: 68                 PLA
0821: 85 07              STA   $07
0823: A0 00              LDY   #$00     ; Set Y up as
        counter.
0825: C8        LOADCMD  INY
0826: B1 06              LDA   ($06),Y  ; Load first
        character of string.
0828: 99 FF 01           STA   INPUT-1,Y ; Save it in INPUT.
082B: C9 8D              CMP   #$8D     ; Is it <return>?
082D: D0 F6              BNE   LOADCMD  ; No, stuff next
        character.
082F: 98                 TYA            ; Done, add Y to
        return address.
0830: 18                 CLC
0831: 65 06              ADC   $06
0833: 85 06              STA   $06
0835: 90 02              BCC   EXIT1
0837: E6 07              INC   $07
```

Listing 18-1. Assembly source to "RUN STARTUP" via a call to SYNTAX.

```
0839: A5 07      41   EXIT1    LDA   $07         ; Stuff new return
         address on stack.
083B: 48         42            PHA
083C: A5 06      43            LDA   $06
083E: 48         44            PHA
083F: 60         45            RTS               ; Go back to byte
         after string.


--End assembly, 61 bytes, Errors: 0


Symbol table - alphabetical order:

   BASERR  =$0818      DOSCMD  =$BE03      EXIT1    =$0839      INPUT
         =$0200
   LOADCMD =$0825      PRINTERR=$BE0C      SENDCMD =$081D


Symbol table - numerical order:

   INPUT   =$0200      BASERR  =$0818      SENDCMD =$081D
         LOADCMD =$0825
   EXIT1   =$0839      DOSCMD  =$BE03      PRINTERR=$BE0C
```

to execute the "RUN STARTUP" command from machine language.

NON-IMMEDIATE PROBLEMS

There is a problem with BASIC.SYSTEM's literal-mindedness: unless an Applesoft program is actually perceived to be RUNning as this command is used, deferred-only commands like OPEN, READ, WRITE, APPEND, etc. won't work. BASIC.SYSTEM will detect that a BASIC program is not running and respond NOT DIRECT COMMAND. There are a few theoretical ways around this:

1. Always CALL your machine language program from a BASIC program. Even if the only program line is a CALL statement, the fact that a BASIC program is RUNning will keep BASIC.SYSTEM off your back.
2. Set the necessary flags in BASIC.SYSTEM's global page locations to indicate a BASIC program is running, even though one isn't.
3. Change the definition of the deferred-only commands to so that they may be used as immediate commands.

These are listed in approximate order of severe side-effects. The first method is "safe", since your programs are in control of the situation. The second method is a little more risky in that the locations that are changed need to be changed back when you exit your program; you don't want to leave BASIC.SYSTEM misinformed about the state of things.

The last method is not recommended as it involves making rash modifications to BASIC.SYSTEM's normal way of doing things, and the changes have to be made internally to BASIC.SYSTEM. Rather than doing this, it is better to use the ProDOS MLI to OPEN the file, etc. (an example will be presented in Chapter 20). The MLI does not care about the state of a BASIC program as far as carrying out commands.

The global page location to change to make BASIC.SYSTEM think a program is running is $BE42 (48706). This location will contain a $00 if no BASIC program is perceived as executing. Simply set the register to a non-zero value to make BASIC.SYSTEM believe a BASIC program is RUNning and deferred-mode commands are permitted.

It would seem one could change this byte to a non-zero value to execute a series of indirect-only commands, then change it back (IMPORTANT!) before returning to immediate-mode BASIC. It turns out that this technique does work for OPEN, but certain other commands that perform file I/O fail to work (see Cecil Fretwell's article on page 19 of the August 1985 issue of *Call-A.P.P.L.E.* for a lengthier description of the problems encountered). Therefore, it's probably best to avoid this method until Apple (or someone else) documents a way to make it work.

After eliminating the last two options, it seems the safest way to issue deferred-mode commands from machine language is to CALL the machine language program from a BASIC program. This seems to be somewhat redundant, as it might be suitable just to issue BASIC.SYSTEM commands from the BASIC program itself. While in machine language,the MLI can be used.

PEEKING AT THE GLOBAL PAGE

There is also a lot of information in the global page about the status of things. These can be read from machine language to check "where things are" while your program is executing. They also can be PEEKed (safe) or POKEd at (which could be disastrous) from BASIC programs.

The default slot and drive values are kept in $BEC3 (48835) and $BE3D (48836) respectively. These will be set to $06 and $01 immediately after booting from slot 6; and will change when the defaults are changed by a command which specifies a new slot and drive, such as CAT S6,D2. When PREFIX is used with a pathname to find a specified volume, the slot and drive to which the volume is assigned (or found) will be placed here. Incidentally, in our program to read directory files earlier in the book, a "PEEK (48835)" was used to detect the default slot number. This is the only easy way to determine it without user intervention.

$BE41 (48705) is a flag indicating whether the Applesoft TRACE display is enabled. If non-zero, TRACE line numbers are sent to the Apple screen or other current output device. If zero, the TRACE output is not seen, but remember that BASIC.SYSTEM keeps TRACE going "behind the scenes" for its own use.

$BE42 (48706) is the aforementioned register that holds the status of immediate versus deferred mode for BASIC, it is $00 if no BASIC program is currently running.

$BE43 (48707) through $BE4F (48719) hold status information for various functions of BASIC.SYSTEM. For file and command statuses, a $00 means no activity and a value grater than $80 means the named status is "active". Other bytes may contain straight data. The assignments are shown in Table 18-1.

For external commands, $BE50-51 (48720-48721) contains the execution address for the command's code, $BE52 (48722) contains the length of the command text string minus one (for example, the length of "NEWCOMMAND" would be $09), and $BE53 (48723) contains the number of the BASIC.SYSTEM command last issued; "00" for an external command (data). The installation of external commands is discussed in Chapter 20.

The next two pairs of bytes at $BE54-55 (48724-48725) and $BE56-57 (48726-48727) hold the permitted parameters and entered parameters for a BASIC.SYSTEM command. These will also be discussed with external commands.

$BE58-$BE6E (48728-48750) hold the last-entered values for the parameters entered with BASIC.SYSTEM commands, as shown in Table 18-2.

For multi-byte parameters (that is, those using more than a single byte), the values are stored into the parameter entry in the reverse order of their significance. As an example, the parameter entry "B$123456" would be stored in $BE5A-$BE5C in the order "56 34 12".

The "V" parameter is generally ignored; the reason it is present at all is to increase compatibility with older DOS 3.3 programs being ported to ProDOS/BASIC.SYSTEM. DOS 3.3 programs use a "volume" parameter which we allude to in the Appendix comparing DOS and ProDOS/BASIC.SYSTEM. BASIC.SYSTEM will allow inputting the parameter but ignores it, thereby eliminating some SYNTAX ERROR messages. Since DOS 3.3 programs using disk commands

Table 18-1. BASIC.SYSTEM Global Page File Status Registers.

$BE43	EXEC file active (status)
$BE44	Input file active (status)
$BE45	Output file active (status)
$BE46	Prefix active (status)
$BE47	Directory file being accessed (status)
$BE48	End of directory data reached (status)
$BE49	Index to free string space (in kilobytes) (data)
$BE4A	Character count for WRITE's temporary buffer (data)
$BE4B	Current character count during keyboard entry (data)
$BE4C	ASCII code of last character sent to output (used in error detection) (data)
$BE4D	Number of open files (does not include an EXEC file) (data)
$BE4E	EXEC file is being closed (status)
$BE4F	DIR file is being read (status)

usually have other problems, this feature is of limited use, one might as well remove *all* non-BASIC.SYSTEM syntax at once. Gary Little, in *ProDOS: Advanced Features for Programmers*, does reveal a bug in the use of "V" with the "@" parameter; they cannot be used together. The bottom line: forget "V"; lose it when converting DOS 3.3 BASIC programs to use with BASIC.SYSTEM.

Table 18-2. Parameter Value Storage Registers.

$BE58-59	A (address)
$BE5A-5C	B (byte offset)
$BE5D-5E	E ("end")
$BE5F-60	L (length)
$BE61	S (slot number)
$BE62	D (drive number)
$BE63-64	F (field)
$BE65-66	R (record)
$BE67	V (volume - see below)
$BE68-69	@ (for BASIC line number execution)
$BE6A	T (numeric value for the file type specification)
$BE6B	IN# or PR# "slot" value

```
10  REM *** READ PATHNAME FROM BUFFER ***
20 P1BUF =  PEEK (48748) +  PEEK (48749) * 256:
      REM PATHNAME BUFFER 1.
30 P2BUF =  PEEK (48750) +  PEEK (48751) * 256:
      REM PATHNAME BUFFER 2.
100  REM *** READ PATHNAME ***
110 LNAME =  PEEK (P1BUF): REM FIRST BYTE IS
      NAME LENGTH.
120 NAME$ = "": REM EMPTY NAME VARIABLE.
130  FOR I = P1BUF + 1 TO P1BUF + LNAME
140 NAME$ = NAME$ +  CHR$ ( PEEK (I) + 128)
150  NEXT I
200  REM *** PRINT RESULT ***
210  PRINT "The pathname in buffer 1 is:"
220  PRINT
230  PRINT  CHR$ (34);NAME$; CHR$ (34)
```

Listing 18-2. Reading a pathname from BASIC.SYSTEM's primary buffer.

The pathname buffers used by BASIC.SYSTEM are pointed to in vectors at $BE6C-BE6D (for the primary pathname) and $BE6E-$BE6F (the secondary pathname). The pathnames consist of a byte which gives the length of the pathname, followed by the pathname itself.

The primary pathname buffer is used for most BASIC.SYSTEM commands where a single pathname is required, such as DELETE, RENAME, RUN, etc. The secondary pathname buffer is used by BASIC.SYSTEM to hold the second pathname required by RENAME. It is also supposed to be used by programmers to hold the value of the prefix while switching *system* programs, as in switching from BASIC.SYSTEM to CONVERT (a system utility on the ProDOS/USERS.DISK).

Apple's literature doesn't bother to tell you where the pathnames are located; it turns out that the primary pathname is sensibly kept within BASIC.SYSTEM itself. This buffer may be moved in future versions of BASIC.SYSTEM.

The secondary pathname is not as sensibly kept in the upper half of the keyboard input buffer at $200, the pathname buffer is actually $280-$2FF. This will cause us headaches later when we talk about clock drivers. This usage has been the same in both BASIC.SYSTEM 1.0 and 1.1.

The current pathname in either of these buffers could be read very easily from either BASIC or machine language, and the current prefix extracted. From BASIC, reading the prefix is easy using the PREFIX command, but from machine language it may be easier to check the primary buffer for it. If you have a *long* pathname, however, the only way to recover it may be by scanning the buffer and reconstructing it. Even the PREFIX command will only let you recover no more than 64 characters if the currently set prefix points to the correct path.

The program in Listing 18-2 attempts to extract the pathname from the primary pathname buffer. There is an anomaly: the program works fine if it is RUN from disk, but not when RUN while resident in memory. If RUN from a disk file with a command such as "RUN READ.BUF.NAME", the program will identify the pathname as "/PROG/READ.BUF.NAME", where "/PROG/" is the volume name. If the program is immediately executed again while in memory with the Applesoft "RUN" command, the name printed in response is "RUN<cr>G /READ.BUF.NAME", where "<cr>" indicates a carriage return. Apparently the buffer is also used in BASIC.SYSTEM's parsing of Applesoft command input, and the "RUN" (followed by a carriage return) we typed has overwritten the first four characters of the pathname ("/PRO").

At $BEE0 (48864) is the text string "(C) 1983 COPYRIGHT APPLE COMPUTER" which is probably included as copyright notification (incidentally, this is *not* the copyright string printed when "VERIFY" is used as a command with no pathname).

OTHER STUFF

Two more subroutine vectors that exist in the global page are for GETBUFR ($BEF5-F7) and FREEBUFR ($BEF8-FA), which are used in managing the Apple's program memory space, a subject we'll attack in the next chapter. In addition, the section of the global page from $BE70 through $BEDE is taken up with code to allow BASIC.SYSTEM to call the ProDOS MLI (well, it has to get to the disk *somehow*), another subject that will be taken up (briefly) later in Part V, which describes some elements of ProDOS proper.

Incidentally, Apple's *ProDOS Technical Reference Manual* calls "FREEBUFR", the name used in Apple's *ProDOS Technical Note #9*, by the name "FREBUFR"; take your pick.

BASIC.SYSTEM GLOBAL PAGE DISASSEMBLY

Listing 18-3 is a disassembly of a real, live BASIC.SYSTEM Global page for BASIC.SYSTEM 1.1. The page appears in the state it was in at the time of a "BSAVE GLOBAL.PAGE.O,A$BE00, L$100,D2" command (used to save the page) and all data contained in it is set accordingly. This listing is included as an exemplar for the descriptions in this chapter. The disassembly was performed with the aid of the SOURCEROR utility program provided with the *Merlin Pro* macroassembler.

```
********************************
*                              *
* BASIC.SYSTEM 1.1 GLOBAL PAGE *
*                              *
********************************
                               ;
                               ;
* The following is a disassembly of an example
BASIC.SYSTEM
* global page from BASIC.SYSTEM 1.1. The state
of the page
* is preserved in the form in which it was
saved via a
* "BSAVE GLOBAL.PAGE.0,A$BE00,L$100" command,
and all
* parameters, etc. are set accordingly.
                               ;
                               ;
* Most of the following entry points to
BASIC.SYSTEM are
* defined for use. Unlabeled entry points (such
as $ABF1
* for BASIC.SYSTEM version 1.1 warmstart entry)
are left
* as such since their internal location may
change in later
* revisions. These addresses should NOT be
"called"; they
* they should only be accessed by calling the
BASIC.SYSTEM
* global page vectors.
```

Listing 18-3. A BASIC.SYSTEM global page disassembly.

```
                                     ;
             WARMDOS  =     $ABF1
             MLI      =     $BF00
             KEYIN    =     $FD1B
             COUT1    =     $FDF0
                                     ;
                      19-DEC-85  18:46
                                     ;
                      ORG   $BE00
                                     ;
             * BASIC.SYSTEM entry call vectors, available
        for user
             * programs.
                                     ;
BE00: 4C F1 AB   CI_ENTRY JMP   WARMDOS    ; Warm entry vector.
BE03: 4C 77 A6   DOSCMD   JMP   $A677      ; Routine to parse
        command line.
BE06: 4C 9E BE   EXTRNCMD JMP   XRETURN    ; Vector to parse
        external command.
                                           ; (pointed to known
        RTS here).
BE09: 4C F0 9A   ERROUT   JMP   $9AF0      ; Jump to error
        handler.
BE0C: 4C 88 9F   PRINTERR JMP   $9F88      ; Routine to print
        error message for code in A.
BE0F: 00         ERRCODE  HEX   00         ; Storage for error
        code encountered.
                                           ;
             * The following tables list the output and
        input vectors
             * assigned for each slot. Normally, they point
        to "$Cn00"
             * for each slot that contains a firmware ROM
        identifiable
             * to BASIC.SYSTEM, or the routine "NODEVERR" if
        no ROM
             * has been identified (NODEVERR produces the
        "NO DEVICE
             * CONNECTED" error when executed). These
        vectors can be
             * altered via the "IN#n,A$addr" and
        "PR#n,A$addr" commands.
                                           ;
BE10: F0 FD      OUTVEC   DA    COUT1      ; Vector used for
        "slot 0" output.
BE12: 00 C1               DA    $C100      ; Slot 1.
BE14: 00 C2               DA    $C200      ; Slot 2.
BE16: 00 C3               DA    $C300      ; Slot 3.
BE18: 00 C4               DA    $C400      ; Slot 4.
BE1A: EE 9A               DA    $9AEE      ; Slot 5.
BE1C: 00 C6               DA    $C600      ; Slot 6.
BE1E: 00 C7               DA    $C700      ; Slot 7.
BE20: 1B FD      INVEC    DA    KEYIN      ; Vector used for
        "slot 0" input.
BE22: 00 C1               DA    $C100      ; Slot 1.
BE24: 00 C2               DA    $C200      ; Slot 2.
BE26: 00 C3               DA    $C300      ; Slot 3.
BE28: 00 C4               DA    $C400      ; Slot 4.
```

```
BE2A: EE 9A                DA    $9AEE       ; Slot 5.
BE2C: 00 C6                DA    $C600       ; Slot 6.
BE2E: 00 C7                DA    $C700       ; Slot 7.
                                             ;
                 * The following two vectors are the output and input vectors
                 * currently in use by BASIC.SYSTEM. When a slot is defined
                 * for I/O, the corresponding vector for the slot is moved
                 * from the OUTVEC or INVEC table to the VECTOUT or VECTIN
                 * location for I/O redirection. These locations can also be
                 * changed by use of the "PR#,Aaddr" or "IN#,Aaddr" commands.
                 * The normal slot 0 assignments point to the monitor I/O
                 * routines COUT1 (send a character to the screen) and KEYIN
                 * (read a key from the keyboard).
                                             ;
BE30: F0 FD      VECTOUT   DA    COUT1
BE32: 1B FD      VECTIN    DA    KEYIN
                                             ;
                 * The following routines are used for ProDOS/BASIC.SYSTEM
                 * communication and BASIC.SYSTEM's internal redirection of
                 * I/O.
                                             ;
BE34: F1 B7      VDOSIO    DA    $B7F1
BE36: F4 B7                DA    $B7F4
BE38: 2F 9A      VSYSIO    DA    $9A2F
BE3A: BA 9A                DA    $9ABA
                                             ;
                 * Status information for BASIC.SYSTEM.
                                             ;
BE3C: 06         DEFSLT    HEX   06          ; Default slot number assumed.
BE3D: 02         DEFDRV    HEX   02          ; Default drive number assumed.
BE3E: 8D         PREGA     HEX   8D          ; Storage for saving A register.
BE3F: 2E         PREGX     HEX   2E          ; Storage for X register.
BE40: 07         PREGY     HEX   07          ; Storage for Y register.
BE41: 00         DTRACE    HEX   00          ; TRACE flag; bit 7 set if enabled.
BE42: 00         STATE     HEX   00          ; Deferred-mode flag, bit 7 set if deferred.
BE43: 00         EXACTV    HEX   00          ; EXEC active if bit 7 set.
BE44: 00         IFILACTV  HEX   00          ; File input active if bit 7 set.
BE45: 00         OFILACTV  HEX   00          ; File output active if bit 7 set.
```

```
BE46: 00          PFXACTV  HEX  00        ; Prefix active (set)
        if bit 7 set.
BE47: 00          DIRFLG   HEX  00        ; Directory file
        being accessed if bit 7 set.
BE48: 00          EDIRFLG  HEX  00        ; Bit 7 set when end
        of directory file reached.
BE49: E6          STRINGS  HEX  E6        ; Indicator of free
        string space.
BE4A: 00          TBUFPTR  HEX  00        ; Buffered character
        count for WRITE.
BE4B: 2E          INPTR    HEX  2E        ; Number of
        characters in last keyboard input.
BE4C: B0          CHRLAST  HEX  B0        ; Last character
        output.
BE4D: 00          OPENCNT  HEX  00        ; Number of OPEN
        files.
BE4E: 00          EXFILE   HEX  00        ; Flag for EXEC (bit
        7 set as file is closed).
BE4F: 00          CATFLAG  HEX  00        ; Flag indicating
        DIR-> CAT(ALOG) translation.
BE50: 00 00       XTRNADDR DA   $0000     ; Address of external
        command ($0000 if none).
BE52: 04          XLEN     HEX  04        ; Length of command
        string (minus one).
                                          ; (last command was
        "BSAVE").
BE53: 0F          XCNUM    HEX  0F        ; BASIC.SYSTEM
        command number (0 = external).
BE54: 0D F4       PBITS    DDB  $0DF4
BE56: 01 90       FBITS    DDB  $0190
BE58: 00 BE       VADDR    DA   $BE00     ; Last "A" parameter
        value.
                                          ; (last file save "A"
        was "$BE00").
BE5A: 00 00 00    VBYTE    HEX  000000    ; Last "B" value.
BE5D: 00 00       VENDA    DA   $0000     ; Last "E" value.
BE5F: 00 01       VLNTH    DA   $0100     ; Last "L" parameter
        value.
                                          ; (last file save "L"
        was "$100").
BE61: 06          VSLOT    HEX  06        ; Last "S" value
        (slot 6 here).
BE62: 02          VDRIV    HEX  02        ; Last "D" value
        (drive 2 here).
BE63: 00 00       VFELD    DA   $0000     ; Last "F" value.
BE65: 00 00       VRECD    DA   $0000     ; Last "R" value.
BE67: 00          VVOLM    HEX  00        ; Last "V" value
        (archaic, from DOS 3.3).
BE68: 00 00       VLINE    DA   $0000     ; Last "?" value.
BE6A: 06          VTYPE    HEX  06        ; Last "T" value
        (numeric equivalent).
BE6B: 00          IOSLT    HEX  00        ; Last slot value for
        "IN#" or "PR#".
BE6C: BC BC       VPATH1   DA   $BCBC     ; Primary pathname
        buffer.
BE6E: 80 02       VPATH2   DA   $0280     ; Secondary pathname
        buffer (used by "RENAME").
                                          ;
```

```
                 * The following routines and tables are used by BASIC.SYSTEM
                 * to conduct all of it's MLI calls for disk access.
                                                ;
BE70: 8D 85 BE   GOSYSTEM STA   SYSCALL
BE73: 8E A8 BC            STX   $BCA8
BE76: 29 1F               AND   #$1F
BE78: AA                  TAX
BE79: BD 05 B8            LDA   $B805,X
BE7C: 8D 86 BE            STA   SYSPARM
BE7F: AE A8 BC            LDX   $BCA8
BE82: 20 00 BF            JSR   MLI
BE85: CB         SYSCALL  HEX   CB
BE86: D5 BE      SYSPARM  DA    $BED5
BE88: B0 01      MLIRTN   BCS   BADCALL
BE8A: 60                  RTS
BE8B: A2 12      BADCALL  LDX   #$12
BE8D: DD EE B9   FNDERRNO CMP   $B9EE,X
BE90: F0 05               BEQ   GOTERRNO
BE92: CA                  DEX
BE93: 10 F8               BPL   FNDERRNO
BE95: A2 13               LDX   #$13
BE97: BD 01 BA   GOTERRNO LDA   $BA01,X
BE9A: AE A8 BC            LDX   $BCA8
BE9D: 38                  SEC
BE9E: 60         XRETURN  RTS
BE9F: 00         BISPARE1 HEX   00
BEA0: 07 BC BC   SCREATE  HEX   07BCBCC30600BE01
BEA3: C3 06 00 BE 01
BEA8: 00 00 00            HEX   00000000
BEAB: 00
BEAC: 01 BC BC   SSGPRFX  HEX   01BCBC
BEAF: 02 BC BC   SRENAME  HEX   02BCBC8002
BEB2: 80 02
BEB4: 0A BC BC   SSGINFO  HEX   0ABCBCE30600BE01
BEB7: E3 06 00 BE 01
BEBC: 01 00 65            HEX   010065AB330D65AB
BEBF: AB 33 0D 65 AB
BEC4: 33 0D               HEX   330D
BEC6: 02 01 BD   SONLINE  HEX   0201BDBC00
BEC9: BC 00
BECB: 03 BC BC   SOPEN    HEX   03BCBC009601
BECE: 00 96 01
BED1: 03 00 7F   SNEWLN   HEX   03007F0D
BED4: 0D
BED5: 04 01 00            HEX   040100BE00012700
BED8: BE 00 01 27 00
BEDD: 01 01               HEX   0101
                                                ;
                 * The following is a "scratch" area, presently holding an
                 * Apple copyright notice.
                                                ;
BEDF: 00                  HEX   00
BEE0: C3 CF D0            ASC   "COPYRIGHT APPLE, 1983"
BEE3: D9 D2 C9 C7 C8 D4 A0 C1
BEEB: D0 D0 CC C5 AC A0 B1 B9
```

```
BEF3: B8 B3
                 ;
       * Next are the call vectors for the GETBUFR AND
   FREEBUFR
       * routines discussed in Chapters 19 and 20.
                 ;
BEF5: 4C B5 A2   GETBUFR JMP   $A2B5
BEF8: 4C 01 A3   FREEBUFR JMP  $A301
BEFB: 96                 HEX   96        ; HIMEM page value.
BEFC: 00 00 00           HEX   00000000  ; Unused at present.
BEFF: 00
--End assembly, 256 bytes, Errors: 0


Symbol table - alphabetical order:

   BADCALL =$BE8B   ? BISPARE1=$BE9F   ? CATFLAG =$BE4F   ?
          CHRLAST =$BE4C
?  CI_ENTRY=$BE00     COUT1   =$FDF0   ? DEFDRV  =$BE3D   ?
          DEFSLT  =$BE3C
?  DIRFLG  =$BE47   ? DOSCMD  =$BE03   ? DTRACE  =$BE41   ?
          EDIRFLG =$BE48
?  ERRCODE =$BE0F   ? ERROUT  =$BE09   ? EXACTV  =$BE43   ?
          EXFILE  =$BE4E
?  EXTRNCMD=$BE06   ? FBITS   =$BE56     FNDERRNO=$BE8D   ?
          FREEBUFR=$BEF8
?  GETBUFR =$BEF5   ? GOSYSTEM=$BE70     GOTERRNO=$BE97   ?
          IFILACTV=$BE44
?  INPTR   =$BE4B   ? INVEC   =$BE20   ? IOSLT   =$BE6B     KEYIN
          =$FD1B
   MLI     =$BF00   ? MLIRTN  =$BE88   ? OFILACTV=$BE45   ?
          OPENCNT =$BE4D
?  OUTVEC  =$BE10   ? PBITS   =$BE54   ? PFXACTV =$BE46   ? PREGA
          =$BE3E
?  PREGX   =$BE3F   ? PREGY   =$BE40   ? PRINTERR=$BE0C   ?
          SCREATE =$BEA0
?  SNEWLN  =$BED1   ? SONLINE =$BEC6   ? SOPEN   =$BECB   ?
          SRENAME =$BEAF
?  SSGINFO =$BEB4   ? SSGPRFX =$BEAC   ? STATE   =$BE42   ?
          STRINGS =$BE49
   SYSCALL =$BE85     SYSPARM =$BE86   ? TBUFPTR =$BE4A   ? VADDR
          =$BE58
?  VBYTE   =$BE5A   ? VDOSIO  =$BE34   ? VDRIV   =$BE62   ?
          VECTIN  =$BE32
?  VECTOUT =$BE30   ? VENDA   =$BE5D   ? VFELD   =$BE63   ? VLINE
          =$BE68
?  VLNTH   =$BE5F   ? VPATH1  =$BE6C   ? VPATH2  =$BE6E   ? VRECD
          =$BE65
?  VSLOT   =$BE61   ? VSYSIO  =$BE38   ? VTYPE   =$BE6A   ? VVOLM
          =$BE67
   WARMDOS =$ABF1   ? XCNUM   =$BE53   ? XLEN    =$BE52
          XRETURN =$BE9E
?  XTRNADDR=$BE50


Symbol table - numerical order:

   WARMDOS =$ABF1   ? CI_ENTRY=$BE00   ? DOSCMD  =$BE03   ?
```

```
        EXTRNCMD=$BE06
? ERROUT   =$BE09   ? PRINTERR=$BE0C   ? ERRCODE =$BE0F   ?
        OUTVEC  =$BE10
? INVEC    =$BE20   ? VECTOUT =$BE30   ? VECTIN  =$BE32   ?
        VDOSIO  =$BE34
? VSYSIO   =$BE38   ? DEFSLT  =$BE3C   ? DEFDRV  =$BE3D   ? PREGA
        =$BE3E
? PREGX    =$BE3F   ? PREGY   =$BE40   ? DTRACE  =$BE41   ? STATE
        =$BE42
? EXACTV   =$BE43   ? IFILACTV=$BE44   ? OFILACTV=$BE45   ?
        PFXACTV =$BE46
? DIRFLG   =$BE47   ? EDIRFLG =$BE48   ? STRINGS =$BE49   ?
        TBUFPTR =$BE4A
? INPTR    =$BE4B   ? CHRLAST =$BE4C   ? OPENCNT =$BE4D   ?
        EXFILE  =$BE4E
? CATFLAG  =$BE4F   ? XTRNADDR=$BE50   ? XLEN    =$BE52   ? XCNUM
        =$BE53
? PBITS    =$BE54   ? FBITS   =$BE56   ? VADDR   =$BE58   ? VBYTE
        =$BE5A
? VENDA    =$BE5D   ? VLNTH   =$BE5F   ? VSLOT   =$BE61   ? VDRIV
        =$BE62
? VFELD    =$BE63   ? VRECD   =$BE65   ? VVOLM   =$BE67   ? VLINE
        =$BE68
? VTYPE    =$BE6A   ? IOSLT   =$BE6B   ? VPATH1  =$BE6C   ?
        VPATH2  =$BE6E
? GOSYSTEM=$BE70      SYSCALL =$BE85     SYSPARM =$BE86   ?
        MLIRTN  =$BE88
  BADCALL =$BE8B      FNDERRNO=$BE8D     GOTERRNO=$BE97
        XRETURN =$BE9E
? BISPARE1=$BE9F   ? SCREATE =$BEA0   ? SSGPRFX =$BEAC   ?
        SRENAME =$BEAF
? SSGINFO =$BEB4   ? SONLINE =$BEC6   ? SOPEN   =$BECB   ?
        SNEWLN  =$BED1
? GETBUFR =$BEF5   ? FREEBUFR=$BEF8     MLI     =$BF00     KEYIN
        =$FD1B
  COUT1   =$FDF0
```

Chapter 19

BASIC Memory Management

Finding safe places for BASIC programs is usually not a problem, unless they have to coexist with machine language routines or data files which are also placed in main memory. Also, data areas such as the high-resolution graphics pages can "collide" with BASIC programs.

Machine language programs can be tough to find a "safe" place for. We can "hide" machine language programs in memory via some tricks, including a trick whereby the machine language program is hidden *within* a BASIC program. There are also situations where the BASIC program itself can be moved out of the way of other data areas in memory.

I'LL TAKE THE LOW ROAD

There were a few nooks and crannies that were used under DOS 3.3, with some care, to hide *short* machine language programs or binary data. One of these was the lower portion of page $3, from location $300 to $3CF (768 to 975). At $3D0, the DOS vectors started. Overwriting these is hazardous to one's programs. That limits the page 3 area to $D0 bytes of storage.

Also, under DOS, one could sometimes use part of the area normally used for getting a line of text input, which is page $2. The input buffer area reserved was $200 to $2FF (512 to 767). Sometimes this area was used contiguously with the area at $300 to form a slightly larger usable memory block.

Another trick was to use an unused portion of the 6502's stack area, which is restricted to bytes $100 to $1FF (256 to 511). This was a little dangerous, but the danger was limited by the fact that DOS always initialized the stack pointer register in the 6502 to point at the "bottom" of the stack area ($1FF) and programs usually did not use much of the stack. This allowed a short amount of storage to be "stolen" at $100. Actually, the only situation where this process could be deemed 100% safe was for programs where the stack usage was exactly known.

ALONG COMES PRODOS

The use of the page $3 area described is still fine with ProDOS; ProDOS and BASIC.SYSTEM also only use the area from $3D0 and higher. The use of the input buffer and the stack area for storage can no longer be considered safe, however. ProDOS manipulates the stack more than DOS, especially during use of interrupts. The input buffer area at $200 is used by the ProDOS clock driver (if active), the area from $280-$2FF is used as a secondary pathname buffer by BASIC.SYSTEM and sometimes by ProDOS. Therefore it is best to stay *out* of these areas for data/program storage.

The problem that will remain with using lonely old page $3 is that, since it is now the only large area of contiguous "safe" memory left at the low end of memory, *everybody* will want to use it. It will be prime real estate for every short program and data block. Even the Apple *IIc* System Utilities disk uses this area for an archaic "error handling" add-on to Applesoft, even *after* Apple itself said that page $3 should be considered "safe" for a clock driver.

Another possibility is to place our program/data areas as *high* in memory as feasible. This entails some rather technical talk about the ProDOS/BASIC.SYSTEM buffers. Remember where you found this section as we'll refer back to it later.

BASIC.SYSTEM'S BUFFERS

BASIC.SYSTEM resides in the memory range from $9600 to $BEFF. Immediately above this, page $BF belongs to the ProDOS kernal as its global page. BASIC.SYSTEM's global page, of course, can always be found at $BE00-BEFF.

Unlike DOS 3.3, which would *statically* allocate space for up to 16 file buffers, BASIC.SYSTEM *dynamically* allocates buffer space for up to 8 file buffers. File buffers are used to store information about a file and the disk the file is on while the file is open.

DOS 3.3 used the command *MAXFILES n*, where "n" was a number from 1 to 16, to define how many buffers were to be allowed to be active at one time. The space for *each* buffer was then reserved in memory; if you had 16 buffers reserved with MAXFILES 16, you used 16 times as much memory as for MAXFILES 1. All that memory was lost as program space until MAXFILES was set to a lower value.

BASIC.SYSTEM's buffers are somewhat larger than DOS 3.3's: 1,024 bytes (4 pages, 1K) versus 595 bytes (2.3 pages, .6K). The one buffer BASIC.SYSTEM always allocates is known as the *temporary command buffer*. It's used by commands such as CATALOG and LOAD that only need a buffer while they are active. This buffer's home is at $9600-$99FF, but, as we shall see, it's on the road a lot.

After that, BASIC.SYSTEM only uses up more memory for file buffers if you open up other files; the file buffer space is not "permanently" reserved as for DOS 3.3. This eliminates the need for MAXFILES and the command is *not* recognized by BASIC.SYSTEM; if you use it, you'll get a SYNTAX ERROR.

When you open a file, BASIC.SYSTEM allocates a second buffer. This buffer will stick around until the file is closed. To make room for this buffer, Applesoft's *HIMEM* (the highest address Applesoft can use; kept at $73-$74) will be lowered by four pages ($400 bytes). The temporary command buffer is moved into the new area, and the newly opened file gets the nice warm buffer that the temporary commands had been using. Normally Applesoft strings reside in the area just below HIMEM. BASIC.SYSTEM moves them down too, automatically, as it adjusts the HIMEM value.

If you open a second file, another ProDOS buffer will be built. Again everything will be moved down. You can open as many as eight buffers, unless you run out of memory. As you close files, buffers will be deallocated. BASIC.SYSTEM will automatically move everything back up.

If you EXEC a file, it will get the highest buffer. The temporary command buffer is always the lowest buffer. To see this in pictures, refer to Figure 19-1. The newly created buffer at $9200 will become the temporary command buffer, and BASIC.SYSTEM's internal buffer at $9600 will become the buffer for the open file.

PLEASE NOTE TECH NOTE #9

If you have one of the newer copies of Apple's *ProDOS Technical Reference Manual* (the *new* version is spiral bound and published for Apple by Addison-Wesley), the following tips on allocation

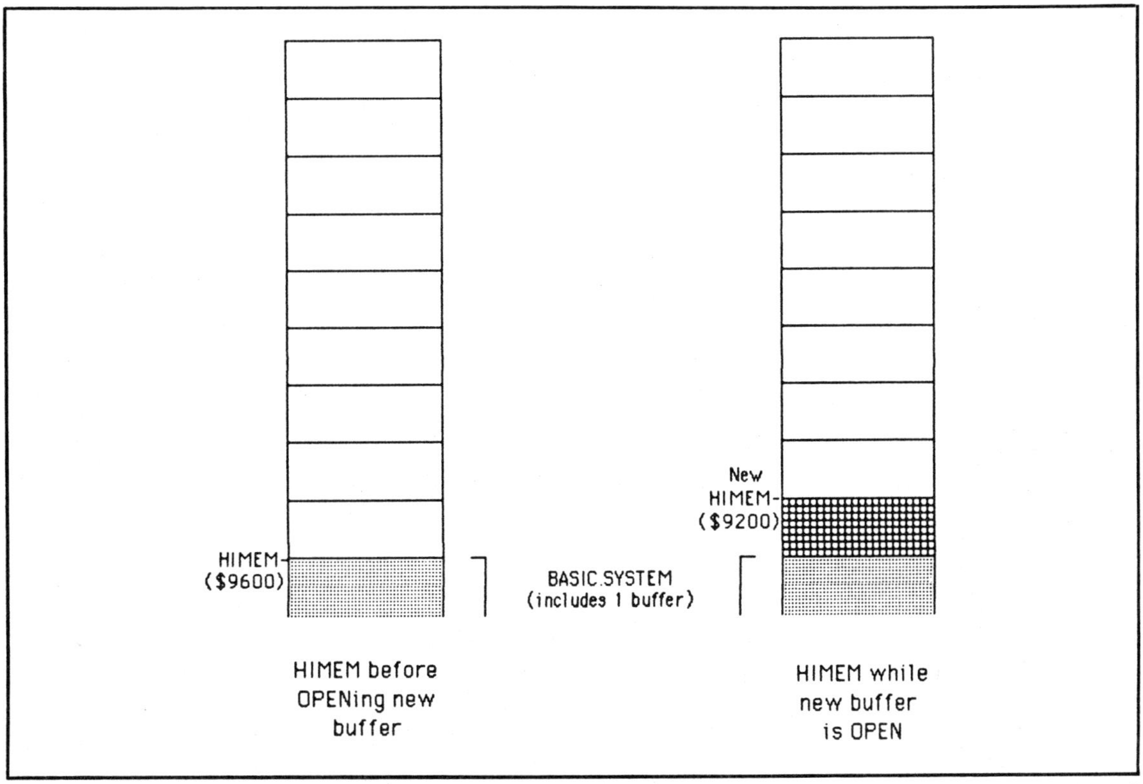

Fig. 19-1. Movement of HIMEM with OPEN.

of buffers are outlined in the manual.

Apple's older ProDOS technical manual (the looseleaf version that requires a separate binder) has its explanation of buffer manipulation on pages 116, 117, and 118. If you have one of these manuals, get a red pen and cross out the warning box on page 117 and everything the manual says on page 118 about putting routines above HIMEM, except for the warning and little grey boxes. Write yourself a note to refer here or to the June 1984 "DOStalk" (in the now sadly defunct *Softalk* magazine) instead. The folowing discussion is primarily for the benefit of those readers who have the *old* manual.

The manual indicates you can obtain space for assembly language routines by adjusting HIMEM yourself, but the procedure is tricky. BASIC.SYSTEM's temporary buffer *always* lies just above HIMEM. Thus, it will move as you adjust the HIMEM value. The space you create by moving HIMEM will be on the other side of the temporary buffer; that is, *1K above HIMEM* (this isn't crystal clear in the manual, but it's true nonetheless). The manual warns you to do this only when no files are open, no string variables are declared, and only in 256-byte ($100) increments.

After the manual was written, the ProDOS development team came up with a much better way to get yourself some space; ask BASIC.SYSTEM for it. This technique is documented in *ProDOS Technical Note* #9, which has been sent to licensed ProDOS developers and is also available as a text file on the disk "/IAC.43" from the International Apple Core.

To use this technique, simply place the number of pages you need in the accumulator and *JSR GETBUFR* ($BEF5). The first space allocated goes just below BASIC.SYSTEM (page $99 and downward), regardless of the number and type of ProDOS buffers that are open. If more allocations are requested, they will be installed immediately below the first. BASIC.SYSTEM will automatically provide for moving all ProDOS buffers and any Applesoft strings that need to be moved.

When BASIC.SYSTEM passes control back to you, the carry flag indicates whether the call was successful. If the carry is set, an error occurred and the accumulator will return the (non-zero) error code. If the carry is clear, on the other hand, the call was successful. In this case the accumulator will hold the high-byte address of the memory space that was assigned to you (the low byte of the address will always be zero). The actual area you get will depend on how many other programs asked for space before yours did.

There are many advantages to this system of letting BASIC.SYSTEM give you space for your programs. Obviously, if you let BASIC.SYSTEM do it, you don't have to worry whether any files are open or any strings declared. BASIC.SYSTEM will give you a secure niche and automatically move anything that needs to be moved.

WHY "NOHELP" IS NO HELP AT ALL

Tech note #9 also refers to the vector called *FREEBUFR* ($BEF8). When you call this vector, *all* of the program memory spaces that have been allocated are freed. There is no way to selectively deallocate these spaces. It's just as well. Assume memory spaces *could* be selectively deallocated. And say your program was the second entity to ask for one. If the first program could then say it didn't need its space anymore, your program would have to be relocated. Who's going to do that and keep your program functioning? In the interests of compatibility, we recommend that you *never call FREEBUFR*. If a user wants to reclaim a buffer, the only safe procedure is to reboot or to rerun BASIC.SYSTEM.

Consider, for example, BASIC.SYSTEM's *HELP* program, provided on the BASIC Examples disk with the Apple manual *BASIC Programming With ProDOS*. HELP includes a *NOHELP* command, which removes HELP and frees its buffer. But if any other routine is loaded after help, NOHELP frees *its* buffer too. If the second routine is a special screen driver or any of several other types of programs, the system will crash soon after you enter "NOHELP".

Even worse is the attitude of *Applesoft Programmer's Assistant*, another program on the ProDOS BASIC Examples disk. It calls FREEBUFR even before it calls GETBUFR. If your program has already received a buffer when *HELP* is run, HELP expires with a *no buffers available* error. *APA*, on the other hand, first knocks you out of your buffer with its FREEBUFR call and asks questions later. This self-centered kind of programming is not welcome, thank you.

DON'T TREAD ON ME

The ProDOS system global page which exists in memory at $BF00- $BFFF includes a *system bitmap*. ProDOS uses the bitmap to keep itself from accidentally overwriting itself, its data, or other sensitive system areas, such as the stack and the text screen. If you like, you can protect the memory space you are assigned by BASIC.SYSTEM. (BASIC.SYSTEM does *not* do this for you; memory protection for this purpose is ProDOS's lookout.)

The advantage to marking the bitmap is that the ProDOS kernal won't allow you or any one else to accidentally load a file into your memory space. However, this can also be a disadvantage. The TYPE command presented in Chapter 20, for example, reads files by repeatedly making 1-byte read calls to the MLI. We tell the MLI to place the byte in an unused part of our memory space. But if our space is marked in the system bitmap, ProDOS will refuse to do this.Thus, our alternatives are to leave the memory space we are assigned unprotected or to clear a location elsewhere in memory for passing the file. It is easier, and far less dangerous than not wearing seat belts, to leave the buffer unprotected.

If you prefer to protect your buffer, the information you need to do so is touched on in the chapter on the ProDOS Global Page, and described in Apple's *ProDOS Technical Reference Manual* on page 124. Also, there is a program at the end of this chapter that shows how to manipulate the system bitmap entirely from BASIC.

CALL THE MOVERS

Any program you write that will insert itself

in a space provided by BASIC.SYSTEM will have two parts. The first part of the program will ask for the memory space, perhaps protect it, tap into whatever vector your program will use, and then actually move the second part to the assigned location. The second part of your program will set up house and can expect to be a part of the system until the computer is turned off or rebooted.

Since you can't predict exactly where BASIC.SYSTEM will give you space (it depends on how many programs asked for space before you did and how long they were), the first part of your program must *relocate* the second part. This means that all absolute memory references in the second part of your program, such as *JMP*s, *JSR*s, and references to data and variables must be changed.

One way to solve this problem is to avoid internal references; that is, make the second part of your program relocatable. This is usually a lot of trouble, however. The more common method of solving this problem is to write a routine that properly relocates your program. In the chapter on adding commands to BASIC.SYSTEM the TYPE-command program demonstrates a simple method of doing this.

MAKING PROGRAM SPACE

The method of using GETBUFR and FREEBUFR to create a space for programs above HIMEM may seem a bit complicated, especially if you just need the space temporarily for your program. So how do you protect your program or data? Several methods have been used.

The Applesoft "end-of-program" pointer can be used to attach a machine language program to the end of a BASIC program. As a variation of this method, a program or data area can be "hidden" internally in an Applesoft program between any two consecutive program lines. Even a *large* program or data area can be created this way; Applesoft programs have even been designed to "wrap around" both high-resolution graphics pages so that a section of the program exists both above and below the high-resolution pages.

The odds are not greatly in favor of using this method; for several reasons. First, after you have played with the program area, the data area and/or machine language portion is "hidden"; which is lousy for someone trying to alter the program later. Plus, editing the program can create real problems. Any CALLs to the machine language portion, for example, will likely have to be re-written if the machine language routine is forced to "move about" in memory as a result of editing. Or, editing can cause the BASIC program to again infringe on a memory area that was meant to be "clear" until the internal structure of the program is shuffled again.

TAKING A LESSON FROM DOS

DOS 3.3 programmers often use an *easy* way to free up a memory block for machine language routines or binary data which is to move a BASIC program "up" in memory from its normal location and use the space created as a "safe" area. Fortunately, the technique still works under ProDOS. You can even alter the system bitmap to reflect the situation, unless you want to BLOAD something into that area.

Unless some specific Applesoft pointers are altered, Applesoft BASIC programs normally typed in or LOADed into memory are placed so that the program starts at $800 (2048), just above the text screen memory area. As lines are added to the program, it "expands" upward toward higher memory addresses, and LOMEM is updated to point to the end of the program in memory.

When the program is RUN, all numeric variables are stored in memory starting from the end of the program (LOMEM) and expanding upward toward HIMEM, the highest location available to Applesoft. Data for string variables is stored starting immediately below HIMEM and starts expanding downward toward LOMEM. When the two sets of variables meet, you get an ?OUT OF MEMORY error.

It's usually safe, though, to move the program up a *small* distance in memory to make room for assembly language routines to be added between $800 and the new starting location of the program. Before we tell you how easy it is to do, we'd better warn you about the number one troublemaker.

A GRAPHIC PROBLEM

A common problem is the use of moderate-sized BASIC programs with the Apple high resolution graphics pages. The high-resolution pages seem to be stuck in the most inconvenient place possible, from $2000 to $3FFF for page 1 and $4000 to $5FFF for page 2. As your program grows, it expands toward $2000. If you move it slightly up in memory, you are moving ever closer to the high-resolution area. The infringement of an Applesoft program into a high-resolution page can usually be seen by one of two occurrences.

In the first case, you RUN your program and when the HGR (or HGR2) statement is executed, you see a lot of "white space" (or even colored space) on various parts of the video screen display as the high-resolution screen is erased to black. Eventually, the program crashes with some type of error or just "locks up", and you list it to find out part of the end of the program is missing; lines are lost, etc.

This occurs because the program extended past $2000 in memory. If the program started at $800, we have $1800 bytes for our program before it passes the $2000 barrier. On page 154, the older version of Apple's *BASIC Programming with ProDOS* claims that BASIC.SYSTEM "protects" the high-resolution pages when they're in use; *cross that section out*. It's *totally* false.

If you want a demonstration and have typed in *and SAVEd* the "directory file to text file" program at the end of Chapter 16, type "VTAB 22" to move the cursor to the bottom of the text screen, type "HGR" to clear the screen and then LOAD the BASIC program. You'll see parts of the screen "colored in"; this is the program infringing into the HGR screen's memory area.

In the second case, the program starts out and runs fine and dandy for a while after the HGR (or HGR2) statement, but eventually you notice white space or colored space "creeping onto" your screen; things that you aren't drawing on the screen. These are your *variables* expanding to fill memory until they have impinged into the area of the high-resolution screen. If your program should happen to issue another HGR (or HGR2) statement while these variables are "visible" in the high-resolution graphics area, the variables will be erased as part of the screen memory and BASIC errors will likely result. This latter problem is easier to solve; simply use the Applesoft *LOMEM:* command in your program as a statement to set the value of LOMEM to just above high-resolution screen 1 ("LOMEM: 16384") or high-resolution screen 2 ("LOMEM: 24576") *before any variables are defined* by program statements.

For the first problem, more drastic measures may be called for.

GETTING OUT OF THE WAY

Seldom are *both* high-resolution pages used from a BASIC program, so two options are open before we have to start moving our program:

1. Use high-resolution page 1. That allows us about $1800 (6144) bytes of BASIC program from the normal starting address of $800 to one byte "below" the start of high-resolution screen 1 at $2000. If the program is any longer than that the end of the program will be "erased" when the high-resolution screen is cleared.
2. Use high-resolution page 2. Comments are the same as for page 1, except the limit is $3800 (14336) bytes, as the available area now extends from $800 to $3FFF.

In both cases remember the use of LOMEM: to protect the graphics page from infringement by variables (and vice versa). So what if your program exceeds 15K bytes?

HIGHER RELOCATION

The easiest technique is to move the BASIC program so that it resides "above" one or both high-resolution pages in memory. This gives us two additional options:

1. Use only high-resolution page 1. The program can be relocated to $4000, which gives us a free area from $4000 to $8FFF, or $5000 (20480) bytes to work with.

2. Using *both* page 1 and page 2, relocate the program to $6000. This leaves $3000 (12288) bytes. Unless you're using both pages, leave the program at $800 and use page 2; it gives you more room.

Another thing to realize in these instances is that you have to subtract the memory usage of any string variables, which are stored beneath HIMEM:, from the program space, as well as the space of any additional buffers BASIC.SYSTEM might have to reserve for your program (one for each OPEN file). Therefore, you may not gain as much memory as you'd like to think.

SCHIZOID APPLESOFT

The last possibility for this scenario is to divide the BASIC program into smaller parts. You can segment the program into logical units and CHAIN the pieces together from disk. This option is sounder from an ease-of-use standpoint, it requires only standard programming practices and a little conservatism on the size of your program segments. Since a working Applesoft CHAIN was not an inherent part of DOS 3.3, this procedure was a little more problematical under DOS and some of the "trickier" methods were relied upon. With ProDOS, CHAIN has been implemented as part of BASIC.SYSTEM. The biggest disadvantage is that all the "segment" programs will have to be on a disk, and the disk will have to be available in a drive when the CHAIN is performed.

OK, SO HOW DO I DO IT?

Relocating BASIC programs is easy, using Applesoft's zero-page program pointers. You check the start-of-program pointer to determine where the program is currently running; if it isn't in the right location you can POKE in the desired values and RUN the program from disk again. As RUN loads the program, it places it at the new pointer value. A sample program to do this is presented in Listing 19-1. You can put whatever you like after line 50, within BASIC reason.

Line 40 does all the work. The variable "START" at the beginning of the line holds the decimal of the page number we wish to relocate our program to. The high byte of the start-of-program pointer is in location 104 and the low byte is in 103, after BASIC. SYSTEM is first initialized this location will point toward $801 (or 2049, if you prefer). We have arbitrarily decided to move our program to $1001 (16 × 256 + 1 or 4097), so "START" in this case is set equal to 16. The "IF PEEK (104) < > START" statement checks to see if the pointer has already been set to this value, otherwise it POKEs the proper pointer into 103 and 104. We have poked $1001 in as the starting address, but Applesoft actually checks the byte immediately preceding the program to see if it is a 0. Therefore, we will say that the BASIC program space starts at $1000 since Applesoft looks at this byte, too.

The third POKE puts a 0 into the byte immediately *preceding* the first byte of the program. This prevents Applesoft from producing a "?SYNTAX ERROR". *Make sure that the location you POKE the zero into is not the current program line*; line 30 in this case. Otherwise, you may destroy one of the statements which is yet to execute. Normally, you

```
10 REM *** RELOCATOR ***
20 TEXT : PRINT CHR$ (21) : HOME : D$ = CHR$ (4)
30 REM "START" EQUALS HIGH BYTE OF DESIRED
      STARTING ADDRESS (PAGE #).
40 START = 16 : IF PEEK (104) < > START THEN
      PRINT "RELOCATING..." : POKE 103,1 : POKE
      104,START : POKE 16 * 256, 0 : PRINT
      D$;"RUN RELOCATOR" : END
50 REM << REST OF PROGRAM HERE >>
```

Listing 19-1. Sample BASIC program relocator.

will want to move the program more than 256 bytes when you re-locate it so if the "relocator" is one of the first few lines this should not be a problem. If you want to check to make sure, make the relocator the first line in the program, then compute the difference between the starting location you want for the program and the present location (from the address in 103 and 104) as part of the relocation line. If this difference is less than 256, your relocator may be at risk of POKEing a "0" into itself (the current line) and the POKEs should be aborted.

After the POKEs are taken care of, the RUN command is issued to re-load the program at the

```
10  REM TEXT PAGE SAVER DEMO.
20  TEXT : PRINT : PRINT  CHR$ (21): HOME
30 D$ =  CHR$ (4)
40  GOSUB 3000: REM INSTALL ROUTINE
50  REM MAKE BUFFER.
60  IF  PEEK (104) <  > 12 THEN  POKE 104,12:
      POKE 103,1: POKE 12 * 256,0: PRINT
      D$;"RUN TEXT.SAVER.DEMO"
100  REM MAKE AND SAVE 4 PAGES.
110  FOR I = 1 TO 4
120  GOSUB 1000
130 A$ = "THIS IS PAGE NUMBER " +  STR$ (I) +
      "."
140  GOSUB 2000
150  PRINT D$;"BSAVE
      PAGEFILE,A$400,L$400,B";1024 * (I - 1)
160  NEXT I
200  REM PROMPT FOR PAGE.
210  HOME : VTAB 3
220  PRINT "PAGE NUMBER TO LOAD (1-4 OR 'ESC')?:
      ";
230  GET A$: IF A$ <  >  CHR$ (27) AND ( VAL
      (A$) < 1 OR  VAL (A$) > 4) THEN 230
235  IF A$ =  CHR$ (27) THEN 900
240  PRINT :I =  VAL (A$)
250  PRINT D$;"BLOAD
      PAGEFILE,A$800,L$400,B";1024 * (I - 1)
260  CALL 768: REM MOVE PAGE TO DISPLAY AREA.
270  POKE  - 16368,0: REM CLEAR KEYBOARD DATA
      STROBE.
280  IF  PEEK ( - 16384) < 128 THEN 280: REM
      WATCH FOR KEYPRESS.
290  POKE  - 16368,0
299  GOTO 200
900  REM FIX POINTERS AND EXIT.
910  HOME
920  PRINT D$;"-BASIC.SYSTEM": REM RE-INIT
      BASIC.
1000  REM MAKE BORDER.
1010  VTAB 1: FOR K = 0 TO 39: PRINT I;: NEXT K
1020  FOR K = 2 TO 22: VTAB K: HTAB 1: PRINT I;:
      HTAB 40: PRINT I;: NEXT K
1030  VTAB 23: HTAB 1: FOR K = 0 TO 39: PRINT
      I;: NEXT K
```

Listing 19-2. Modified version of "text screen saver" program.

```
1040  RETURN
2000  REM CENTER STRING
2010  VTAB 11: HTAB  INT ((40 - ( LEN (A$))) /
       2)
2020  PRINT A$
2030  RETURN
3000  REM ML DATA TO RESTORE TEXT PAGE FROM
       BUFFER.
3010  FOR I = 768 TO 823: READ X: POKE I,X: NEXT
       I
3020  DATA 162,119,189,0,8,157,0,4,189
3030  DATA 128,8,157,128,4,189,0,9,157
3040  DATA 0,5,189,128,9,157,128,5,189
3050  DATA 0,10,157,0,6,189,128,10,157
3060  DATA 128,6,189,0,11,157,0,7,189
3070  DATA 128,11,157,128,7,202,224,255,208
3080  DATA 203,96
3099  RETURN
```

new location and start execution. This entire set of commands should be combined on the same BASIC program line, otherwise Applesoft may lose its place after the POKE command when it tries to find the next program line which causes the program to crash.

Listing 19-2 is a second version of the "text screen saver" first presented in Chapter 11. It uses this method of relocation to create a data buffer at \$800-\$BFF to load the screen data into prior to moving it into the text screen area. Notice that a few lines (including some of the DATA values) have been changed. Also notice that the program exits by executing the BASIC.SYSTEM file to re-initialize the Applesoft program space. Otherwise, our start-of-program pointer would remain at \$C00 and our next LOADed BASIC program would be placed at the odd place in memory.

SMALL BITS OF PROTECTION

A few points about the system bitmap.

Apple's *ProDOS Technical Reference Manual* warns that no area of memory is "safe" other than the lower portion of page 3, even the area below LOMEM, unless protected by the system bitmap. In truth, page 3 is also not "safe", because it is not marked as protected in the bitmap when ProDOS is booted. However, as far as BASIC.SYSTEM and ProDOS are concerned, your reserved memory area should only be threatened by the possibility of BLOADING a file below LOMEM: or by having a buffer OPENed there.

We assume that for *your* program you will be responsible for making sure no file is BLOADed into your reserved area unless you want it there. Secondly, BASIC.SYSTEM should not open a buffer in low memory (unless you have altered HIMEM). You can prevent these occurrences by "protecting" the area you want to reserve with the system bitmap; just remember to "un-protect" the area when you are done with it.

Also, even if marked as "reserved" in the system bitmap, the area will *not* be protected against POKEs or programs that relocate data into the "protected" area.

CLEARING OUT

The two-edged sword here is the fact that clearing the Applesoft pointers is a bit sticky under ProDOS. Under DOS 3.3, there was an FP command that reinitialized Applesoft and cleared any Applesoft LOMEM: and HIMEM: settings, including POKEd values like those we're using. Issuing "FP" as you exited a DOS program insured that the pointers were re-set. There is no similar intrinsic command in BASIC.SYSTEM. To restore the start-of-program pointer, you must either POKE the former values into memory or execute BASIC.SYS-

```
10  REM *** BASIC.SYSTEM "FP" SIMULATOR ***
20 HIMEM =  PEEK (112) * 256 +  PEEK (111): REM
       HIGHEST MEMORY LOCATION.
30  IF HIMEM <  > 38400 THEN  GOTO 100
40  POKE 104,8: POKE 103,1: POKE 2048,0: NEW :
       REM RESET LOMEM.
99  END
100  REM *** EXIT VIA "-BASIC.SYSTEM" ***
105  HOME
110  PRINT "Can't reset 'HIMEM'.": PRINT : PRINT
       "Run 'BASIC.SYSTEM'?: ";
120  GET A$
130  IF A$ <  > "Y" AND A$ <  > "y" AND A$ <  >
       "N" AND A$ <  > "n" THEN 120
140  PRINT
150  IF A$ = "N" OR A$ = "n" THEN  VTAB 22: END
200  ONERR  GOTO 210
210  HOME
220  PRINT "Insert disk with 'BASIC.SYSTEM'
       into"
230  PRINT "drive 1 and press a key: ";
240  GET A$
250  PRINT
260  PRINT  CHR$ (4);"-BASIC.SYSTEM,D1"
```

Listing 19-3. Program to "reset" BASIC program space.

TEM with the "dash" command ("-BASIC.SYSTEM) as was done in the new version of the "text screen saver". The latter approach will re-initialize the Applesoft program area but will also re-RUN STARTUP (if present); plus you will have to have BASIC.SYSTEM available on a disk.

Earlier it was said that there was no BASIC.SYSTEM equivalent of the DOS 3.3 "FP" command which re-initializes the BASIC program space. By POKEing the normal start-of-program values into memory, however, we can reset the Applesoft program space, as shown in Listing 19-3. Lines 20 and 30 check to see if HIMEM has been lowered for some reason; if so, this version of the program assumes that you will want to re-run BASIC.SYSTEM to initialize all of the Applesoft program space. If you want to leave HIMEM where it is (you may have a perfectly useful program hiding up there) and simply reset the start-of-program pointer, you could eliminate this step and simply go on to line 40, which resets the pointer and NEWs the program away. This program could be incorporated into a larger program as a subroutine.

A "CONVERT" BUG

Another problem is that if a relocated program is SAVEd from its relocated position (so that it is not saved with all of its internal pointers reflecting a starting address of $800) under either DOS or BASIC.SYSTEM, the CONVERT utility on the "/USERS.DISK" will not correctly transfer the program to the other operating system. Under DOS, this could be fixed by using *FP* to initialize the Applesoft pointers, LOADing, and reSAVEing the program. Under BASIC.SYSTEM, you will have to reset the program pointers manually via "NEW" followed by "POKE 103,1 : POKE 104,8 : POKE 2048,0" (or run BASIC.SYSTEM); then LOAD and SAVE the program anew.

BASIC BITMAP

The use of the system bitmap when "hiding" programs in main memory is usually not necessary,

```
100  REM *** BASIC BITMAP EDITOR ***
110  TEXT : PRINT  CHR$ (21): HOME
120  INVERSE : PRINT  SPC( 9);"PRODOS BITMAP
       EXAMINER"; SPC( 9);"": NORMAL
130  GOSUB 380: REM GET BITMAP.
140  GOSUB 580: REM PRINT BITMAP.
150  HTAB 1: VTAB 22: PRINT "Type M)odify,
       Q)uit, or ?)Help: ";: GOSUB 730: REM GET
       KEY.
160  IF KEY$ = "Q" THEN  TEXT : HOME : END
170  IF KEY$ = "M" THEN  GOSUB 790: REM EDITOR.
180  IF KEY$ = "?" THEN  GOSUB 210
190  GOTO 150
200  END
210  REM *** DESCRIPTION ***
220  VTAB 4: HTAB 1: CALL  - 958
230  PRINT "This program does simple
       manipulation"
240  PRINT "of the ProDOS bitmap from BASIC.
       Why?"
250  PRINT "Just to show it can be done!"
260  PRINT : PRINT "The display is as follows:"
270  PRINT : HTAB 5: PRINT " 1 ";: INVERSE :
       PRINT "0123456789ABCDEF";: NORMAL : PRINT
       "  <<Page # Low"
280  HTAB 6: PRINT "^";: PRINT "
       0001000000000000  << Bitmap"
290  HTAB 6: PRINT "^": HTAB 6: PRINT "^": HTAB
       6: PRINT "High digit of page number."
300  PRINT : PRINT "In the above example, page
       $13 is"
310  PRINT "'reserved' by ProDOS. This program"
320  PRINT "is only for experimentation. Use at"
330  PRINT "your own (considered) risk!"
340  VTAB 22: PRINT "Press a key to return:
       ": GOSUB 730
350  GOSUB 580
360  RETURN
370  END
380  REM *** BITMAP PARSER ***
390  DIM BM%(23),MAP$(23)
400  VTAB 6: CALL  - 958: REM CLREOP FROM LINE
       6.
410  VTAB 10: HTAB 6: INVERSE : PRINT "
       CALCULATING BITMAP DATA... ": NORMAL
420  REM *** READ BITMAP BYTES ***
430  FOR I = 0 TO 23
440 BM%(I) =  PEEK (48984 + I)
450  NEXT I
460  REM *** CONVERT TO "BINARY" ***
470  FOR I = 0 TO 23
480 TEST% = BM%(I)
490 MAP$(I) = ""
500  FOR K = 0 TO 7
510 BIT% = 0
```

Listing 19-4. BASIC program to manipulate the ProDOS system bitmap.

```
520  IF (( INT (TEST% / 2)) * 2) <  > TEST% THEN
       BIT% = 1
530 MAP$(I) =  STR$ (BIT%) + MAP$(I)
540 TEST% = TEST% / 2
550  NEXT K
560  NEXT I
570  RETURN
580  REM *** PRINT BITMAP ON SCREEN ***
590  VTAB 4: HTAB 1: CALL  - 958
600  PRINT "0 ";: INVERSE : PRINT
       "0123456789ABCDEF";: NORMAL : PRINT "  1
       ";: INVERSE : PRINT "0123456789ABCDEF":
       NORMAL
610  PRINT  SPC( 2);MAP$(0);MAP$(1); SPC(
       4);MAP$(2);MAP$(3): PRINT
620  PRINT "2 ";: INVERSE : PRINT
       "0123456789ABCDEF";: NORMAL : PRINT "  3
       ";: INVERSE : PRINT "0123456789ABCDEF":
       NORMAL
630  PRINT  SPC( 2);MAP$(4);MAP$(5); SPC(
       4);MAP$(6);MAP$(7): PRINT
640  PRINT "4 ";: INVERSE : PRINT
       "0123456789ABCDEF";: NORMAL : PRINT "  5
       ";: INVERSE : PRINT "0123456789ABCDEF":
       NORMAL
650  PRINT  SPC( 2);MAP$(8);MAP$(9); SPC(
       4);MAP$(10);MAP$(11): PRINT
660  PRINT "6 ";: INVERSE : PRINT
       "0123456789ABCDEF";: NORMAL : PRINT "  7
       ";: INVERSE : PRINT "0123456789ABCDEF":
       NORMAL
670  PRINT  SPC( 2);MAP$(12);MAP$(13); SPC(
       4);MAP$(14);MAP$(15): PRINT
680  PRINT "8 ";: INVERSE : PRINT
       "0123456789ABCDEF";: NORMAL : PRINT "  9
       ";: INVERSE : PRINT "0123456789ABCDEF":
       NORMAL
690  PRINT  SPC( 2);MAP$(16);MAP$(17); SPC(
       4);MAP$(18);MAP$(19): PRINT
700  PRINT "A ";: INVERSE : PRINT
       "0123456789ABCDEF";: NORMAL : PRINT "  B
       ";: INVERSE : PRINT "0123456789ABCDEF":
       NORMAL
710  PRINT  SPC( 2);MAP$(20);MAP$(21); SPC(
       4);MAP$(22);MAP$(23)
720  RETURN
730  REM *** GET KEYSTROKE ***
740  POKE  - 16368,0
750 KD =  PEEK ( - 16384): IF KD < 128 THEN 750
760 KEY$ =  CHR$ (KD - 128)
770  POKE  - 16368,0
780  RETURN
790  REM *** EDITOR ROUTINES ***
800 VP = 6:HP = 3: REM UPPER LEFT-HAND CORNER.
810  REM *** MOVE CURSOR ***
```

```
820  VTAB 22: HTAB 1: PRINT "Type command, or
       '?' for Help.        "
830  VTAB VP: HTAB HP: PRINT "^";: IF UF% = 1
       THEN  VTAB VP: HTAB HP: FLASH : PRINT
       "^";: NORMAL
840  GOSUB 730: REM GET KEYSTROKE.
850  IF KEY$ = "M" AND VP < 21 THEN  VTAB VP:
       HTAB HP: PRINT " ":VP = VP + 3
860  IF KEY$ = "I" AND VP > 6 THEN  VTAB VP:
       HTAB HP: PRINT " ":VP = VP - 3
870  IF KEY$ = "J" AND HP > 3 THEN  VTAB VP:
       HTAB HP: PRINT " ":HP = HP - 1: IF (HP >
       18) AND (HP < 23) THEN HP = 18
880  IF KEY$ = "K" AND HP < 38 THEN  VTAB VP:
       HTAB HP: PRINT " ":HP = HP + 1: IF (HP >
       18) AND (HP < 23) THEN HP = 23
890  IF (KEY$ = "1") OR (KEY$ = "0") THEN NP =
       HP - 2: GOSUB 1120: REM FIX BYTE.
900  IF KEY$ = "?" THEN  GOSUB 950: GOSUB 580:
       GOTO 820
910  IF KEY$ = "Q" THEN  VTAB VP: HTAB HP: PRINT
       " ": GOSUB 580: RETURN
920  IF KEY$ = "U" THEN  GOSUB 1220: REM UPDATE
       BITMAP.
930  GOTO 820
940  STOP : REM BREAKPOINT.
950  VTAB 4: HTAB 1: CALL  - 958
960  PRINT "I,J,K,M - Move cursor (diamond)."
970  PRINT "  0,1   - Set bit to that value."
980  PRINT "  ?     - Display this page."
990  PRINT "  U     - Update bitmap (manual)."
1000  PRINT "  Q     - Quit editing phase."
1010  PRINT : PRINT "NOTE: A flashing '";: FLASH
       : PRINT "^";: NORMAL : PRINT "' indicates
       bits"
1020  PRINT "have been toggled. The map will not
       be"
1030  PRINT "changed unless you specifically
       order"
1040  PRINT "an U)pdate to store the new map."
1050  PRINT : PRINT "Display - numbers at left
       are high"
1060  PRINT "digit of page, inverse row is low
       digit"
1070  PRINT "of page. See page 88 of APPLE
       PRODOS"
1080  PRINT "TECHNICAL MANUAL (or equivalent)."
1090  VTAB 22: PRINT "Press a key to return: "
1100  GOSUB 730: RETURN
1110  RETURN
1120  REM *** FIX BIT IN MAP BYTE ***
1130 NP = HP - 2: IF NP > 16 THEN NP = NP - 4
1140 I = (( INT ((VP - 6) / 3)) * 4) +  INT ((NP
       - 1) / 8): REM BYTE/LINE OFFSET.
1150 K = (NP - ( INT (8 * ( INT (NP / 8)))):
```

```
        REM BIT TO DEFINE.
1160  IF K = 1 THEN MAP$(I) = KEY$ +  RIGHT$
        (MAP$(I),7): GOTO 1190
1170  IF K = 8 THEN MAP$(I) =  LEFT$ (MAP$(I),7)
        + KEY$: GOTO 1190
1180 MAP$(I) =  LEFT$ (MAP$(I),K - 1) + KEY$ +
        RIGHT$ (MAP$(I),8 - K)
1190  IF UF% = 0 THEN UF% = 1: REM SET UPDATE
        FLAG.
1200  GOSUB 580: REM UPDATE DISPLAY.
1210  RETURN
1220  REM *** UPDATE BITMAP ***
1230  IF UF% = 0 THEN  RETURN : REM NO CHANGES
        THIS TIME.
1240  VTAB 22: HTAB 1: CALL  - 958
1250  PRINT "UPDATE IMMINENT: Are you sure?: ";
1260  GOSUB 730
1270  IF KEY$ <  > "Y" THEN  RETURN
1280  VTAB 22: HTAB 1: PRINT "Please wait - slow
        program at work..."
1290  FOR I = 0 TO 23
1300 WB% = 0
1310  FOR K = 1 TO 8
1320 WB% = WB% + ( VAL ( MID$ (MAP$(I),K,1)) *
        (2 ^ (8 - K)))
1330  NEXT K
1340 BM%(I) = WB%
1350  NEXT I
1360  REM *** REPLACE OLD BITMAP WITH NEW ***
1370  FOR I = 0 TO 23
1380  POKE 48984 + I,BM%(I)
1390  NEXT
1400 UF% = 0
1410  RETURN
```

nor even desirable, when using machine language or binary files in conjunction with BASIC programs. The exception is the use of GETBUFR to put programs high in memory. You may wish to mark the bitmap to protect that region.

For the die-hards, however, Listing 19-4 presents a BASIC program that allows viewing (and altering) the state of the bitmap. There are a couple of "help" screens incorporated into the program. Since it is in BASIC, it sometimes is a bit slow, so have patience.

Observing the initial bitmap display of this program is interesting. If the program is RUN after booting a disk with only the "PRODOS" and "BASIC.SYSTEM" programs on it, the following areas of memory are not "protected": pages \$2 and \$3, page \$8 through \$95, and pages \$BA through \$BD. What makes this interesting is that the \$BA-\$BD range is within the BASIC.SYSTEM program area, which means ProDOS would allow us to load a file into the BASIC.SYSTEM interpreter while it is running!

Chapter 20

Adding New Commands

BASIC.SYSTEM has an advantage over DOS 3.3 in its ability to "gracefully" accept additional external commands. DOS 3.3 doesn't provide any formal way to add commands nor do Apple's DOS manuals support such an action; doing it requires that you learn a good deal of information about DOS 3.3's internal structure. In addition, unless you make major modifications, adding a command to DOS 3.3 requires the deletion of an existing command.

We are going to implement such a command, TYPE, which lets you see what's in text files. It's an indispensable command for people who write programs that use text files; it lets you see if what's *supposed* to be in a file is actually there. TYPE is also handy for sending text files to your printer or any other device.

IF WE'RE ALL FRIENDS, WHO'S AN ALIEN?

BASIC.SYSTEM includes special features that make it quite easy for assembly language programmers to add new commands. In fact, Apple's *ProDOS Basic Programming Examples* disk includes a file that adds a *HELP* command to ProDOS.

Just as DOS 3.3 has no formal technique for adding commands, it has no defined protocol for assigning memory space to machine language utilities. In the world of DOS 3.3, machine language utilities from various publishers rarely work together. Since there is no formal way to add them, there is usually a memory conflict somewhere. If you try to use two or more utilities from different publishers at once, your computer usually crashes.

ProDOS, on the other hand, does provide a way for assembly language programs to ask for and to be assigned memory space. By following a few *extra* rules, in fact, programmers of ProDOS utilities can make their software completely compatible with any other software that follows the same rules.

This is significant. We feel so strongly about the advantages of compatibility that as we develop our ProDOS *TYPE* command, we'll also demonstrate this protocol. Our TYPE-command installation program includes all the routines an assembly language programmer needs to add utilities or other machine language programs to ProDOS.

The complete source code for our ProDOS TYPE command can be found at the end of this chapter. The program line numbers we refer to in the following material can be seen in all their glory there. The listing also uses the techniques described in Chapter 19 on memory management involving GETBUFR to install the routine at the "high" end of memory.

You should know that Mark Simonsen, one of the assembly language wizards in the Beagle Bros kennel, helped us with this protocol and its routines. But the routines are in the public domain; use them, *please*. Mark says his life will be a lot easier when alien software stops stepping on his programs.

PRODOS AND ASSEMBLY LANGUAGE

If you are an assembly language programmer interested in ProDOS, the first thing you need to do after reading this chapter, if you haven't done it already, is get a copy of Apple's *ProDOS Technical Reference Manual*. This book is where you'll find all the basic information about how to deal with ProDOS from assembly language. If you're serious about ProDOS programming, you'll need this book.

From an assembly language programmer's point of view, ProDOS consists of two distinct parts. One is the ProDOS kernel that resides in the language-card memory area. In addition, the ProDOS kernel always uses page $BF ($BF00-$BFFF) in lower RAM memory for a *system global page*. This page contains a lot of interesting stuff, such as vectors for disk-device drivers, a system bitmap you can use to protect vital memory areas from being overwritten, the date and time, and a machine identification byte that indicates what kind of Apple II is in use, how much memory it has, and whether it has an 80-column card or a clock.

But most importantly, the first three bytes of this page always contain the ProDOS *Machine Language Interface* vector. Assembly language programs use ProDOS by making calls to this machine language interface, or MLI.

There are 26 different calls that can be made to the ProDOS MLI. These include housekeeping calls, such as create and rename; filing calls, such as open and read; and system calls, such as GET_TIME and ALLOC_INTERRUPT. Each time you call the MLI you must build a command parameter table somewhere and pass its address to the MLI. Calls to the MLI always look like Listing 20-1.

```
CALLMLI JSR    MLI          ; call the MLI
                              vector at $BF00
        DFB    CMDNUM       ; a one-byte number
                              indicating the
                              command
        DA     CMDLIST      ; a two-byte
                              pointer to a
                              command parameter
                              list
        BCS    ERROR        ; the MLI returns
                              here-- error if
                              carry set
```

Listing 20-1. A sample MLI call.

As you can see, the MLI command number and parameter table address are actually embedded in your program's code. The MLI finds them by referencing the call's return address in the stack. While messing with the return address, the MLI bumps it by three bytes so that control will be passed back to your BCS instruction. The embedded information, obviously, cannot be executed.

Each MLI command has its own command number and parameter table format. These are (exceedingly briefly) described in Chapter 22. The *ProDOS Technical Reference Manual* describes the parameter tables in great detail. These tables may scare you at first, but after working with them awhile you'll find this system is really very elegant. Later in the chapter we'll show you an actual MLI call, complete with parameter table.

BASIC.SYSTEM'S RESPONSIBILITY

If you write assembly language programs that have nothing to do with BASIC, all you have to learn about to use ProDOS is the machine language interface. You can save your work as a ProDOS *system program* (see Chapter 5 of the *ProDOS Techni-*

cal Reference Manual for complete information). Your program will have lots of memory (the entire "lower 48K", with the exception of page $BF) available to use however you like.

As mentioned earlier, if asked politely, BASIC.SYSTEM will allocate memory to assembly language programs. These can be Applesoft *&* (*ampersand*) or *USR* routines, special device drivers, new DOS commands, or any other kind of assembly language routine. The beauty of BASIC.SYSTEM is that it provides a way any number of these routines, written by anyone, can co-exist and *work together*. This is something that was never possible with DOS 3.3.

To install the TYPE command, we use the memory-management tricks involving GETBUFR discussed in Chapter 19. In the TYPE-command program listing, we ask for memory space in lines 68 through 84.

TAPPING THE COMMAND LINE

Whenever a command is entered, BASIC.SYSTEM looks to see if it is one of its commands. If not, BASIC.SYSTEM does a JSR *EXTRNCMD* ($BE06) to give other routines, such as our TYPE, a chance to claim the command. If no external command routine is installed, EXTRNCMD contains a jump to $BE9E, which is an *RTS* that will return control to BASIC.SYSTEM.

To hook in your own command, you must change the jump at $BE06 so it points to your routine rather than to the RTS at $BE9E. However, don't just wildly go in and overwrite what's there.

Always assume your program will be the *second* one to connect itself to the external command vector. When BASIC.SYSTEM gets a command it doesn't recognize, it will pass the command to you. *If you don't recognize it either, you should pass control to whatever was in $BE06 before you.* This way, any number of separate routines can share the external command vector. See lines 89-97 of the TYPE-command program for an example of how to do this.

If your program doesn't use the external command vector but connects itself to the system elsewhere, such as the ampersand vector or the input/output links, *use the same procedure*. If the call is not for you, be nice to the rest of us and pass it on. We'll do the same for you.

You determine whether the command is yours by PEEKing in the keyboard input buffer at $200. You will always find the command here, even if it was executed from inside a BASIC program with a PRINT D$ command. In our TYPE-command program, this occurs in lines 224 through 235, with the help of the *GET.CHR* subroutine at lines 329 through 338.

If the command is yours, and if your command allows parameters such as the slot and drive to be given, you have the option of allowing BASIC.SYSTEM to *parse* the command for you. This means BASIC.SYSTEM will dig out the correct numbers from the command, check for range errors, update all necessary flags and tables, and so on. Unless your command doesn't have any parameters at all, or unless it has some parameters not used by BASIC.SYSTEM, we highly recommend you let BASIC.SYSTEM parse your command for you.

Complete information on how to do this is in the ProDOS technical manual on pages 124-127. In the TYPE command program you can see the basic procedure in lines 237 through 251.

GOSYSTEM GO

We now come back to the subject of relocatable code and imbedded data. This requirement of no embedded data may seem in conflict with the technique used to call the MLI, which we discussed earlier. And it would be, except that BASIC.SYSTEM provides a way around the problem. In BASIC.SYSTEM's global page there is a vector called *GOSYSTEM* that is used to make MLI calls while BASIC.SYSTEM is active. The GOSYSTEM vector uses a set of ready-made command parameter tables that are also contained in BASIC.SYSTEM's global page. Before calling GOSYSTEM, you must fill in the appropriate table. Complete information on these ready-made tables is in the ProDOS technical manual on pages 122 to 124. Listing 20-2, for example, shows the parameter table for the MLI's *OPEN* call.

To open a file, you put the address of the

```
BECB- 03        SOPEN  DFB $03        ; OPEN's command parameter
        table has three parameters.
BECC- BC BC            DA  TXBUF-1    ; Pointer to the file's
        pathname--this is provided by BASIC.SYSTEM.
BECE- 00 00    OSYSBUF DA  $0000      ; Pointer to the file's
        buffer--you must provide this.
BED0- 00       OREFNUM DFB $00        ; Reference number of opened
        file--this is returned by the ProDOS Kernal.
```

Listing 20-2. BASIC.SYSTEM's parameter table for the OPEN call.

buffer the file will use in *OSYSBUF*, load the A (accumulator) register with the number for the open command ($C8), and "JSR GOSYSTEM". ProDOS will open the file and pass back a reference number in *OREFNUM*. This reference number is used in other command parameter tables to indicate this file.

The TYPE command opens the file to be *TYPE*d in BASIC.SYSTEM's temporary command buffer, which is always found just above

```
BE70- 8D 85 BE  GOSYSTEM STA SYSCALL     ; Embed command number
        below.
BE73- 8E A8 BC           STX CALLX       ; Save X register
        temporarily.
BE76- 29 1F              AND #$1F        ; Strip off high bits of
        command
BE78- AA                 TAX             ;    number and use as an
        index to
BE79- BD 5F B8           LDA SYSCTBL,X   ;    find low byte of this
        command's
BE7C- 8D 86 BE           STA SYSPARM     ;    parameter table.
        Embed it.
BE7F- AE A8 BC           LDX CALLX       ; Retrieve X.
BE82- 20 00 BF           JSR MLI         ; Call MLI.
BE85- 00        SYSCALL  DA  #0          ; Command number and
        parameter table
BE86- 00 BE     SYSPARM  DA  $BE00       ;    address. (High byte
        always $BE.)
BE88- B0 01              BCS BADCALL     ; Branch if error
        encountered.
BE8A- 60                 RTS

BE8B- A2 12     BADCALL  LDX #18         ; Compare ProDOS error
        number (30
BE8D- DD 40 BA  MLIERR1  CMP MLIERTBL,X  ;    possible) with the 19
        errors
BE90- F0 05              BEQ MLIERR2     ;    BASIC.SYSTEM has
        messages for.
BE92- CA                 DEX
BE93- 10 F8              BPL MLIERR1
BE95- A2 13              LDX #19         ; Use I/O ERROR if not
        recognized.
BE97- BD 53 BA  MLIERR2  LDA BIERRTBL,X  ; Convert to BASIC.SYSTEM
```

Listing 20-3. The GOSYSTEM routine.

```
        error #.
BE9A- AE A8 BC          LDX CALLX       ; Retrieve X.
BE9D- 38                SEC             ; Set carry to denote
        error.
BE9E- 60                RTS             ; BASIC.SYSTEM error #
        returned in A.
```

HIMEM. Lines 264 to 271 of the TYPE program show how simple an OPEN call can be.

Listing 20-3 shows what happens when you call *GOSYSTEM*. Note that all of the code in Listing 20-3 is inside BASIC.SYSTEM's global page.

After our TYPE command has opened the appropriate file, the file's reference number is retrieved from OREFNUM. We place this number in the parameter table used for reads and writes (lines 276-277). In addition, the table must include the address of a buffer (*BYTEBUF*) ProDOS can use to pass us the bytes it reads. We also tell ProDOS to give us just one byte at a time (lines 279-287).

We then load A with the ASCII code for a carriage return and enter the main loop of the program. The carriage return is printed, the keyboard is checked for a press of the escape key (which would halt execution of *TYPE*), and we *JSR GOSYSTEM* to read the next byte in the file (lines 289-297).

When control returns to us we check for an error. ProDOS stores all file bytes in the positive (bit 7 "clear") ASCII format. If no error has occurred, we pick up the byte ProDOS found in the file from *BYTEBUF*, convert it to the negative (bit 7 "set") ASCII format so it will appear correctly on the screen, and loop back to the beginning of our main loop to print it (lines 298- 302).

This normally continues until ProDOS gets to the end of the file. When the end of the file is reached our *GOSYSTEM* call will return with the carry set. We then branch to an error handler (lines 307-318) that will close the file for us and tell BASIC.SYSTEM to handle the error, unless it was "END OF DATA". In that case we tell BASIC.SYSTEM no error occurred and life goes on.

COMMANDING THE "TYPE" COMMAND

The syntax of our ProDOS TYPE command is

TYPE *pathname*,Sn,Dn

Our ProDOS TYPE command also neglects to check filetypes. This means you can *TYPE* any kind of file: text, basic, binary, even directories and subdirectories! However, the display you get is usually completely devoid of meaning unless the file is a text file. Other filetypes rarely contain the ASCII-encoded data we humans need to make sense of things. If you have a robot, he or she may find a use for *TYPE* with non-ASCII files, but few humans will.

Whenever a zero byte is encountered in a file, the ProDOS TYPE command will return an inverse-@, indicating a "00" (zero) byte. ProDOS doesn't use internal markers at the end of files, but instead keeps an end-of-file *pointer* with each file's director y entry. Zero bytes in ProDOS files always indicate that nothing has been stored in that part of the file yet.

If you have a few hours, try *TYPE*ing the file called *HELPSCREENS* on the ProDOS *BASIC Programming Examples* disk. This file, which takes up a mere 60 blocks (30720 bytes) on the disk, is well over 12 million bytes long (note the number under *ENDFILE* for this file when you do a CATALOG). Nothing has ever been stored in 99.7 percent of this file. ProDOS and *TYPE* will be glad to show you all those zeros if you don't believe us. Listing 20-4 contains the complete source code for the ProDOS TYPE command.

```
*---------------------------------------------------
   *        : ProDOS TYPE command
   *        :
   *        :    This program demonstrates the use
   *        :    of the "DOStalk Protocol" for
adding
   *        :    machine language utilities to
ProDOS.
   *        :
   *        : by Tom Weishaar and Mark Simonsen
   *        :    June 1984
   *        :
   *        : a public domain program
*---------------------------------------------------
                                  ;
   POINTER =    $3C               ; Zero-page locations
used by section one.
   HIMEM   =    $73
                                  ;
   RANGE_STRT = $3C               ; Addresses related
to Monitor's 'move' routine.
   RANGE_END =  $3E
   MOVE_TO  =   $42
   MOVE     =   $FE2C
                                  ;
   INBUF    =   $200              ; Locations used by
section two.
   COUT     =   $FDED
                                  ;
   EXTRNCMD =   $BE06             ; BASIC.SYSTEM's
external command vector.
   ERROUT   =   $BE09             ; BASIC.SYSTEM's
error vector.
   GOSYSTEM =   $BE70             ; BASIC.SYSTEM's
machine language interface vector.
   GETBUFR  =   $BEF5             ; BASIC.SYSTEM's
buffer allocation vector.
                                  ;
   XTRNADR  =   $BE50             ; Command execution
vector.
   XLEN     =   $BE52             ; Command string
length minus 1.
   XCNUM    =   $BE53             ; Command number
(should be zero if external command).
   PBITS    =   $BE54             ; Command parameter
flags.
   BITMAP   =   $BF58             ; ProDOS system bit
map.
                                  ;
   MLI_OPEN =   $C8               ; Number for MLI's
open command.
   OSYSBUF  =   $BECE             ; Address of system
```

Listing 20-4. A BASIC.SYSTEM TYPE command.

```
buffer for this file.
        OREFNUM  =     $BED0       ; Reference number
assigned to this file by MLI.
                                   ;
        MLI_READ =     $CA         ; Number for MLI's
read command.
        RWREFNUM =     $BED6       ; File's reference
number.
        RWDATA   =     $BED7       ; Address of data
buffer.
        RWCOUNT  =     $BED9       ; Number of bytes to
be read.
        RWTRANS  =     $BEDB       ; Number of bytes
actually read.
                                   ;
        MLI_CLOSE =    $CC         ; Number for MLI's
close command.
        CFREFNUM =     $BEDE       ; File's reference
number.
                                   ;
                 ORG   $2000
                                   ; SAV TYPE.CMD
                                   ;

*-----------------------------------------------------------
-----
        *
        *  Section I
        *   This section asks BASIC.SYSTEM for a memory
space we
        *     can place our routine in.  After the
buffer has been
        *     allocated to us, we hook our routine into
BASIC.SYSTEM's
        *     external command vector, while saving the
current contents
        *     of that vector for daisy-chaining.
        *  Next, we adjust all addresses inside our
routine to reflect
        *     the routine's assigned location.
        *  Then we move the routine into place.
        *  Finally, we send the user a "type
installed"
        *     message.
        *

*-----------------------------------------------------------
-----
                                   ;
        PREP_CMD =     *
2000: 18          CLC              ; Check memory
        availability so that memory
2001: AD BC 20    LDA   END_ADR+1  ; allocation doesn't
        overwrite our
2004: 6D BD 20    ADC   PAGES      ; program.
        End-of-program plus number
```

```
2007: C5 74              CMP   HIMEM+1     ; of pages to be
        requested must be
2009: 90 05              BCC   GET_BUF     ; less than the
        current himem value.
                                           ;
             NOBUFS  =         *
200B: A9 0E              LDA   #14         ; Code for PROGRAM
        TOO LARGE error.
             NOBUFS_1 =        *
200D: 4C 09 BE           JMP   ERROUT      ; New command cannot
        be installed.
                                           ;
             GET_BUF  =        *
2010: AD BD 20           LDA   PAGES
2013: 20 F5 BE           JSR   GETBUFR     ; Ask for a buffer A
        pages in length.
2016: B0 F5              BCS   NOBUFS_1    ; Error encountered,
        no buffer allotted.
2018: 8D BF 20           STA   OUR_BUF+1   ; Save start of
        allotted buffer space
201B: 38                 SEC
201C: ED BA 20           SBC   CODE_STRT+1 ; Compute increment
        for address adjustments.
201F: 8D C0 20           STA   INCREMENT
                                           ;
             SET_HOOKS =       *
2022: AE 07 BE           LDX   EXTRNCMD+1
2025: AD 08 BE           LDA   EXTRNCMD+2
2028: 8E 3B 21           STX   CMDLINK+1   ; Link into external
        command vector,
202B: 8D 3C 21           STA   CMDLINK+2   ; saving current
        external vector
202E: AE BE 20           LDX   OUR_BUF     ; for daisy-chaining.
2031: AD BF 20           LDA   OUR_BUF+1
2034: 8E 07 BE           STX   EXTRNCMD+1
2037: 8D 08 BE           STA   EXTRNCMD+2
                                           ;
             ADJ_CODE =        *
203A: A0 00              LDY   #0          ; Adjust routine's
        internal address references...
203C: B1 3C              LDA   (POINTER),Y ; Get instruction
        byte.
203E: F0 18              BEQ   ADJ_TABLES  ; 0 (brk) MUST
        separate code from address tables.
2040: 20 8E F8           JSR   $F88E       ; Ask monitor if this
        is a 1-, 2-, or
2043: A4 2F              LDY   $2F         ; 3-byte instruction.
2045: C0 02              CPY   #2          ; If monitor returns
        a 2 at $2F it is a 3-byte
2047: D0 07              BNE   LOOP1       ; instruction.  Else
        skip it.
2049: B1 3C              LDA   (POINTER),Y ; Get high byte of
        embedded address.
204B: 20 9C 20           JSR   FIX_ADR     ; Make adjustment for
        new location.
204E: 91 3C              STA   (POINTER),Y ; Store result.
2050: C8         LOOP1   INY
```

```
2051: 98                 TYA                ; Add one to index,
2052: 20 AD 20           JSR  INC_PNTR      ; adjust pointer,
2055: 4C 3A 20           JMP  ADJ_CODE      ; and repeat.
                                            ;
          ADJ_TABLES =   *
2058: A0 01              LDY  #1            ; Adjust routine's
        address tables...
205A: B1 3C              LDA  (POINTER),Y ; Get high byte of
        address
205C: F0 0D              BEQ  MOVE_CMD      ; 0000 MUST separate
        tables from data/strings.
205E: 20 9C 20           JSR  FIX_ADR       ; Make adjustment for
        new location.
2061: 91 3C              STA  (POINTER),Y ; Store result.
2063: A9 02              LDA  #2
2065: 20 AD 20           JSR  INC_PNTR      ; Increment pointer 2
        bytes,
2068: 4C 58 20           JMP  ADJ_TABLES ; and repeat.
                                            ;
          MOVE_CMD =     *
206B: AE B9 20           LDX  CODE_STRT
206E: AD BA 20           LDA  CODE_STRT+1 ; Set up parameters
        for monitor's move command.
2071: 86 3C              STX  RANGE_STRT
2073: 85 3D              STA  RANGE_STRT+1
                                            ;
2075: AE BB 20           LDX  END_ADR
2078: AD BC 20           LDA  END_ADR+1
207B: 86 3E              STX  RANGE_END
207D: 85 3F              STA  RANGE_END+1
                                            ;
207F: AE BE 20           LDX  OUR_BUF
2082: AD BF 20           LDA  OUR_BUF+1
2085: 86 42              STX  MOVE_TO
2087: 85 43              STA  MOVE_TO+1
                                            ;
2089: A0 00              LDY  #0            ; Ask monitor to move
        routine into
208B: 20 2C FE           JSR  MOVE          ; allotted buffer.
                                            ;
208E: A0 00              LDY  #0
2090: B9 C1 20    LOOP2  LDA  MSG,Y         ; Tell user that type
        command has
2093: F0 06              BEQ  INSTALL_END ; been successfully
        installed.
2095: 20 ED FD           JSR  COUT
2098: C8                 INY
2099: D0 F5              BNE  LOOP2
                                            ;
          INSTALL_END
209B: 60                 RTS                ; End of installation
        program, return to BASIC.
                                            ;
          *---------------------------
          *
          * Section I: subroutines
          *
```

```
                *---------------------------
                                          ;
                FIX_ADR =     *
209C: CD BA 20            CMP   CODE_STRT+1 ; Is this address
        lower than routine's start?
209F: 90 0B               BCC   LOOP4      ; yes--don't change
        it.
20A1: CD BC 20            CMP   END_ADR+1  ; Is it higher than
        routine's end?
20A4: F0 02               BEQ   LOOP3
20A6: B0 04               BCS   LOOP4      ; yes--don't change
        it.
20A8: 18        LOOP3     CLC
20A9: 6D C0 20            ADC   INCREMENT  ; Add distance from
        here to buffer location.
20AC: 60        LOOP4     RTS
                                          ;
                INC_PNTR =    *
20AD: 18                  CLC
20AE: 65 3C               ADC   POINTER    ; Add value in A (1,
        2, or 3) to 'pointer'.
20B0: 85 3C               STA   POINTER
20B2: A5 3D               LDA   POINTER+1
20B4: 69 00               ADC   #0
20B6: 85 3D               STA   POINTER+1
20B8: 60                  RTS
                                          ;
                *---------------------------
                *
                * Section 1: data
                *
                *---------------------------
                                          ;
20B9: 00 21     CODE_STRT DA    ROUTINE_STRT ; address of
        beginning of routine
20BB: C4 21     END_ADR   DA    ROUTINE_END ; address of end of
        routine
20BD: 01        PAGES     DFB   #1         ; number of pages
        needed for routine
                                          ;
20BE: 00 00     OUR_BUF   DA    $0000
20C0: 00        INCREMENT HEX   00
                                          ;
20C1: 8D        MSG       HEX   8D
20C2: A2 D4 D9            ASC   !"TYPE" COMMAND NOW AVAILABLE.!
20C5: D0 C5 A2 A0 C3 CF CD CD
20CD: C1 CE C4 A0 CE CF D7 A0
20D5: C1 D6 C1 C9 CC C1 C2 CC
20DD: C5 AE
20DF: 8D 8D 00            HEX   8D8D00
                                          ;
20E2: 00 00 00            DS    \          ; Fill program with
        empty bytes so following
20E5: 00 00 00 00 00 00 00 00
20ED: 00 00 00 00 00 00 00 00
20F5: 00 00 00 00 00 00 00 00
20FD: 00 00 00
                                          ; section will start
```

```
                                       ; make things easy on the relocation routine.  (on a page boundry to)
                                       ;
*----------------------------------------------------------------
*
* Section II
* This section holds the routine that is actually moved into
*    the space allocated by BASIC.SYSTEM.  It has two parts.
* BASIC.SYSTEM passes control to the first part of this routine
*    whenever a command is entered that BASIC.SYSTEM doesn't
*    recognize.  Our routine looks at the command.  If the
*    command isn't ours either, we pass it to the next routine
*    on the daisy-chain.  If the routine is ours, we notify
*    BASIC.SYSTEM and pass back control so the rest of the
*    command can be parsed.
* After the command is parsed, BASIC.SYSTEM sends control to
*    the second part of this section, where the type command is
*    actually executed.
*
*
-------------------------------------------------------------
                                       ;
*---------------------------
*
* Section II: part 1
*
*---------------------------
                                       ;
              ROUTINE_STRT = *
2100: D8                CLD            ; (identification byte)
2101: A2 00             LDX  #0        ; DOS has a command it doesn't recognize,
2103: A0 00             LDY  #0        ; let's take a look at it.
2105: 20 A6 21    LOOP5 JSR  GET_CHR   ; Get a character of the command.
2108: F0 2F             BEQ  NOT_US    ; Character was comma or return--cmd not ours.
210A: 29 DF             AND  #$DF      ; Convert to U/C - DJD.
210C: D9 BE 21          CMP  CMDNAME,Y ; Compare character to our command string.
```

```
210F: D0 28           BNE   NOT_US     ; Not equal--cmd not
        ours.
2111: C8              INY              ; Increment command
        index.
2112: C0 04           CPY   #4         ; Compare index to
        length of command.
2114: 90 EF           BCC   LOOP5      ; less--check next
        character.
                                       ;
                ITS_US  =   *
2116: 88              DEY              ; The command is
        ours, so...
2117: 8C 52 BE        STY   XLEN       ; Save cmd length
        minus 1 at 'xlen'.
211A: AE B8 21        LDX   DO_ADR
211D: AD B9 21        LDA   DO_ADR+1   ; Save command
        execution address
2120: 8E 50 BE        STX   XTRNADR    ; at 'xtrnaddr'.
2123: 8D 51 BE        STA   XTRNADR+1
2126: A9 00           LDA   #0         ; Put a zero at
        'xcnum' so BASIC.SYSTEM
2128: 8D 53 BE        STA   XCNUM      ; Knows the command
        was recognized.
212B: AE C2 21        LDX   PARMS
212E: AD C3 21        LDA   PARMS+1    ; Flag the parameters
        we allow with our
2131: 8E 54 BE        STX   PBITS      ; command in 'pbits'.
2134: 8D 55 BE        STA   PBITS+1
2137: 18              CLC              ; Ask BASIC.SYSTEM to
        finish parsing command.
2138: 60              RTS
                                       ;
                NOT_US  =   *
2139: 38              SEC              ; The command isn't
        ours, so...
                CMDLINK =   *
213A: 4C 00 00        JMP   $0000      ; Pass it down the
        daisy chain (address
                                       ; filled in by
        Section I).
                *--------------------------
                *
                * Section II: part 2
                *
                *--------------------------
                                       ;
                DO_CMD  =   *
213D: A6 73           LDX   HIMEM      ; Actual command
        execution starts here.
213F: A5 74           LDA   HIMEM+1    ; Use BASIC.SYSTEM's
        temporary buffer
2141: 8E CE BE        STX   OSYSBUF    ; for type command's
        buffer.
2144: 8D CF BE        STA   OSYSBUF+1  ; (Adr of temp buf
        always same as himem.)
                                       ;
2147: A9 C8           LDA   #MLI_OPEN  ; Put number for open
        in A.
```

```
2149: 20 70 BE              JSR   GOSYSTEM    ; Open file.
214C: 90 03                 BCC   INIT_READ
214E: 4C 09 BE              JMP   ERROUT      ; If error on open,
        pass control to error handler.
                                              ;
                 INIT_READ =      *
2151: AD D0 BE              LDA   OREFNUM     ; Get file's
        reference number
2154: 8D D6 BE              STA   RWREFNUM    ; for read command
        table.
                                              ;
2157: AE BA 21              LDX   BUF_ADR
215A: AD BB 21              LDA   BUF_ADR+1   ; A one-byte data
        buffer where ProDOS
215D: 8E D7 BE              STX   RWDATA      ; can put our data.
2160: 8D D8 BE              STA   RWDATA+1
                                              ;
2163: A2 01                 LDX   #1
2165: A9 00                 LDA   #0          ; We want one byte at
        a time.
2167: 8E D9 BE              STX   RWCOUNT
216A: 8D DA BE              STA   RWCOUNT+1
                                              ;
216D: A9 8D                 LDA   #$8D        ; (carriage return)
                                              ;
                 MAINLOOP =       *
216F: 20 ED FD              JSR   COUT        ; Print it!
2172: AD 00 C0              LDA   $C000       ; Check keyboard.
2175: C9 9B                 CMP   #$9B        ; Is it escape?
2177: F0 10                 BEQ   HALT        ; yes--halt
2179: A9 CA                 LDA   #MLI_READ   ; no--read next
        character
217B: 20 70 BE              JSR   GOSYSTEM
217E: B0 0E                 BCS   ERROR       ; End of file or
        other error?
2180: AD C4 21              LDA   BYTEBUF     ; no--get character
        from one-byte buffer
2183: F0 EA                 BEQ   MAINLOOP    ; and print it if
        control-@,
2185: 09 80                 ORA   #$80        ; else change it to
        hi-value ASCII.
2187: D0 E6                 BNE   MAINLOOP    ; (always branchs)
                                              ;
2189: A9 05      HALT       LDA   #5          ; Fake end-of-data
        error.
218B: 8D 10 C0              STA   $C010       ; Clear keyboard
        strobe.
                                              ;
                 ERROR    =       *
218E: AA                    TAX               ; Save error code in
        X.
218F: AD D0 BE              LDA   OREFNUM     ; Put file's
        reference number in
2192: 8D DE BE              STA   CFREFNUM    ; close
        command-table.
2195: A9 CC                 LDA   #MLI_CLOSE  ; Close file.
2197: 20 70 BE              JSR   GOSYSTEM
219A: B0 07                 BCS   REALERR     ; If error on close,
```

```
        pass control to error handler.
219C: 8A                    TXA               ; Retrieve error code
        from before.
219D: C9 05                 CMP   #5          ; Is it end-of-data?
219F: D0 02                 BNE   REALERR     ; no--pass control to
        error handler.
21A1: 18                    CLC               ; yes--tell system no
        error occurred.
21A2: 60                    RTS               ; Done.
                                              ;
             REALERR   =     *
21A3: 4C 09 BE              JMP   ERROUT      ; Problem
        encountered, let BASIC.SYSTEM fix it.
                                              ;
             *---------------------------
             *
             * Section II: subroutines
             *
             *---------------------------
                                              ;
             GET_CHR   =     *
21A6: BD 00 02              LDA   INBUF,X     ; Get a character
        from the input buffer.
21A9: E8                    INX               ; Increment character
        index.
21AA: C9 8D                 CMP   #$8D        ; Test for return.
21AC: F0 08                 BEQ   LOOP6
21AE: C9 AC                 CMP   #","        ; Test for comma.
21B0: F0 04                 BEQ   LOOP6       ; If comma or return,
        pass back 'equal'.
21B2: C9 A0                 CMP   #$A0        ; Test for blank.
21B4: F0 F0                 BEQ   GET_CHR     ; If blank, skip it
        and get next character.
21B6: 60     LOOP6          RTS
                                              ;
21B7: 00                    BRK               ; Separates code from
        data for relocator.
                                              ;
             *---------------------------
             *
             * Section II: data
             *
             *---------------------------
                                              ;
21B8: 3D 21  DO_ADR         DA    DO_CMD
21BA: C4 21  BUF_ADR        DA    BYTEBUF
                                              ;
21BC: 00 00                 DA    $0000       ; Separates address
        tables for relocator.
21BE: D4 D9 D0  CMDNAME     ASC   "TYPE"
21C1: C5
21C2: 01 04  PARMS          HEX   0104        ; Pathname required /
        slot,drive allowed.
21C4: 00     BYTEBUF        HEX   00
                                              ;
             ROUTINE_END =   *-1
                                              ;
```

```
--End assembly, 453 bytes, Errors: 0


Symbol table - alphabetical order:

   ADJ_CODE=$203A      ADJ_TABLES=$2058   ? BITMAP  =$BF58
         BUF_ADR =$21BA
   BYTEBUF =$21C4      CFREFNUM=$BEDE      CMDLINK =$213A
         CMDNAME =$21BE
   CODE_STRT=$20B9      COUT    =$FDED      DO_ADR  =$21B8
         DO_CMD  =$213D
   END_ADR =$20BB      ERROR   =$218E      ERROUT  =$BE09
         EXTRNCMD=$BE06
   FIX_ADR =$209C      GETBUFR =$BEF5      GET_BUF =$2010
         GET_CHR =$21A6
   GOSYSTEM=$BE70      HALT    =$2189      HIMEM   =$73        INBUF
         =$0200
   INCREMENT=$20C0      INC_PNTR=$20AD      INIT_READ=$2151
         INSTALL_END=$209B
? ITS_US  =$2116      LOOP1   =$2050      LOOP2   =$2090      LOOP3
         =$20A8
   LOOP4   =$20AC      LOOP5   =$2105      LOOP6   =$21B6
         MAINLOOP=$216F
   MLI_CLOSE=$CC       MLI_OPEN=$C8        MLI_READ=$CA        MOVE
         =$FE2C
   MOVE_CMD=$206B      MOVE_TO =$42        MSG     =$20C1    ?
         NOBUFS  =$200B
   NOBUFS_1=$200D      NOT_US  =$2139      OREFNUM =$BED0
         OSYSBUF =$BECE
   OUR_BUF =$20BE      PAGES   =$20BD      PARMS   =$21C2      PBITS
         =$BE54
   POINTER =$3C      ? PREP_CMD=$2000      RANGE_END=$3E
         RANGE_STRT=$3C
   REALERR =$21A3      ROUTINE_END=$21C4      ROUTINE_STRT=$2100
         RWCOUNT =$BED9
   RWDATA  =$BED7      RWREFNUM=$BED6    ? RWTRANS =$BEDB    ?
         SET_HOOKS=$2022
   XCNUM   =$BE53      XLEN    =$BE52      XTRNADR =$BE50


Symbol table - numerical order:

   POINTER =$3C        RANGE_STRT=$3C        RANGE_END=$3E
         MOVE_TO =$42
   HIMEM   =$73        MLI_OPEN=$C8        MLI_READ=$CA
         MLI_CLOSE=$CC
   INBUF   =$0200    ? PREP_CMD=$2000    ? NOBUFS  =$200B
         NOBUFS_1=$200D
   GET_BUF =$2010    ? SET_HOOKS=$2022      ADJ_CODE=$203A
         LOOP1   =$2050
   ADJ_TABLES=$2058      MOVE_CMD=$206B      LOOP2   =$2090
         INSTALL_END=$209B
   FIX_ADR =$209C      LOOP3   =$20A8      LOOP4   =$20AC
         INC_PNTR=$20AD
   CODE_STRT=$20B9      END_ADR =$20BB      PAGES   =$20BD
         OUR_BUF =$20BE
   INCREMENT=$20C0      MSG     =$20C1      ROUTINE_STRT=$2100
         LOOP5   =$2105
```

```
?  ITS_US   =$2116      NOT_US   =$2139      CMDLINK =$213A
           DO_CMD   =$213D
   INIT_READ=$2151      MAINLOOP=$216F      HALT     =$2189
           ERROR    =$218E
   REALERR =$21A3      GET_CHR =$21A6      LOOP6    =$21B6
           DO_ADR   =$21B8
   BUF_ADR =$21BA      CMDNAME =$21BE      PARMS    =$21C2
           BYTEBUF =$21C4
   ROUTINE_END=$21C4      EXTRNCMD=$BE06      ERROUT   =$BE09
           XTRNADR =$BE50
   XLEN     =$BE52      XCNUM    =$BE53      PBITS    =$BE54
           GOSYSTEM=$BE70
   OSYSBUF =$BECE      OREFNUM =$BED0      RWREFNUM=$BED6
           RWDATA   =$BED7
   RWCOUNT =$BED9   ?  RWTRANS =$BEDB      CFREFNUM=$BEDE
           GETBUFR =$BEF5
?  BITMAP   =$BF58      COUT     =$FDED      MOVE     =$FE2C
```

Chapter 21

BASIC.SYSTEM Interaction With The Apple Firmware

This chapter is the last to be based almost solely on pure BASIC.SYSTEM subjects before a foray into ProDOS matters of interest to BASIC programmers. Before moving on, a few miscellaneous subjects having to do with the interaction of the Apple's firmware/hardware and BASIC.SYSTEM will be discussed.

IDENTIFYING PERIPHERAL CARDS

Most presently available interface cards can be tentatively identified using the *Pascal 1.1 Protocol*. Yes, it says "Pascal". The reason it appears in a book on BASIC.SYSTEM is that ProDOS and BASIC.SYSTEM use this protocol to identify certain devices attached to the Apple slots, and it provides a guideline for writing programs which will hopefully utilize peripherals that follow the protocol on nearly any Apple *II*. The Apple versions of the CP/M operating system also normally follow these conventions.

Essentially, the Pascal 1.1 protocol was an attempt by Apple to standardize the interfacing of Apple programs to the "intelligent" peripheral cards that the Apple tends to use. The cards are referred to as "intelligent" because they can contain a certain amount of ROM programming to control the card, eliminating the need for your program to know how to control the device attached to the card. The idea behind the protocol was to be able to identify the *type* of interface represented by the card, and to provide standardized entry point addresses into the firmware to perform input and output.

Normally, each peripheral card has two ROM areas available to it. The first is a 256 ($100) byte area located in the address range $Cs00-$CsFF, where "s" is the slot number. This address is slot-specific; an interface card in slot 1 would, for example, have the address range $C100-$C1FF reserved for a ROM.

In addition, a second area from $C800-$CFFF is reserved for use by *any* peripheral card; a second 2 kilobyte ROM can be assigned here to augment its 0.25 kilobyte ROM. The $C800 space is "released" by attempting to store a value into location $CFFF (via a "STA $CFFF" instruction, for example); this activates a switching mechanism in the Apple that keeps any ROM from owning that address area exclusively. The area can then be assigned to a ROM by accessing any location within the $Cs00- $CsFF peripheral card slot ROM area; the peripheral card in that slot can "take over" the $C800-$CFFF ROM area also until a "STA $CFFF" or similar instruction "removes" it again.

The Pascal 1.1 protocol uses four bytes in the 256 byte slot ROM area to identify the type of peripheral card assigned to the slot. The bytes at $Cs05 and $Cs07 are always $38 and $18 respectively, the byte at $Cs0B is to be a $01 to indicate a firmware ROM is present, and the final identifier byte at $Cs0C is used to contain a *device signature* byte value. Apple currently recognizes the device signature values listed in Table 21-1. The "x" representing the second hexadecimal digit of each byte is used by Apple for a unique identifier for a particular product. As an example, the value of "x" for an Apple *II*e 80-column text card is "8", making its device signature byte value a "$88".

In addition, standard entry points are maintained for initializing the peripheral card and performing I/O in conjunction with it. We'll leave that discussion for others; the information was originally available in a booklet named *Apple IIe Design Guidelines* from Apple Computer (part number 030-0621A), which is now reportedly extinct (just the book, not the protocol).

A device interface can be tentatively identified by reading the four protocol bytes to determine if they match the accepted values for a firmware card ROM. ProDOS does this at boot-up and keeps a record of slots that appear to contain a ROM for its use; BASIC.SYSTEM also keeps some of these records in its global page. That is how BASIC.SYSTEM is able to reply with a "NO DEVICE CONNECTED" error on certain commands before it even accesses a slot; it checks its internal records of slots with ROMs to see if a peripheral card was detected.

NON-PASCAL PROTOCOL DEVICES

In addition to the device signature codes above, other common types of devices are detected by ProDOS. The first of these is the Apple Disk *II*-type disk drives, which do not follow the Pascal 1.1 protocol. The Disk *II* controller card in slot number "s" is identified specifically by the following byte values: $20 at $Cs01, $00 at $Cs03, and $03 in $Cs05.

There is an extended protocol for use with mass storage devices necessitated by the advent of

Table 21-1. Pascal 1.1 Protocol Signature Byte Values.

Signature Byte	Device Class
0x	reserved (not specified at present)
1x	printer
2x	X-Y input device
3x	serial or parallel input/output card
4x	modem
5x	sound or speech device
6x	clock
7x	mass storage device
8x	80-column display device
9x	network or bus interface
Ax	special purpose
Bx	reserved

ProDOS, which can access volumes of up to 32 megabytes in size. This protocol is described in Apple's "ProDOS Technical Note #3". In addition to the three bytes used by the Pascal protocol to identify a Disk *II*-type device, ProDOS examines the byte at $CnFF to determine if the drive controller actually belongs to a Disk *II*. If this byte equals $00, ProDOS assumes the drive controller belongs to a Disk *II*-type drive and uses its (ProDOS's) internal disk driver routines for the Disk *II*. If the byte value is non-zero, ProDOS assumes that the disk controller found is "intelligent" and contains its own routines for accessing the drive. A further description of these routines can be found in the technical note or in Chapter 7 of Gary Little's book *Apple's ProDOS: Advanced Features for Programmers.*

A second type of device, a ProDOS-compatible clock, does not use the Pascal protocol. The clock can be identified by four byte values: $Cs00 ($08), $Cs02 ($28), $Cs04 ($58), and $Cs06 ($70). Additionally, older Apple peripheral cards that do not follow the Pascal 1.1 protocol may be recognized by ProDOS so that accessing the slot containing one of these cards does not produce a "DEVICE NOT CONNECTED" error. A common example is the Apple Parallel Interface card. These devices must be detected by specific bytes (as for the ProDOS-compatible clock) since they do not follow a generalized identification protocol. A program to identify several interfaces via the Pascal 1.1 protocol plus certain other devices is presented in Listing 21-1.

```
10  REM *** ID.SLOT.ROMS ***
20  TEXT : PRINT : PRINT  CHR$ (21): HOME
30  DIM ID$(16): REM FOR ID STRINGS.
40  FOR ID = 0 TO 16: READ ID$(ID): NEXT ID
100  REM *** TITLE ***
110  HOME
120  PRINT
       "========================================"
130  PRINT
140 A$ = "Slot Configuration Check": HTAB  INT
       ((40 -  LEN (A$)) / 2): PRINT A$
150  PRINT
160  PRINT
       "========================================"
170  PRINT
180  PRINT
200  REM *** SCAN SLOTS FOR I/O DEVICES ***
210  FOR SLOT = 1 TO 7
220 SROM = 49152 + SLOT * 256: REM FIRST BYTE OF
       SLOT ROM.
300  REM *** LOOK FOR PASCAL 1.1 FIRMWARE ID ***
310 ROM(SLOT) = 16: REM NO DEVICE TO START.
320  IF  PEEK (SROM + 5) = 56 AND  PEEK (SROM +
       7) = 24 AND  PEEK (SROM + 11) = 1 THEN
       GOSUB 1000: REM IF ID FOUND, DETERMINE
       TYPE OF ROM.
400  REM *** LOOK FOR DISK CONTROLLER ROM ***
410  IF  PEEK (SROM + 1) = 32 AND  PEEK (SROM +
       3) = 0 AND  PEEK (SROM + 5) = 3 THEN
       ROM(SLOT) = 12: REM DISK ][-TYPE.
420  IF ID = 12 AND  PEEK (SROM + 255) =  < > 0
       THEN ROM(SLOT) = 13): REM INTELLIGENT
       CONTROLLER.
```

Listing 21-1. Checking slot ROMs per the Pascal 1.1 protocol.

```
500  REM *** LOOK FOR PRODOS-COMPATIBLE CLOCK
       CARD ***
510  IF  PEEK (SROM) = 8 AND  PEEK (SROM + 2) =
       40 AND  PEEK (SROM + 4) = 88 AND  PEEK
       (SROM + 6) = 112 THEN ROM(SLOT) = 14: REM
       SPECIFIC CLOCK ID.
600  REM *** DO NEXT SLOT ***
610  NEXT SLOT
700  REM *** PRINT THE RESULTS ***
710  PRINT "Slot Configuration:"
720  PRINT
730  FOR SLOT = 1 TO 7
740  PRINT  SPC( 3);SLOT;": ";ID$(ROM(SLOT))
750  NEXT SLOT
760  VTAB 22
999  END
1000  REM *** GET DEVICE ID CODE ***
1010 ID =  INT ( PEEK (SROM + 12) / 16)
1020  IF ID > 11 THEN ID = 15: REM UNKNOWN CODE.
1030 ROM(SLOT) = ID
1099  RETURN
10000  REM *** DATA STRINGS ***
10010  DATA "<reserved>","Printer
       interface","X-Y Device Interface"
10020  DATA "Serial/Parallel I/O
       Interface","Modem","Sound/Speech Device"
10030  DATA "Clock","Mass Storage
       Device","80-column Display Device"
10040  DATA "Network/Bus Interface","Special
       Purpose Interface","<reserved>"
10050  DATA "Disk ][-type
       Controller","Intelligent Drive
       Controller","ProDOS-compatible Clock"
10060  DATA "<unknown device>","<no device
       identified>"
```

STANDARD SLOT ASSIGNMENTS

When the Apple *II* was first introduced, Apple allowed the purchaser to configure his own system by placing peripheral interface cards in whichever slots he desired (the only exception was slot 0, which was reserved for the use of specific types of cards). This meant that originally, an Apple owner might have his printer attached to slot 1, 4, 5, or even another slot depending on his own whim. Some standardization was eventually enforced through the expectations of software. For example, it was often assumed that the Disk *II* drive's controller card existed in slot 6 on the computer, slot 1 was assumed to contain the printer interface card, etc.

Apple's Pascal operating system, in addition to setting a protocol for identifying peripheral interface cards, normally expected to find these interface cards in specific slots. This added to the impetus for setting "standards" regarding the location of specific peripheral cards within the Apple. Basically, the "standard" assignments are

Slot 0: Firmware ROM or RAM card (RAM card required by Pascal)
Slot 1: Printer interface card
Slot 2: Remote terminal interface; communications interface
Slot 3: Auxiliary console or system terminal (usually an 80-column card)
Slot 4: <no formal assignment>
Slot 5: < no formal assignment>

Slot 6: Disk *II*-type controller
Slot 7: <no formal assignment>

Recall that the Apple *II*e has no slot 0 (to the software, its RAM memory resembles a 48K Apple *II* with a RAM card in slot 0), and that an 80-column text card in the *II*e's auxiliary slot resembles (to the software) an 80-column display device in slot 3.

The use of slots 4, 5 and 7 is not rigidly defined by Pascal, with the exception that interfaces for additional Disk *II* devices are normally expected to be added to slots 5 and 4 (sequentially). Devices not inherently supported or recognized by the original Pascal 1.1 implementation are often placed in these slots.

Slot 4 has come to be used for either an AppleMouse interface card, a clock card, or an auxiliary coprocessor (a second microprocessor to be operated as an adjunct to the 6502).

Slot 7 is occasionally used for an RGB monitor interface (a specialized color display) since it is the only Apple *II* slot that provides the necessary video signals (on the Apple *II*e, the auxiliary slot also has the video signals needed for an RGB interface). It is presently also often used for either a coprocessor peripheral or a mass storage device such as Apple's ProFile hard disk drive.

Although the Apple *II*c has no real slots inside the case, it does have hardware and firmware designed so that its internal interfaces resemble peripheral cards in slots. The assignments are:

Slot 0: RAM card (as for *II*e)
Slot 1: Serial interface (printer interface)
Slot 2: Serial interface (remote communications)
Slot 3: 80-column text display (as for *II*e)
Slot 4: AppleMouse interface
Slot 5: <none or UniDisk interface >
Slot 6: Disk *II*-type controller
Slot 7: <none>

In the original *II*c ROMs, a "PR#7" command would cause the *II*c to attempt to boot a disk placed in the external drive. The new ROMs provided with the *II*c for use with the 3.5" UniDisk have removed this feature.

Although ProDOS does not have "hard and fast" rules about which device is attached to a slot, most programs have come to expect peripheral cards to exist in the slots indicated by these general rules.

THE ULTIMATE ERROR TRAP: TRAPPING RESET

One vexing "feature" of BASIC.SYSTEM is the memory management routine that causes the Applesoft variable space to be "cleared" whenever you perform a reset. If a program "locks up" mysteriously, you often cannot escape without using reset; but your variables are then gone which complicates troubleshooting. Also, sometimes you *want* to be able to trap the reset operation to prevent someone from exiting your program rudely. So how do you do this with BASIC.SYSTEM?

First, you should know that the reset operation does several things before returning you to Applesoft (or wherever "reset" is supposed to send you). Among these, "reset" scrambles the contents of the 6502's stack register. Applesoft uses a small section of the stack to parse command lines. If the stack register accidentally points at this area after a reset, BASIC trips over its own feet and tumbles to the ground.

In addition to scrambling the stack pointer, pressing "Reset" disables interrupts (on the Apple itself and often on any peripheral cards causing interrupts) and causes the 6502 to fetch the address stored at $FFFC and jump there. On all but the earliest Apples $FFFC points to $FA62. The routine there is called, appropriately enough, *RESET*. That routine puts the 6502 in binary (rather than decimal) mode; turns on normal (rather than inverse) characters; turns off graphics and turns on full-window, 40-column text with the cursor at the bottom of the screen; connects the keyboard for input and the display screen for output (disconnecting DOS from the I/O hooks in the process); turns off annunciators 0 and 1 and turns on annunciators 2 and 3; clears the keyboard strobe; turns off any active peripheral card ROM; and rings the Apple's bell.

In the *II*e and *II*c, special hardware circuits also turn on the motherboard ROM and the main bank of RAM. Auxiliary RAM is disabled. On earlier Apples with 64K of memory, on the other hand, RESET does not change the memory configuration.

After doing all of the above, the RESET routine takes a look at byte 1012 ($3F4). If this byte, called the *power-up byte*, contains the proper value, the routine next jumps to the address stored in a place called the *soft-entry vector*, which is at 1010 ($3F2). If the power-up byte contains any other value, as it always does immediately after you turn on your computer, RESET will attempt to boot a disk. The proper value is defined by RESET as being equal to the exclusive-OR of the contents of $3F4 and $A5. The address usually stored in the soft-entry vector is the warmstart address for the system program in use; 48640 ($BE00) for BASIC.SYSTEM.

Thus, the next thing RESET normally does is warmstart BASIC.SYSTEM. Under DOS 3.3, a "reset" meant the language card/ROM area was switched back to whatever language had been in use when "Reset" was pressed; DOS is reconnected to the I/O hooks; a NOMONICO is executed; and a jump occurs to BASIC's warmstart address, 54332 ($D43C). The BASIC prompt and cursor appear on your screen. Your program and data are intact, but your program is no longer running.

ProDOS's BASIC.SYSTEM, on the other hand, handles warmstarts a little differently. It first jumps to the CLEAR command inside Applesoft at 54885 ($D665), which empties out all your variables and leaves them filled with zeros. This isn't real handy if you'd like to recover from a "reset" without losing any data. The CLEAR routine also fixes the stack register, however; something DOS 3.3 neglected to do. Next BASIC.SYSTEM reconnects itself to the I/O links, pushes the cursor over to the left edge of the screen, and warmstarts BASIC at 54335 ($D43F). The Applesoft prompt and cursor appear on your screen. Your program is intact but no longer running; your data is gone.

Note the two BASIC warmstart addresses are different by three bytes. BASIC.SYSTEM skips the first warmstart instruction, which sends a carriage return to the screen. A BASIC.SYSTEM "reset" doesn't make the screen scroll. A DOS 3.3 "reset" does. This is why. It's also why BASIC.SYSTEM has to push the cursor to the left edge of the screen by hand.

The exercise in Figure 21-1 is instructive for looking at the differences between DOS 3.3 and ProDOS/BASIC.SYSTEM reset operations. BASIC.SYSTEM will *not* reply "HI THERE" to the Applesoft "PRINT A$" command, its reset cycle makes Applesoft forget its variables' values.

Now you know everything there is to know (and much more than you probably wanted to know) about RESET. The original question remains, however; how do you keep a BASIC program running and send control to a special error routine when "Reset" is pressed (with the variables intact)?

In theory, all you have to do is change BASIC.SYSTEM so that instead of warmstarting BASIC, it jumps to a BASIC error handler. Applesoft

```
]10 A$ = "HI THERE!"     Enter these lines into Applesoft.
]20 GOTO 20

]RUN                     The program hangs in line 20
                         (you press Reset).

]PRINT A$                Print out the value of A$.
HI THERE!                DOS 3.3 replies with the value of A$
                         (BASIC.SYSTEM will respond with a
                          blank line.).
```

Fig. 21-1. Testing RESET.

doesn't have a "reset" error, thus we'll have to use another one. There's a good one at 58123 ($E30B); the Applesoft "*ILLEGAL DIRECT*" error. This error occurs when you try to do an INPUT, GET, or a few other commands from the keyboard. It never occurs in a running program. So let's modify the BASIC.SYSTEM reset operation a little; a simple task.

The bytes you have to change move around from one BASIC.SYSTEM version to another. Luckily, they're easy to find; first look at the BASIC.SYSTEM warmstart vector at 48640 ($BE00) to determine where the actual warmstart code lies; the bytes that must be changed are the 11th and 12th bytes of the warmstart code (at least that's where they've been in all BASIC.SYSTEM versions to date). After we make these modifications, RESET, in conjunction with an ONERR GOTO statement in your program, will pass control to ONERR with the code for an ILLEGAL DIRECT error (149) stored where you can fish it out with the standard PEEK(222).

That's the theory, anyhow. But BASIC.SYSTEM still makes us lose all our data. Let's fix this problem, too; we'll change the jump to the CLEAR subroutine into a jump to just the stack initialization subroutine, which lives at byte 54915 ($D683).

—Whew—. A little program that does all this stuff is shown in Listing 21-2. Run the program (nothing will seem to happen; it locks up in line 100) and press "Reset". Line 100's message should appear on your screen. Since the ILLEGAL DIRECT error won't ever occur naturally inside a program, you can always be sure its appearance means somebody pressed the "Reset" key.

Delete line 80's ONERR and RUN the program again. Now Applesoft's built-in message center will print "?ILLEGAL DIRECT ERROR IN 100".

If you haven't saved the program to disk yet, *do it now*. Then put line 80 back in and add "210 RESUME". RUN and press "Reset". You'll find yourself in an eternal cycle of errors. Too many things get changed when "Reset" is pressed to simply resume execution. Instead, warmstart your program with a GOTO. In this case, use "210 GOTO 100".

```
10 REM Reset trap

20 V1=58123 : REM address of Applesoft illegal
      direct error
25 V2=54915 : REM address of Applesoft stack
      initialization

60 A2=1+PEEK(48641)+PEEK(48642)*256 : REM
      ($BE01)+1
62 A1=A2+10 : REM fish out BASIC.SYSTEM
      warmstart address

70 REM 2-byte pokes adr,value
72 POKE A1+1,V1/256 : POKE
      A1,V1-(PEEK(A1+1)*256)
74 POKE A2+1,V2/256 : POKE
      A2,V2-(PEEK(A2+1)*256)

80 ONERR GOTO 200

100 GOTO 100 : REM lockup

200 PRINT "ERROR #"; PEEK(222); " IN LINE
      ";PEEK(218) + PEEK(219)*256
```

Listing 21-2. A RESET trapper.

RUN again and try pressing control-C as well as "Reset". That is how you direct a program to line x after "Reset" has been hit. The only way to get out of our sample program now is with a hard "Reset" ("control open-Apple reset" on an Apple *II*e or *II*c) or to turn the computer off (losing your program). *Sure hope you saved it like you were supposed to.*

Remember that RESET turns off graphics and 80-column displays, reconfigures memory, and makes other subtle system changes. Your ONERR routine (or your warmstart) may have to take special steps to set these things alright again. The modifications we made here should never be permanently added to BASIC.SYSTEM. They cause a lot of trouble if you don't want "reset" trapped; among these things 3D00G (which JMPs to our warmstart entry) does strange stuff.

Since this is becoming a definitive explanation of RESET, let's mention a couple more things. If you ignore my advice and try to change the soft-entry vector (instead of leaving it pointing to the BASIC.SYSTEM warmstart routines), issue a "CALL 64367" ($FB6F) after the change to correct the power-up byte. If you don't, the disk will boot when you press "Reset" (there goes the program in memory again). On the other hand, if that's what you *want* to happen, just poke a zero into the power-up byte (POKE 1012,0).

ZERO PAGE (AND DASTARDLY $D6)

Every once in a while, it's useful for a programmer to be able to find a few uncommitted zero page locations for his own use. Between ProDOS, Applesoft, the system monitor, and BASIC.SYSTEM (all of which use zero page in some manner) there are not many "free" locations left. Apple's *ProDOS Technical Reference Manual* shows the following ranges available: $06-$09, $19-$1E, $CE, $CF, $D6, $D7, $EB-$EF, and $F9-$FF.

At least one of these, $D6 (214), is *not* truly available and should not be used. $D6 is used as an Applesoft "protection" register; if a value greater than 128 ($80) is stored there Applesoft will not allow you to enter *any* command at an Applesoft prompt other than a "return" without issuing a "clandestine RUN" command. Thus, any attempt to use LIST or NEW on a program will result in running the program in memory. RESET also has no effect on escape from the dilemma, but may get you out of your BASIC program to the Applesoft prompt.

BASIC.SYSTEM will, fortunately (and unlike DOS 3.3's SAVE command), apparently ignore this register for its commands. If you notice the above symptoms and you have a program in memory, try SAVEing the program to a disk file. Then reboot to eliminate the Applesoft protection.

Part 5

BASIC.SYSTEM with the ProDOS Kernel

Chapter 22

Introduction To ProDOS

The important thing to remember about BASIC.SYSTEM is that, for the most part, it serves as an intermediary between BASIC and ProDOS proper. BASIC.SYSTEM runs straight to ProDOS to execute certain commands, and cannot function properly without ProDOS active in the computer memory.

ProDOS, however, couldn't give a hoot about whether BASIC.SYSTEM is in the computer or not. ProDOS never runs to BASIC.SYSTEM to execute one of its commands. ProDOS is like the "Tibetan Wise Man" to BASIC.SYSTEM's disks requests; BASIC.SYSTEM always asks for information from ProDOS and ProDOS patiently answers. ProDOS, however, has nothing to ask of BASIC.SYSTEM.

Here, Part V turns to look at ProDOS itself for the sole purpose of using it to advantage with BASIC.SYSTEM and ancillary routines. This is not going to be an exhaustive examination of ProDOS and its Machine Language Interface (MLI) as that would fill another book, and many good references on the MLI exist (see the Bibliography). Instead, the discussion will focus on the description of ProDOS and its command structure so that we can add routines which may be of importance to BASIC programs. We have already seen one example, the TYPE command of Chapter 20.

For now, the discussion starts by looking at the ProDOS global page, then taking a cursory tour of the MLI calls (similar to the ones used for the TYPE command) used by BASIC.SYSTEM. Then we'll tackle the BASIC issues of device drivers and interrupts.

THE PRODOS GLOBAL PAGE

Just as BASIC.SYSTEM was designed to have its internal structure changed at will (or, hopefully, by design), so was the ProDOS code. To provide a standard interface, just as for BASIC.SYSTEM, ProDOS has a global page, which lies at \$BF00-\$BFFF in the Apple's RAM memory. The biggest chunk of ProDOS's global page is concerned with the presence and locations of *device drivers* for peripherals. Most of the rest of the page is taken up with data registers and vectors for calling various ProDOS functions.

The standard access to ProDOS is performed through the machine language interface (MLI). Since standard ProDOS I/O functions are usually invoked through MLI calls, most of the ProDOS call vectors are to very specialized routines, such as interrupts.

NOTICE: ProDOS lives in the RAM card, and is *not* accessible by a simple "JMP" to the appropriate address of a function you wish to call. For example, the clock routine vector is kept at $BF06, but the Thunderclock driver that ProDOS installs is in the RAM card area, which is normally "turned off". If you do a JMP $BF06 without activating the RAM card, you'll end up JMPing into the Applesoft ROM code! Also, if you "switch on" the language card from machine language without putting everything right when you're done, you can make ProDOS lose its place and die. Don't get fancy unless you have to; use the MLI.

THE MLI VECTORS

At $BF00-$BF02, we have the infamous JMP to the ProDOS MLI command handler. Once you have prepared your MLI command table (the tables and sample calls are illustrated in Chapter 23) you can LDA with the command number and JMP $BF00 to have ProDOS take over and try to execute the command.

$BF03-$BF05 is the JMP instruction ProDOS calls to invoke the system death code, which can be used in the event of a catastrophic error. Executing the code causes a prompt indicating the error (number) detected, and that you should re-boot ProDOS and your application.

$BF06-$BF08 is a JMP to the current routine to set DATE and TIME. The first byte of this vector is initially a RTS ($60) if no clock driver or similar routine is installed. The next two bytes define the address (low-order byte, then high-order byte) of the clock driver; ProDOS initially has these set to its internal driver for the Thunderware Thunderclock. When it is executed, the ProDOS system program attempts to identify a Thunderclock by examining each slot for a card containing certain values in its firmware ROM. If the proper identifying codes are found, ProDOS changes the $60 at $BF06 to a $4C, converting it to a JMP instruction. Some clock cards have copied the "signature" bytes used to identify the clock so that they, too, will be automatically installed and accessed by ProDOS.

$BF09-$BF0B contains a JMP to the system error handler for ProDOS MLI errors.

$BF0C-$BF0E contains a JMP to the system death handler, which prints an error message and then calls up the "death code". This routine will be accessed when a severe ProDOS error is detected.

$BF0F is used as a data register to hold the system/MLI error return code.

DEVICE VECTORS

$BF00-$BF2F holds the addresses for a sequence of device drivers assigned to (potential) disk devices (*only*), including a driver for the "/RAM" volume if it is installed. The assignments are listed in Table 22-1. Both "Slot 0" assignments are assigned an address pointing to a section of code that provides the "NO DEVICE CONNECTED" error when executed. These are kept for use by ProDOS since slot 0 cannot contain a disk controller under ProDOS.

ProDOS checks all slots during bootup for a valid disk controller ROM via the protocol mentioned in Chapter 21. If found, the appropriate vector is set in the device table to reflect the presence of a disk drive at that location. Additionally, if ProDOS detects the "extra" 64K RAM memory of an Apple *II*c or 128K *II*e, it will create the "/RAM" volume (and "format" the auxiliary RAM area) and assign its driver's address to slot 3, drive 2 in the table.

$BF30 contains a single byte representing the last device accessed (slot and drive); the form is "DSSSxxxx" bitwise (in binary). "D" is 0 for drive 1, "1" for drive 2. "SSS" is a slot number from "000" (0 decimal) to "111" (7). The lower four "x" bits are unused in this byte.

$BF31 contains a number representing the number of active disk (mass storage) devices, minus one.

$BF40-$BF4F contain the text of an Apple copyright notice.

Table 22-1. Device Driver (Disk) Vector Table within the ProDOS Global Page.

$BF10-11	Slot 0, Drive 1
$BF12-13	Slot 1, Drive 1
$BF14-15	Slot 2, Drive 1
$BF16-17	Slot 3, Drive 1
$BF18-19	Slot 4, Drive 1
$BF1A-1B	Slot 5, Drive 1
$BF1C-1D	Slot 6, Drive 1
$BF1E-1F	Slot 7, Drive 1
$BF20-21	Slot 0, Drive 2
$BF22-23	Slot 1, Drive 2
$BF24-25	Slot 2, Drive 2
$BF26-27	Slot 3, Drive 2
$BF28-29	Slot 4, Drive 2
$BF2A-2B	Slot 5, Drive 2
$BF2C-2D	Slot 6, Drive 2
$BF2E-2F	Slot 7, Drive 2

MEMORY MANAGEMENT

$BF50-$BF55 contains a brief machine language routine used to activate the RAM card space at $D000-$FFFF and call the ProDOS interrupt handler. $BF56-$BF57 is used as storage for the interrupt request handler. A more complete discussion of interrupts will be offered in a later chapter.

$BF58-$BF6F contains the *system bitmap* for the lower 48K of memory. ProDOS sets one bit in this table for each memory page in use (there is a BASIC program to examine the bitmap described in Chapter 19).

$BF70-$BF7F contains a series of 8 addresses for each of a maximum of eight file buffers in ascending order; that is, $BF70-71 is the address for the first currently active buffer OPENed, $BF72-73 for the second buffer, etc.

Back to more interrupt information: at $BF80-$BF87 is room for the addresses of up to four interrupt handlers, in the order of reverse priority. The first address in the table has the highest priority, etc. Register storage for A, X, Y, S, and P respectively is at $BF88-$BF8D (one byte each). $BF8E-$BF8F holds the return address for the ultimate RTI after ProDOS is satisfied that the interrupt has been handled.

The DATE and TIME information is contained in the registers $BF90-BF93. The DATE is in $BF90-91 in two bytes. The form in binary, with symbols representing binary digits, "YYYYYYYM MMMDDDDD"; seven bits ("Y"s) for a year value of 0-99, four bits ("M"s) for a month value from 1-12, and five bits ("D"s) representing a day-of-month value 0-31. The TIME is stored with the hour ("H" digits) in $BF92 as "xxxHHHHH" and the minutes (new "M" digits) in $BF93 as "xxMMMMMM"; the bits marked "x" are unused and should be zero.

The current file level is kept at $BF94, a backup byte is kept at $BF95. These are listed by Apple but no description of their use is provided.

THE MACHINE ID BYTE

$BF98 is used for an identification of the machine size and type; this byte is automatically filled in by ProDOS. You can read this byte to determine the hardware configuration of the Apple that ProDOS was booted on. The values are shown in Table 22-2. At present, only these bit combinations (bits 7, 6, and 3 for the machine model, bits 4-5 for the memory size, bit 1 for the 80-column display status, and bit 0 for the clock status) were defined. Any other patterns may be used for future expansion.

$BF99 contains a single-byte bitmap of slots in which an expansion ROM was identified by ProDOS. A "1" in a position indicates a ROM was found in the corresponding slot.

MLI STATUS BYTES

$BF9A contains a flag to indicate whether or not a prefix has been set. This would include use by BASIC.SYSTEM, so that you can PEEK the value at this location (49050) from a BASIC program to determine whether the prefix has been set before resorting to the PREFIX command. The value is non-zero if there is a set prefix.

$BF9B contains the status of the MLI; if non-zero then the MLI is active and in the midst of a call. You might wonder how this location could be

Table 22-2. The MACHID Byte's Bit Values.

Bit values	Indication
00..0...	Apple][
01..0...	Apple][Plus
10..0...	Apple //e
11..0...	Apple /// (// series emulation)
10..1...	Apple //c
..01....	48K RAM memory
..10....	64K RAM memory
..11....	128K RAM memory (//e extended memory- or //c-type)
.....0..	No native //e-//c 80-column display
.....1..	//e or //c native 80-column display present
.......0	No ProDOS-compatible clock found
.......1	ProDOS compatible clock found

used; if the MLI is busy how can you be mucking about in memory to read this location? The answer is that the status will indicate whether the MLI was in the midst of a call when an interrupt was generated. Your interrupt handling routine can detect whether the MLI was through (status < $80) or not (status > = $80) and make *sure* that the MLI gets a chance to complete its call.

$BF9C-$BF9D contains the last MLI call return address, also used with interrupt handling.

$BF9E and $BF9F are used to save the X and Y registers, respectively, during MLI calls.

$BFA0-$BFCF contains the routines needed to activate and deactivate the RAM card area during entry and exit to the MLI.

$BFD0-$BFF3 contains the entry and exit routines for ProDOS's interrupt handling.

$BFF4 and $BFF5 are used for storage of the bytes found at $E000 and $D000 respectively.

$BFF6-$BFFB contains the code to activate the RAM card area and call the system death handler.

$BFFC-$BFFF contain version numbers for determining compatibility, one byte each. $BFFC and $BFFD are to be set by the resident system program (such as BASIC.SYSTEM) upon its initialization; $BFFC to the minimum version of the ProDOS kernel needed to run the current interpreter, and $BFFD to the system program's version number. $BFFE is supposed to contain the minimum version of ProDOS compatible with the specific version of the ProDOS kernel currently active, and $BFFF contains the actual version number of the specific ProDOS kernel in memory.

USING THE INFORMATION

Normally, the ProDOS global page information is useful only to machine language programs. However, it is apparent that the various status byte's information can be used when read into BASIC programs via PEEK statements.

One example is the "machine ID byte" at $BF98 (49048). It's easy to determine whether you are running on a *II*, *II*e, or *II*c by PEEKing the ROM, but Apple's routine to detect a *II*e 80-column card (presented in the text card manuals) is a little lengthy. Since ProDOS has already done that work for you, that information can be extracted from the machine ID by

```
10  C8 = 0 : ID = PEEK (49048)
20  IF (ID - INT (ID/4)) > 1 THEN C8 = 1
```

C8 will be set to "1" in line 20 if the ID byte indicates an 80-column card is present.

Chapter 23

Your Basic MLI

BASIC.SYSTEM uses a subset of ProDOS MLI calls for all of its file handling; ProDOS does more types of operations on files than BASIC.SYSTEM but *all* of BASIC.SYSTEM's disk operations require ProDOS calls. The complete description of these commands usually fills a good portion of a book on the MLI. For the purposes of this book, we are going to describe the parameter lists that BASIC.SYSTEM maintains for these commands and give brief synopses for the commands, then add the synopses for the remaining MLI commands not used by BASIC.SYSTEM.

Please be aware that this is an informational tour only with terse explanations; for a more complete explanation, please refer to one of the references listed in the Bibliography. In particular, *Apple's ProDOS: Advanced Features for Programmers* by Gary Little is recommended; it contains programming examples for many of the MLI calls documented.

THE BASIC.SYSTEM MLI CALLS

BASIC.SYSTEM keeps a small number (9, to be exact) of MLI parameter tables in its global page, along with a short routine to call the MLI and handle any errors detected on returning from the MLI. The MLI calls used are *CREATE, GET_PREFIX, SET_PREFIX, DESTROY, RENAME, GET_FILE_INFO, SET_FILE_INFO, ON-LINE , SET_MARK, GET_MARK, SET_EOF, GET_EOF, SET_BUF, GET_BUF , OPEN, SET_NEWLINE, READ, WRITE, CLOSE, QUIT,* and *FLUSH.* That's 21 of the 26 available MLI calls accounted for!

Notice that some of the MLI calls above have the same name as a BASIC.SYSTEM command (such as "CLOSE" and "RENAME"). These calls are involved in performing the BASIC.SYSTEM command of the same name, but the ProDOS code for the command is distinct from the BASIC.SYSTEM code for the command. For CLOSE, as an example, BASIC.SYSTEM first performs its interpretation of CLOSE as its command, then converts the command into a CLOSE call to the MLI to perform the necessary functions. The MLI never directly sees nor would understand the "CLOSE" you type at the keyboard or include in a BASIC program.

These parameter tables do not fill the global page with data because most of the tables are similar in structure so that several calls can use the same parameter table. This is how, in the case of BASIC.SYSTEM's global page, the above calls reduce to using only 9 distinct parameter tables.

CALLING THE MLI

At $BE70 within BASIC.SYSTEM's global page is a short routine that calls the MLI using one of the tables, which includes the MLI call form we listed earlier. The JMP MLI occurs at $BE82, immediately following the JMP at $BE85 is the required command code (one byte), and the (two-byte) address of the parameter list for the call.

When the MLI returns from the call, it has set the program counter to "skip over" these three bytes so that execution resumes at $BE88. This is the start of a routine which sniffs out any error that the MLI may report; if none is found, control passes back to BASIC.SYSTEM straightaway. If an error is found, the routine converts the MLI error code to a BASIC.SYSTEM error code number and reports it as it passes control back to BASIC.SYSTEM.

THE PARAMETER LISTS

The BASIC.SYSTEM global page parameter lists are divided up for the following MLI calls into 9 lists. Remember that the names that follow refer to MLI calls and not BASIC.SYSTEM command words.

THE "CREATE" PARAMETER LIST

$BEA0 is the starting location of the parameter list for CREATE (MLI code = $C0), presented in Listing 23-1. PATHNAME is a two-byte pointer to the address of the pathname to use. The pathname is defined with a leading "length" byte so that the name "NEWFILE" could be stored at $280 as

```
280:07 4E 45 57 46 49 4C 45
```

The leading byte "07" (hex) indicates there are 7 characters in the pathname; the bytes following are the hex values for the ASCII characters with the high bit of each character set to "0" (positive ASCII). If the pathname does not begin with a "/", then the prefix is "pre-pended" to the name to form a complete pathname.

The ACCESS byte value determines what actions can be performed on a file; and can be used to limit access to the file from BASIC.SYSTEM until the ACCESS is changed via a MLI call. The actions listed in Table 23-1 are allowed at the time of creation if the corresponding bit is set to "1". Bits 2-4 are reserved for future use. The BACKUP bit is always "set" by this call. Although access can be restricted to other levels by setting only certain of these bits, the common settings use DESTROY, RENAME, and WRITE. If all three are enabled, the file is "unlocked". If any or all of the three are not enabled, then the file is locked.

```
DFB     $07             ; Number of parameters
                          to follow this byte.
DA      PATHNAME        ; Pointer to buffer of
                          pathname to use.
DFB     ACCESS          ; File access
                          privileges.
DFB     TYPE            ; File type to create.
DFB     AUX_TYPE        ; Auxiliary data
                          dependent on TYPE.
DFB     STORAGE_TYPE    ; File storage type.
DDB     CREATE_DATE     ; DATE of creation.
DDB     CREATE_TIME     ; TIME of creation.
```

Listing 23-1. The CREATE parameter list.

Table 23-1. The ACCESS Byte's Bit Values.

Bit Number	Name	Indication (when set)
Bit 7	DESTROY	File can be deleted.
Bit 6	RENAME	File can be renamed.
Bit 5	BACKUP	File needs to be backed-up.
Bit 1	WRITE	File can be written to.
Bit 0	READ	File can be read from.

The TYPE is a numerical designation for the file type to be created. The file types in Table 23-2 are currently defined.The unused type codes from $02 to $BF are reserved for the Apple III SOS operating system; they are mentioned in the *ProDOS Technical Reference Manual.*

AUX_TYPE is used to hold either the record length of a text file (the "L" parameter) or the binary file "A" (load address) parameter value for the creation of those type of files.

STORAGE_TYPE is either $0D (for a linked directory file) or $01 (for a standard file); no other values are currently documented by Apple. This value describes the actual organization of the file on the disk for ProDOS's internal use.

The CREATE_DATE and CREATE_TIME registers are set in the parameter list; the values can be copied from the values kept in ProDOS's global page. The form of their storage is the same as in the ProDOS global page.

THE "GET_PREFIX", "SET_PREFIX", AND "DESTROY" LIST

The next call parameter list at $BEAC is used for the three MLI calls GET_PREFIX ($C7), SET_PREFIX ($C6), and DESTROY ($C1). Each

Table 23-2. ProDOS (Numeric) Type Designations.

Type Number	File Type Denoted
$00	Typeless file.
$01	BAD BLOCK file (created by FILER on damaged disks).
$04	"TXT" file.
$06	"BIN" file.
$C0-$EF,$F9	<reserved>.
$F0	Added command ("CMD") file.
$F1-$F8	User-defined files 1-8.
$FA	"INT" (Integer BASIC) file.
$FB	Integer BASIC variable file.
$FC	"BAS" (Applesoft BASIC) file.
$FD	"VAR" (Applesoft variables) file.
$FE	"REL" (relocatable code) file.
$FF	"SYS" (ProDOS system) file.

```
DFB     $01             ; Parameter count.
DA      PATHNAME        ; Pointer to pathname.
```

Listing 23-2. The parameter list for GET_PREFIX, SET_PREFIX, and DESTROY.

of these calls requires only one parameter; the list is in the form of Listing 23-2. For DESTROY, the pathname is for the file or directory file to be removed. For SET_PREFIX, the pathname is the prefix that is to be set. For GET_PREFIX, the pointer is instead used to show the MLI where to put the prefix that it has determined is set.

THE "RENAME" LIST

$BEAF holds the parameter list for an MLI RENAME ($C2) call. The parameter list looks like Listing 23-3.The command changes the name in the buffer defined by OLD_PATH to the name defined in the buffer defined by NEW_PATH. Each pathname is in the form described under the CREATE parameter list description.

THE "GET_FILE_INFO" AND "SET_FILE_INFO" LIST

$BEB4-$BEC5 holds the parameter list for the GET_FILE_INFO ($C4) and SET_FILE_INFO ($C3) calls, depicted in Listing 23-4. PATHNAME, ACCESS, FILE_TYPE, AUX_TYPE, and STORAGE_TYPE are all defined under CREATE; the exception is that these parameters are returned from ProDOS for the call GET_FILE_INFO rather than being set by the call.

SET_FILE_INFO can be used to modify all of these parameters except STORAGE_TYPE and BLOCKS_USED, which were set by ProDOS at the time of the file's creation. The three bytes used for these values are not used, but room is left for these parameters in the SET_FILE_INFO parameter list so that it and the GET_FILE_INFO parameter list can be "overlapped" to save space, which was done in BASIC.SYSTEM's global page. Also, SET_FILE_INFO cannot set the date or time the file was created, but it can set the date and time the file was last modified. Since SET_FILE_INFO does not use the last two entries (CREATE_DATE and CREATE_TIME), its number of parameters for PARM_COUNT is $07.

GET_FILE_INFO returns all of the listed data for the above parameters with the exception of the pathname, which is set by the caller so that GET_FILE_INFO knows which file it is to look at. PARM_COUNT for GET_FILE_INFO is therefore $0A.

CALLS USING THE "ONLINE" PARAMETER LIST

$BEC6-BECA contains a parameter list used for several calls. One of these is ONLINE ($C5) shown in Listing 23-5. This call returns the volume name of the device corresponding to UNIT_NUM into the data buffer. UNIT_NUMBER is defined bitwise as DSSSxxxx, where "D" = the drive number ("0" for drive 1, "1" for drive 2), "SSS" is three

```
DFB     $02             ; Parameter count.
DA      OLD_PATH        ; Pointer to original
                          pathname.
DA      NEW_PATH        ; Pointer to new
                          pathname.
```

Listing 23-3. The RENAME parameter list.

```
DFB     PARM_COUNT      ; Parameter count
                          (varies dependent on
                          call type).
DA      PATHNAME        ; Pointer to pathname
                          buffer.
DFB     ACCESS          ; File access
                          definition.
DFB     FILE_TYPE       ; File type.
DA      AUX_TYPE        ; Auxiliary data word.
DFB     STORAGE_TYPE    ; Storage type (unused
                          by SET_FILE_INFO).
DA      BLOCKS_USED     ; Blocks allotted
                          (unused by
                          SET_FILE_INFO).
DDB     MOD_DATE        ; Date modified.
DDB     MOD_TIME        ; Time modified.
DDB     CREATE_DATE     ; Date CREATEd (unused
                          by SET_FILE_INFO).
DDB     CREATE_TIME     ; Time CREATEd (unused
                          by SET_FILE_INFO).
```

Listing 23-4. The SET_FILE_INFO and GET_FILE_INFO parameter list.

bits defining a slot from 0 to 7 ("000" to "111") and the bits marked "xxxx" are presently not defined for use with the call. If the unit number used is given as $00, ProDOS will search for *all* attached volumes and return the volume name of each into the buffer.

The names are returned with the first byte denoting the unit number as above, but the last four bits are used to denote the length of the pathname which follows. The names are returned without bracketing "/" characters. When the UNIT_NUMBER sent with the ONLINE call is "$00" so that multiple names may be returned, the last name will be followed by a byte value of $00.

This same form is used for the calls SET_BUF ($D2) and GET_BUF ($D3), but with a minor difference shown in Listing 23-6. In this case, REF_NUM is a reference number assigned to a file when it is opened by an MLI OPEN call (we'll look at this just a little later in these descriptions). The SET_BUF call assigns the address of the I/O buffer used by the file to the address defined by DATA_BUFFER. GET_BUF will return the address of the currently assigned buffer in DATA_BUFFER when the REF_NUM is provided to the call.

The reserved storage byte "DS 1" is actually unused by these parameter lists, but is used by the slightly expanded parameter lists for GET_EOF ($D1), SET_EOF ($D0), GET_MARK ($CF), and SET_MARK ($CE), as shown in Listing 23-7.

The position-in-file mark data is allowed three bytes for these calls, which allows us to either set or recover the position-in-file pointer for a

```
DFB     $02             ; Parameter count.
DFB     UNIT_NUM        ; Unit number.
DA      DATA_BUFFER     ; Pointer to low end of
                          data buffer.
DS      1               ; Unused for this set.
```

Listing 23-5. The ONLINE parameter list.

```
DFB     $02            ; Number of parameters.
DFB     REF_NUM        ; File reference
                         number.
DA      DATA_BUFFER    ; Address of start of
                         data buffer area.
DS      1              ; Unused by this list.
```

Listing 23-6. The GET_BUF and SET_BUF parameter list.

"marked" position ("MARK") or for the end-of-file marker ("EOF"). GET_EOF and GET_MARK retrieve the current EOF position or position-in-file pointer (respectively) for the file designated by REF_NUM and place the value in the last three bytes of the parameter list. SET_EOF and SET_MARK set the EOF value or the position-in-file marker for a write-enabled file to the value in the last three bytes of the parameter table.

For SET_MARK, the position-in-file pointer may not be moved past the current EOF. For SET_EOF, the block size of the file is reduced by the appropriate amount if the new EOF is less than the original EOF.

Finally, this list's format is used for the QUIT code (called by the BASIC.SYSTEM BYE command), denoted as MLI code $65. The parameter format for this call is shown in Listing 23-8. According to Apple's *ProDOS Technical Reference Manual*, all four parameters are "reserved", they must be present and all initialized to zeroes.

THE "OPEN" PARAMETER LIST

At $BECB-$BED0 is the parameter list for the MLI OPEN ($C8) call, outlined in Listing 23-9. The DATA_BUFFER used here is the dynamically assigned buffer as we described being created by the BASIC.SYSTEM OPEN command, which uses this MLI call namesake.

THE "NEWLINE" PARAMETER LIST

At $BED1-BED4 is the parameter list for the NEWLINE ($C9) call shown in Listing 23-10. This call determines whether, during a READ (MLI) operation, data will be read from the file until a requested number of bytes is read (as with the binary file BLOAD commands) or the end of the file is reached. If the ENABLE_MASK equals zero, then the file will be read in that manner.

If ENABLE_MASK is non-zero, then it and NEWLINE_CHAR are used to determine whether a "line" has been read from the file, and the read is halted at the end of that line. If the last character read logically "anded" with the value of ENABLE_MASK equals the value of NEWLINE_CHAR, then it is assumed that a line has been read. If you wished to use a linefeed character (ASCII $0A) as a "newline" character, for example, you could set ENABLE_MASK to $7F and NEWLINE_CHAR to $0A. If either a $8A or $0A value was read from the file, the read would stop at that point until a subsequent call to

```
DFB     $02            ; Number of parameters.
DFB     REF_NUM        ; File reference
                         number.
DS      $03            ; Three bytes for
                         position-in-file
                         value,
                       ; from low- to
                         high-byte.
```

Listing 23-7. The parameter list for GET_EOF, SET_EOF, GET_MARK_ and SET_MARK.

```
DFB     $04             ; Parameter Count.
DFB     $00             ; Reserved.
DA      $0000           ; Reserved.
DFB     $00             ; Reserved.
DA      $00             ; Reserved.
```

Listing 23-8. The QUIT parameter list.

```
DFB     $03             ; Parameter count.
DA      PATHNAME        ; Pointer to pathname
                          buffer.
DA      DATA_BUFFER     ; Pointer to
                          input/output buffer.
DFB     REF_NUM         ; Reference number for
                          file.
```

Listing 23-9. The OPEN parameter list.

```
DFB     $03             ; Parameter count.
DFB     REF_NUM         ; File reference
                          number.
DFB     ENABLE_MASK     ; Code to select
                          function.
DFB     NEWLINE_CHAR    ; Character to use to
                          denote end-of-line.
```

Listing 23-10. The NEWLINE parameter list.

the MLI READ operation.

THE "READ" AND "WRITE" PARAMETER LIST

$BED5-$BEDC holds the parameter list for BASIC.SYSTEM's calls to the MLI READ ($CA) and WRITE ($CB) operations. The list is shown in Listing 23-11.The READ call attempts to transfer the REQUEST_COUNT number bytes starting at the address referenced by DATA_BUFFER to the file denoted by REF_NUM. TRANS_COUNT holds the actual number of bytes transferred. WRITE reverses the procedure, attempting to copy REQUEST_COUNT bytes from the file to the address at DATA_BUFFER. Both calls access the file starting at the value of the position-in-file pointer for the file.

THE "CLOSE" AND "FLUSH" PARAMETER LIST

Finally(!) at $BEDD-BEDE is the parameter list used by CLOSE ($CC) and FLUSH ($CD), outlined in Listing 23-12. FLUSH writes any data in the current input/output buffer to the file denoted by REF_NUM. and leaves the file open for further access. CLOSE also writes out the contents of the I/O buffer but also secures the file, frees its REF_NUM for use by another file and releases its buffer. After CLOSE, the file must be opened with another MLI OPEN call before it can be accessed.

```
DFB     $04                ; Parameter count.
DFB     REF_NUM            ; File reference
                             number.
DA      DATA_BUFFER        ; Pointer to data
                             buffer.
DA      REQUEST_COUNT      ; Number of bytes to
                             read/write.
DA      TRANS_COUNT        ; Actual number of
                             bytes transferred.
```

Listing 23-11. The READ and WRITE parameter list.

THE NON-BASIC.SYSTEM CALLS

Here are the remaining MLI calls *not* used by BASIC.SYSTEM.

GET_TIME ($82) attempts to update the ProDOS DATE and TIME registers in the global page. It uses *no* parameter list, just define the parameter list address as "$0000" in the MLI call for it.

ALLOC_INTERRUPT ($40) adds an interrupt-handling routine to the ProDOS table of interrupt handlers. The table is limited to four of these routines at a time; ProDOS will call these routines one after the other in the order of their assigned priority if an IRQ occurs. The parameter list is shown in Listing 23-13.

The interrupt handler will be installed at the first "open" location in the table, and its priority is returned as INT_NUM. INT_NUM should be saved for reference by the call, DEAL LOC_INTERRUPT ($41), which can be used to remove an interrupt routine when it is no longer needed. It uses the parameter list shown in Listing 23-14.

The last two MLI commands allow direct access to disk blocks. READ_BLOCK ($80) is used to read one disk block into memory from a device; its parameter list is contained in Listing 23-15.

WRITE_BLOCK ($81) uses the same format, except it attempts to write the contents of the data buffer specified by DATA_BUFFER to the UNIT_NUM device at block number BLOCK_NUM.

MLI ERROR CODES

Any time that you perform an MLI call, any error is reported by returning a code in the 6502 accumulator. A non-zero return code results if an error occurs, in addition the processor status's carry flag will be set to "1". If no error occurs the accumulator will contain a zero and the carry will be cleared to "0".

To insure that all is right with the world after an MLI call, the first instruction after the call should be either a "BCS ERROR" or "BNE ERROR" (where "ERROR" is the address of an error handler) to verify if the MLI call was successfully completed. Table 23-3 is a brief description of the possible MLI errors, their return codes, and (where not obvious) explanations of their cause.

There are also errors called *system failure errors* that may occur. When one of these errors occurs, the MLI directly jumps to the system death code entry at $BF0C, it doesn't return to your pro-

```
DFB     $01                ; Parameter count.
DFB     REF_NUM            ; File reference
                             number.
```

Listing 23-12. The CLOSE and FLUSH parameter list.

```
DFB     $02              ; Parameter count.
DFB     INT_NUM          ; Assigned priority
                           number, returned by
                           MLI.
DA      INT_CODE         ; User-supplied address
                           of interrupt routine.
```

Listing 23-13. An ALLOC_INTERRUPT parameter list.

```
DFB     $01              ; Parameter count.
DFB     INT_NUM          ; Number of
                           interrupt-handler to
                           remove.
```

Listing 23-14. A DEALLOC_INTERRUPT parameter list.

```
DFB     $03              ; Parameter count.
DFB     UNIT_NUM         ; Unit number of device
                           to access.
DA      DATA_BUFFER      ; Starting address of
                           512 byte data buffer.
DA      BLOCK_NUM        ; Number of disk block
                           to access.
```

Listing 23-15. The READ_BLOCK and WRITE_BLOCK parameter list.

gram. Apple's *ProDOS Technical Reference Manual* mentions that in event of a fatal unclaimed IRQ request that you should attempt to CLOSE any open files; they neglect to say how this should be accomplished since the system death handler locks up the system. "Reset" allows you to escape, but may not fix the world; you may wish to go ahead and close files before re-booting ProDOS and checking your files.

ISSUING MLI CALLS FROM BASIC (SORT OF)

The easiest way to issue MLI calls from BASIC programs is to simply POKE the needed information into a parameter list table along with a short routine to call the MLI and then CALL the routine. As an example, to issue the GET_TIME ($82) MLI call which is not included in the BASIC.SYSTEM list of calls, we can use the program in Listing 23-16. Line 20 pokes in the instruction to perform a subroutine jump to the MLI entry point. The byte following the JSR instruction is the value of the MLI code for GET_TIME, the next two bytes define the address of the parameter list which for GET_TIME is $0000 since GET_TIME uses no parameters. The next byte in line 40 is a "return from subroutine" instruction to send us back to BASIC when the MLI has finished. We are not concerned with an MLI error in this case since GET_TIME cannot return an MLI error.

Line 50 executes the routine, which causes ProDOS to update the DATE and TIME registers in the ProDOS global page from any installed clock driver. The actual routine looks like Listing 23-17.

For a more complicated call, we can now reveal that we used an MLI call to "cheat" in the BASIC "/RAM copy" in Chapter 11. The lines that

Table 23-3. MLI Errors.

ERROR TYPE	CODE	COMMENTS
No error	$00	
Non-existant call number	$01	
Incorrect parameter count	$04	
Interrupt vector table full	$25	
I/O error	$27	
No device detected	$28	
Write protect error	$2B	
Disk switched	$2E	The expected volume/disk was not found during an attempt to WRITE, CLOSE or FLUSH using a file on it.
Invalid pathname syntax	$40	
Too many files OPEN	$42	
Invalid reference number	$43	A file reference number specified in a parameter list does not correspond to an open file.
Path not found	$44	
Volume not found	$45	
File not found	$46	
Duplicate filename	$47	Occurs if you try to CREATE a file in a directory with a name matching an existing file.
Overrun error	$48	Either the output volume is full or an incorrect EOF parameter was specified.
Volume directory full	$49	
Incompatible file format	$4A	The version of ProDOS used to attempt the specified file is unable to use the file's format (may occur when accessing a "modern" file format with an "archaic" version of the PRODOS system program booted).
Unsupported storage type	$4B	ProDOS cannot recognize the file type in it's attempted use.
End-of-file encountered	$4C	
POSITION out of range	$4D	
Access error	$4E	Caused by attempting to access a file in oppostion to it's ACCESS settings.
File open	$50	An OPEN, RENAME, or DESTROY call was attempted on an open file.
Directory count error	$51	A descrepancy existed between the number of files in a DIR file indicated by it's header information, and the actual number of files found.
Not a ProDOS disk	$52	ProDOS/SOS directory format was not found.
Invalid parameter	$53	
Volume control block full	$55	In addition to ProDOS's limit of 8 open files (at a time), ProDOS can only keep track of 8 volumes. If you attempt to use ONLINE on a ninth volume while already having to keep track of 8 open

		files on 8 distinct volumes, this error results.
Duplicate volume	$57	Warns that two volumes on-line have the same name.
Volume bit map error	$5A	The disk volume's map of available blocks exceeds the block size of the volume.

```
10 REM *** CHEAP MLI CALL ***
20 POKE 768, 32 : POKE 769, 0 : POKE 770, 191 :
      REM JMP $BF00.
30 POKE 771, 130 : POKE 772, 0 : POKE 773, 0 :
      REM MLI # AND POINTER.
40 POKE 774, 96 : REM RTS.
50 CALL 768 : REM CALL "GET_TIME" SUBROUTINE.
```

Listing 23-16. BASIC program that calls the MLI.

```
300:    JSR     $BF00
        DFB     $082
        DA      $0000
        RTS
```

Listing 23-17. The MLI call hidden within Listing 23-16.

```
405 X1=0 : X2=0 : CMD=0

455 CMD=196 : GOSUB 600 : X1=PEEK(48825) :
      X2=PEEK(48826)
475 CMD=195 : POKE 48820,7 : POKE 48825,X1
      POKE 48826,X2 : GOSUB 600

600REM*** MLI caller for use with BASIC.SYS
      ***
601 POKE 48728,169 : POKE 48729,CMD : POKE
      48730,32
602 POKE 48731,112 : POKE 48732,150 : POKE
      48733,176
603 POKE 48734,170 : POKE 48735,96 : CALL 4
      : RETURN
```

Listing 23-18. "BASIC copy" program lines which perform an MLI call.

were used in the program to perform the call are contained in Listing 23-18. This particular example uses the BASIC.SYSTEM *GOSYSTEM* routine and parameter tables to conduct its MLI call. The purpose of these lines is to use the MLI GET_FILE_INFO call to find out the AUX_TYPE information for a file immediately after BLOADing it so that it can be BSAVED with the proper information using SET_FILE_INFO. Line 405 allocates "X1" and "X2" as bytes used

```
BE58:   LDA     #CMD            ; Load command code.
        JSR     GOSYSTEM        ; Have BASIC.SYSTEM
                                  call the MLI.
        BCS     ERROUT          ; If an error occurs,
                                  have BASIC.SYSTEM
                                  report it.
        RTS
```

Listing 23-19. The GOSYSTEM call hidden in Listing 23-18.

to hold the AUX_TYPE information, and "CMD" to represent the MLI command value.

Line 455 sets CMD to 196 for GET_FILE_INFO ($C4) and calls the routine at 600 that POKEs the MLI call routine (including the command) on top of the existing MLI call routine in BASIC.SYSTEM's global page. The actual routine disassembles to the form of Listing 23-19.

The PEEKs in line 455 recover the AUX_TYPE information for the file and hold it for later use. The information is loaded into the BASIC.SYSTEM parameter list used for GET_FILE_INFO (and several other) MLI calls. This saves us setting up our own parameter list and call functions, but when using the global page in this manner, you must be careful to make sure that you use the correct locations and, for the sake of your program, that you not trust BASIC.SYSTEM to leave your information intact during any of its MLI calls.

Line 475 performs a similar sequence for the MLI call SET_FILE_INFO; the AUX_TYPE information is POKEd back into the BASIC.SYSTEM parameter list for SET_FILE_INFO and the MLI call is performed. The reason the MLI call was needed was to extract the length (ENDFILE) magnitude for any BASIC programs to be transferred.

Chapter 24

Adding a (Clock) Driver to ProDOS

Normally, it is hazardous to make internal modifications to ProDOS or BASIC.SYSTEM for a reason we've mentioned before: the internal structure of ProDOS and BASIC.SYSTEM was designed to be easily modified by Apple in the event that bugs needed to be rectified or features added or removed. Therefore, internal modifications by the user (which might conflict with Apple's changes) should be avoided if at all possible.

Apple has provided for external routines to be "installed" for recognition by ProDOS and BASIC.SYSTEM via function calls and the design of the global pages; we've already seen how such an external command (TYPE) can be added to BASIC.SYSTEM. Generally, these methods are adequate to support ancillary routines. We'll look at such an ancillary driver for the clock.

STRAIGHT TIME

Although internally modifying ProDOS is usually not recommended, one notable exception is the clock driver routine that exists internal to ProDOS, which is used to provide the system date and time if you have a Thunderware Thunderclock (or a clock peripheral that emulates the Thunderclock). There are two reasons for wanting to modify this routine: first, to install a clock other than a Thunderclock; and second, to get rid of a problem that may arise with the generation of the "year" data.

One notable clock card that needs support is the Mountain Hardware (now called "Mountain Computer") Apple Clock. This was the *original* "official" Apple clock peripheral; Apple even advertised it in their product catalog in 1980. This peripheral card supplies the time in hours, minutes, seconds and milliseconds and also the day (date) and month; it does not supply data for the day-of-week or the current year. This peripheral is no longer in Apple's favor; endorsement of it has been dropped in favor of the Thunderclock for ProDOS and ProDOS does not recognize or install the Apple Clock.

Lest you think this means that the Thunderclock is free-and-clear where ProDOS is concerned, you should realize that the current Thunderclock driver also does not read data for the current year from the clock card. The year that ProDOS arrives at when a Thunderclock is installed is determined by a short perpetual- calendar routine (actually, a lookup table for the year based on the day-of-week and month data that the Thunderclock *does* provide) within ProDOS's clock driver routine. Unless Apple updates the routine, this calculation will go awry beginning in 1987 due to limitations in the data table for the routine (for ProDOS versions up to 1.1.1, anyway).

In the case of the Apple Clock, the Thunderclock routine internal to ProDOS can be replaced with a new driver for the Apple Clock. The year data can either be entered from the keyboard or updated from a disk file.

Although we haven't provided a program to do it here, the same method can be used with the Thunderclock to keep track of the year if the perpetual calendar can be eliminated. This requires patching the ProDOS driver for the Thunderclock.

THE DATE AND TIME REGISTERS

ProDOS uses four bytes in the ProDOS global page to store the current system date and time: locations $BF90 and $BF91 for the date and locations $BF92 and $BF93 for the time. These pairs are not surprisingly called DATE and TIME, respectively.

The format for TIME is straightforward: $BF92 holds the value of the hour, which ranges from 0 to 23 (binary 00000000 to 00010111, or hex $00 to $17), and $BF93 holds the value of the minute from 0 to 59 (binary 00000000 to 00111011, or hex $00 to $3B).

The format of DATE has been compressed to allow condensing three items of data (the year, month, and day) into two bytes. Seven bits are allotted to hold the magnitude of the last two (decimal) digits of the year, four bits are allotted to the month, and five bits are allotted to the day. We can show this arrangement (bitwise) as "YYYYYYY MMMM DDDDD" where "YYYYYYY" is a binary number from 0000000 to 1100011 (0 to 99 decimal) representing the year, "MMMM" is a binary number from 0001 to 1100 (1 to 12 decimal) representing the number of the month, and "DDDDD" is a binary number which can range from 00001 to 11111 (1 to 31 decimal) to represent the current day-of-month.

These three items would require three bytes to store separately, but can be combined into two bytes by dividing the month like this—"YYYYYYYM MMMDDDDD"—so that the high-order bit of the month is paired with the year to form an 8-bit byte, and the remaining three bits of the month are paired with the day to form another 8-bit byte. ProDOS uses this compacted format to hold the date.

If the four TIME and DATE register bytes all contain $00, ProDOS will assume the time is invalid or no clock is present. When you create or modify a file under this circumstance, "<NO TIME>" will be displayed in the respective field of the directory display.

CALLING FOR THE TIME

The TIME and DATE register are updated every time ProDOS performs a disk access by using a ProDOS MLI called GET_TIME. The function call number for this MLI call is $82, so that the call looks like that in Listing 24-1. The "dummy" parameter list address tells the MLI that this call requires no actual parameter list. There is no check for an error before the "RTS" instruction, because GET_TIME cannot return an error.

```
DO_TIME     JSR    MLI     ; Go to the MLI.
            DFB    $82     ; Function call number
            DA     $0000   ; Dummy parameter list
                             address.
            RTS
```

Listing 24-1. The GET_TIME call.

Passing control to the routine at $BF06 (labeled as the DATETIME vector in the map of ProDOS's global page) causes GET_TIME to be executed. The DATETIME vector's first byte will be an RTS instruction if no clock is installed in ProDOS, so that update of DATE and TIME will occur. Otherwise, the vector is supposed to contain a JMP to the correct clock driver location. You *cannot* use the DATETIME vector directly via a BASIC CALL statement because it assumes ProDOS is active (not Applesoft) in high memory and has "banked in" the RAM segment with the clock driver.

WHERE'S IT GO?

The default vector is $F1 42 for ProDOS version 1.0 and revisions, and $D742 for ProDOS version 1.1 and revisions. Notice that the "$D742" space exists in the 4K "banked" segment of the RAM card area. It turns out that the driver is installed in bank 1; so that in addition to activating the RAM card area, the proper bank must be activated to access the routine.

If you wish, you can re-define this vector to point to another area of memory and install the driver there. "Where" to install the driver is another problem. Some programs (such as APA, which we've mentioned before) clear out any programs installed in high memory beneath BASIC.SYSTEM; besides, a clock driver there would be lost when system programs are changed. Page 3 of memory seems a likely choice; unfortunately, you can expect that just about everybody else will want to put any ancillary routines there, too (the *IIc* /UTILITIES disk put an archaic "stack correcting" routine there, for example).

The safest place seems to be where Apple put the Thunderclock driver; within ProDOS itself. The original driver is 127 bytes long, which should give us enough room.

THE CLOCK DRIVER

The clock driver itself has the responsibility to read the clock peripheral, translate the information into the proper format for TIME and DATE, and store the data in those registers before returning to ProDOS via RTS. These routines are dependent on how your clock card functions and how it presents its data.

The clock driver also has to stay out of ProDOS's (and BASIC.SYSTEM's) way, which means that you cannot use any area of memory that ProDOS and BASIC.SYSTEM expect you to leave untouched, unless you restore them before returning to ProDOS. This is not as easy to do as it sounds due to some "holes" in the ProDOS manuals.

First, a lot of clock cards copy their data to the keyboard (GETLIN) input buffer at $200 for your program to read. Apple designed ProDOS to stay out of the way of the Thunderclock, which stores its string starting at $200. For the Apple Clock, however, the time string is stored in the buffer starting at $280. Possibly this was to leave the first 128 bytes of the input buffer undisturbed for later review.

ProDOS, unfortunately, uses the area at $280 to store a pathname under certain circumstances. One, which Apple documents as a "standard", is for use when system programs are "switched." Before the first system program exits, it is supposed to save the prefix in this buffer area for recovery by the next system program.

The next use is *not* explicitly documented in Apple's manuals; the buffer area at $280 is also used as a secondary pathname buffer. One of its uses is to save the second filename during execution of a RENAME command by BASIC.SYSTEM.

If not discovered and taken into account, this causes a very interesting problem with the Apple Clock: RENAME will consistently reply "SYNTAX ERROR" (BASIC.SYSTEM error message) with the clock installed because the clock data will overwrite the second pathname as BASIC.SYSTEM executes the command. Then ProDOS will attempt to use the time data as the second pathname, and the string format is *not* that of a valid pathname.

HIDE AND SEEK

Apple's "ProDOS Technical Bulletin #6" addresses this problem by stating that the input buffer should not be modified, and recommending that if there is a conflict of use, the buffer should be "copied to a safe area of memory" and restored before returning to ProDOS. If anyone knows of a guaranteed contiguous 256-byte safe area of memory under ProDOS and/or BASIC.SYSTEM for *all* programs, let us know.

Fortunately, Apple itself does not follow their own doctrine. As we said, the lower end of the buffer at $200 is overwritten by the Thunderclock driver. We therefore assume that we can use this area.

That leaves two solutions: modify the Apple Clock's firmware so that the time string is stored at $200 instead of $280, or include a short routine in the clock driver to move the area that the Apple Clock overwrites at $280 to $200 *before* accessing the clock. After we get the data, we move the possible filename data back to $280 from $200, return to ProDOS, and no one's the wiser.

KEEPING UP-TO-DATE

The year is a simpler problem; we use a STARTUP program written in BASIC to look for the clock and install it if found (and if no other clock has been installed). We then check for a previously saved DATE and TIME on disk. If none is found, we get the time from the Apple Clock and request that the person at the keyboard enter the last two digits of the current year. We then save the time and date, including the year, for reference.

Each time the program is run, it will again check the disk for the last updated value of the time and date. It compares this to the *current* date read from the clock card. If the number of the month has *decreased*, we assume we have passed the first of the year and so we increment the last value of the year by one before saving the new date and time.

If the number of the month is *higher* than the previously saved value, we assume we are still in the same year, and use the saved value of the year. We then save the current date and time in a disk file for reference and continue.

As long as the disk gets booted a few times a year, and you keep the time on your clock card set correctly, this STARTUP program should handle keeping the year up to date. It does require that the program be run from a write-enabled disk. Just to be safe, you are given a chance to override the current value of the year manually.

```
100  REM *** STARTUP FOR MOUNTAIN CLOCK ***
110  TEXT
120  PRINT  CHR$ (21)
130 D$ = CHR$ (4)
140 EFLAG = 0
150  ONERR  GOTO 1330
160  HOME
170  POKE  - 16368,0
180  PRINT
       "--------------------------------------"
190  PRINT
200  PRINT  SPC( 5);"ProDOS Mountain Clock
       STARTUP"
210  PRINT
220  PRINT "   Copyright 1985 Dennis Doms, KCMO"
230  PRINT
240  PRINT
       "---------------------------------------";
       PRINT
```

Listing 24-2. STARTUP file to install a clock driver and update the year.

```
250  IF  PEEK ( - 16634) = 76 THEN  VTAB 10:
       HTAB 1: CALL  - 958: PRINT "A clock has
       already been installed.": GOTO 730: REM
       EXIT.
260  VTAB 10
270  PRINT "Press 'ESC' to reset year manually."
280  IF  NOT EFLAG THEN  PRINT D$;"BLOAD
       AUTO.CLK.BAS"
290  IF (EFLAG = 1 AND (ECODE = 6 OR ECODE = 7))
       THEN  VTAB 10: HTAB 1: CALL  - 958: PRINT
       "File 'AUTO.CLK.BAS' not found.": PRINT :
       PRINT "Unable to find/install Mountain
       Clock.": GOTO 730: REM EXIT.
300  IF EFLAG THEN  VTAB 10: HTAB 1: CALL  -
       958: PRINT ECODE$: PRINT : PRINT "Unable
       to continue; clock not installed.": GOTO
       730: REM EXIT.
310  CALL 8196
320 C = PEEK (7) - 192
330  IF C = 8 THEN  VTAB 10: HTAB 1: CALL  -
       958: PRINT "Mountain Clock not found.":
       GOTO 730: REM EXIT.
340  VTAB 10
350  HTAB 1
360  CALL  - 958
370  PRINT "Installing clock found in slot
       ";C;"."
380  IF  NOT EFLAG THEN  PRINT D$;"BLOAD
       DATE,A$2000"
390  IF EFLAG THEN EFLAG = 0: REM PATH
       'DATEFILE/DATE' NOT FOUND.
400  REM *** CONVERT STORED DATE TO YE)AR,
       MO)NTH, HO)UR, AND MI)NUTE ***
410 DH = 8193:DL = 8192:TH = 8195:TL = 8194: REM
       DATE AND TIME HIGH AND LOW BYTES FROM
       STORED DATE.
420 D1 = PEEK (DH):D2 = PEEK (DL)
430 T1 = PEEK (TH):T2 = PEEK (TL)
440  GOSUB 860
450  REM *** CHECK FOR YEAR ***
460  IF YE = 0 OR MO = 0 THEN  GOSUB 1050
470 YR = YE:LM = MO: REM SAVE YR (LAST YEAR) AND
       LM (LAST MONTH) RECORDED.
480  GOSUB 930: REM GET DATE/TIME FROM MOUNTAIN
       CLOCK.
490  IF LM > MO THEN YR = YR + 1: REM INCREMENT
       YEAR IF MONTH HAS DECREASED.
500  REM *** PRINT CURRENT TIME AND DATE TO
       SCREEN ***
510  VTAB 10
520  HTAB 1
530  CALL  - 958
540 AM$ = "AM":HP = HO
550  IF HP > 11 THEN AM$ = "PM": IF HP > 12 THEN
       HP = HP - 12
560 MN$ = "JANFEBMARAPRMAYJUNJULAUGSEPOCTNOVDEC"
570 MN$ = MID$ (MN$,((MO - 1) * 3) + 1,3)
580  PRINT "Currently set time: ";HP;":";
```

```
590  IF  LEN ( STR$ (MI)) < 2 THEN  PRINT "0";
600  PRINT MI;" ";AM$
610 YE = YR: REM SET TO PRESENT YEAR.
620  GOSUB 780
630  POKE DH,D1: POKE DL,D2: POKE TH,T1: POKE
       TL,T2: REM SET DATE FOR FILE SAVE.
640  POKE 49041,YE * 2
650  CALL 8276: REM EQUALS $2054, 'INSTALL CLOCK
       DRIVER' ROUTINE.
660  REM ATTEMPT TO SAVE DATE FOR FUTURE
       REFERENCE.
670  IF  NOT EFLAG THEN  PRINT D$;"BSAVE
       DATE,A$2000,L$04"
680  IF EFLAG THEN EFLAG = 0: VTAB 18: CALL  -
       958: PRINT ECODE$: PRINT : PRINT "Unable
       to update 'DATE'."
690  REM *** CHECK IF 'ESC' TYPED TO UPDATE YEAR
       ***
700 KD = PEEK ( - 16384)
710  POKE  - 16368,0
720  IF KD = 128 + 27 THEN  GOSUB 1050: GOTO 510
730  VTAB 22
740  HTAB 1
750  CALL  - 958
760  POKE 216,0: REM CLEAR ONERR GOTO FLAG.
770  END : REM TO LINK NEXT PROGRAM, REPLACE
       'END' WITH BASIC.SYSTEM COMMAND.
780  REM *** SET DATE ***
790 HB = 0
800  IF MO > 7 THEN HB = 1
810 D1 = YE * 2 + HB
820 D2 = INT ((MO - (HB * 8)) * 32) + DA
830 T1 = HO
840 T2 = MI
850  RETURN
860  REM *** READ DATE (PRODOS) ***
870 YE = INT (D1 / 2)
880 MO = ((D1 - (YE * 2)) * 8) +  INT (D2 / 32)
890 DA = D2 - (MO * 32)
900 HO = T1
910 MI = T2
920  RETURN
930  REM *** READ DATE (MT CLOCK) ***
940  PRINT D$;"IN#";C
950  PRINT D$;"PR#";C
960  INPUT TI$
970  PRINT D$;"PR#0"
980  PRINT D$;"IN#0"
990  REM GET MO, DA, HO, AND MI.
1000 MO = VAL ( LEFT$ (TI$,2))
1010 DA = VAL ( MID$ (TI$,4,2))
1020 HO = VAL ( MID$ (TI$,7,2))
1030 MI = VAL ( MID$ (TI$,10,2))
1040  RETURN
1050  REM *** GET CURRENT YEAR (MANUAL) ***
1060  VTAB 10
1070  HTAB 1
1080  CALL  - 958
```

```
1090  PRINT "Please enter current year: YY"
1100  VTAB 10
1110  HTAB 28
1120  GET A$
1130  IF A$ < "0" OR A$ > "9" THEN  GOTO 1120
1140  PRINT A$;
1150 YE$ = A$
1160  VTAB 10
1170  HTAB 29
1180  GET A$
1190  IF A$ < "0" OR A$ > "9" THEN  GOTO 1160
1200  PRINT A$
1210 YE$ = YE$ + A$
1220  VTAB 22
1230  HTAB 1
1240  PRINT "Is this the correct year?: "
1250  VTAB 22
1260  HTAB 28
1270  GET A$
1280  IF A$ <  > "Y" AND A$ <  > "y" AND A$ <  >
       "N" AND A$ <  > "n" THEN  GOTO 1270
1290  IF A$ = "N" OR A$ = "n" THEN  GOTO 1050
1300 YE = VAL (YE$): REM FIX TO NEW ENTRY.
1310  PRINT
1320  RETURN
1330  REM *** ERROR HANDLER ***
1340  REM RESERVED VARIABLES:
1350  REM     ECODE  (FOR ERROR NUMBER)
1360  REM     EMESSAGE$ (FOR ERROR MESSAGE
       STRING)
1370  REM     EFLAG  (FOR ERROR FLAG, = 1 IF
       ERROR)
1380  REM     ELINE (FOR ERROR LINE NUMBER)
1390  GOSUB 1430: REM get error info.
1400  IF EFLAG = 1 AND ECODE = 255 THEN  VTAB
       20: HTAB 1: CALL  - 958: PRINT EMESSAGE$:
       PRINT "at # ";ELINE".": VTAB 22: CALL  -
       3288: POKE 216,0: END : REM EXIT ON
       CONTROL-C.
1410  RESUME
1420  STOP : REM shouldn't happen.
1430  REM *** MAKE UP ERROR STRING ***
1440 ECODE = PEEK (222)
1450 ELINE = PEEK (218) +  PEEK (219) * 256
1460 EMESSAGE$ = ""
1470  REM APPLESOFT ERRORS
1480  IF ECODE = 0 THEN EMESSAGE$ = "NEXT
       WITHOUT FOR"
1490  IF ECODE = 16 THEN EMESSAGE$ = "INCORRECT
       SYNTAX"
1500  IF ECODE = 22 THEN EMESSAGE$ = "RETURN
       WITHOUT GOSUB"
1510  IF ECODE = 42 THEN EMESSAGE$ = "OUT OF
       DATA"
1520  IF ECODE = 53 THEN EMESSAGE$ = "ILLEGAL
       QUANTITY"
1530  IF ECODE = 69 THEN EMESSAGE$ = "OVERFLOW"
1540  IF ECODE = 77 THEN EMESSAGE$ = "OUT OF
```

```
        MEMORY"
1550  IF ECODE = 90 THEN EMESSAGE$ = "UNDEFINED
        STATEMENT"
1560  IF ECODE = 107 THEN EMESSAGE$ = "BAD
        SUBSCRIPT"
1570  IF ECODE = 120 THEN EMESSAGE$ =
        "REDIMENSIONED ARRAY"
1580  IF ECODE = 133 THEN EMESSAGE$ = "DIVISION
        BY ZERO"
1590  IF ECODE = 163 THEN EMESSAGE$ = "TYPE
        MISMATCH"
1600  IF ECODE = 176 THEN EMESSAGE$ = "STRING
        TOO LONG"
1610  IF ECODE = 191 THEN EMESSAGE$ = "FORMULA
        TOO COMPLEX"
1620  IF ECODE = 224 THEN EMESSAGE$ = "UNDEFINED
        FN"
1630  IF ECODE = 255 THEN EMESSAGE$ = "CONTROL-C
        ABORT"
1640  REM BASIC.SYSTEM ERRORS
1650  IF ECODE = 2 THEN EMESSAGE$ = "RANGE
        ERROR"
1660  IF ECODE = 3 THEN EMESSAGE$ = "NO DEVICE
        CONNECTED"
1670  IF ECODE = 4 THEN EMESSAGE$ = "WRITE
        PROTECTED"
1680  IF ECODE = 5 THEN EMESSAGE$ = "END OF
        DATA"
1690  IF ECODE = 8 THEN EMESSAGE$ = "I/O ERROR"
1700  IF ECODE = 9 THEN EMESSAGE$ = "DISK FULL"
1710  IF ECODE = 10 THEN EMESSAGE$ = "FILE
        LOCKED"
1720  IF ECODE = 11 THEN EMESSAGE$ = "INVALID
        OPTION"
1730  IF ECODE = 12 THEN EMESSAGE$ = "NO BUFFERS
        AVAILABLE"
1740  IF ECODE = 13 THEN EMESSAGE$ = "FILE TYPE
        MISMATCH"
1750  IF ECODE = 14 THEN EMESSAGE$ = "PROGRAM
        TOO LARGE"
1760  IF ECODE = 15 THEN EMESSAGE$ = "NOT DIRECT
        COMMAND": REM SUPERFLUOUS.
1770  IF ECODE = 16 THEN EMESSAGE$ = "INCORRECT
        SYNTAX": REM REDUNDANT.
1780  IF ECODE = 17 THEN EMESSAGE$ = "DIRECTORY
        FULL"
1790  IF ECODE = 18 THEN EMESSAGE$ = "FILE NOT
        OPEN"
1800  IF ECODE = 19 THEN EMESSAGE$ = "DUPLICATE
        FILENAME"
1810  IF ECODE = 20 THEN EMESSAGE$ = "FILE BUSY"
1820  IF ECODE = 21 THEN EMESSAGE$ = "FILE(S)
        STILL OPEN"
1830 EFLAG = 1
1840  IF (ECODE = 0 OR ECODE > 21) THEN
        EMESSAGE$ = "A/S error: " + EMESSAGE$
1850  IF (ECODE > 0 AND ECODE < 21 AND ECODE <
        > 16) THEN EMESSAGE$ = "BASIC.SYSTEM
```

```
      error: " + EMESSAGE$
1860  IF (ECODE = 16) THEN EMESSAGE$ = "A/S or
      BASIC.SYSTEM error: " + EMESSAGE$
1870  RETURN
```

```
********************************
*                              *
*  Mountain Clock Driver for   *
*  ProDOS versions to 1.1.1    *
*                              *
********************************
*                              *
*  Assumes that ProDOS has     *
*  saved registers and set     *
*  proper interrupt status     *
*  before calling this code.   *
*                              *
********************************
*                              *
*   In the midst of revision   *
*             9/2/84           *
*                              *
*   by Dennis Doms             *
*                              *
*   Assembler: Merlin Pro      *
*                              *
* All commercial rights are    *
* reserved. Non-commercial     *
* distribution is encouraged   *
* provided all original com-   *
* ments are retained (leave    *
* what little documentation    *
* there is!).                  *
*                              *
********************************
                          ;
                          ;
* This version of the routine is designed for use with the
* BASIC installation program.
                          ;
                          ;
* Various label definitions.
                          ;
                          ;
KSWH    =     $39         ; high byte of Keyboard vector.
DATA    =     $3A         ; Zero page workspace.
MIN     =     $3A         ; minute
HOUR    =     $3B         ; hour
DAY     =     $3C         ; day
MONTH   =     $3D         ; month
```

Listing 24-3. The Apple Clock driver for ProDOS.

```
        INPUT    =     $0200       ; Keyboard input
  buffer.
        TINDEX   =     $0289       ; index for clock's
  time string
        CLOCKSTR =     $0280       ; base location for
  clock data string.
        TEMP1    =     $0478       ; from flaky //e
  ROMs.
        YEAR     =     $BF91       ; since Mountain
  Clock does not provide year,
                                   ; this register
  should be set before clock
                                   ; driver is loaded
  and then used thereafter.
        DATE     =     $BF91       ; high byte of DATE
  register pair.
        TIME     =     $BF93       ; high byte of TIME
  register pair.
        MACHID   =     $BF98       ; Machine ID Byte.
        CLOCKROM =     $C400       ; assume slot 4
        XROMOFF  =     $CFFF       ; Softswitch to turn
  off $C800 ROM.
        COUT     =     $FDED       ; for bell later.
                                   ;
                                   ;
                  16-DEC-85  14:43
                                   ;
                                   ;
                  ORG   $2000      ; but clock driver is
  actually relocatable.
2000: 00 00 00    DS    4          ; Create 4 byte area
  for DATE
2003: 00
2004: A9 00   SLOTCHK  LDA   #$00  ; Set for slot 1
2006: 85 06            STA   $06
2008: A9 C1            LDA   #$C1
200A: 85 07            STA   $07
200C: AD FF CF CHKCLK  LDA   XROMOFF  ; turn off extension
  ROM.
200F: A0 13            LDY   #$13  ; check Mountain's ID
  bytes for clock values.
2011: B1 06            LDA   ($06),Y
2013: C9 03            CMP   #$03
2015: F0 0C            BEQ   MAYBECLK
2017: C9 B1            CMP   #$B1
2019: F0 08            BEQ   MAYBECLK
201B: C9 EC            CMP   #$EC
201D: F0 04            BEQ   MAYBECLK
201F: C9 2C            CMP   #$2C
2021: D0 20            BNE   NXTSLOT
2023: C8      MAYBECLK INY               ; set index to #$15.
2024: C8               INY
2025: B1 06            LDA   ($06),Y
2027: C9 F8            CMP   #$F8
2029: F0 0C            BEQ   GOTCLK
202B: C9 FD            CMP   #$FD
202D: F0 08            BEQ   GOTCLK
202F: C9 07            CMP   #$07
```

```
2031: F0 04                BEQ   GOTCLK
2033: C9 68                CMP   #$68
2035: D0 0C                BNE   NXTSLOT
2037: A5 07          GOTCLK LDA   $07        ; found clock if we
       make it to here
2039: 8D 97 20             STA   FIX1       ; so get Cx value and
       fix driver
203C: 8D A0 20             STA   FIX2
203F: AD FF CF             LDA   XROMOFF    ; turn off extension
       ROM.
2042: 60                   RTS              ; Return to BASIC
       driver.
2043: E6 07          NXTSLOT INC  $07        ; set to next page to
       check.
2045: A5 07                LDA   $07        ; get byte to look
       over.
2047: C9 C8                CMP   #$C8       ; are we off the
       motherboard?
2049: D0 C1                BNE   CHKCLK     ; no, Keep looking
204B: A9 87                LDA   #$87       ; yes, beep and
       return before damage is done
204D: 20 ED FD             JSR   COUT
2050: AD FF CF             LDA   XROMOFF    ; turn off extension
       ROM.
2053: 60                   RTS
                                            ;
                     * Subroutine to install driver internal to
       ProDOS.
                                            ;
2054: AD 07 BF       INSTALL LDA  $BF07      ; move vector to page
       0 for indirect address
2057: 85 06                STA   $06
2059: AD 08 BF             LDA   $BF08
205C: 85 07                STA   $07
205E: AD 89 C0             LDA   $C089      ; Write-enable slot 0
       RAM card bank 1.
2061: AD 89 C0             LDA   $C089
2064: A0 7A                LDY   #FIN-BEG   ; put length of
       routine into Y
2066: B9 81 20       MOVECD LDA   BEG,Y      ; get driver byte
2069: 91 06                STA   ($06),Y    ; put in ProDOS clock
       driver space
206B: 88                   DEY
206C: C0 FF                CPY   #$FF       ; moved everything?
206E: D0 F6                BNE   MOVECD     ; not yet
2070: AD 81 C0             LDA   $C081      ; set bank 2 and read
       ROM.
2073: A9 4C                LDA   #$4C       ; change to JMP
       instruction
2075: 8D 06 BF             STA   $BF06
2078: AD 98 BF             LDA   MACHID     ; Get machine ID
       byte.
207B: 29 01                AND   #$01       ; Say compatible
       clock installed (fib?).
207D: 8D 98 BF             STA   MACHID     ; Put back new value.
2080: 60                   RTS              ; go home.
                                            ;
```

```
                * Clock driver.
                                               ;
2081: AD 78 04      BEG      LDA   TEMP1       ; get TEMP1 and save
        it on stack.
2084: 48                     PHA
2085: A2 21                  LDX   #$21        ; now move this area
        of INPUT...
2087: BD 80 02      MOVBUFDN LDA   CLOCKSTR,X  ; down low in the
        buffer before
208A: 9D 00 02               STA   INPUT,X     ; CLOCKROM call
        overwrites it.
208D: CA                     DEX
208E: 10 F7                  BPL   MOVBUFDN
2090: A5 39                  LDA   KSWH        ; get keyboard vector
        and save...
2092: 48                     PHA
2093: A5 38                  LDA   KSWH-1
2095: 48                     PHA
2096: A9 C4                  LDA   #>CLOCKROM  ; ...then replace it
        with clock vector. This
                    FIX1     =     *-1         ; byte value is slot
        dependent!
2098: 85 39                  STA   KSWH
209A: A9 00                  LDA   #<CLOCKROM
209C: 85 38                  STA   KSWH-1
209E: 20 00 C4               JSR   CLOCKROM    ; put time string
        into $280-$293. This call
                    FIX2     =     *-1         ; vector is slot
        dependent!
20A1: 68                     PLA               ; put back the
        keyboard vector and TEMP1.
20A2: 85 38                  STA   KSWH-1
20A4: 68                     PLA
20A5: 85 39                  STA   KSWH
20A7: 68                     PLA
20A8: 8D 78 04               STA   TEMP1
20AB: 18                     CLC               ; SHOWTIME (pun
        intended)
20AC: A2 03                  LDX   #$03        ; four values to calc
        and save.
20AE: A0 0A                  LDY   #$0A        ; offset to month (to
        start)
20B0: B9 89 02      CALCTIME LDA   TINDEX,Y    ; get 10's (ASCII
        char) value...
20B3: 29 07                  AND   #$07        ; ...take last three
        bits...
20B5: 95 3A                  STA   DATA,X      ; ...and save for a
        millisecond or two.
20B7: 0A                     ASL               ; multiply by four.
20B8: 0A                     ASL
20B9: 75 3A                  ADC   DATA,X      ; now multiplied by
        five.
20BB: 0A                     ASL               ; now (wala!)
        multiplied by ten total.
20BC: 79 88 02               ADC   TINDEX-1,Y  ; add in ones place
20BF: 38                     SEC               ; make sure carry set
20C0: E9 B0                  SBC   #$B0        ; and subtract out
```

```
        ASCII offset of ones.
20C2: 95 3A                      STA   DATA,X      ; completed this
        conversion
20C4: 88                         DEY               ; decrement to point
        at next pair.
20C5: 88                         DEY
20C6: 88                         DEY
20C7: CA                         DEX               ; one less pair to do
20C8: 10 E6                      BPL   CALCTIME    ; go back if
        someone's left
20CA: AD 91 BF        FIXDATE    LDA   DATE        ; get year/month high
        byte
20CD: 6A                         ROR               ; keep just the year
20CE: 48                         PHA               ; save for the nonce.
20CF: A5 3D                      LDA   MONTH       ; get month value
20D1: 4A                         LSR               ; shift to keep only
        highest bit in month.
20D2: 4A                         LSR
20D3: 4A                         LSR
20D4: 6A                         ROR               ; Put last bit into
        carry.
20D5: 68                         PLA               ; Get back year.
20D6: 2A                         ROL               ; Shift up w/high bit
        of month.
20D7: 8D 91 BF                   STA   DATE        ; done here
20DA: A5 3D                      LDA   MONTH       ; get month
20DC: 0A                         ASL               ; shift bits 2-0 to
        7-5
20DD: 0A                         ASL
20DE: 0A                         ASL
20DF: 0A                         ASL
20E0: 0A                         ASL
20E1: 05 3C                      ORA   DAY         ; combine with 5 bits
        (4-0) of day
20E3: 8D 90 BF                   STA   DATE-1      ; done with date
20E6: A5 3B           FIXTIME    LDA   HOUR        ; just move these to
        ProDOS
20E8: 8D 93 BF                   STA   TIME
20EB: A5 3A                      LDA   MIN
20ED: 8D 92 BF                   STA   TIME-1
20F0: A2 21                      LDX   #$21        ; put back the buffer
        as we found it (almost).
20F2: BD 00 02        MOVBUFUP   LDA   INPUT,X
20F5: 9D 80 02                   STA   CLOCKSTR,X
20F8: CA                         DEX
20F9: 10 F7                      BPL   MOVBUFUP
20FB: 60              FIN        RTS               ; that's all,
        folks...


--End assembly, 252 bytes, Errors: 0


Symbol table - alphabetical order:
   BEG     =$2081      CALCTIME=$20B0      CHKCLK  =$200C
        CLOCKROM=$C400
   CLOCKSTR=$0280      COUT    =$FDED      DATA    =$3A        DATE
        =$BF91
```

```
   DAY      =$3C        FIN      =$20FB      FIX1     =$2097      FIX2
         =$20A0
 ? FIXDATE =$20CA    ? FIXTIME =$20E6      GOTCLK   =$2037      HOUR
         =$3B
   INPUT    =$0200    ? INSTALL =$2054      KSWH     =$39
         MACHID   =$BF98
   MAYBECLK=$2023      MIN      =$3A        MONTH    =$3D
         MOVBUFDN=$2087
   MOVBUFUP=$20F2      MOVECD   =$2066      NXTSLOT  =$2043    ?
         SLOTCHK  =$2004
   TEMP1    =$0478      TIME     =$BF93      TINDEX   =$0289
         XROMOFF  =$CFFF
 ? YEAR     =$BF91


Symbol table - numerical order:

   KSWH     =$39        DATA     =$3A        MIN      =$3A        HOUR
         =$3B
   DAY      =$3C        MONTH    =$3D        INPUT    =$0200
         CLOCKSTR=$0280
   TINDEX   =$0289      TEMP1    =$0478    ? SLOTCHK  =$2004
         CHKCLK   =$200C
   MAYBECLK=$2023      GOTCLK   =$2037      NXTSLOT  =$2043    ?
         INSTALL  =$2054
   MOVECD   =$2066      BEG      =$2081      MOVBUFDN=$2087      FIX1
         =$2097
   FIX2     =$20A0      CALCTIME=$20B0    ? FIXDATE  =$20CA    ?
         FIXTIME  =$20E6
   MOVBUFUP=$20F2      FIN      =$20FB    ? YEAR     =$BF91      DATE
         =$BF91
   TIME     =$BF93      MACHID   =$BF98      CLOCKROM=$C400
         XROMOFF  =$CFFF
   COUT     =$FDED
```

The two programs in Listing 24-2 and 24-3 are a "STARTUP" program for the Apple Clock and its machine-language clock driver. The "STARTUP" program expects to find the driver under the pathname "DATEFILE/AUTO.CLK.BAS" (the driver also contains a routine to find the clock and install the driver in ProDOS). "STARTUP" also uses the DATEFILE directory to save the last date recorded by the system (in the file "DATE") so that it can attempt to keep the year current.

Chapter 25

Installation of Interrupt Handlers

Interrupts seem to be largely left as a mystery subject, but they are a part of everyday life. Actually, a computer's interpretation of interrupts is very close to the same thing that happens to a human under the same conditions. It's just that, true to form, the computer is a lot more literal in its interpretation.

PARDON, MAY I INTERRUPT?

You're sitting at the computer, entering your latest figures and getting ready for the final calculation and printout. Suddenly someone leans in the door and asks "Can you come help me with this for a minute? . . . ".

Being a helpful sort of person, you decide that, yes, you will go tend to whatever task they have for you; unloading groceries from the car, perhaps. But first, you don't want the four hours you spent typing in figures lost while you walk away from the computer. So you take a few seconds to put things in order, save the file, etc. Satisfied that you have everything put away so you can recover your place later, you go off to haul in groceries.

A little while later, done with the manual labor, you return to the computer. You recover your stored data and continue entering data just as you were doing before you changed tasks for a few moments.

That was an interrupt. You were doing one task, an event caused you to reach a quitting place in the task, you saved the state of your work, went to do another task, returned and recovered your place in your original task, and went on with the original task.

INTERRUPTS IN THE UNREAL WORLD

In the microcomputer world, the handling of interrupts follows the same pattern but with the rigid logic that computers thrive on. The 6502 microprocessor at the heart of the Apple has two provisions for *hardware* interrupts; interrupts which are caused by an electrical signal to the microprocessor. These are referred to as *IRQ* and *NMI* interrupts. There is also the *BRK* instruction, which is sometimes referred to as a *software* interrupt.

THE PATIENT IRQ

The IRQ (*i*nterrupt *req*uest) interrupt is the most common type of hardware interrupt on the Apple *II* series computers. The primary reason for this has to do with the Apple Disk *II* drives and work-alikes, which cannot be interrupted while actually writing to the disk without destroying data on the disk. The IRQ can be ignored through use of some 6502 instructions, while the NMI cannot be ignored and will *always* interrupt the program flow.

The BRK (*BR*ea*K*) instruction is initially handled in the same manner as an IRQ interrupt, but a BRK is initiated in software only, via the BRK (6502 machine language $00) instruction.

WHEN I'M READY

Obviously, for our "help unload the groceries" scenario, there may be times when you cannot afford to be interrupted. You may have left a sign on the door ordering "Do Not Disturb".

There are times the Apple's 6502 can't afford to be stopped in the middle of some things, too. Notably, if an interrupt was allowed while ProDOS was using a Disk *II* drive to write to a disk, part of the disk's format would likely be destroyed.

Before a specific IRQ is signaled to the 6502, an Apple program has the option of causing the 6502 to ignore the interrupt. It does this by using the assembly instructions *SEI* and *CLI*. SEI (*SE*t *I*nterrupt disable) causes bit 2 of the processor status register to be set to 1 and serves as a "flag" to notify the 6502 that it should not react to the hardware IRQ request. If the signal for an IRQ is present it is ignored while this flag is set.

If CLI (*CL*ear *I*nterrupt disable) is issued as a 6502 instruction, the flag at bit 2 in the processor status register is set to 0. This tells the 6502 that it is indeed to respond to an IRQ request. Between SEI and CLI, your program has control over whether or not interrupts from the IRQ are allowed. BRK does "not" recognize the SEI or CLI state.

If IRQ interrupts are allowed, when the interrupt occurs it causes the 6502 to take certain actions. First, the 6502 pushes the program counter's current contents onto the stack, followed by the current value of the status register. Next, the 6502 sets bit 2 of the processor status register to disable further IRQ interruptions for the moment and begins execution at the address specified by the contents of $FFFE-$FFFF. In the standard Apple monitor, which resides on the motherboard in that area, this location points to an interrupt handler within the monitor that takes care of IRQ and BRK requests.

A SILICON BUG

The code in the monitor is an elementary built-in IRQ/BRK handler. When executed, it first proceeds to save the accumulator. Apple *II* and unenhanced Apple *II*e computers saved the accumulator at $45, which causes problems if certain monitor routines are called, or if another interrupt is allowed before this register is saved elsewhere. The newer Apple ROMs save the value of A on the stack, which eliminates the problem.

It then checks to see if an IRQ is present or if BRK instruction has been executed. If it was an IRQ, the bit will be 0; and a JMP ($03FE) will be performed. $03FE-$03FF should contain the address of the interrupt handler you wish to use. Under ProDOS, this will point to ProDOS's interrupt handler at $BFEB.

TAKE A BREAK

If the interrupt was caused by a break, bit 4 of the processor status at the time of the interrupt (which was saved on the stack) will be set to 1 and (on most Apples) a "JMP ($03F0)" will be performed. Location $3F0 is initially set by the monitor to point to $FA59, which is a monitor routine which prints the contents of the 6502 registers in the form illustrated by Figure 25-1. The asterisk shows you have been left in the Apple's monitor.

Note: on Apple *II* computers with the "old" non-Autostart monitor ROMs, BRK will *always* send you directly to this "display registers" routine. The vector at $03F0 was not implemented un-

```
2002-    A=00 X=12 Y=00 S=F1 P=14
*
```

Fig. 25-1. Monitor BRK display.

til the advent of the Autostart ROM.

It is important to realize that BRK causes the program counter to be incremented by two before it is pushed onto the stack, even though BRK is a one-byte instruction. BRK was designed as a debugging tool to use with machine language programs. A BRK can be inserted into your Apple program and, when encountered, it stops your program, prints the status of the registers at the time of the interruption, then drops you back into the monitor so you can review your code easily. The designers of the Apple ROM went ahead and included the BREAK code to facilitate this use of the BRK instruction. The vector pointing to this routine (at $03F0) can be altered; but ProDOS does not inherently change this vector.

INTERRUPT HANDLERS AND PRODOS

Under DOS, some strange things could happen with interrupts. First, DOS used some zero-page locations that were also used by the interrupt routines; this could cause the supposedly "safe" values to be altered. DOS itself usually was altered to bypass the use of these locations. Second, some DOS programs, notably FID, also used some of these locations. The designers of ProDOS have tried to eliminate any problems of this nature between ProDOS and use of interrupts.

As we have already mentioned, the specific use of $45 by the older Apple II and *II*e monitor programs also causes a conflict. In the old monitors, $45 was used to save the value of the accumulator during IRQ handling. Unfortunately, $45 was also defined as A5H, a general purpose register used by some other monitor routines. Therefore, it was important to make sure $45 was saved elsewhere *first* during an IRQ handler before any monitor routines were used. It is probably best to continue this practice for compatibility, although the problem has been solved by the *II*c and enhanced *II*e ROMs, which save the accumulator on the stack instead of in $45.

ON WITH THE INTERRUPTION

With these considerations aside, the normal course of an interrupt handling routine on the Apple is to move any "saved" registers to other, safer, locations; re-enable interrupts if the interrupt handler is interruptable, and proceed with the action you wish to take on the current interrupt.

Each interrupt handler is basically a machine language routine, which should be as succinct as possible to do the necessary task that the interrupt was designed to initiate. If an interrupt indicates that you should increase the value of location $800 by one (for whatever reason), then the actual working portion of the routine would have to be no more than an INC $0800 instruction. The difference between this routine and a standard 6502 subroutine is that a 6502 *RTI* (*Re**T*urn from *I*nterrupt) is used to return from the routine rather than an RTS. Also, you should *not* alter the state of the stack or stack pointer from within an interrupt handler under most circumstances. When RTI is encountered, you want the interrupt handler to return to the original program as if nothing (adverse) has happened.

The action you take will depend on what caused the interrupt. Often, a device such as a clock card is used to generate IRQ interrupts so that an action can be performed at regular intervals. Your interrupt routine would then verify that the clock card *issued* the IRQ signal and, if so, perform the scheduled task.

Other cards for the Apple also use interrupts to get the Apple's attention, notably the Apple Mouse interface card. If you were using interrupts from a clock card *and* from a Mouse, your interrupt handler would have to determine which card issued the current IRQ, and take the corresponding action. Perhaps the respective action would be to update the system's TIME and DATE registers for use by a program, or to read the current position of the Mouse.

Two devices increase the complexity of the problem, because one device *could* issue an IRQ at the same time that you are handling an interrupt from the other device. That means not only is your main program put "on hold", but the interrupt handler must also be put on hold for the *first* device while you service the second device. After you finish each stage of the process, you release control back to the previous stage.

PRODOS INTERRUPT SUPPORT

ProDOS contains its own interrupt handler which does most of the tasks except for determining which device produced the interruption and servicing it. ProDOS also allows for the assignment of four prioritized *levels* of interrupt handlers.

ProDOS maintains a bevy of status locations and data areas in its global page to save the "state" of various ProDOS functions at the time of an interrupt. For one thing, ProDOS saves all registers (including taking care of the "$45" bug) and the program counter's return address so that you do not need to worry about those details. ProDOS also keeps a record of whether the MLI is in use, which can be detected by an interrupt handler.

ProDOS reserves 16 locations of the stack from $1E0 to $1FF for use by your interrupt routine. You can't *leave* data on the stack, however, because this assigned usage is only for the purposes of servicing the interrupt. ProDOS will restore its location in the stack upon your return from the interrupt subroutine.

USING THE PRODOS IRQ SUPPORT

Under ProDOS, you can write your "interrupt handler" as a normal subroutine and install it into ProDOS's interrupt handler. ProDOS then takes over the normal interrupt handling responsibilities with the exception of actually servicing the interrupt.

Upon receiving an IRQ, ProDOS will take care of saving the registers and return address and pass control to your routine. Your routine must identify itself to ProDOS by beginning with a CLD instruction, which ProDOS uses to identify an external routine which has been assigned to ProDOS. It should contain the necessary code to identify the interrupting device (including examining the processor status register to see if the interrupt is from a BRK instruction) and process the interrupt, then return to ProDOS via an *RTS*. An RTI is *not* used to return because ProDOS handles that portion of the interrupt handling.

A few situations within the routine require special attention. First, if you are going to use the 6502 stack, the stack pointer should be initialized to $FF so that you are using the 16 bytes of the stack reserved by ProDOS for you.

Second, if you wish your subroutine to *not* be interruptable, you should perform a PHP to save the current state of the processor status followed by an SEI instruction to lock out further interrupts. A PLP instruction issued shortly before the RTS (remember, the stack operations should all be paired) used to exit will restore the initial interrupt enable flag's state.

Third, if you wish to call routines in the motherboard ROM (including the monitor), you must activate the motherboard ROM by "bank-switching" it in. ProDOS enables the RAM card area while it is active, as it will be when the interrupt handler is called. ProDOS maintains a byte to indicate which RAM card bank was in use at the time of the interrupt and that byte can be used to reactivate the proper area on exit.

MLI CALLS AND INTERRUPTS

If you are going to use an MLI call as part of your subroutine, you must check $BF9B to see if the MLI is active. If bit 7 of $BF9B is set, then the MLI was interrupted while issuing a call and you must allow it to complete that call before issuing yours. You can do this and vector the MLI to return to *your* routine by placing the contents of $BF9C-$BF9D in a JMP vector to be used as your final exit, and placing the address to which you want the MLI to return within $BF9C-$BF9D.

Next, clear the carry with a CLC and then issue an RTS. The MLI will complete the call and transfer control to the address contained in $BF9C-$BF9D, which now points to your routine. Your routine *must* save all registers upon entry, it can then do any processing required including MLI calls and exit through a JMP to the address initially found in $BF9C-$BF9D.

These gymnastics are dangerous and caution is recommended; you are responsible for making sure that your routine is not interrupted and overwrites $BF9C-$BF9D *twice* in sequence, or the initial return vector will be lost!

Also, calling the MLI is a bit of a time consuming task; usually, interrupt servicing routines should be as *short* as possible and do only the minimum amount needed to handle the interrupt. Saving data to disk from a buffer, for example, is probably *not* a good thing to do within such a routine. Set a flag in memory for your main program to recognize and let the main program save the data from a specifically constructed buffer after the interrupt handler returns.

INSTALLING INTERRUPT HANDLERS IN PRODOS

ProDOS maintains four addresses for interrupt handlers. Rather than writing a single interrupt handler to process four devices, you can write four separate subroutines (one for each device) and install them in ProDOS. ProDOS will then sequentially call each subroutine until one identifies itself as having found the source of the interrupt.

Less than four such routines can be assigned, but four is the maximum. To provide for more than four interrupting devices at one time, one or more of the subroutines will have to check for and process more than one device. The interrupt subroutines are installed by the MLI call ALLOC_INTERRUPT, which is shown in Listing 25-1. The value returned by the MLI into the one-byte storage register in the parameter list is the priority number of the routine. The first routine installed will be 1, the second installed will be 2, etc. up to a maximum of four. "INT.ROUT" is the address you provide for your subroutine.

One of two errors can be returned in the accumulator for this MLI call; $25, if all four vectors have been assigned, and $53, for an invalid parameter. As always, $00 will be returned in A if no error occurs.

The routine should be installed before interrupts on the device are enabled to insure that ProDOS knows where to go to process the device before the device cries out to be processed. When the address is installed, interrupts can be enabled via CLI and the device can be set to allow it to generate interrupts.

For an interrupt subroutine to notify ProDOS that it has or hasn't found its device, the carry flag is used. If the carry is cleared immediately before returning to ProDOS, ProDOS assumes the device was handled by the subroutine and does not call any of the lower-priority routines. If the carry is set with SEC, ProDOS assumes the device was not found or processed and will call the next lower priority subroutine and give it a chance to look for its device. If *no* device claims an interrupt, ProDOS will

```
ALLOC   JSR    MLI          ; Call MLI.
        DFB    $40          ; Code for
                              ALLOC_INTERRUPT.
        DA     PARMON       ; Parameter list.
        RTS

PARMON  DFB    $02          ; Parameter count (2).
        DS     $01          ; One byte storage for
                              interrupt priority
                            ; returned from MLI (1
                              to 4, if valid).
        DA     INT.ROUT     ; Address of interrupt
                              routine entry.
```

Listing 25-1. The ALLOC_INTERRUPT call.

```
        JSR     MLI             ; Call MLI.
        DFB     $41             ; Code for
                                  DEALLOC_INTERRUPT.
        .DA     PARMOFF         ; Parameter list.
        BCS     ERROR           ; Go if error (invalid
                                  parameters) occurs.
        RTS

PARMOFF DFB     $01             ; Parameter count (1).
        DS      1               ; Byte to contain
                                  interrupt priority
                                  number.
```

Listing 25-2. The DEALLOC_INTERRUPT call.

print a message on the screen telling you that an unclaimed interrupt occurred and call the system death code to "lock up" the Apple. To exit, you will be advised to re-boot.

To *remove* a device from ProDOS's list, it should first have its interrupt capability disabled. Then the MLI call DEALLOC_INTERRUPT is used to clear it from the list, as in Listing 25-2. The interrupt priority number defined in the parameter list should be the number originally given to the subroutine you are de-allocating when it was allocated by the MLI. In other words, if the MLI assigned routine as number 2 when it was installed, that number 2 should be used in the parameter list

```
********************************
*                              *
* Interrupt Driver for H. O.   *
*                              *
* Dennis Doms    11/20/85      *
*                              *
* Based on information in the  *
* TIMEMASTER ][ HO Manual.     *
*                              *
********************************
                            ;
                            ;
MLI      =      $BF00       ; MLI call vector.
GET_TIME =      $82         ; Code for "get time"
routine.
ALLOC_I  =      $40         ; Code for "allocate
interrupt vector".
DEALL_I  =      $41         ; Code for
"de-allocate interrupt vector".
CSLOT    =      $40         ; Clock slot times 16
(assume slot 4).
INPUT    =      $0200       ; GETLIN input
buffer.
DRA      =      $C080       ; PIA PortA/DDRA.
CRA      =      $C081       ; Offset to control
register A.
DRB      =      $C082       ; PIA PortB/DDRB.
CRB      =      $C083       ; Offset to control
```

Listing 25-3. Source for an IRQ program to update the DATE and TIME registers periodically.

```
         register B.
                MLIACTV  =     $BF9B      ; MLI "active" flag
         (bit 7).
                                          ;
                         19-DEC-85  19:24
                                          ;
                         ORG   $300       ; Assume page 3 is
         "safe".
                *
                * Call MLI to install interrupt handler in
         ProDOS.
                *
0300: D8        INSTALL  CLD              ; For ProDOS's
         benefit.
0301: 78                 SEI              ; Not ready for IRQ
         yet.
0302: 20 00 BF           JSR   MLI        ; Allocate interrupt
         vector.
0305: 40                 DFB   ALLOC_I    ; Code.
0306: 50 03              DA    ALLOC      ; Table address.
0308: D0 4C              BNE   ERROR1     ; Something went
         wrong.
030A: AD 51 03           LDA   ALLOC+1    ; Get device
         priority.
030D: 8D 55 03           STA   DEALL+1    ; Save for
         de-allocation.
                *
                * Following is based on 6821 PIA data sheet and
         HO docs.
                *
0310: A9 00     ENABLE   LDA   #$00       ; Set Timemaster for
         1 sec. interrupts.
0312: A2 40              LDX   #CSLOT
0314: 9D 81 C0           STA   CRA,X
0317: 9D 83 C0           STA   CRB,X
031A: 9D 80 C0           STA   DRA,X
031D: A9 FF              LDA   #$FF
031F: 9D 82 C0           STA   DRB,X
0322: A9 0C              LDA   #$0C
0324: 9D 81 C0           STA   CRA,X
0327: A9 04              LDA   #$04
0329: 9D 83 C0           STA   CRB,X
032C: A9 2F              LDA   #$2F       ; Set PIA to enable
         interrupts.
032E: 9D 82 C0           STA   DRB,X
0331: BD 81 C0           LDA   CRA,X      ; Clear previous
         interrupt.
0334: BD 83 C0           LDA   CRB,X
0337: 58                 CLI              ; Ready to enable.
0338: 60                 RTS
                *
                * Call MLI to remove interrupt driver.
                *
0339: D8        REMOVE   CLD              ; Identify for
         ProDOS.
033A: 08                 PHP              ; This time, don't
         assume IRQ status.
033B: 78                 SEI              ; Stop IRQ
```

```
        recognition.
033C: A9 04          LDA   #$04       ; Stop interrupts
        from Timemaster.
033E: A2 40          LDX   #CSLOT
0340: 9D 81 C0       STA   CRA,X
0343: 9D 83 C0       STA   CRB,X
0346: 20 00 BF       JSR   MLI        ; De-allocate
        interrupt handler.
0349: 41             DFB   DEALL_I    ; Code.
034A: 54 03          DA    DEALL      ; Table address.
034C: D0 0D          BNE   ERROR2     ; Something went
        wrong.
034E: 28             PLP              ; Restore entry IRQ
        status, etc.
034F: 60             RTS
           *
           * Tables, etc.
           *
0350: 02       ALLOC DFB   $02        ; Two parameters.
0351: 00             DFB   $00        ; Device priority
        (returned by MLI).
0352: 61 03          DA    NEW_TIME   ; Address of IRQ
        handler.
                                      ;
0354: 01       DEALL DFB   $01        ; One parameter.
0355: 00             DFB   $00        ; Device priority
        (set at installation).
                                      ;
0356: 8D 60 03 ERROR1 STA  ERCODE     ; For allocation
        error.
0359: 18             CLC              ; Make BASIC happy.
035A: 60             RTS
                                      ;
035B: 8D 60 03 ERROR2 STA  ERCODE     ; For deallocation
        error.
035E: 28             PLP              ; Balance stack use.
035F: 60             RTS
0360: 00       ERCODE DS   1
                                      ;
                                      ;
           *
           * Interrupt processor.
           *
                                      ;
0361: D8       NEW_TIME CLD           ; Identify for
        ProDOS.
0362: 08             PHP              ; Save status.
0363: 78             SEI              ; Go deaf for a few
        millisecs.
0364: A2 40          LDX   #CSLOT
0366: BD 81 C0       LDA   CRA,X      ; Get interrupt state
        (bit 7).
                                      ; (supposedly clears
        CRA bit 7).
0369: 10 2F          BPL   NOTCLOCK   ; It wasn't the HO.
036B: AD 9B BF       LDA   MLIACTV    ; Is MLI in midst of
        something?
036E: 30 24          BMI   IGNORE     ; Yes, don't call
```

```
        GET_TIME.
0370: A2 1C              LDX   #28        ; Move 28 bytes
0372: BD 00 02  SAVEPG2  LDA   INPUT,X    ; Save lower portion
        of INPUT.
0375: 9D 9D 03           STA   SAVINPUT,X ; Into safe area.
0378: CA                 DEX
0379: 10 F7              BPL   SAVEPG2
037B: AD 00 04           LDA   $0400      ; Signal IRQ "alive"
        by "flashing" on screen.
037E: 49 80              EOR   #$80
0380: 8D 00 04           STA   $0400
0383: 20 00 BF           JSR   MLI        ; Go get time/date.
0386: 82                 DFB   GET_TIME   ; Code.
0387: 00 00              DA    $0000      ; Null data address.
0389: A2 1C              LDX   #28
038B: BD 9D 03  FIXPG2   LDA   SAVINPUT,X ; Put INPUT right.
038E: 9D 00 02           STA   INPUT,X
0391: CA                 DEX
0392: 10 F7              BPL   FIXPG2
0394: 20 10 03  IGNORE   JSR   ENABLE     ; Re-activate IRQ
        after firmware call.
0397: 28                 PLP              ; Recover processor
        status.
0398: 18                 CLC              ; Say IRQ handled.
0399: 60                 RTS
                                          ;
039A: 28        NOTCLOCK PLP
039B: 38                 SEC              ; Wasn't Timemaster.
039C: 60                 RTS
                                          ;
039D: 00 00 00  SAVINPUT DS    28         ; 28 bytes for INPUT
        storage.
03A0: 00 00 00 00 00 00 00 00
03A8: 00 00 00 00 00 00 00 00
03B0: 00 00 00 00 00 00 00 00
03B8: 00


--End assembly, 185 bytes, Errors: 0


Symbol table - alphabetical order:

   ALLOC   =$0350     ALLOC_I =$40       CRA     =$C081     CRB
        =$C083
   CSLOT   =$40       DEALL   =$0354     DEALL_I =$41       DRA
        =$C080
   DRB     =$C082     ENABLE  =$0310     ERCODE  =$0360
        ERROR1  =$0356
   ERROR2  =$035B     FIXPG2  =$038B     GET_TIME=$82
        IGNORE  =$0394
   INPUT   =$0200   ? INSTALL =$0300     MLI     =$BF00
        MLIACTV =$BF9B
   NEW_TIME=$0361     NOTCLOCK=$039A   ? REMOVE  =$0339
        SAVEPG2 =$0372
   SAVINPUT=$039D
```

```
Symbol table - numerical order:

  ALLOC_I =$40        CSLOT   =$40        DEALL_I =$41
        GET_TIME=$82
  INPUT   =$0200   ?  INSTALL =$0300      ENABLE  =$0310   ?
        REMOVE  =$0339
  ALLOC   =$0350      DEALL   =$0354      ERROR1  =$0356
        ERROR2  =$035B
  ERCODE  =$0360      NEW_TIME=$0361      SAVEPG2 =$0372
        FIXPG2  =$038B
  IGNORE  =$0394      NOTCLOCK=$039A      SAVINPUT=$039D      MLI
        =$BF00
  MLIACTV =$BF9B      DRA     =$C080      CRA     =$C081      DRB
        =$C082
  CRB     =$C083
```

for DEALLOC_INTERRUPT.

DOING THE IRQ

Listing 25-3 contains a short assembly language program that uses the IRQ from an Applied Engineering Timemaster HO clock card to "continuously" (actually, once per second) update the ProDOS DATE and TIME registers through the MLI GET_TIME call. The BASIC program in Listing 25-4 then reads and reports the time.

HO owners note: the identification of whether the clock issued the IRQ is based on the HO literature to determine the memory-mapped location of the 6821 PIA used by the HO and on the 6821 PIA specification sheets. Where the two differed, I used the data in the spec sheet. As far as I can deter-

```
1000  REM *** HO.IRQ.DISPLAY ***
1100  REM DJD - 11/21/85
1200  TEXT
1300  PRINT  CHR$ (21)
1400 D$ .EQCHR$ (4)
1500 EF = 0
1600  ONERR  GOTO 20000
2000  REM *** TITLE ***
2100  HOME
2200  POKE  - 16368,0
2300  PRINT
        "---------------------------------------"
2400  PRINT
2500  PRINT  SPC( 7);"TIMEMASTER INTERRUPT
        CHECK"
2600  PRINT
2700  PRINT
        "---------------------------------------";
        PRINT
3000  REM *** FIND CLOCK PER TIMEMASTER MANUAL
        (SLOT 4) ***
3100  IF  PEEK (50176) <  > 8 AND  PEEK (50177)
        <  > 120 AND  PEEK (50430) <  > 178 THEN
        VTAB 10: HTAB 1: CALL  - 958: PRINT
        "CAN'T FIND CLOCK IN SLOT 4.": GOTO 7200:
        REM EXIT.
```

Listing 25-4. BASIC program to read and display the DATE and TIME values.

```
3200  IF  PEEK ( - 16634) <  > 76 THEN  VTAB 10:
       HTAB 1: CALL  - 958: PRINT "CLOCK NOT
       INSTALLED!!!": GOTO 7200: REM EXIT.
3300  IF EF = 0 THEN  PRINT D$;"BLOAD
       HO.IRQ.RTN"
3400  IF EF <  > 0 THEN  VTAB 10: HTAB 1: CALL
       - 958: PRINT "FILE NOT FOUND": GOTO 7200:
       REM EXIT.
3500  CALL 768: REM INSTALL.
4000  REM *** CONVERT PRODOS DATE TO YE)AR,
       MO)NTH, HO)UR, AND MI)NUTE ***
4100 DH = 49041:DL = 49040:TH = 49043:TL =
       49042: REM DATE AND TIME HIGH AND LOW
       BYTES.
4200  GOSUB 10000: REM GO READ TIME/DATE.
5000  REM *** PRINT CURRENT TIME AND DATE TO
       SCREEN ***
5100 AM$ = "AM"
5200  IF HO > 11 THEN AM$ = "PM": IF HO > 12
       THEN HO = HO - 12
5300 MN$ =
       "JANFEBMARAPRMAYJUNJULAUGSEPOCTNOVDEC"
5400 MN$ .EQMID$ (MN$,((MO - 1) * 3) + 1,3)
5500  VTAB 8: HTAB 1
5600  PRINT "CURRENTLY SET TIME: ";HO;":";
5700  IF  LEN ( STR$ (MI)) < 2 THEN  PRINT "0";
5800  PRINT MI;" ";AM$
5900  PRINT : PRINT "CURRENTLY SET DATE:
       ";MN$;". ";DA;", 19";YE
6200  IF  PEEK ( - 16384) < 128 THEN  GOTO 4200
7000  REM *** EXIT (W/IRQ DISABLED) ***
7100  CALL 825: REM DE-ALLOCATE INTERRUPT
       HANDLER.
7200  POKE  - 16368,0
7300  VTAB 22
7400  POKE 216,0: REM CLEAR ONERR GOTO FLAG.
7500  END
10000  REM *** READ DATE ***
10100 D1 .EQPEEK (DH):D2 .EQPEEK (DL)
10200 T1 .EQPEEK (TH):T2 .EQPEEK (TL)
10300 YE .EQINT (D1 / 2)
10400 MO = ((D1 - (YE * 2)) * 8) +  INT (D2 /
       32)
10500 DA = D2 - ( INT (D2 / 32) * 32)
10600 HO = T1
10700 MI = T2
10800  RETURN
20000  REM *** CHEAP ERROR HANDLER ***
20100 ER .EQPEEK (222)
20200 EF = 1
20300  IF (ER = 0 OR ER > 21) THEN ER$ =
       "APPLESOFT ERROR: " +  STR$ (ER)
20400  IF (ER > 0 AND ER < 21 AND ER <  > 16)
       THEN ER$ = "BASIC.SYSTEM ERROR: " +  STR$
       (ER)
20500  IF (ER = 16) THEN ER$ = "A/S OR
       BASIC.SYSTEM ERROR: " +  STR$ (ER)
```

```
20600  IF EF = 1 AND ER = 255 THEN  VTAB 18:
       HTAB 1: CALL  - 958: PRINT ER$: CALL  -
       3288: GOTO 7200: REM FIX STACK AND EXIT.
20700  RESUME
```

mine, bit 7 of the PIA control register A (which should signify the interrupt) *always* is set when IRQ in enabled, which means this routine will always execute GET_TIME when an interrupt occurs. The bit does *not* appear to reset when CRA is accessed. Therefore, if you are going to use the IRQ capability of the HO based on this algorithm, manipulate the ProDOS interrupt vector table to assign the routine the *lowest* priority possible. I was awaiting clarification from Applied Engineering about this use of IRQ at the time this book was completed; the specific information needed is not in the HO manual.

THE USER-HOSTILE NMI

We have so far talked about only the IRQ type of interrupt under ProDOS. There is a second type of interrupt signal to the 6502 that will stop the 6502 and force it to respond to the interrupt regardless of the use of the SEI and CLI. It is tantamount to someone coming into your room and forcibly dragging you away from whatever you are doing, without giving you a chance to tie up loose ends.

This NMI (*n*on-*m*askable *i*nterrupt) of the 6502 is a problem. It *cannot* be disabled by SEI or any other software technique. Upon an NMI, the 6502 again saves the program counter and processor status on the stack, then grabs the address at location $FFFA-FFFB and uses it to resume execution. The Apple monitor contains the address $03FB as the NMI execution address vector. Anytime an NMI interrupt occurs with a monitor ROM active at $F800-$FFFF, the Apple will (nearly) immediately transfer execution to $03FB. It does *not* attempt to save the 6502 registers A, X, Y, and S.

ProDOS understandably does not want any part of the NMI and leaves its vector pointed to $FF59 in the monitor. That causes a bell ("BEEP!") and a sudden entry to the monitor if an NMI occurs. NMI is supported on some devices but is very seldom used. An NMI during a write-to-disk operation on a DISK *II* would be fatal to the disk. The only time it is safe to use NMI interrupts is when *all* devices to be in use are fully interruptable. If you have enough control over the programming environment to know *absolutely* that that situation is going to be true, then you can probably use IRQ instead, anyway.

The only reason to use NMI is if you want a completely sure-fire way to interrupt whatever program the Apple is executing. If you want to chance it, the NMI is handled in the same manner as the IRQ, except that there is no need to look at the BRK flag, and that SEI will obviously not protect your NMI handling routine from a subsequent NMI.

Appendices

Appendix A

BASIC.SYSTEM Commands And Other Tables

The following is a listing of BASIC.SYSTEM command syntax, in loose groupings, followed by possible BASIC.SYSTEM and Applesoft errors. Required arguments for the commands are underlined:

DIRECTORY COMMANDS

CAT	pathname,Sn,Dn,Ttyp
CATALOG	pathname,Sn,Dn,Ttyp
PREFIX	pathname,Sn,Dn
CREATE	pathname,Sn,Dn,Ttyp

PROGRAM FILE COMMANDS

SAVE	pathname,Sn,Dn
LOAD	pathname,Sn,Dn
RUN	pathname,@ln,Sn,Dn
CHAIN	pathname,@ln,Sn,Dn
BSAVE	pathname,Aaddr,Lnbyt,Sn,Dn,Bnbyt,Ttyp
	or
BSAVE	pathname,Aaddr1,Eaddr2,Sn,Dn,Bnbyt,Ttyp
BLOAD	pathname,Aaddr,Lnbyt,Sn,Dn,Bnbyt,Ttyp
	or
BLOAD	pathname,Aaddr1,Eaddr2,Sn,Dn,Bnbyt,Ttyp
BRUN	pathname,Aaddr,Lnbyt,Sn,Dn,Bnbyt,Ttyp
	or
BRUN	pathname,Aaddr1,Eaddr2,Sn,Dn,Bnbyt,Ttyp
-	pathname,Sn,Dn

GENERAL FILE COMMANDS

LOCK	pathname,Sn,Dn
UNLOCK	pathname,Sn,Dn
DELETE	pathname,Sn,Dn
RENAME	pathname1,pathname2,Sn,Dn
VERIFY	pathname,Sn,Dn

TEXT FILE COMMANDS

OPEN	pathname,Sn,Dn,Lnbyt,Ttyp
READ	pathname,Rn,Fn,Ln,Bnbyt
WRITE	pathname,Rn,Fn,Bnbyt
APPEND	pathname,Sn,Dn,Lnbyt,Ttyp
POSITION	pathname,Fn
	or
POSITION	pathname,Rn
EXEC	pathname,Sn,Dn,Fn
	or
EXEC	pathname,Sn,Dn,Rn
CLOSE	pathname

OTHER COMMANDS

FRE	
IN#	n
	or
IN#	Aaddr
PR#	n,Aaddr
	or
PR#	Aaddr
STORE	pathname,Sn,Dn
RESTORE	pathname,Sn,Dn

NUMERIC PARAMETERS AND MAXIMUM (INTEGER) RANGES

Sn	Slot number 0-7
Dn	Disk drive number 1-2
@ln	BASIC program line number 0-63999
Aaddr	Memory address 0-65535 ($0-$FFFF)
Eaddr	Memory address 0-65535 ($0-$FFFF)
Lnbyt	Number of bytes in length, 0-65535 ($0-$FFFF)
Rn	Record number 0-65535 ($0-$FFFF)
Fn	Field number 0-65535 ($0-$FFFF)
Bnbyt	Number of bytes to offset 0-16,777,215 ($0-$FFFFFF)

BASIC.SYSTEM ERROR CODES AND MESSAGES

2	RANGE ERROR
3	NO DEVICE CONNECTED
4	WRITE PROTECTED
5	END OF DATA
6,7	PATH NOT FOUND
8	I/O ERROR
9	DISK FULL
10	FILE LOCKED
11	INVALID OPTION
12	NO BUFFERS AVAILABLE
13	FILE TYPE MISMATCH
14	PROGRAM TOO LARGE
15	NOT DIRECT COMMAND
16	SYNTAX ERROR
17	DIRECTORY FULL
18	FILE NOT OPEN
19	DUPLICATE FILENAME
20	FILE BUSY
21	FILE(S) NOT OPEN

APPLESOFT ERRORS

0	NEXT WITHOUT FOR
16	SYNTAX ERROR
22	RETURN WITHOUT GOSUB
42	OUT OF DATA
53	ILLEGAL QUANTITY
69	OVERFLOW
77	OUT OF MEMORY
90	UNDEF'D STATEMENT
107	BAD SUBSCRIPT
120	REDIM'D ARRAY
133	DIVISION BY ZERO
163	TYPE MISMATCH
176	STRING TOO LONG
191	FORMULA TOO COMPLEX
224	UNDEF'D FUNCTION
254	(?EXTRA IGNORED, does not halt program)
255	Control-C "break" attempted

Appendix B

Counting By 16's

Most of us deal with numbers every day, and assume that the numerals we see are the only useful ones. Notice the use of the word *numeral* instead of *number* in the last phrase. Numerals are distinct from numbers; the numeral is a symbol, and the number is the actual quantity that the symbol stands for. For a short time, let's insist on thinking of a symbol like "456" as a *numeral,* and the quantity it represents ("four hundred fifty-six", in English) as a number.

The symbols "XI", "11", "1011", and "0B" are just some of the numerals representing the quantity "eleven" in Roman numerals, Arabic numerals (our "normal" *decimal* system), binary representation, and hexadecimal representation.

In dealing with computers, the latter two methods of representing numbers sometimes make things easier. The reason is that the computer tends to "break things down" into multiples of two, just as we humans presently tend to break down our numbers into groups of ten.

BREAKING THINGS INTO "TENS"

Having ten fingers, we count in the fashion of "0, 1, 2, 3, 4, 5, 6, 7, 8, 9, 10, 11, 12 . . . ". The magic happens at "10", where we switch from using a single character to using two "number" characters, or *digits*. The left digit, a "1", tells us we have reached the point of having more than ten items. For the numeral "12", we know that we have ten items, plus two more. For the numeral "45", we have four groups of ten items plus five more. We call this decimal notation; it follows through into fractions, but fractions are (thankfully) not needed for our discussion here.

The fact that the "4" in "45" means forty items (and not four) is based upon our recognition that, as we move to the left one place in one of our "normal" numerals, the symbols stand for ten times as many items. As we move to the right one place, the symbol's representative value decreases in magnitude by ten. Therefore, "784" means we have seven times ten times ten, plus eight times ten, plus four times one of something. Expanding our decimal notation into a mathematical expression, we can write this as

784 = (7 × 10 × 10) + (8 × 10) + (4 × 1)

We can now use *exponential notation* to replace the multiples of ten by something easier to write:

784 = (7 × 10^2) + (8 × 10^1) + (4 × 10^0)

where "10^2" means two tens multiplied together,

"10^1" means one ten multiplied together(?), and "10^0" means no tens multiplied together. Take our word that mathematically *any* number multiplied by itself 0 times equals 1, so the last "4 × 10^0" equals "4 × 1" or 4.

This system always works because, as we move "left" across one of our decimal representations, the value of the digit at that location is multiplied times ten relative to the previous digit. So, moving right to left across "8192", we realize that we have

(2 × 10^0) + (9 × 10^1) + (1 × 10^2) + (8 × 10^3)

or "eight thousand, one hundred, and ninety-two". Remember, all this is based on a system of ten basic digits: "0", "1", "2", "3", "4", "5", "6", "7", "8", and "9".

COUNTING ON TWO FINGERS

The "brain" of the Apple is based on *binary digital logic.* The adjective "binary" essentially means that the number of digits the Apple has to count with is two instead of our ten (fingers).

The Apple "fingers" are based on electrical signals; either the signal is there or it isn't, which gives us two possible values. We start the representative binary digits at "0" and, since we only have one digit left to count to, stop at "1".

The fun starts when you try to take our decimal numeral "19", which stands for nineteen items, and try to represent it using only a group of "1"s and "0"s. It turns out that we can use the same type of symbolic system that we used with decimal notation, but with the symbols in their places meaning something a little different.

"0" and "1" still mean the same thing. "0" means you have "zero" of an item, and "1" means you have one of an item. But since we are now counting by *twos* (rather than *tens*) we cannot count higher than "1" in a position before we have to add a "1" to the position to the left. We have re-defined the value of the place of the digit in using binary numerals so that it now stands for "multiply by a power of two" rather than "multiply by a power of ten". Example: the *binary* numeral "1011" does *not* mean

(1 × 10^3) + (0 × 10^2) + (1 × 10^1) + (1 × 10^0)

because we have replaced counting by ten with counting by two. Therefore, we make each digit worth *two* (rather than *ten*) times as much as the digit to it's right, and the value (calculated using decimal math) becomes

(1 × 2^3) + (0 × 2^2) + (1 × 2^1) + (1 × 2^0)

Try adding this up and see what you get:

(1 × 2^3) + (0 × 2^2) + (1 × 2^1) + (1 × 2^0) = 8 + 0 + 2 + 1 = 11

That's right: "1011" as a binary numeral means the same quantity as "11" in our "normal" system of numerals; both stand for a magnitude of "eleven". Each place in the binary numeral is based on the multiplication of "twos" rather than "tens", which is why binary numbering is often referred to as *base two* and our decimal system is referred to as *base ten*. You can have a numbering system based on *any* number you want to use, from one to ten to a million to the square root of two. However, we will get by for now with base two and base ten. And base sixteen, which gives us a shorthand way to write base two numerals.

COUNTING ON SIXTEEN FINGERS

Binary notation is used when talking in detail about the Apple because it makes some very "unround" numbers in base 10 come out nice and "even". For example, the Apple's high-resolution screen number one lies in main memory from the decimal location 8192 up to one byte below location 16384. Those numbers don't just roll right into place for memorization.

However, the Apple counts memory locations in its numbering system, not ours. Counting the Apple's way (in binary), the high-res screen starts at

10000000000000 and ends one byte before 100000000000000. Using our numbering system and powers of 2, that corresponds to 2^13 and 2^14 respectively.

Having a little trouble reading those numbers? So did everybody else. So they adopted a shorthand method to make it easier. It turns out that the shorthand corresponds to using a system of numerals based on *base 16.*

Let's break the first numeral down into groups of four digits, starting from the right-hand end. We'll use spaces to show the divisions, but the numeral still represents a single value:

10 0000 0000 0000

Now we will assign a numeral to each of the groups of four (we just pretend the leftmost set of two digits has two zeros in front of it, making it "0010" instead of "10"), based on each group's magnitude, so that we have

2 0 0 0

Putting the numeral back together, we now have "2000". But this is no longer binary notation (else we could not use the "2").

Looking at the original groups of 4 binary digits, each group has it's minimum value when all of it's digits are "0", and it's maximum value when all digits in a group are "1". The minimum value for a group is therefore zero, and the maximum (for "1111") works out (in decimal) to

$$(1 \times 2^3) + (1 \times 2^2) + (1 \times 2^1) + (1 \times 2^0) = 8 + 4 + 2 + 1 = 15$$

Our new numeral "2000" therefore is made up of four digits, each digit of which can take on 16 values, from zero to fifteen. We only have ten digits in our system of numerals, so we use letters to make up the difference. The resulting correspondence between the symbols works out like the list in Table B-1.

This system gives us a way to write out longer binary numbers in four times less space. Since we are grouping four binary digits to form each of the new digits, each new digit can represent a value from 0 to 15 (using base 10 notation) or 0 to F (using the new numerals) and the system turns out to be base 16. Base 16 is used so commonly that it is referred to as *hexadecimal notation*, which is sometimes abbreviated "hex notation" or just "hex".

As you can see, the reason it is used is that once the system is learned, it is easier to remember that high-res page 1 starts at "2000" than "8192". To prevent confusion between hexadecimal and decimal (base ten), usually hexadecimal numbers are prefaced with a "$" to indicate the number is base 16. Therefore, "$2000" means the hexadecimal representation of the value we express as "8192" in our decimal system.

The other reason for using hexadecimal is that it is relatively easy to "re-expand" a hexadecimal numeral into binary. "$FBB3" becomes "1111101110110011" in binary notation, which is obviously easier than converting it to the decimal symbol "64435".

Now, we will slip back into sloppy English and allow you (and ourselves) to call numerals "numbers" again . . .

OTHER TRICKS OF MEMORY

A common collision between needing to convert to hexadecimal (or binary) from decimal or back is in using Apple memory locations explicitly from Applesoft, which has no innate way of using hexadecimal numbers from within a program. (assemblers almost universally can do hexadecimal math). Therefore, you end up converting them to the decimal numbers that PEEK, POKE, and CALL statements can use.

Here are a few fine points about "why" certain things are done with PEEK, POKE, and CALL statements, although these explanations are not complete and are just in the hope that it makes you believe that there *is* a logic, no matter how perverse, to the way things are done.

BIG NUMBERS IN SMALL HOLES

One thing you will see happen is a combination

Table B-1. Binary and Hexadecimal Equivalents..

Decimal Numeral	Base 2 Numeral	Base 16 Numeral
0	0000	0
1	0001	1
2	0010	2
3	0011	3
4	0100	4
5	0101	5
6	0110	6
7	0111	7
8	1000	8
9	1001	9
10	1010	A
11	1011	B
12	1100	C
13	1101	D
14	1110	E
15	1111	F

of two PEEKs or POKEs being used in apparent tandem, as in the BASIC line

```
10 PRINT PEEK (104) × 256 + PEEK
(103) : REM PRINT START OF PROGRAM.
```

If you type in this line and RUN it, it will tell you where the program line itself starts in memory! It does this by PEEKing the locations that Applesoft uses to store it's "start-of-program" pointer. The reason that two PEEK statements are required is that the range of memory in the Apple is from location 0 ($0000) to 65535 ($FFFF), each location representing a byte. The largest value that a byte can contain is 255 ($FF), so two bytes are required to hold the value of $FFFF.

The normal Applesoft start-of-program value is $0801 (2049); that value is divided and stored in the two locations $67-$68 (103-104). When divided into two halves, the "left" half ($08, in this case) is called the *high order byte* since it is the one-byte value representing the two "higher" magnitude digits. The remaining two digits are referred to as being the *low order byte*. To get the value of the digit, you can add the value of the low order byte to the value of the high order byte *times 256 ($100)*. $08 + $01 mathematically equals $09; to get $0801 the $08 must be multiplied by 256 to restore it's true relative value $0800 before the $01 is added.

The second point of curiosity is that since PEEK (103) = 1 and PEEK (104) = 8; you might think that the value would be $0108. It turns out that the Apple always splits it's address data into bytes by storing the high order byte ($08) in the higher of two adjacent locations. The reasons for this lie in the design of the 6502 MPU that controls the Apple. So when we are reading data used by 6502 programs as in this case, the high order byte is always one byte "above" the low order byte in memory.

The above line 10 reads the high order byte, multiplies it by 256, and then adds the low order byte to compute the address.

POSITIVE/NEGATIVE NUMBERS

The other "mystery" calculation is often why commands can use two different numbers, like "CALL-151" and "CALL 65385", for the same function. This again is based on the way the Apple processor interprets numbers from Applesoft.

Applesoft does not directly accept hexadecimal or binary numbers (numerals), so we enter addresses for Applesoft's use as decimal numbers. The decimal range of acceptable addresses to the Apple (as positive numbers) is 0 to 65535. How, then, do we get "CALL – 151"?

The answer again lies in the interface between Applesoft and the 6502. The number representation that Apple sends to the 6502 for either "-151" and "65385" ends up looking the same, each ends up representing the hexadecimal address $FF69. To get the negative number equivalent, subtract 65386 from the positive decimal representation.

Applesoft will accept either the positive or negative equivalent, so "PEEK (– 1101)" and "PEEK (65459)" (both pointing to $FBB3) will return the same value under the same circumstances. The historical reason that negative values are used for several common PEEKs, POKEs, and CALLs is that an older version of BASIC for the Apple, *Integer BASIC* (not currently available under ProDOS) would not allow entering a decimal value greater than 32767. In Integer BASIC, all accesses to the "upper" half of the Apple memory required using negative values for PEEK, POKE, or CALL arguments.

Appendix C

A Brief Look Inside the Apple

Unfortunately, when Apple as a company decided home computer users would be "confused" by complete and adequate documentation, it decided to cut the cost of its computers by discontinuing the inclusion of several essential manuals with the computers. The "Resources" Appendix contains a partial list of those manuals.

In order to do any practical programming it is necessary to know a certain amount about the basic Apple hardware and software. This is a short tour around the Apple II in its various incarnations. First we'll hit the general features of the common basic Apple configuration (64K memory, disk drive, display, printer); then we'll attack the differences/exceptions for the II+, *II*e, and *II*c models.

COMPUTER BASICS

Any computer must contain several components: a *processor* unit that executes instructions, *memory* to contain the instructions and other information, and a method of communicating ("talking") with other devices. The purpose of these components is to allow the computer to remember and execute a recorded set of instructions (program) that can be altered to perform a desired task.

The Apple contains the processor and a block of *fast* memory in the large rectangular box that also houses the typewriter-style keyboard, we'll refer to this box as the CPU (Central Processing Unit). The processor is the electronic device that fetches and processes (executes) instructions and does the actual work of performing a task. Processors vary from computer to computer, the Apple II is based upon the MOS Technology 6502 microprocessor (abbreviated MPU), if you are curious.

A BYTE AT A TIME

The Apple's memory can be thought of as a series of 65,536 ($10000) "pigeonholes" of information numbered from 0 to 65,534 ($FFFF), each holding one *byte* of information. The number identifying a specific byte in memory is known as its *address*. Due to binary math, it turns out that a grouping of 256 bytes turns out to be a convenient way to "bundle" a group of bytes; a group of 256 bytes starting at address 0 or an address evenly divisible by 256 is call a *page* of memory.

A byte is sufficient to hold 8 *bits* of binary data which can represent a number ranging from 0 to 255. Often these numbers are used as codes to represent things other than numbers; for example, a byte is often used to represent a character via a code. Apple uses a code system called ASCII (acronym for American Standard Code for Information Interchange) to represent characters.

See Figure C-1 for a 64K "map" of the Apple memory, which we will describe.

TYPES OF APPLE MEMORY

There are several types of memory used in computers; the Apple itself uses different types for different purposes. The Apple II computer uses both RAM (Random Access Memory) memory and ROM (Read Only Memory) in its CPU, as well as external devices like the disk drive to record infor-

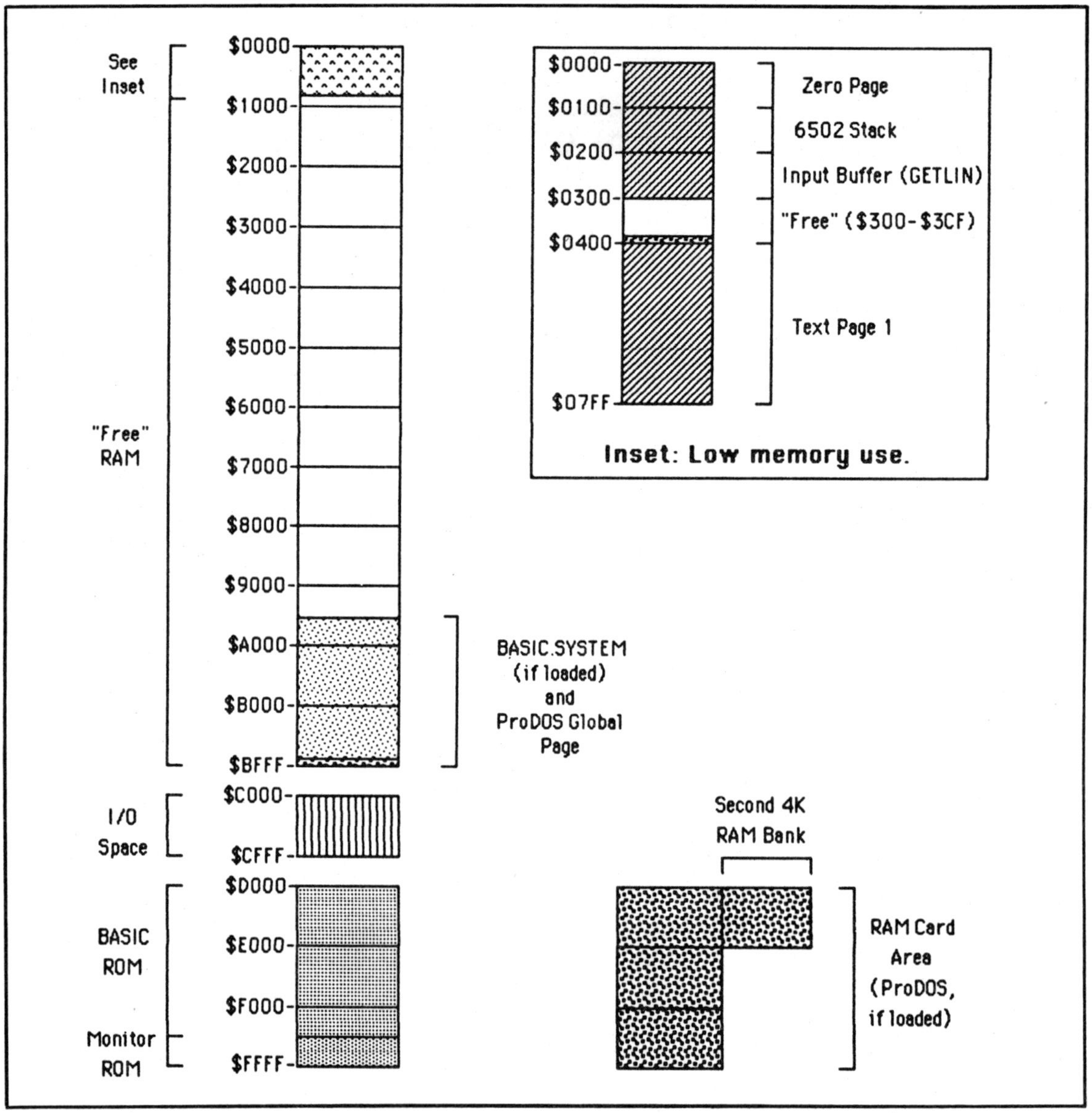

Fig. C-1. Apple II memory map (64K plus ROM area).

mation for later recall.

RAM is designed to hold information temporarily; it is "loaded" with information when the computer is turned on and all information must be brought into the RAM memory to be worked on. Information in RAM can be altered by simple commands typed at the keyboard, or by running programs. When the computer's power is turned off, all information in RAM is lost. This is very important to remember so that you don't lose any work. Any files you work on and alter must be saved to the disk or other similar device before you turn off the power to the CPU or your work will be lost.

ROM on the Apple holds programs and data that are not meant to be easily changed or lost; information in ROM does not disappear when the computer is turned off. It also cannot be changed by programs or by typing keyboard commands. "Permanent" programs, like the Applesoft interpreter that runs BASIC programs and the system monitor, which helps you to communicate with the Apple, are stored in ROM.

The now-ubiquitous Apple disk floppy drive (either the Unidisk, Disk II, or *II*c internal drive) is used as a *mass storage* device for the Apple's RAM. The disk drive, as you should know, is used to "record" programs and data similar to the manner in which a tape recorder can record or play music; the information can then be read back from the disk into RAM at a later time. Any information in RAM you wish to save should always be written to the disk or similar device before you turn off the power to the computer. Otherwise, the information will be lost. Once the information is on the disk, it is safe unless the disk is erased or damaged.

RAM MEMORY USE

The Apple has some areas of its RAM reserved for specific purposes, due to the way that the Apple's 6502 and other devices work. The first 256 (addresses $0-$FF) bytes of memory are referred to as *zero page* since the first address in the page is $0 (or $0000, if you prefer). Due to the way the 6502 operates, they are used to store information that is needed often by the computer. The second 256 bytes ($100-$1FF) are used by the 6502 microprocessor as its *stack*, which is used by the MPU to store its internal values for quick retrieval later. Changing values in either of these areas indiscriminately is often fatal to a program.

The area from $200-$2FF is usually used by the Apple as an *input buffer* to hold keystrokes you type at the keyboard until you hit the "return" key (the word "buffer" is computerese for a temporary storage area). This area is also used for other purposes by ProDOS and BASIC.SYSTEM.

Part of page 3 ($300-$3FF) from $3D0 to $3FF is reserved for use by the Apple, the rest is normally available as space for very short programs (or data areas) that will fit in $300-$3CF.

The four pages from $400 to $7FF (1024 to 2047) are reserved for the 40-column and/or low-resolution graphics video display data; the 40-column screen can display 24 lines of 40 characters each. That calculates up to 960 bytes (characters) used out of 1024 locations available, the other 64 locations are used for special storage for the peripheral cards (described later).

The area from $800 (2048) to $BFFF (49151) is normally free RAM memory available for programs, although any time you boot a disk part of this area is used by the program that allows you to communicate with the disk. The normal amount of memory left available after booting ProDOS and BASIC.SYSTEM is from $800 to $95FF, ProDOS and BASIC.SYSTEM use the rest (from $9A00 to $BFFF) of this space.

Parts of the area from $800 to $BFFF are sometimes used for various display options. A second 40-column text page area can be reserved and displayed using the memory from $800 to $BFF, although this is seldom done. More often, part of the memory is used to display high-resolution graphics. The data area for the first high-resolution screen (displayed by "HGR" from Applesoft) lies in the area from $2000 to $3FFF; that for the second screen (displayed by "HGR2") lies in the area from $4000 to $5FFF. If these areas are being used for holding graphics data then the area is unavailable for a program.

THE I/O AREA

The area from $C000 to $CFFF is reserved for performing communications (or *input* and *output*) between devices "hooked" to the Apple and programs running in the Apple. For example, when information is being read from a disk drive, the disk drive "stores" a byte of information in a (specific) memory location in this area and the program (let's say ProDOS) that is loading the data from the disk "reads" that same location to get a byte of data. The information is passed through the memory location until enough bytes have been read to satisfy the program. Information can be sent to a disk drive or other "external" device (called a *peripheral*) in a similar manner. The exact structure of this page is complicated and you are referred to the Apple technical manual for your computer to discover the addresses and functions of the input/output locations. What follows is only a brief overview.

Page $C000-$C0FF is reserved for "softswitches" that control various hardware functions of the Apple itself, such as reading keyboard data (if you wish to "do-it-yourself"), switching "active" areas of memory (referred to later), reading a joystick or game paddle, etc.

Each of the seven succeeding memory pages ($C100-$C1FF, $C200-$C2FF, etc.) is reserved for use by a *peripheral interface card* that may be assigned to that area. $C100-$C0FF is assigned to slot 1, $C200-$C2FF is assigned to slot 2, etc. Normally, this area is used for a ROM on the peripheral card that controls the peripheral card's ability to communicate with the Apple. For example, the slot 6 area from $C600-$C6FF normally contains a ROM that bootstraps the Apple disk drive when the computer is "started up".

The area from $C800 to $CFFF can contain another two-kilobyte ROM for a peripheral card that needs more programming space than the 256-byte area can provide. This area is held in common by *all* of the slots and it is the responsibility of a peripheral card to "switch in" its ROM when it is needed.

THE MOTHERBOARD ROM SPACE, AND OTHERS

The area from $D000 to $FFFF gets to be complicated; you can see from the diagram that it looks like this area is assigned to both RAM and ROM memory. It is, but only one type of memory at a time actually has control. The RAM and ROM can be "switched in" to this area via some of the softswitches in page $C0.

When the ROM area is in control, the program in ROM on the Apple *motherboard* (the large board inside the Apple containing most of the Apple's circuitry) is visible to a program running in the lower 48K of the Apple's RAM. Usually, there are two programs in this area of the Apple's ROM; the *BASIC interpreter* (we'll assume Applesoft since we are concerned with BASIC.SYSTEM in this book) and the *system monitor.*

The Applesoft BASIC interpreter is the program that allows you to enter and RUN BASIC programs. It was originally designed to use a tape recorder for mass storage and does *not* recognize the disk drive by itself.

The system monitor (the program, not the display device) is the overseer of the hardware; it usually does the real work of reading characters from the keyboard and transferring them to Applesoft, placing characters on the text screen display, beeping the speaker, etc. In addition, the monitor can be used without Applesoft to enter and examine machine language programs (programs written in the actual "language" of the 6502).

BYE TO ROM, HELLO TO RAM

By using the softswitches in page $C0, it is also possible to make the ROM "disappear" from the area $D000-$FFFF and replace it with the RAM in the same area of the memory map. The RAM is a bit trickier than ROM, however. One problem: there is no program like the system monitor or Applesoft in RAM when the computer is powered up. That means that if RAM is activated before a program is loaded in there, the 6502 gets garbage for instructions and the computer will do unpredictable things. Most often, it just appears to go "dead".

Another problem is that Applesoft can't use the RAM in the area from $D000-$FFFF directly because the Applesoft interpreter has to be "mapped into" that area in order for a BASIC program to be running. Therefore, machine language must be used to access the RAM from a BASIC program if RAM is to be used as a data area, etc.

Under the DOS 3.3 disk operating system, often a second version of BASIC called *Integer BASIC* (somewhat incompatible with Applesoft but good for games and some types of educational programming) and other utilities were loaded into this area for use as alternatives to Applesoft. Apple's version of Pascal (another computer language) also used this area, which on older Apple IIs was often referred to as the *language card* or simply the *RAM card* area.

If you didn't want a second language, most of DOS 3.3 itself could be moved into the RAM card area, freeing up additional RAM in the Apple's $800-$BFFF programming area. Although Apple itself didn't support this practice, and it caused problems with some of the Apple DOS 3.3 disk utilities and other programs unless they were modified, several programmers developed this practice to gain the extra 10 kilobytes of usable RAM space that it provided.

With ProDOS and BASIC.SYSTEM, this area is now used to hold the ProDOS program which handles disk operations. The area which DOS 3.3 once occupied is now occupied by BASIC.SYSTEM if it is loaded into the computer.

AN EXTRA 4 KILOBYTES?

The last thing to look at is the "extra" RAM block at $D000- $DFFF, labeled BANK 2, which "overlaps" the address area of the RAM area labeled BANK 1.

Under DOS 3.3, BANK 1 was unused by Apple's BASIC (and ancillary programs) loaded into the RAM card area by the DOS system master disk. BANK 2 was normally active and contained either part of BASIC or some utility programs, depending on which version of BASIC DOS loaded into the card.

Under ProDOS, both banks are used. Just as ROM and RAM in the same address range cannot *both* be active at the same time, both of these RAM banks cannot be active at the same time. ProDOS uses (nearly) the entire combined 16 kilobytes of this area (the RAM in $D000-$FFFF plus the additional $D000-$DFFF in the second 4K bank). Some space is reserved within ProDOS for device drivers (small programs used to access hardware devices) so that the entire area may not be totally consumed by ProDOS depending on how many drivers you have installed. ProDOS switches these banks into activity as needed.

It should be noted that the ProDOS machine-language program is capable of operating these switches safely while it is running (which it normally is while loaded). An Applesoft program by itself cannot access the "guts" of ProDOS since the program requires the Applesoft interpreter be "switched" in to run. Applesoft accesses ProDOS by sending commands to BASIC.SYSTEM, which turns control over to ProDOS (effectively putting the Applesoft program "on hold"). ProDOS then returns control to BASIC.SYSTEM when its task is complete, and BASIC.SYSTEM lets Applesoft get on with running the program.

That completes the nickel tour. Now to look at the differences in the Apple computers.

VARIETIES OF APPLES

There are several different incarnations of the Apple computer. We will separate them as the Apple II (pre-1983), the Apple *II*e (post 1983) and the Apple *II*c (1984 to ???).

The first design was the Apple II. It was available with a maximum of 48K memory and had an upper-case (capital letters only) keyboard.

The original Apple II computer did not have Applesoft installed in ROM, it instead used a language called Integer BASIC. This computer did not contain the upper 16K RAM area we call the RAM card area; instead it had a *slot 0* peripheral connector which was able to contain a card with a second set of ROM memory. Applesoft was originally available in a ROM version on this type of slot 0 card, and in a RAM version that could be loaded *from cassette* into RAM memory and executed.

Because of some limitations of the Integer BASIC language, Applesoft became preferred by some programmers, especially for business and other "serious" applications. Apple offered a second version of the Apple it called the Apple II Plus with Applesoft installed in the computer's internal ROM memory. Integer BASIC could then be purchased on a ROM peripheral card for slot 0 and added. Either combination (Apple II with Applesoft ROM card or Apple II Plus with Integer ROM card) gave you access to both versions of BASIC with their respective advantages. Apple also had, by this time, added disk drives to the Apple.

Later, Apple was adding the Pascal language to its software offerings for the Apple and needed a minimum total of 64K memory in the Apple to make it capable of handling the Pascal program. Apple added a new 16K of memory by replacing the ROM card in slot 0 with a RAM card configured with the 12K plus 4K "bank-switched" system we have described.

While using Pascal, the BASIC in the Apple's ROM was disabled and ignored. To restore the ability to use both BASICs when Pascal was not being used, Apple released versions of its disk operating system (for BASIC) with the ability to fill the RAM card with the versions of BASIC (either Integer or Applesoft) which was not installed in the computer's ROM. The RAM card then appeared to function just as the ROM card had before, except that it had to be loaded when the computer was started up.

Eventually, the Apple II (Integer BASIC in ROM) was phased out and Apple manufactured essentially only the Apple II Plus version. Since the price of the RAM card was about the same as the Integer BASIC ROM card, nearly all Apple purchasers bought Apple II Plus computers with 48K memory and added the 16K RAM card for use with Integer BASIC. The 5 1/4" floppy disk drive became the standard storage device, and DOS 3.3 became the standard operating system.

CHANGING OF THE GUARD

The Apple *II*e computer was an "enhancement" of the popular Apple II Plus configuration. At the *II*e's introduction in 1983, RAM prices were low enough that 64K RAM was made standard on the Apple *II*e; this RAM was configured to look like the same arrangement as the 48K Apple II Plus with a 16K RAM card. The Apple *II*e was available only with Applesoft BASIC in ROM; Integer BASIC was available only to be loaded into the RAM card area by DOS 3.3.

The Apple *II*e also was supplied with an upper/lower case keyboard that could reproduce capital and "small" letters, as well as some common symbols that the original Apple keyboard could not produce.

The Apple *II*e also had a "standardized" method of adding an 80-column text display and 64K extra memory through a new *auxiliary slot.* The new *II*e had no "slot 0" connector (the other 7 slot connectors are still there, visible if you remove the lid) but had a new slot specifically designed for adding an 80-column display and extra memory. The extra 64K memory uses bank-switching techniques similar to the RAM card's to be accessed; but the 6502 MPU used in the Apple IIs (and *II*e) cannot access more than a 64K range of memory at a time.

The *II*e also had a set of ROM programs, essentially an extension of the monitor program, for operating the 80-column display that could be "banked" into the $C100-$CFFF address space. In particular, the ROM code for the 80-column card used the area at $C3 so as to appear to be a peripheral card ROM assigned to that slot. This was done for compatibility with standards that had arisen among software for the Apple II.

THE LITTLEST APPLE

In mid-1984, Apple took most of the features of the popular configuration of the Apple *II*e and assimilated them into a transportable computer, the

Apple *II*c. Like the Apple *II*e, the Apple *II*c had an upper/lower case keyboard. The Apple *II*c came standard with the 128K capability of the Apple *II*e.

In order to make the *II*c as compact as possible, Apple "built in" the features of several popular peripheral cards for the Apple *II*e so that they appeared the same to software. In other words, the *II*c appears to have a disk interface card in a "slot 6" (the *II*c has a disk drive installed in the computer itself), but there are *no* actual slots in the *II*c. The *II*c configuration is "wired in". That allowed the Apple *II*c to be compact; it also makes it more difficult to re-configure (not impossible, however; some companies have developed internal modifications).

The *II*c also used an updated version of the 6502 MPU, called the *65C02*, which is slightly more powerful. This MPU and some other features were made available to *II*e owners in a kit, resulting in a version called the *Enhanced II*e.

Late news: as this book was being "wrapped up", Apple had just announced a new enhancement to the *II*c which is included with the purchase of the new 800K 3 1/2″ version of the UniDisk. This enhancement requires a change of the *II*c motherboard and included a revised set of ROMs.

Appendix D

The DOS-ProDOS Debate

We are about to critique ProDOS. About halfway through this chapter you may decide that we *hate* ProDOS; please do not draw that conclusion. ProDOS is a tool which is necessary for some programming tasks, and an enhancement to the world of Apple software as any new tool would be. We *do* have some qualms about saying ProDOS is inherently "superior" to the older Apple disk operating system, DOS 3.3, which Apple is proffering. We are going to make a point for retention *and support* of *both* operating systems. Be aware that some of the comments within are "editorial" (personal) viewpoints.

Apple declared DOS to be more or less defunct after they released ProDOS; that is to say, Apple "retired" DOS 3.3 as an operating system to be used when writing new software. ProDOS is now to be the "operating system of choice" for Apple products.

As a ProDOS user, you will of course not be *required* to work with DOS 3.3, but if you can avoid it entirely you are the exception. At the time this manuscript was being prepared it was estimated that the majority of all Apple programs were *still* being developed using DOS 3.3. So the question arises: if ProDOS is so amazingly great, why hasn't everyone switched?

We will attempt to answer that question by addressing the strengths and weaknesses of ProDOS, both independently and versus DOS 3.3. Throughout this book, we'll try to point out differences between ProDOS and DOS that might concern programmers. For right now, we'll just look at the big picture.

IN THE LAND OF THE GIANTS

Probably the biggest obvious difference to most people is the touted ability of ProDOS to access very large disk storage devices, such as Winchester drives which may store 10-20 megabytes of data (or more!) and are rapidly becoming affordable. However, for years manufacturers of these drives have modified regular old DOS 3.3 to also handle these drives. One scheme involved the fact that DOS 3.3 had a provision to identify disks by an assignable volume number of 1-254 ("0" matched any volume number, and "255" was unavailable). Manufacturers used this numbering system to create "virtual volumes" on a large disk; the modified version of DOS saw the hard disk being divided up into a large number of smaller storage areas, each of which looked like a floppy disk with a distinct volume number.

The biggest restriction of the size of the disk that DOS 3.3 can work with is the way it keeps track of the number of tracks and sectors on the drive. It turns out that with no modifications other than a few POKEs to re-define the number of tracks and sectors, DOS 3.3 can operate a floppy disk of 50 tracks with 32 sectors per track for a total raw storage capacity of 400K, versus 140K for the standard Apple 5 1/4″ disk format.

With more severe modifications, even this number can be increased but we'll use it as a conservative estimate. Assuming we create 400K volumes numbered 1-254 on a hard disk, we will have about 99 *megabytes* of storage available! That should keep things well in hand for what is basically a 64K computer.

One advantage ProDOS *does* offer with the newer types of Apple drives is the capability ProDOS has to use specialized software interface routines called *device drivers* to access many types of peripherals, including mass storage devices. ProDOS treats all disk drives (including /RAM) as simply indexed sequences of disk blocks. The routines to fetch or store blocks are an integral part of ProDOS, but the definition of how many blocks are on a disk and how they are accessed is left to these alterable drivers. Usually, DOS itself had to be customized to a specific disk drive.

FILE SIZES

As for the size of a *file* that DOS 3.3 can access, it is basically limited (at least for text files) to the size of the disk; 400K without internally modifying DOS routines. ProDOS obviously comes out a winner in this aspect because it can support a single file up to 16 megabytes in size. Text files are really all that matter; it does no good to have a 16 megabyte program file on disk when you only have 64K (actually, less) memory to load it into. So let's point out that the *true* advantage of ProDOS over DOS in this respect is not the size of the *disk device*, but the maximum size of a *file*, and the ease with which ProDOS can handle different drives.

SPEEDING WITH PRODOS

One bona-fide enhancement of ProDOS is speed of file access, especially for text files, over standard DOS 3.3. Several "fast" versions of DOS 3.3 are available which greatly improve DOS's performance with files other than text files; but ProDOS is significantly faster with standard text file commands than any of these.

A DISK BY ANY OTHER NAME

One other seeming advantage of ProDOS is the hierarchical directory structure used to manage its large disk device. It's supposedly a lot easier to remember that a file is on a disk named "GEORGE" than to remember a file is on (DOS) "volume 127". ProDOS does allow the segmentation of a large disk into a hierarchy of directories, as we've discussed. The luxury of this "files within files" structure is not without problems, however. How do you find a file that is *somewhere* on the ProDOS disk, but you have forgotten where?

With a hard disk divided up for DOS, the problem is simple (well, by comparison); you simply read the files in each DOS volume's directory (let's say a maximum of 254 tries before you find it). With ProDOS, you can open only 51 subdirectories within the volume directory, but you can put literally *thousands of* files and subdirectories in each of these and in each subdirectory on the disk; you are no longer searching "just" 254 directories. How long will it take you to search *all* of these?

Operating systems for larger computers that also use hierarchical file structure usually have utility commands that allow you to search for a lost file. These utilities will often allow the use of *wildcard* characters, so that when you need to find a file named "GEORGE . . . something or other" you can tell the operating system to look for "GEORGE=", where "=" tells the system that you don't care what the filename ends with. The system can then reply with all valid pathnames that contain the name you mention, so that the whereabouts of "GEORGE.1" and "GEORGE.2" will be revealed to you.

Sound nice? Forget it, ProDOS doesn't have

such a utility supplied when you purchase it. FILER (the /USERS.DISK utility) will *not* allow the use of wildcards at the beginning of a pathname or within a pathname, which is necessary for this type of program. The reason that ProDOS does not have such a command "ready" for use is part of our next point.

A luxury that is provided by the use of pathnames is that BASIC.SYSTEM will search all attached devices for the name if a pure pathname is used, rather than a single device (although BASIC.SYSTEM can be instructed to search only a single device.

(NO) THANKS FOR THE MEMORY

ProDOS's ability to handle the complexity of the hierarchical file structure comes from a lot of programming effort. Unfortunately, this resulted in a lot of program. At this juncture we're talking quantity, not necessarily quality.

DOS 3.3 does most everything you need a normal microcomputer operating system to do. It handles the majority of the same file functions ProDOS does, with the restriction that ProDOS will work with larger files and subdirectories. But what's the penalty if you don't need files over 3-400K, or hierarchical file structure?

Look at the comparative memory use of DOS 3.3 versus ProDOS. DOS 3.3 occupies (with three files in use) about a 10K segment of memory from \$9600-\$BFFF. ProDOS uses *all* of the "RAM card" area from \$D000-\$FFFF (there is a second "switchable" 4K segment of memory in this region that brings this total to 16K RAM used!), and you still must have an interface program to ProDOS like BASIC.SYSTEM to really do any work! In the case of BASIC.SYSTEM, the extra space required with three files in use is \$7600-\$BFFF, for a grand total of 32.25K. That is *over half* of the Apple's main memory dedicated to running a simple BASIC program from disk. If you count the fact that certain applications moved DOS 3.3 into the language card area to free up an additional 8-10K of program space, the difference (on a 64K system, remember) is staggering.

With DOS, the memory penalty for each additional file in use is 565 bytes. That is, if we have three files in use and wish to activate a fourth file we will lose 565 bytes of memory which we must relinquish to the file's use. ProDOS takes 1024 bytes from us for each file we are using, but ProDOS does automatically "free up" that memory when we are done with the file, which DOS does not do. With DOS, the memory must be put aside "manually" with a command called *MAXFILES*.

The advantage of ProDOS's method is that it is one of the factors that speeds up ProDOS's disk access versus DOS. The disadvantages are that you can only have a maximum of 8 files active at one time with ProDOS (you could have twice as many active at one time with DOS), and that the shuffling of the buffer space in ProDOS brought the advent of "memory management", or routines to handle shuffling the memory around. And the intelligence of these routines had to be limited since ProDOS already consumes a monstrous amount of memory.

NO LONGER BASICALLY BILINGUAL

Another "feature" of ProDOS memory gluttonage: Integer BASIC is not supported, only Applesoft, and BASIC.SYSTEM must be in memory to use Applesoft. Unless you are a *pure* assembly language programmer, you *must* have at least a 64K Apple computer with Applesoft on the motherboard. Apple *II* owners are out in the cold, as are 48K *II* Plus owners. Schools, in particular, own hundreds of thousands of these machines.

DISK SPACE FREE?

Just to point out; not only does the BASIC programming environment of ProDOS and BASIC.SYSTEM take up a lot of memory in the computer, they take up a lot of room on the disk; 50 blocks, to be precise. The amount of free space left on an Apple standard formatted 5 1/4" floppy disk with ProDOS and BASIC.SYSTEM is about 111.5K; a DOS 3.3 disk with DOS (no separate BASIC interpreter interface required) could leave you 124K (no files).

A note about the space requirements; ProDOS's utilities (either FILER or the *II*c /UTIL-

ITIES) do allow you to create a "DOS-less" data disk for more space; the space sans *any* files is 273 blocks (136.5K). As a matter of fact, that's the *only* way the disk is initially prepared; you must copy any programs you need to the formatted disk, including PRODOS and BASIC.SYSTEM. DOS's INIT command always puts DOS on the disk; using DOS 3.3 this meant a loss of about 8K of space. A commonly available DOS utility allows you to regain all except the space on track 0 (not accessible to the standard DOS file manager) and track 17 ($11, the "directory" track); this makes a DOS-less data disk of 132K (no files).

Also, we need to compare file storage space for small files. The minimum space assignable to a ProDOS file is 512 bytes or one disk block. If the file is even one byte longer, it will take 3 disk blocks or 1536 bytes of disk space to store. Under DOS, the minimum space allotted to a non-text file is two disk sectors of 256 bytes each, or 512 bytes. If the file requires one byte over 256 to store then the file will consume three disk sectors or 768 bytes.

What this works out to show is that ProDOS is *very* inefficient for the storage of a large number of small individual files. For large files, the difference in storage requirements is slightly in favor of ProDOS. And, of course, ProDOS can work with much larger files than DOS.

COMMANDS POSITIVE

Now that we have about convinced you that ProDOS may not be the ideal operating system, we enter one of the areas where ProDOS does have concrete advantages: enhancements to the DOS command set.

There are three parts to the DOS 3.3 program, although all of these are not documented in Apple's manuals on DOS (for a complete discussion, see *The DOSTalk Scrapbook*, By Tom Weishaar and Bert Kersey). They are the *command interpreter*, the *file manager*, and *RWTS*. Notably, the file manager interface is *not* described in Apple's *The DOS Manual*.

The command interpreter reads the command words (such as "CATALOG") you type or use within programs and decides what DOS routines must be used to complete the command. For disk access commands, many of these routines are within the file manager, which is responsible for finding, saving, restoring, and altering file data as requested. The RWTS (*r*ead/*w*rite *t*rack/*s*ector) routines are responsible for locating, loading, and reading specific sectors on the DOS disk.

RWTS can be accessed *directly* to access any specific disk sectors, but it knows nothing about files. The file manager contains the logic necessary to do the file bookkeeping, but it knows nothing about the "English-like" commands we usually associate with DOS, which the command interpreter must handle.

We can compare these sections of DOS to their ProDOS counterparts. In the terms of commands issued from BASIC, BASIC.SYSTEM is the (external) ProDOS equivalent of the command interpreter. BASIC.SYSTEM is responsible for taking English-like commands and converting them into machine language which sends commands to, among other things, the ProDOS file management routines.

The file manager interface, undocumented for the end user under DOS, compares to ProDOS's *m*achine *l*anguage *i*nterpreter, or *MLI*. Apple did the programming community a service by documenting the commands for the MLI in *The ProDOS Technical Reference Manual*, although they still have some holes in their coverage. Lastly, the RWTS became ProDOS's own block read/write routines.

BASIC.SYSTEM GAINS AND LOSSES

BASIC.SYSTEM has added several commands, although we will tend to discount the commands PREFIX and CREATE (a subdirectory) dealing with pathnames, since their "enhancements" have been previously argued.

CHAIN for Applesoft programs is now an integral portion of BASIC.SYSTEM. Under DOS, there was a CHAIN command which was only valid for Integer BASIC programs. The BASIC.SYSTEM CHAIN is (naturally) for Applesoft only.

The "@" parameter has been added to the BASIC.SYSTEM RUN command.

Binary file commands have been enhanced to

include the "E" and "B" parameters. "E" makes saving files easier sometimes; the "B" parameter used with the other binary file command parameters including "T" allows tricks that were formally available under DOS only via direct use of the file manager. Yes, such use was largely undocumented in print until *Beneath Apple DOS*, but people who had a necessity for use of the file manager seemed to be able to figure it out despite Apple.

Many features of BASIC.SYSTEM such as the I/O vectors are now consolidated into a defined (and thankfully documented) area called the *BASIC.SYSTEM global page*.

A fast set of Applesoft string "clean up" (*garbage collection*) routines have been added to BASIC.SYSTEM. Unless the old, slow, Applesoft "FRE (0)" command is explicitly used, BASIC.SYSTEM will clear unused string storage out of memory *quickly*.

BASIC.SYSTEM does not require a carriage return to precede its deferred-mode commands (those imbedded in Applesoft programs) as DOS did. This makes BASIC.SYSTEM commands work with TRACE under all circumstances (this can also be done under DOS by insuring each command is preceded *immediately* with a carriage return and a control-D) and makes it more difficult to disconnect BASIC.SYSTEM from a running program unintentionally. Since BASIC.SYSTEM also has to monitor *all* program statement input during execution to do this, it means that programs run slightly slower under BASIC.SYSTEM than they would under DOS; at least, until they access the disk drive, where ProDOS's greater speed tends to negate the loss.

BASIC.SYSTEM does *not* have the equivalent of DOS's MON and NOMON for debugging. This can be circumvented but is a real pain, especially since there is now no way to "monitor" an EXEC file in progress (Beagle Brothers had just announced a "MON/NOMON" utility for ProDOS as this book was being completed).

Another undesirable feature is from BASIC.SYSTEM's "memory management"; RESET will clear all active BASIC variables. Apparently, BASIC.SYSTEM's designers wanted to make debugging an adventure.

Lastly, BASIC.SYSTEM is out in at least two versions as of this date. The available commands have changed between versions as have the performance of some of the commands.

PRODOS GAINS AND LOSSES

On 128K Apple *II*e's or *II*c's the pseudo-disk volume /RAM is created using the auxiliary 64K memory by ProDOS. DOS had no such provision (there are commercial programs available to create a DOS RAM disk, however).

Date/time stamping has been added to the file information, along with the random-access file record length. The number of distinct filetypes has been increased, including eight user-definable types. The file information can be easily read from a ProDOS directory; this was not as straightforward under DOS.

Individual filenames have been cut from 30 characters (under DOS) to 15 characters under ProDOS, and a lot of characters are illegal. This eliminates some of the problems which occurred under DOS, such as accidentally imbedding invisible control characters in filenames when SAVEing them (which kept them from being reLOADed later, for no apparent reason). Pet peeve: it makes using mnemonic names under ProDOS more difficult.

File accesses under ProDOS can be partially restricted to read only, execute only, etc. This must be done directly through use of the MLI since there is no BASIC.SYSTEM command to facilitate this.

One *big* problem: you cannot initialize ProDOS data disks (with or without the disk operating system) under ProDOS as you could with the DOS INIT command. Outside of your programs, you can use the provided formatting utility within FILER (on the /USERS.DISK) or on the *II*c /UTILITIES disk. To have this capability for your programs, you must license Apple's (separate) formatter utility or write your own.

Finally, while booting, ProDOS attempts to verify whether it is running on an Apple-manufactured CPU (Apple *II* Plus, *II*e, or *II*c). If not, it crashes. No comment.

SUPPLIED SOFTWARE AND DOCUMENTATION

ProDOS comes in two "usable" forms: *The ProDOS User's Kit* sold separately and with Apple *II*e Computers, and also the *II*c /UTILITIES disk. Both contain programs to copy and format disks, copy files, perform disk file maintenance, and convert files from DOS to ProDOS and back (except random-access text files).

As this book was being completed, a new set of utilities, called "Apple *II* System Utilities", had just been released. The provided programs in this set support the new 3.5″ UniDisk drive from Apple. They also require a 128K enhanced *II*e or *II*c.

First, *major* complaint: neither of the manuals provided with these programs supplies one-tenth of the necessary knowledge to literally "use" ProDOS or BASIC.SYSTEM. The *II*c manual has a few token comments about BASIC (and BASIC.SYSTEM) commands; the *User's Kit* manual does not include *one single immediate or deferred mode BASIC.SYSTEM command.* This is ludicrous and indefensible for a product as expensive and complicated as a personal computer.

Second, CONVERT (on the /USERS.DISK) has bugs from irritating to devastating. It does not work on single-drive systems without trickery. It displays "highlighted" filenames for transfer in MouseText characters on the *II*c and Enhanced *II*e. It won't transfer random-access text files. There also is a bug in transferring large text files (requiring more than one DOS track/sector list sector) from ProDOS to DOS, reported by (among others) Glen Bredon in the May, 1985, issue of *Open-Apple* (in the same issue, Val Golding reports a bug in the *II*c /UTILITIES in transferring files larger than 46 DOS sectors from ProDOS to DOS).

FILER (also on the /USERS.DISK) is also flakey; for one thing it just seems to be hard to use. The previously mentioned restrictions on where filenames can use wildcards is one problem. A second problem is the inability to perform file copy operations via slot and drive numbers rather than pathnames, if desired (even Apple Pascal allows file copy operations using unit numbers!). Directories must be explicitly created on a target disk before files can be copied into them. This last feature must make FILER very amusing for masochistic hard-drive owners.

The *II*c /UTILITIES are much more user-friendly, but do not show file statistics. The file copy function does automatically copy a subdirectory's contents, creating the target directory if necessary. We cannot, however, make /UTILITIES function with a *II*c clock device (yes, there are a few) without it crashing upon exit; does ProDOS support time-stamping or not? Also, /UTILITIES does not allow the use of the full 128 character pathnames "supported" by ProDOS. /UTILITIES is programmed to be *II*c-specific. And, again, there is a reported error in transferring large text files from ProDOS to DOS using /UTILITIES.

The new "System Utilities" can be run on a 128K *II*e, and works with a clock, but it also cannot handle 128 character pathnames. The authors have not checked it's ability to convert large files from ProDOS to DOS.

OTHER SOFTWARE

The ultimate test of *any* operating system is the software base available. Here, DOS is *still* winner and champion. Look for a ProDOS-based Applesoft compiler (DOS compilers are available from several companies), ProDOS-based educational software (rare), ProDOS-based games (also rare); in almost every category a larger base of selection exists for DOS 3.3 versus ProDOS. The strongest piece of software operating exclusively under ProDOS at present is undoubtably *Appleworks* and its support programs. Admittedly, ProDOS has been on the market a shorter time, but new DOS products *still* outnumber ProDOS products overall.

Why the delay, if ProDOS is *the* Apple *II* operating system? We think it is due to the following:

1) ProDOS manuals have been hard to come by. Apple took over six months after the introduction of ProDOS to deliver signifi-

cant quantities of the technical manual to end users. After this period, it was often necessary to special order the manuals to receive one (and, at one time, orders were not accepted for quantities less than five manuals at once). The need to special- order the manuals is still largely true two years after the fact; most Apple dealers do not routinely stock them. Apple itself still refers you to Addison-Wesley, their new publisher, for some of the manuals.

2) The ProDOS manuals contain many inaccuracies, some irritating to programmers, some fatal. Elsewhere, essential information is simply omitted. We approach some of these subjects in the course of this book.
3) ProDOS is hardware restrictive. It will not run unmodified except on a minimum 64K Apple with Applesoft ROMs on the motherboard. It will attempt to "crash" during boot on Apple "clones". It uses most of precious memory. Why restrict your software audience?
4) Programs often cannot be easily "ported" to ProDOS and executed. Machine language programs which interface with DOS have the most problems. BASIC programs may require more restructuring than some people feel is worth the effort.
5) The impetus to use ProDOS and Apple *III* SOS in a "combined" disk has been negated by Apple's subsequent withdrawal of the Apple *III* from the market, within months of announcing ProDOS.
6) Apple itself does not bring enough software to market to aggressively swing opinion toward ProDOS, and does not appear to be truly supporting ProDOS. Indeed, Apple Pascal 1.3, which was announced two years after ProDOS had arrived (and is the second Apple Pascal update released after the announcement of ProDOS), still runs under the UCSD p-system. Despite the existence of SOS-based Pascal, Apple has *still* not announced Pascal for ProDOS (a non-Apple product named *Kyan Pascal* is ProDOS-based, however). Apple's *II*c /UTILITIES disk does not support 128 character pathnames. Apple's training disks are largely written using Pascal. If Apple doesn't fully believe in its operating system to the point of porting software to it and using it for development, why should non-Apple developers?
7) ProDOS is still being "actively" revised; as of this writing, four versions have been released and each has distinct bugs either in ProDOS itself or in BASIC.SYSTEM. Programs must compensate for this by checking the version and acting accordingly. DOS was difficult to alter and therefore most bugs were never "changed" (for better or worse) and could be programmed around. Some patches *were* made to DOS as recently as 1985, most having to do with the APPEND function.
8) Connected with the "bug" issue, Apple has no apparent organized policy of upgrading ProDOS versions (to be fair; this problem is common among microcomputer manufacturers. It needs to be remedied.) or reporting bugs to end users. News of new versions is often passed by "word-of-mouth"; again, as with the manuals, Apple does not seem to be working with dealers to insure the end user is supported.

ALL IN FAVOR OF PRODOS?

The decision to use ProDOS rests with your need for its features, as with any software. The strong points of ProDOS and BASIC.SYSTEM summarize as:

1. Programming features: more BASIC programming commands available, the support of device drivers, the documented MLI access.
2. The ability to deal with large files.
3. Speed of disk access.

If you need one or more of these features, ProDOS is indeed advantageous. drivers, the documented MLI access.

APPENDIX E
ProDOS/DOS Program Conversions

We have tried to cover some of the programming differences between DOS and ProDOS in the body of this book for those who are working with both operating systems. This is a summary of that information, plus some tips.

BASIC.SYSTEM COMMANDS NOT FOUND IN DOS

The following BASIC.SYSTEM commands are not used or recognized by DOS 3.3: CAT, PREFIX, CREATE, - (dash, "smart RUN"), STORE, RESTORE, FRE, and FLUSH. They must be removed.

The following BASIC.SYSTEM parameters are not recognized when used with the (parenthetically) associated commands: @ (RUN), E and B (BLOAD, BSAVE, and BRUN), F and R (EXEC, READ, and WRITE), F (POSITION), R (APPEND), B (READ and WRITE), L (READ), A (IN# and PR#), T (BSAVE, BLOAD, OPEN).

DOS COMMANDS NOT FOUND IN BASIC.SYSTEM

The following DOS commands are not recognized by BASIC.SYSTEM: FP, INT, MON, and MAXFILES.

The NOMON command is recognized in that it does not force a "SYNTAX ERROR" message, but it (and any text that follows on the same line, prior to a carriage return) is ignored.

The "V" parameter used with any DOS command is ignored by BASIC.SYSTEM. It can cause a problem when used with the "@" parameter of the BASIC.SYSTEM RUN command.

SAME COMMAND, DIFFERENT MEANING

The CHAIN command under DOS is reserved for Integer BASIC programs *only*. "Chaining" Applesoft programs is not a provision of DOS, it requires a separate "chain" utility program. Since you shouldn't be CONVERTing Integer BASIC programs to ProDOS anyway (unless also re-writing them for Applesoft), this should be a rare problem.

When CONVERTing Applesoft programs from use under ProDOS to DOS, however, the CHAIN command must be changed to utilize one of the Applesoft "chain" utilities. As a further restriction, these utilities will usually only allow "chaining" to the starting line of a program.

OTHER "DIFFERENT" COMMANDS

You may wish to shorten the DOS "CATA-

LOG" command to the BASIC.SYSTEM "CAT" command if you are using the 40-column screen format.

Under BASIC.SYSTEM, the use of "APPEND" to open a file also implies that you wish to WRITE to the file. DOS's APPEND command does not; a "WRITE" command must be explicitly used.

Under DOS, "READ" would OPEN the file if it wasn't open. Not so for BASIC.SYSTEM's READ command.

Under DOS 3.3, "VERIFY" would check all disk space assigned to a file to see if it could detect damage to the file. Under BASIC.SYSTEM, "VERIFY" only checks to see if the specified file exists in the directory.

DIFFERENCES IN ERRORS

BASIC.SYSTEM and DOS generally use the same error codes and messages, but there are a few differences. BASIC.SYSTEM has five new error messages/codes: DIRECTORY FULL (17), FILE NOT OPEN (18), DUPLICATE FILENAME (19), FILE BUSY (20), and FILE(S) STILL OPEN (21). In addition, the following error messages/codes have been changed from their meaning under DOS.

Error code 11 produces an "INVALID OPTION" error under BASIC.SYSTEM; under DOS, it was "SYNTAX ERROR".

Error code 6 and 7 under DOS were originally "FILE NOT FOUND" and "VOLUME MISMATCH" errors respectively, both represent "PATH NOT FOUND" under BASIC.SYSTEM.

Error code 3, which was "RANGE ERROR" under DOS, represents "NO DEVICE CONNECTED" with BASIC.SYSTEM.

In addition, BASIC.SYSTEM now shares error code 16 with Applesoft as "SYNTAX ERROR".

COMMAND SYNTAX

Within a DOS 3.3 program, each DOS command must be preceded by a carriage return, followed by a control-D, followed by the DOS command terminated by a carriage return. The requirement of a carriage return before the control-D led some programmers to define D$ as equal to CHR$ (13) + CHR$ (4), so that the carriage return *always* preceded a control-D.

BASIC.SYSTEM finds its commands by watching the BASIC program execute; if it sees a PRINT statement executed and the *first* character PRINTed is a control-D, then the following string is taken as a BASIC.SYSTEM command. It does not require that the last character printed before the "control-D + command string" is a carriage return. Therefore, the definition of D$ must be changed to simply "CHR$ (4)" for BASIC.SYSTEM programs. Also, you may need to check PRINT statements for any occurances of the type:

```
10 PRINT CHR$ (13);CHR$ (4);"CATALOG"
```

where "CATALOG" could be any BASIC.SYSTEM command.

In the reverse direction, you may *want* to redefine D$ as "CHR$ (13) + CHR$ (4)" for BASIC.SYSTEM programs being ported to DOS. Check the text-file operations, however: defining D$ in this way will often add an extra (undesirable) carriage return to the end of a DOS text file. To CLOSE a DOS text file, you should only use a control-D in the PRINT statement containing the rest of the DOS command.

"OPEN" AND "CLOSE"

DOS 3.3 was lax about forcing OPENed text files to be CLOSEd before using the commands OPEN, DELETE, or RENAME on them. BASIC.SYSTEM requires that you CLOSE any open file before performing one of these operations.

Unfortunately, it became common practice when emptying text files under DOS to OPEN a file, DELETE it, then re-OPEN it. The initial OPEN was used to insure the file existed before the DELETE command, avoiding a "FILE NOT FOUND" error for the DELETE operation. Apple itself recommended this in the original "DOS Manual" for the Apple II (page 59). Under BASIC.SYSTEM, you must re-write programs to insure that OPEN files are CLOSEd before these using these operations on it or you will receive a "FILE BUSY" error.

THE WOES OF MACHINE LANGUAGE

The biggest headache in transferring DOS programs to use with BASIC.SYSTEM is for binary programs or data, including the use of PEEK, POKE, and CALL. Similar problems exist in the reverse direction (BASIC.SYSTEM to DOS). For PEEK, POKE, and CALL, any access to addresses normally occupied by DOS is suspect. BASIC.SYSTEM's internals do not resemble DOS's.

For machine language programs that do not use DOS internals, the main problem is where they reside in memory. Some programs resided in high memory between DOS and its buffers; to install these programs with BASIC.SYSTEM requires that you alter them to use the protocol described in Chapters 19 and 20 (for the "TYPE" command). The process must be reversed when going from BASIC.SYSTEM to DOS.

Additionally, the program must not clash with BASIC.SYSTEM's and ProDOS's use of memory, including that from \$0-\$2FF, \$3D0-\$3FF, buffers in the main program area, \$9A00-\$BFFF and the RAM card (or DOS's, in the reverse direction).

DOS ACCESS FROM MACHINE LANGUAGE

Also, machine language programs under DOS could send DOS commands via DOS's I/O link by "printing" a sequence of a carriage return, control-D, and the ASCII codes of the command (plus terminating carriage return) through COUT (\$FDED) or DOS's I/O itself. This no longer works with BASIC.SYSTEM. Instead, the command is sent by placing it in the INPUT buffer at \$200 and calling BASIC.SYSTEM to scan INPUT for the command. Such programs must be converted to the proper method.

DOS programs that use DOS file manager calls must also be re-written to use BASIC.SYSTEM and/or MLI calls.

CONVERSION PROBLEMS

The /USERS.DISK "CONVERT" utility also has a few problems. First, random access text files cannot be transferred, they must be converted to sequential text files via a program. Once CONVERTed to the target operating system, they can be converted back to their original form as random access files. An example of one side of the conversion (going from sequential to random access) is presented in Chapter 16 (Listing 16.3). Watch out for ProDOS *sparse* files, which may expand to fill the DOS disk.

Second, programs that have used the "POKE 103, AL : POKE 104, AH" relocation trick discussed in Chapter 19 may not CONVERT properly (they LIST having no recognizable form as BASIC programs). To solve this problem, *before transferring the file,* type the following BASIC commands in immediate mode (under BASIC.SYSTEM).

]POKE 103,1	fix Applesoft start-of-program pointers
]POKE 104,8	
]POKE 2048,0	
]LOAD PROGRAM	load program at \$800
]SAVE PROGRAM.NEW	save properly located program.

"PROGRAM.NEW" should now transfer fine, and the relocation will still work correctly under DOS. For DOS 3.3, you use the same procedure, but the three POKEs can be replaced by a single DOS FP command (there is no equivalent in ProDOS).

There is also a problem with CONVERT transferring *large* files from ProDOS to DOS (files small enough to fit on a DOS disk, however). Additionally, you must remember that some ProDOS-sized files may not be accessible by simple DOS programming methods, or that such a file may not fit on a DOS disk.

Appendix F

An "Input Almost Anything" Routine

The following programs are presented without much explanation since Applesoft internals and other technical details are involved, but they may prove useful. The programs are designed to provide an "input anything" routine for use with BASIC programs by installing a machine language routine which is accessed via the Applesoft & ("ampersand") command. This command passes control to a user-installed routine via a specific page 3 vector assigned for use of the "&" command.

The following programs were adapted from the September and October 1985 issues of *Open-Apple* magazine, which also contained descriptions of the history of "input anything" routines and information on the development of this specific version.

THE PROGRAMS

The program in Listing F-1 creates the needed binary file containing the actual input routine. Type in and RUN this program to create the binary program file "IAA.OBJ" on your disk. Then, to install the routine for use, you can use the technique outlined in Listing F-2. This installation will fail if the ampersand vector appears to be in use; you'll be notified of such an occurrence. Incidentally, this program supports both DOS 3.3 and ProDOS installation.

Once the IAA.OBJ utility is in place, you invoke it by using the ampersand command followed *immediately* by the string variable you want the string input to appear in:

```
10  REM *** INPUT ANYTHING CALL ***
20  PRINT "Give me a line";: REM Prompt line.
30  &ANS$ : REM Get input into "ANS$".
40 ? ANS$ : REM Print line out for verification.
```

This short program will demonstrate the routine, you can enter commas and colons with no "?EXTRA IGNORED" to worry about.

The routine will stay in effect unless the user (or a program) re-defines the ampersand vector, or you re-boot, or you "trash" page three where the IAA.OBJ program resides. It also can be used for input from disk files; just substitute "& IN$" (or whatever variable) for "INPUT IN$".

/UTILITIES SECRETS

Back when the Apple *II*e 80-Column Text Card

```
10  REM *** MAKE IAA.OBJ ***
100  REM *** INSTALL INPUT ALMOST ANYTHING IN
       PAGE 3 ***
110  GOSUB 1000
200  REM *** SAVE IT TO FILE ***
210  PRINT  CHR$ (4);"BSAVE IAA.OBJ,A$300,E$37E"
999  END
1000  REM ML DATA
1010  FOR I = 768 TO 894: READ X: POKE I,X: NEXT
       I
1020  DATA 169,132,133,51,32,227,223,32,108,221
1030  DATA 162,0,32,12,253,168,41,127,201,13
1040  DATA 8,72,240,7,201,32,176,3,105,64
1050  DATA 168,152,32,237,253,104,40,240,13,157
1060  DATA 0,2,232,224,255,208,221,169,13,32
1070  DATA 237,253,134,253,32,57,213,166,253,138
1080  DATA 160,0,209,131,240,2,176,31,145,131
1090  DATA
       200,177,131,133,113,72,200,177,131,133
1100  DATA 114,197,112,104,144,13,197,111,144,9
1110  DATA 138,162,0,160,2,32,226,229,96,138
1120  DATA 32,82,228,162,0,160,2,32,226,229
1130  DATA 160,0,165,253,145,131,200,165,111,145
1140  DATA 131,200,165,112,145,131,96
```

Listing F-1. Program to create the "input anyting" program file "IAA.OBJ."

was released, Apple promised a machine language version of the "blinking underline cursor" routine presented in MAGIC MENU (in *The Applesoft Tutorial* for the *II*e). The routine never surfaced. However, there is a "secret" routine used in the 128K version of the Apple *II* system utilities which is close.

Originally, the system utilities was sold as part of the *II*c CPU package on a disk named "/UTILITIES". These utilities were designed for an Apple *II*c computer; they utilize most of the 128K of memory and the MouseText character set. These utilities were easy to adapt for use on an enhanced Apple *II*e when it arrived. With the introduction of the 3.5" UniDisk disk drive, Apple has since elected to release a newer version of the system utilities that will run a *II*c or a 128K (enhanced only?) *II*e computer and support the new device. The information presented here is based on version 2.1 of these utilities.

There are several program files on the disk; the file "SU2.OBJ" happens to contain several ampersand utilities named "& GET", "& INPUT", "& PRINT", and "& EXIT". These utilities can be installed by using a program sequence:

```
10 HIMEM: 32266 : REM RESERVE MEMORY
   ABOVE $7E00.
20 PRINT CHR$(4);"-SU2.OBJ" : REM RUN
   AMPERSAND UTILITIES.
```

With the *II*c /UTILITIES disk, you can simply "-SU.OBJ" to enable its version of the routines; the routines apparently do not require the HIMEM statement.

Upon experimenting with the "& INPUT" command, a rough outline of its use falls into place. The statement "& INPUT ANS$" will read a line of input into the variable "ANS$", including commas and colons, making it in effect an "input anything". The line can also be edited during input with the keys listed in Table F-1 ("^" signifies a control character). Typed characters are inserted into the line at the position of the cursor, and all

```
10  REM *** INSTALL IAA.OBJ ***
100  REM *** GET CONTENTS OF '&' HOOK ***
110 AMP =  PEEK (1014) +  PEEK (1015) * 256
200  REM *** DETERMINE WHETHER DOS 3.3 OR PRODOS
      IS IN USE ***
210  IF  PEEK ( PEEK (977) +  PEEK (978) * 256)
      = 76 THEN 400
300  REM *** DOS 3.3 ***
310  IF AMP <  > 65368 THEN 600: REM & HOOK IN
      USE IF NOT $FF58 (RTS).
320 X = 191: REM A $BF TO STUFF AT $301 FOR
      PROMPT.
330  GOTO 500: REM SKIP PRODOS STUFF.
400  REM *** PRODOS/BASIC.SYSTEM ***
410  IF AMP <  > 48643 THEN 600: REM & HOOK IN
      USE IF NOT $BE03 ("SYNTAX ERROR").
420 X = 132: REM A $84 TO STUFF AT $301 FOR
      PROMPT.
500  REM *** FINISH INSTALL ***
510  POKE 1014,0: POKE 1015,3: REM CONNECT TO
      HOOK.
530  PRINT  CHR$ (4);"BLOAD IAA.OBJ,A$0300"
540  POKE 769,X: REM FIX PROMPT FOR DOS IN USE.
550  PRINT "IAA.OBJ installed and ready for
      use."
599  END
600  REM *** CAN'T USE VECTOR ***
610  PRINT "Ampersand vector in use."
620  PRINT "IAA.OBJ not installed."
699  END
```

Listing F-2. Program to install "IAA.OBJ".

characters to the right of the inserted character are moved to the right to create room.

In addition, if a string value is defined before the "& INPUT" is used to read input into it, the first character of the string is presented on screen as a default(?). Possibly, with some questioning letters from Apple owners, Apple Computer might deign to document these routines for end users.

Table F-1. Command Keys Recognized by the "& INPUT" Routine Found in "SU2.OBJ".

Keys	Effect
Right and Left Arrow keys	Move cursor right and left in line.
RETURN (^M) or ESC	Accept entire line as displayed.
^X, ^Z, or ^R	Clear line and restart entry.
^D or DELETE	Delete character to left of cursor.
^F	Deletes character at cursor.

Appendix G

Resources and Acknowledgments

We have mentioned several products and books about ProDOS (and even DOS) during the course of this book. This Appendix is meant to contain a brief list of some resources available for ProDOS programmers; notably manuals, books, magazines, and software. The list is not meant to be complete, but only to be used when starting the search for materials. Readers are cautioned to check with dealers, friends, and other information sources for further recommendations and opinions; the realm of computer products is a fast-changing domain. In advance, apologies for any worthy companies overlooked here, and for any errors.

PRODOS STARTER KITS

Apple Computer, *The ProDOS User's Kit*, part number A2D2010.

Apple Computer, *Applesoft Programmer's Kit* (ProDOS version), part number A2D2039.

BOOKS ON PRODOS

Apple Computer, *BASIC Programming with ProDOS,* part number A2D2037.

Apple Computer, *ProDOS Technical Reference Manual,* part number A2W0010.

Don Worth and Pieter Lechner, *Beneath Apple ProDOS,* Quality Software/Reston 1984.

BOOKS ON APPLESOFT BASIC PROGRAMMING

Apple Computer, *The Applesoft Tutorial,* Apple Computer.

Apple Computer, *Applesoft BASIC Programmer's Reference Manual,* Apple Computer.

GENERAL BOOKS ON APPLE COMPUTERS

Apple Computer, *Apple II Reference Manual.*

Apple Computer, *Apple IIe Reference Manual.*

Apple Computer, *Apple IIc Technical Reference Manual.*

Gary Little, *Apple ProDOS: Advanced Features for Programmers,* Brady Communications.

Gary Little, *Inside the Apple IIe*, Brady Communications.

Gary Little, *Inside the Apple IIc*, Brady Communications.

Jim Sather, *Understanding the Apple II,* Quality Software/Brady Communications.

Jim Sather, *Understanding the Apple IIe*, Quality Software/Brady Communications.

Tom Weishaar and Bert Kersey, *The DOSTalk Scrapbook*, TAB Books.

PUBLISHERS

Addison-Wesley Publishing Company
Jacob Way
Reading, MA 01867
(617) 944-3700
[Addison-Wesley now publishes many of the Apple manuals]

Apple Computer, Inc.
20525 Mariani Avenue
Cupertino, CA 95014
(408) 996-1010

Brady Communications Co., Inc.
Bowie, Maryland 20715

TAB Books Inc.
Blue Ridge Summit, PA 17214

APPLE-SPECIFIC MAGAZINES

IIComputing
Antic Publishing, Inc.
P.O. Box 1922
Marion, OH 43306
(614) 383-3141

A+
P.O. Box 2964
Boulder, CO 80321
(212) 503-5444

Assembly Lines
S-C Software Corporation
P.O. Box 280300
Dallas, TX 75228
(214) 324-2050

Call-A.P.P.L.E.
c/o Apple Pugetsound Program Library Exchange
290 S.W. 43rd Street
Renton, WA 98055
(206) 251-5222

InCider
CW Communications/Peterborough
P.O. Box 911
Farmingdale, NY 11737
(800) 343-0728

Open-Apple
P.O. Box 7651
Overland Park, KS 66207

Nibble
Nibble Publications
45 Winthrop Street
Concord, MA 01742-9990

COMPANIES MARKETING PRODOS UTILITY PROGRAMS

A.P.P.L.E. Co-op
c/o Apple Pugetsound Program Library Exchange
290 S.W. 43rd Street
Renton, WA 98055
(206) 251-5222

Apple Computer, Inc.
20525 Mariani Avenue
Cupertino, CA 95014
(408) 996-1010

Beagle Brothers
3990 Old Town Avenue, Suite 102C
San Diego, CA 92110
(649) 296-6400

Central Point Software
9700 S.W. Capitol Hwy. #100
Portland, OR 97219
(503) 244-5782

MicroSPARC, Inc.
45 Winthrop Street
Concord, MA 01742
(617) 371-1660

Nite Owl Software
5734 Lamar
Mission, KS 66202
(913) 362-9898

Roger Wagner Publishing, Inc.
P.O. Box 582
Santee, CA 92071
(619) 562-3670

Quality Software
21601 Marilla Street
Chatsworth, CA 91311
(818) 709-1721

S-C Software Corporation
P.O. Box 280300
Dallas, TX 75228
(214) 324-2050

PRODUCT ACKNOWLEDGMENTS

In addition to the above, the following manufacturer's names and products mentioned in the course of this book are proprietary to the listed manufacturers:

APPLE COMPUTER, INC.: Apple II, Apple II Plus, Apple *II*e, Apple *II*c, Apple III, Applesoft BASIC, Integer BASIC, AppleMouse, AppleWorks, AppleWriter, ProDOS, SOS, DOS 3.3, Apple Pascal, Apple Dot Matrix printer, Imagewriter, MacIntosh.

APPLIED ENGINEERING: Timemaster H.O.

BELL LABORATORIES: UNIX

DIGITAL RESEARCH, INC.: CP/M

KYAN SOFTWARE: Kyan Pascal

MICROSOFT CORP.: SoftCard

MOUNTAIN COMPUTER: Apple Clock

THUNDERWARE, INC.: Thunderclock

Index